Innovative Methodologies in Enterprise Research

Innovative Methodologies in Enterprise Research

Edited by

Damian Hine

Senior Lecturer, University of Queensland Business School, University of Queensland, Australia

David Carson

Professor of Marketing, School of Marketing, Entrepreneurship and Strategy, University of Ulster, UK

Edward Elgar
Cheltenham, UK • Northampton, MA, USA

Published by
Edward Elgar Publishing Limited
The Lypiatts
15 Lansdown Road
Cheltenham
Glos GL50 2JA
UK

Edward Elgar Publishing, Inc.
William Pratt House
9 Dewey Court
Northampton
Massachusetts 01060
USA

Paperback edition 2008

A catalogue record for this book
is available from the British Library

Library of Congress Cataloguing in Publication Data
Innovative methodologies in enterprise research / edited by Damian Hine,
David Carson.
    p. cm.
  Includes bibliographical references and index.
  1. Small business—Research—Methodology. 2. Entrepreneurship—
Research—Methodology. 3. Business enterprises—Research—Methodology.
I. Hine, Damian. II. Carson, David, 1947-
  HD2341.I556 2006
  338.7072—dc22   2006018298

ISBN 978 1 84542 211 0 (cased)
ISBN 978 1 84844 313 6 (paperback)

Printed by Biddles Ltd, King's Lynn, Norfolk

Contents

Figures

Tables

Abbreviations

4Ps	product, price, promote, place
ACAD	Alberta College of Art and Design
APPA	average pairwise percent agreement
B2B	business to business
B2C	business to consumer
CEO	chief executive officer
GEM	Global Entrepreneurship Monitor
GNP	gross national product
ICT	information and communication technologies
IPO	initial public offering
IT	information technology
MNCs	multinational corporation
MNP	marketing network processes
OBM	original brand marketing
OECD	Organisation for Economic Co-operation and Development
OEM	original equipment manufacturing
OHP	overhead projector
PEG ratio	price-earning-growth ratio
PI	pioneering-innovative
R&D	research and development
RAE	research assessment exercise
SB	small business
SMEs	small and medium-sized enterprises
SPSS	Statistical Package for the Social Sciences
TCP/IP	transmission control protocol/internet protocol
TEA	total entrepreneurial activity
TNC	transnational corporation
VC source	venture capital source

Contributors

Lars Bengtsson, Lund University, Sweden

Nancy J. Birch, Eastern Washington University, Cheney, WA, USA

Martins Bumbieris, University of Flensburg, Germany

David Carson, University of Ulster, Jordanstown, Northern Ireland

Nicole Coviello, University of Auckland, New Zealand

Audrey Gilmore, University of Ulster, Jordanstown, Northern Ireland

Andrew Griffiths, University of Queensland, Brisbane, Australia

Mary F. Hazeldine, Georgia Southern University, Statesboro, GA, USA

Helge Helmersson, Lund University, Sweden

Damian Hine, University of Queensland, Brisbane, Australia

David A. Kirby, University of Surrey, Guildford, England and Adjunct Professor, University of South Australia, Adelaide, SA, Australia

Rikard Larsson, Lund University, Sweden

Jan Mattsson, Roskilde University, Denmark

Andrew McAuley, University of Stirling, Scotland

Asko Miettinen, Tampere University of Technology, Finland

Morgan P. Miles, Georgia Southern University, Statesboro, GA, USA

Hugh Munro, Wilfrid Laurier University, Waterloo, ON, Canada

Rachel Parker, University of Queensland, Brisbane, Australia

Chad Perry, formally University of Southern Cross, Coolangatta, QLD, Australia

Sally Rao, University of Adelaide, Adelaide, SA, Australia

Steve Rocks, University of Ulster, Coleraine, Northern Ireland

Susanne Royer, University of Flensburg, Germany

Robert G. Schwartz, Eastern Washington University, Spokane, WA, USA

Wai-sum Siu, Hong Kong Baptist University, Hong Kong

Robyn Stokes, Queensland University of Technology, Brisbane, Australia

Richard D. Teach, Georgia Institute of Technology, Atlanta, GA, USA

Ellen Kittel-Wegner, University of Flensburg, Germany

1. Introduction

Damian Hine and David Carson

In any research project, there is a hierarchy of objectives, the first and foremost of which relates to the purpose of the research in terms of expanding knowledge about a social phenomenon. Then the research methodology is the instrument through which the research objective is fulfilled. The objective of the research methodology, whatever the objective of the research, is to achieve high quality information, that is data, which are free from bias in relation to the social phenomenon under investigation (Wass and Wells, 1993, p. 91).

INTRODUCTION

Enterprise research incorporating entrepreneurship and small business is gaining an elevated standing within universities, reflecting the recognition small and medium-sized enterprises (SMEs) have garnered as a critical sector in national economies. This standing is reflected in the call for papers for the Academy of Management Learning and Education Journal special edition on Entrepreneurship which remarked:

Entrepreneurship education has been the testing ground for many important techniques in business education. Today virtually every university offers some sort of entrepreneurship course or program. In addition, entrepreneurship is a field that generates strong interest and intrigues practitioners and policy makers at many levels and in many countries. Entrepreneurship education has been touted as a "cure" for economic and social ills and proposed as a part of curriculum for students at all ages and levels (*Call for Papers*, Special Issue of AMLE on Entrepreneurship Education, 2002).

Correspondingly, research encapsulated under the title of enterprise research has taken enormous strides forward in the last two decades. Yet the research frontier is still wide and can be served by encouraging research designs and methodologies as diverse as the content to be covered. The title of this book is deliberately broad to permit an inclusive approach to the diverse content and research processes desired.

RATIONALE FOR THE BOOK

Enterprise research, whether it be small business, entrepreneurship, or innovation, could not be regarded as a cohesive discipline as yet. As research disciplines gain the attention of researchers and the public, more research studies are conducted in ever narrowing areas of interest, with increasingly standardized research techniques. Enterprise research has the advantage of sufficient immaturity as a research discipline to still permit a wide scope for new and innovative research studies to probe under-explored concepts. It also means that researchers are not channelled down the well-worn ruts of research methodology, enabling them to select from a plethora of research methods and techniques. Delving into this unexplored terrain requires exploratory research methods supported by inductive research techniques.

From this inductive, interpretist approach to research has emanated a rich diversity of innovative research techniques. Unfortunately, this diversity can be problematic for the researcher seeking an interpretist perspective. The rationale for the development of this book is to provide a sample of these diverse but valuable techniques in a cohesive form. The cohesiveness is underwritten by a thematic approach to the book that pervades each chapter. The theme is the necessity of inductive/interpretist/humanist approaches to the research of enterprises, to match the individualism and uniqueness of the people and businesses being researched. The book encourages the maintenance of diversity in the research agenda as it matures to ensure innovation and entrepreneurship are not simply the content focus of the research, but that researchers can feel that they themselves can be entrepreneurial and innovative in their research agenda.

THE PURPOSE AND FORMAT OF THIS BOOK

This book has been developed to meet the needs of researchers in the broad field of enterprise research. This ranges from venture creation and firm formation, to small business management, to the study of individual entrepreneurs to innovation and entrepreneurship. An important area of endeavour such as this requires methodological developments which offer rigour and choice for those researching in the area. The unit of analysis may vary widely between the project, the business unit, the individual, the firm, its market or industry, even nations and across nations. As this realm of research endeavour ever expands we need to ensure that the range of methodological techniques available do not hinder its growth and development, and are themselves as innovative as the phenomenon under scrutiny.

The content of this book is international in its appeal and its substance. Contributors from Sweden, Denmark, Scotland, Northern Ireland, Finland, Hong Kong, the United States, Australia, New Zealand, Germany, England and Canada bring with them their own cultural and philosophical perspectives, which ensure expansive views and experience of enterprise research. This is matched by a rich diversity of topics and techniques supported by case examples from the researchers' own experiential discoveries.

Specific chapters will hold value for enterprise researchers and research students, academic institutions and libraries, undergraduate and postgraduate courses on research methods, enterprise advisors and consultants. Overall, the book will provide researchers and research students, with a cohesive body of material on the use of interpretist research techniques in all areas of enterprise research, including small business, entrepreneurship and innovation. It is hoped that the book will provide a major contribution as both a text in research methods programs and as a central reference guide for the increasing number of enterprise researchers, as it provides a distinct body of knowledge in an important and emerging research agenda, which to this point has been disparate.

The diversity of the methodologies described in the book is enhanced by the international flavour of the authorship of each chapter. This book is not, however, proposed to be simply a collection of selected readings with no definable direction or purpose. This book has a clear theme running through sections and chapters chapter authors did not simply contribute pre-existing readings.

WHERE THE MATERIAL IN THIS BOOK SITS IN RELATION TO RESEARCH PARADIGMS

At the outset it is important to clarify that this book focuses not on ontological or epistemological concerns, as important to research and understanding as these are. The focus of the book is squarely on selected methodologies, while maintaining a post-positivist stance. To clarify, ontology is the fundamental assumptions made about the nature of reality (Easterby-Smith et al., 1991); epistemology concentrates on the relationship between reality and the researcher; and methodology outlines the available research tools and techniques to conduct the research (Guba and Lincoln, 1994). In this book we do not seek to question the fundamental belief systems upon which researchers base their research decisions. We seek to offer, rather than prescribe, alternative methodological techniques which have already been applied in research projects conducted by the chapter authors.

As you read through the chapters of this book, you will see that the research paradigms of critical theory, constructivism and realism are all tackled, and corresponding methodologies outlined and exemplified. The only paradigm which is not extensively incorporated into the text of this book is that of positivism. There are numerous reasons for this however, the fundamental reason is that enterprise research is an emerging area. As a content area it is focused upon innovation, change and dynamism. A positivist approach has limited value in the theory building desires of researchers in this realm. Table 1.1 below provides summary clarification of the stances which can be taken. Our focus in this book is on the methodological assumptions under critical theory, constructivism and realism as applied to enterprise research.

Positivism considers that reality in natural and social sciences is composed of discrete variables that can be quantified, measured and classified (Guba and Lincoln, 1994). Researchers observe, collect, measure and

Table 1.1   Philosophies underpinning research paradigms

Philosophical Assumptions	Research Paradigms			
	Positivism	Critical Theory	Constructivism	Realism
Ontology	Reality exists driven by natural mechanisms. Discrete variables can be measured	Reality is shaped by social, ethnic, economic, political and other forces over time	Reality is constructed by people based on beliefs, feelings and experiences	Reality is imperfectly understood because of human mental limitations
Epistemology	Researcher is remote from reality	Researcher is involved with those being researched	Researcher is a passionate participant	Mutual interaction between researcher and interviewee
Methodology	Experiments and surveys. Mainly quantitative methods	Action research. Researcher is transformative, changing the participant's social world	In-depth interviews. Individual beliefs, feelings and views sought	Case studies. Convergent interviewing. Interpretation by qualitative and/or quantitative methods

Source: Adapted from Chew, 2002; Perry, Riege and Brown, 1999, p. 91; Easterby-Smith, Thorpe and Lowe, 1991, p. 90; Guba and Lincoln, 1994, p. 89; and Huberman and Miles, 2002.

classify data on the variables (Easterby-Smith et al., 1991). The positivism paradigm does not fit with the research problem in many areas of enterprise research because there is relatively little previous research in many areas and theory testing would be difficult, as constructs have not yet been established.

A good proportion of the material in this book involves not only inductive, interpretist approaches, rather than hypothetico-deductive research, it is also qualitative research. According to Sarantakos (1993, p. 32) there are three dominant paradigms in the social sciences: positivistic, interpretist and critical. Sarantakos believes the positivist and non-positivist (interpretive and critical) to be considered incompatible, the critical and interpretive paradigms not. For the purposes of this book and of good research, these major paradigms are not considered to be incompatible.

It is important at this point to define the quantitative and qualitative approaches to research, while remembering that these two approaches are not necessarily the two extremes of a philosophical continuum. Reichardt and Cook (1979, pp. 9–10), provide a sound juxtaposition of the two approaches:

> the quantitative paradigm is said to have a positivistic, hypothetico-deductive, particularist, objective, outcome oriented and natural science world view. In contrast, the qualitative paradigm is said to prescribe to a phenomenological, inductive, holistic, subjective, process oriented and social anthropological world view.

Romano (1989) supports this approach: 'If qualitative data is collected in a structured manner it can be used to produce measures which can be tested by quantitative scales. This approach will give better guidance in collecting and analysing the data'.

Inductive research is necessary in the exploratory phase of research as the empirical literature is generally insufficient to permit a deductive approach. The quantitative paradigm is implemented in at a more mature phase of the research field. It is then appropriate to utilize the quantitative hypothetico-deductive approach to test and confirm results, findings and theory.

In comparison to quantitative research, qualitative research:

> considers words rather than numbers as the major element of data; tends to be more inductive than deductive, emphasising theory building rather than hypothesis testing; that is, it aims at internal validity through information richness, coherence and insight from triangulated sources rather than external validity from statistical measures of generalisability; tends to use data within its context; that is, from the field rather than from experiments in the laboratory; includes subjective information collected from interviews, rather than concentrating only on objective, value free data tends to pay more attention to particulars while also being more broadly focused (Perry and Coote, 1994, p. 103).

Parkhe (1993) explicitly endorses the combination of quantitative and qualitative approaches by suggesting that:

'there is no competition (between quantitative and qualitative approaches), but rather an essential continuity and inseparability between inductive and deductive approaches to theory development. Bougeois (1979) correctly pointed to the complementarity between induction and deduction, insisting that the process must continually weave back and forth between them'.

CONCLUSION

As you will see as you read on, the diversity of methodologies explored throughout this book is substantial. The range of study content and context is no less so. Yet, the purpose and focus of this book remains on the methodologies.

REFERENCES

Academy of Management Learning & Education (AMLE) (2002), 'Call for papers', special issue of AMLE (*Entrepreneurship Education*).

Chew, D. (2002), 'The impact of relationship marketing on management of Sino-Singapore joint venture industrial parks in China', doctoral thesis for Southern Cross University, Tweed Gold Coast.

Easterby-Smith, M. (1997), 'Disciplines of organisational learning: contributions and critiques', *Human Relations*, **50**(9), 1085–113.

Easterby-Smith, M., R. Thorpe and A. Lowe (1991), *Management Research: An Introduction*, London: Sage.

Guba, E.G. and Y.S. Lincoln (1994), 'Competing paradigms in qualitative research' in N.K. Dendin and Y.S. Lincoln (eds), *Handbook of Qualitative Research*, Thousand Oaks, CA: Sage.

Miles, M.B. and A.M. Huberman (1994), *Qualitative Data Analysis: An Expanded Sourcebook*, 2nd edn, Thousand Oaks, CA: Sage.

Parkhe, A. (1993), 'Messy research, methodological predispositions and theory development in international joint ventures', *Academy of Management Review*, **18**(2), 227–68.

Perry, C. and L. Coote (1994), 'Process of a cases study research methodology: tool for management development?', presentation to the annual meeting of the Australia and New Zealand Association for Management.

Perry, C., A. Riege and L. Brown (1999), 'Realism's role among scientific paradigms in marketing research', *Irish Marketing Review*, December.

Reichardt, C. (1979), 'The statistical analysis of data from non-equivalent control group designs', in T. Cook and D. Campbell (eds), *Quasi-experimentation: Design and Analysis Issues for Field Settings*, Boston, MA: Houghton-Mifflin.

Romano, C.A. (1989), 'Research strategies for small business: a case study approach', *International Small Business Journal*, **7**(4), 35–43.

Sarantakos, S. (1993), *Social Research*, South Melbourne: Macmillan Education Australia.

Wass, V.J. and P.L.E. Wells (1993), *Principles and Practice in Business and Management Research*, Aldershot: Dartmouth.

2. Teaching and research in small business enterprise marketing: a critique and some alternatives*

Audrey Gilmore and David Carson

INTRODUCTION

In the context of small business (SB) enterprise the interface is that of marketing and entrepreneurship. Teaching and researching at the interface implicitly requires some consideration of the 'commonality' between entrepreneurship and marketing teaching. Teaching marketing is dominated by tools and techniques of marketing, for example the four 'Ps' and management decision-making frameworks such as target marketing and market positioning. It is also about concepts, focus and attitude. Teaching entrepreneurship is about concepts, focus and attitudes based on the characteristics of entrepreneurs and emphasising the common traits. Therefore, teaching at the interface involves considering marketing decision making issues from the perspective of common themes (*not* marketing tools and techniques) and new ways of doing and adapting marketing to suit entrepreneurial activity. Thus the issues arising suggest that marketing frameworks and emphasis *must be* different when addressed at the interface.

A MODEL OF SB ENTERPRISE MARKETING

This chapter offers a pragmatic model of SB enterprise marketing. This model is an amalgam of the following: adapting marketing techniques for SB enterprises, competency marketing, networking marketing, and innovative marketing. It is illustrated in Figure 2.1. These approaches are based on the notion that all SB enterprise business is carried out in a unique context. Cognisance of this context must be carefully taken into account, particularly the limitations of resources, and the inherent characteristics of the entrepreneur/owner/manager upon marketing and related decision making, as well as the industry in which it operates.

7

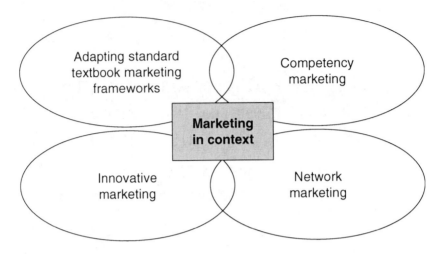

Source: Carson, D. and A. Gilmore (2000), 'Marketing at the interface: not "what" but "how"', *Journal of Marketing Theory and Practice*, **8**(2), 1–7.

Figure 2.1   A model of small business enterprise marketing

The model requires adopting an 'experienced', 'real-world' perspective of marketing. It represents 'how to do marketing' rather than 'what marketing is', and as such is highly compatible with SB enterprise entrepreneurs/owners/managers' ways of thinking, and indeed, way of 'doing business'.

DIMENSIONS OF THE MODEL

The approaches that both reflect and contribute to SB enterprise marketing are:

- Adapting standard textbook marketing frameworks
- Network Marketing
- Competency marketing
- 'Innovative' marketing.

These contribute to:

- Marketing in 'context' (or 'Situation Specific' Marketing).

Although each of these approaches are about marketing, they will be performed as part of 'doing business' and taking decisions by the SB enterprise owner/manager. As an illustration of this notion, consider the marketing activity of pricing. Decisions on pricing will probably be driven by considerations with regards to cost or cash flow, as much as any specific pricing policy. Of course, such decisions will impact upon pricing and an entrepreneur will be intuitively aware of this in the same way that s/he will be aware of a price change because of competitive pressure and how this will impact upon bottom line costs and cash flows within the business.

Thus, although the following descriptions focus upon marketing aspects, they must be considered in the wider context of overall business decision making as much as marketing decision making. Let us consider each of the components of the model in a little more detail.

ADAPTING STANDARD TEXTBOOK MARKETING FRAMEWORKS

In most SB enterprises marketing will be performed in some form or other. Marketing is inherently and intuitively performed in SB enterprises. Since most SB enterprise will have a Product or Service which they will offer at a Price and they will Promote this through some kind of medium that reaches their market Place, it can be easily determined that SB enterprise marketing can be described under the frameworks of the '4Ps'. At the general level, this is undoubtedly true, however, in just about every circumstance an entrepreneur/owner/manager will 'adapt' this concept to suit the situation specific of his/her firm. Since this situation specific will be structured around the functions and activities of the firm itself, the marketing activity will be closely allied to this.

For an SB enterprise practitioner to accept a concept such as the '4P's' it must have relevance. Therefore, if a simple '4Ps' description is not relevant to an entrepreneur it will not be used. There is a significant point here, that is, marketing activities in SB enterprise will always be pragmatic, practical and relevant to the individual SB enterprise; anything that does not meet these conditions is of little value to them. Thus, SB enterprise will pragmatically adapt any marketing theory to make it relevant to the way they do business. Whether this looks like or meets the criteria of good textbook marketing has no consideration with an entrepreneur, it is the intuitive performance in practice which is the prime consideration. Take for example, the marketing concept of the 'marketing planning process'. The conventional textbook literature describes this as a complex and comprehensive process involving extensive evaluation of a wide range of external environmental factors that are deemed to impact upon an SB enterprise's marketing.

Similar extensive evaluation is required of the SB enterprise's internal environment. Without going into the detail of this comprehensive and complex concept, it is suffice to say that such a 'framework' and process is beyond the scope of expertise and, more significantly, resource of the average SB enterprise. However, the concept itself is a sound one and indeed, one which SB enterprise should and can employ. However, in the main they will minimize the comprehensiveness and complexity of the concept to suit their own unique abilities and circumstance. Most entrepreneurs/owners/managers who might employ this concept will consider only those relevant issues outside the SB enterprise's influence and control and all those issues that are within the SB enterprise's control. In doing so the entrepreneur/owner/manager is implicitly following a marketing planning approach, albeit loosely, but in such a way that is compatible with the SB enterprise's circumstances. The essence of 'implicit marketing planning' is that it does not adhere at all to the formal, sequential frameworks of the textbook description but instead is implicitly informal, intuitive and generally reflects the inherent characteristics of SB enterprise and entrepreneurs/owners/managers (Carson, 1993).

COMPETENCY MARKETING

Competency marketing is a term that means using inherent and learned skills (competencies) to do marketing. To do marketing means anything that impacts upon, or which influences marketing, as well as actually performing marketing activity. This is in recognition that marketing decisions are often inseparable from any other decisions in an SB enterprise. Many entrepreneurs/owners/managers will perceive themselves to have limited marketing ability, primarily because their prior interests and background mean that they are unlikely to bring meaningful marketing experience and skills to a business. Many will bring a 'technical' competency to the SB enterprise. Many will learn new competencies as the business develops. Primary among these learned competencies is that of 'doing business', which is the manifestation of a range of competencies coming together as contributors to decision making. Much has been written about management and decision making competencies, as many as several hundred such competencies have been identified (Gilmore and Carson, 1996).

Consideration of what the marketing job entails helps to differentiate two distinct competency categories, those that are analytical and those that are creative. However, in once again taking account of the influential characteristics of SB enterprise and entrepreneurs/owner/managers, such competency groupings need to be adapted and refined to suit these inherent characteristics. Given the interactive relatedness of SB enterprise decision making, it is important that competency marketing in SB enterprise is compatible with this dimension.

Taking cognisance of the above dimensions and focusing upon the one most significant core competency concept for SB enterprise it is that of experiential learning (Carson and Gilmore, 2000). Experiential learning involves four significant marketing competencies that are compatible with the entrepreneurial way of doing business: experience, knowledge, communication, and judgement.

Experience is derived from accumulated knowledge of doing business and is evolved and developed by the accumulation of experience over time, learning from successes and failures. Knowledge will cover a range of aspects, particularly about how to do business and what is needed to do it successfully. Knowledge is a significant competency, in a variety of ways; it can relate to technical expertise and business acumen, including knowledge of the market environment. A communication competency is a reflection of an ability to communicate to and with all interactive parties. This competency can be improved through the development of knowledge and experience competencies. Judgement is derived from the accumulation of the others, and obviously impacts upon the quality and timing of decision making.

From an SB enterprise marketing perspective, these four competencies can be considered together, because of their interaction and interconnection in job-related activities. Thus, we can describe marketing competency in SB enterprise to be that of Experiential Learning, that is, learning acquired through experience and developed as an accumulation of knowledge and experience built upon and from communication and judgement. Such experiential learning represents a powerful SB enterprise marketing tool that can significantly compensate for the inherent SB enterprise limitations, particularly with regards to marketing activity.

Experiential learning is something that every entrepreneur/owner/manager will acquire over time. It will develop intuitively as the SB enterprise becomes established and as customs and practices emerge and evolve. The point here is that it will develop naturally; the question is whether the level and quality of experiential learning is of the best possible or just mediocre. An entrepreneur/owner/manager can utilize experiential learning proactively and in an accelerated way by concentrating on developing his/her experiential learning and therefore competency marketing. This will substantially strengthen the SB enterprise's marketing effectiveness.

NETWORK MARKETING

Networking is both a natural and an acquired skill or competency of the entrepreneur. Entrepreneurs may not be aware that they have a 'network' as such, since the way they perform networking is a process which is haphazard, disjointed, spontaneous and opportunistic, and consists of one-to-one interactions with a few or a variety of individuals. Sometimes entrepreneurs will consciously seek out information from certain individuals believed to have a contribution to make, on other occasions information will be gleaned sub-consciously as part of naturally doing business or as part of an informal conversation. Networking can be both proactive and passive depending upon the issue at hand. Indeed, on the same issue it can be proactive with some individuals in the network and passive with others. Similarly, it can be both overt and covert depending on the closeness or otherwise of individuals to the entrepreneur.

Timescales within networking can vary enormously, some individuals may be networked continuously and frequently, while others may only be contacted infrequently and occasionally. Sometimes, the entrepreneur will have a clear issue in mind and will raise this issue with individuals in a way that is deemed to be appropriate for that individual to respond with meaningful feedback. On other occasions, knowledge or information will be acquired as part of other apparently unrelated conversation or observation. Some individuals may receive a flurry of contact at a particular time and then find that no contact is made for some time before contact is re-established. It is unlikely that any one aspect of networking will lead to decisive decision making by the SB enterprise entrepreneur, instead networking will represent an array of assessments which all contribute towards a final decision. The point here is that normally, entrepreneurial networking has no fixed or standard mechanism in operation, there is seldom an agenda or objective because there is no demonstrative 'process' in operation. Networking can be likened to a cloud, when observed it can be seen but it is difficult to make tangible contact with all its dimensions. It will appear to be in constant flux, but at the same time it is always recognisable (Gilmore and Carson, 1999).

Networking is very useful to SB enterprise entrepreneurs/owners/managers, mainly because it is integral to doing business, it does not have to be constructed and contrived, it is not a task to be completed, it is simply part of everyday business activity and therefore happens anyway. All entrepreneurs do networking in some form or other, indeed, like in any aspect of life, some will be better at networking than others. Since networking is such an intuitively natural dimension of entrepreneurial SB enterprise activity, it represents a significant strength for marketing purposes. As SB enterprise are invariably 'close' to their customers, aspects of marketing such as relationship and communication are important. Networking is the mechanism used by SB enterprise to achieve aspects of marketing activity in a way that is compatible with their resource constraints.

Networking and using the appropriate competencies together can represent the core essence of SB enterprise marketing that impacts upon the nature, type and style of SB enterprise marketing activity. These dimensions represent significant strengths that contribute to successful SB enterprise marketing.

INNOVATIVE MARKETING

A vast majority of the literature on innovation in SB enterprise is focused on 'Product Innovation'; assuming that this is where most SB enterprise are innovative. It may be true to say that SB enterprise display a high degree of product innovation since many new SB enterprise will be founded upon a new and innovative product or service, and such innovations are easily identified. However, in most cases, SB enterprise develops products that are only marginally differentiated from others and much of the product innovation is in response or reaction to customer demand.

It is contended here that 'Innovative Marketing' in SB enterprise is much wider than simply product innovation, and indeed, much research in the area recognizes this wider spectrum (see the UIC/AMA Marketing/ Entrepreneurship Interface Proceedings 1987–2004). Innovative marketing is not simply focused on product innovation, instead it covers the whole spectrum of marketing activity within an SB enterprise. Consequently, there is likely to be more innovation in other aspects of marketing activity than there will be around the product or service.

Innovative marketing is driven by several inherent factors surrounding SB enterprise. The SB enterprise characteristics and limitations mean that such SB enterprise cannot engage in comprehensive and expensive marketing programmes. Also, most SB enterprise will have minimal differentiation from other competitors. These factors combined therefore, require entrepreneurs/owners/managers to be 'innovative' in how they 'do marketing'. For example, how they present the product or service; how they create 'added-value' within the scope of product/service offering – and in the delivery of this offering; equally, the level or degree of overall service they can provide. None of this marketing innovation in itself is strikingly differentiated, but packaged together, amounts to innovative marketing entirely compatible with SB enterprise characteristics.

These three dimensions of SB enterprise marketing (networking, competencies and innovation), are used inherently and contribute to the fourth dimension of adapting marketing tools and techniques to suit the unique characteristics of SB enterprise. This results in marketing activities which can be described as 'marketing in context' for SB enterprise.

MARKETING IN CONTEXT – IMPLICATIONS FOR RESEARCHING SMALL BUSINESS ENTERPRISE

Small Business enterprise marketing, in practice, is intuitively performed and is set within the specific situation 'context' of the firm. Some indication of how this marketing is manifested has been described in terms of incorporating influencing factors that must be taken into account in the 'context' of marketing and how certain marketing characteristics will impact upon the type, style and how marketing is carried out by an SB enterprise (Carson et al., 2002).

Therefore researching SB enterprise owner/managers and how they run their business calls for research methodologies that can be adapted and designed to reach an in-depth understanding of business activity with the SB enterprise's specific context. Key questions pertaining to refining research methods in this context are:

- If managers in SB enterprise do not manage conventionally or take decisions according to literature conventions, how do they take business decisions?
- What are the influences on business decision-making?
- How can we judge and assess the quality of small firm marketing decision-making?

Research should try to mirror SB enterprise decision-making processes that are themselves unlikely to be orderly and structured. In-depth understanding of the influences upon the series of processes involved in managerial decision-making and activity would benefit from a research approach that allows the phenomenon to be studied closely, longitudinally, recognizing the 'insider' perspectives. So it is unlikely that conventional quantitative research will reach the required level of penetration. Studying SB enterprise owner/managers is not about testing variables, not about testing techniques but about determining key issues, for example how SB enterprise owner/managers carry out business decision-making.

Recognizing the holistic dimension of entrepreneurial owner/manager decision-making practices, a qualitative approach that encourages a holistic approach to data gathering has many advantages. Given that SB enterprise owner/managers tend not to take decisions along functional frameworks, marketing decisions are likely to be intertwined in decisions concerned with the holistic running of the business. For example a decision on pricing is likely to be stimulated by cash flow and considerations of cost as it is to stimulate customers to buy. Qualitative research allows the researcher to take account of the holistic, contextual dimensions of the environment in which SB enterprise owner-managers operate.

CARRYING OUT FIELD RESEARCH WITH SMALL BUSINESS ENTERPRISE OWNER/MANAGERS

When carrying out any fieldwork specific consideration must be given to the nature of the environment in which data gathering will take place; and perhaps more importantly, the characteristics of the individuals involved in the phenomena under study. In a longitudinal study it will be advantageous to prepare for at least two visits to the key informants. The first part of a study may involve face-to-face in-depth interviews with the owner-managers of small companies; with follow-up interviews at a later date. The objective of such interviews would be to allow owner-managers to describe their views in relation to what they do, how, why, when and where. Therefore a suitable interview approach is one which takes account of SB enterprise owner-managers characteristics and individuality. In-depth interviews which follow a relatively unstructured pattern using the 'tell me about . . .' approach for investigating business decision-making activity, allows respondents to describe opinions and views in relation to what they do, how, when, where and why, in their own words. These in-depth interviews can then provide an open, flexible, experiential and illuminating way to study complex, dynamic interactive situations, such as management decision making. Such an interview technique provides all the advantages of in-depth interviewing; covering a wide area of interest, allowing the researcher to become familiar with the areas of interest as the research progresses; identification and exploration of the key issues as they are revealed due to the open-ended nature of the interview protocol; and allowing opportunity for further probing and examining until mutual understanding is reached.

Furthermore, the interview approach needs to take account of SB enterprise owner-managers' characteristics and individuality. This is particularly applicable to the language used for researching SB enterprise entrepreneurs/owners-managers. The language used by the interviewer should deliberately exclude marketing terminology but focus instead on what the owner-manager does in relation to various aspects of business. This is a vital prerequisite for understanding SB enterprise owner-managers motivations behind decision making.

INTERPRETATIVE ANALYSIS OF DATA

The emphasis on interpretation as being integral to qualitative methodologies is particularly suitable in the context of SB enterprise marketing phenomena, where most decision-making and marketing delivery involves actions and performances which are impacted upon and will have influence on all other aspects of running the business. The aim should be to elicit an interpretative understanding of action where phenomena are considered within the specific context, taking account of the subject's view and their understanding and meaning of the situation in any given situation. Interpretative analysis can be ongoing throughout the study. This allows data to be initially coded in several ways (according to the research topic), then re-analysed and interpreted as further data are gathered.

CRITERIA FOR ANALYSIS

The purpose of using criteria for analysis in a qualitative research study is to provide a framework for analysing data in a holistic manner, that is, within the context of occurrence. The most commonly used technique for this is critical incidence, but this is often too restrictive and limiting in the context of aiming to achieve the integrative approach described above. Therefore consideration of SB enterprise owner-managers behaviour, actions, need to be analysed in the context of the holistic nature of SB enterprise decision-making. Thus, the purpose of criteria for analysis should be to involve the inclusion of 'components' of key aspects of marketing activity; and to develop criteria which assesses these in terms of their use and how they are performed.

However, it is well recognised that it is often difficult to analyse qualitative data in the social sciences where measuring tools are often crude and behavioural activities and processes are complex and multi-faceted. A notion encapsulated by Mintzberg (1970, p. 101): 'Eggs can easily be measured and graded, using well-defined criteria, but managerial activities frequently cannot. For example, consider the challenge of: categorising data relating to managerial decision making into different research areas/issues; how to categorise each participants involvement and in the context of different functional areas; clearly these difficulties arise as the "neat functional categories we tend to use are not very neat in practice"' (Mintzberg, 1970, p. 101). Therefore, the development of criteria for analysis must come from the data. Above all 'measurements need to be in real organisational terms which means . . . measuring things that really happen in organisations, as they experience them' and guarding against 'misunderstanding the organisation by forcing it into abstract categories that have nothing to do with how it functions' (Mintzberg, 1979, p. 583).

Criteria for analysis creates and evolves meaningful categories which can be used to link the raw data with relevant recognized theories, and focus on the important concepts and issues which explain the interactions and activities of the phenomenon under study. The initial stage of data analysis involves two steps: one of convergence and one of divergence. An evaluator of qualitative data must first deal with the problem of convergence; that is, figuring out what things fit together and subsequently working towards a classification system for the data. Divergence occurs where the evaluator must deal with how to 'flesh out' the categories. This involves processes of: extension (that is, building on items of information already known); bridging (making connections among different items); and surfacing (proposing new information that ought to fit and then verifying its existence).

The process ends when 'Sources of information have been exhausted, when sets of categories have been saturated so that new sources lead to redundancy, when clear regularities have emerged that feel integrated, and when the analysis begins to "overextend" beyond the boundaries of the issues and concerns guiding the analysis' (Patten, 1987, p. 154). Uncovering patterns, themes and categories is a creative process that requires making carefully considered judgements about what is really significant and meaningful in the data. Criteria for analysis can evolve over time from further in-depth consideration of the categories identified in the data; and can be built around the various levels of occurrence of activity identified in the longitudinal study. Overall criteria for analysis should link the theory to the data and should be indicative of the interrelationships, links, sequentiality and general interdependencies of the phenomena within the context of the enterprise and the environment in which it operates.

CONCLUSION

This chapter has been framed around building a pragmatic model of the influences on how SB enterprises do business. The model incorporated adapting standard textbook frameworks, using competencies and networks and innovative approaches to doing business. These aspects of SB enterprise business are carried out in a unique context and will be influenced by the life stage of the company and the traditional practices and norms of the industry in which the company operates. The unique context of SB enterprise business activity is built upon recognition of the influence of the inherent characteristics of SB enterprise, particularly the limitations of resources, and the inherent characteristics of the entrepreneur/owner/manager upon business decision-making.

The model should be viewed as a model of marketing 'application' in SB enterprise. It requires the reader to adopt an 'experienced', 'real-world' perspective of marketing, representing 'how to do marketing' rather than 'what marketing is' and as such is highly compatible with SB enterprise entrepreneurs/owners/managers way of thinking, and doing business.

NOTE

*   This chapter is based on the following articles: Carson, D. and A. Gilmore (2000), 'Marketing at the interface: not "what" but "how"', *Journal of Marketing Theory and Practice* **8**(2), pp. 1–7; Gilmore, A. and D. Carson (2000), 'The demonstration of a methodology for assessing SME decision making', *Journal of Research in Marketing and Entrepreneurship* **2**(2), pp. 108–24 and Carson, D. (1999), 'Marketing for small-to-medium enterprises', in *The Marketing Book*, M. Baker (ed.), 4th edn, Oxford: Butterworth-Heinemann, pp. 621–38.

REFERENCES

Carson, D. (1993), 'A philosophy for marketing education in small firms', *Journal of Marketing Management*, **9**(2) (April), 189–204.

Carson, D. (1999) 'Marketing for small-to-medium sized enterprises', in M. Baker (ed.), *The Marketing Book*, 4th edn, Oxford: Butterworth-Heineman, pp. 621–38.

Carson, D. and A. Gilmore (2000a), 'SB marketing management competencies', *International Business Review*, **9**(3), 363–82.

Carson, D. and A. Gilmore (2000b), 'Marketing at the interface: not "what" but "how"', *Journal of Marketing Theory and Practice*, **8**(2), 1–7.

Carson, D., M. Enright, A. Tregear, P. Copley, A. Gilmore, D. Stokes, C. Hardesty and J.H. Deacon (2002), 'Contextual marketing', paper presented at The Academy of Marketing/AMA/UIC Special Interest Group on the Marketing and Entrepreneurship Interface, University of Hertfordshire, January.

Gilmore, A. and D. Carson (1996), 'Management competencies for services marketing', *Journal of Services Marketing*, **10**(3), 39–57.

Gilmore, A. and D. Carson (1999), 'Entrepreneurial marketing by networking', *New England Journal of Entrepreneurship*, **2**(2), 31–38.

Gilmore, A. and D. Carson (2000), 'The demonstration of a methodology for assessing SB decision making', *Journal of Research in Marketing and Entrepreneurship*, **2**(2), 108–24.

Mintzberg, H. (1970), 'Structured observation as a method to study managerial work', *The Journal of Management Studies*, February, 87–104.

Mintzberg, H. (1979), 'An emerging strategy of "direct research"', *Administrative Science Quarterly*, **24** (December), 582–89.

Patton, M.Q. (1987), *How to Use Qualitative methods in Evaluation*, Newbury Park: Sage.

UIC/AMA (1987–2004), 'Marketing entrepreneurship interface proceeding', *Annual Research Symposia Proceedings on Marketing and Entrepreneurship*, University of Illinois, at Chicago.

3. 'If a picture paints a thousand words' – reaching beyond the traditional for alternative insights

Andrew McAuley

INTRODUCTION

This chapter is not intended to be a catalogue or an exhaustive guide to qualitative methods. There are already enough texts around to give the scholar an adequate overview of the possibilities (Carson et al., 2001; Seale et al., 2004). Instead the intention here is to raise ideas, stimulate thoughts, question the myths and outline the realities of doing qualitative research in the context of micro and small businesses.

The stimulus for much of what this chapter is about is a BBC programme which was first broadcast over 30 years ago called 'Ways of Seeing'. It first raised my consciousness to consider different ways of looking at the world, the people and the objects in it. John Berger challenged conventional thinking on this subject and brought many philosophical ideas into a sharper and more accessible focus. Yet seeing is what we all begin with as infants: 'Seeing comes before words. The child looks and recognizes before it can speak' (Berger, 1972). As researchers, looking is an essential first step and yet training people to observe receives little if any attention in the broad business and management curriculum. We know from personal experience that often we look and yet do not see the things we are looking for – the car keys, the purse or wallet. Yes, we searched everywhere and the item is not there; yet it is there, somehow missed in our overdrive to find it. Looking but not seeing; hearing but not listening; speaking but not communicating; touching but not feeling; smelling but not detecting. In many ways our senses play tricks on us. We are in the picture but it is a different picture to the one we think we are in. More confusing still is the fact that the other people we see in our picture are in pictures of their own and we probably play different roles in their pictures to the ones we think we play. Given all of this it is a wonder at all that we manage to communicate our research to students, colleagues, at conferences or in publications in words or pictures or anything else for that matter!

In essence the central theme of this chapter is about encouraging micro and small businesses researchers to see better, look for the real stories and experiment with different ways of presenting the story. The first part begins with a discussion of how our perceived difficulties in dealing with our knowledge of the external world are shaped and influenced by the methods we use and the ways in which we present our findings. The approach to methodology by researchers working on small and micro firms at the marketing-entrepreneurship interface is then used as an illustration of the benefits of flexibility. Finally, this chapter explores how the lessons learned could be applied to other areas of marketing through a re-birth of story telling.

ON METHODS AND PRESENTATION

Part of my own research interests has focused on the internationalization process of small and medium-sized enterprises (SMEs). However, it is regrettable (McAuley, 1995) that there is little research in this area which would be of use to the SME owner. Even allowing for the division between pure and applied research one could have hoped for a better outcome.

Despite the provision of work over the last 30 years many of the studies appear to be 'more of the same', offering few concrete outcomes with X, Y and Z being important determinants of exporting one week and A, B and C being the key influences the following week. It is also possible to bemoan the fact that there is little reapplication of existing methodologies to test previous findings, nor are there many attempts at longitudinal work. International cross-cultural studies are also in short supply.

Internationalization has come to remind me of the old story of the blind people and the elephant. When asked to describe it one person, grabbing its tail, said: 'Why, it's thin and rather long and feathery at the end'. Another, clasping a foot, said: 'No, it's solid and round like a tree'. A third, feeling the tusk, disagreed and compared it more to a pointed spear. So it is with internationalization, we see many beasts depending on our approach and methods used.

To be fair, some reflective articles do exist but they are often few and far between and appear as 'voices crying in the wilderness'; eg Aaby and Slater (1989) have called for better research design and longitudinal studies and this can only be endorsed. However, other authors (eg Miesenbock, 1988), faced with a lack of progress fall back on the call for greater sophistication of our techniques and statistical analysis. I somehow feel that this is the wrong direction to go in. Rather than throwing ever more powerful computer programs (after 30 odd years of such attempts to 'explain' exporting) at the problem let's do something simple for a change.

This is not an isolated concern within internationalization research, it can, I believe, be applied to the generic methods used in research in marketing. I worry about these methods. I worry about our findings derived from them and I worry about the policies developed on the basis of these findings. Compare the answers given to a mail survey to the answers given if you conduct a personal interview with the same person. The nuances can be altered and the meaning becomes entirely different. How often does the real story emerge after the tape recorder is switched off or the questionnaire completed? Yet we structure the presentation of our research papers as if certainty is achievable and the all sacred methodology is the surrogate for trust. If the methodology is appropriate then the findings must be solid. Too often our peers are too conservative in their expectation of our methodologies. There is not enough experimentation, not enough trying new ways of seeing. That which does go on is at the margins and when it comes to report its work in the academic journals it, in order to get published, forces itself into the straightjacket of conventional practice. This is not good for the health of any discipline and yet the most radical researchers are often amongst the tamest when it comes to presenting our knowledge.

Perhaps I worry too much and, with my 'tongue in my cheek', who decided that knowledge/meaning must be contained within the confines of 4–6,000 words? Who decided that the size of the overhead projector (OHP) screen would structure our presentations? As one of my students said recently at a class presentation: 'I had to make it very simple so as it could fit in the computer'. I worry about the words we use, the ways we chose to present our work. The narrowness of our audience; Narcissus would be proud, don't we look lovely? There is still too much emphasis on the use of the academic article as the key measure of our output. Researchers should also be encouraged to seek a wider audience via more popular media. Of course, we will have to accept a trade-off between accuracy and the greater coverage achieved by alternative media, whether this be the press or the Internet. There is a pressing need to revolutionize the way we disseminate our work.

We need also to find more engaging ways of writing. Why can't we write more freely? Why is the pseudo scientific approach adopted in conventional journals the dominant mode? I'm not sure it's because we think it is the most effective. Take the enormous impact of Fergal Keane's 'Letter to Daniel' (Keane, 1996) or the lines from 'Do not stand at my grave and weep', a soldier's prophetic imagery of being shot in Northern Ireland (BBC, 1996). Where is the equivalent impact of writing in marketing? Can we not write to communicate with a wider audience in a more direct way? The overriding necessity, it seems, is to encounter experiences in the business world and write about them as they are. Better one story of a business venture told well than a mail survey of 5,000 respondents wrapped up and packaged along the lines of the academic article. We should free ourselves from the tyranny of its structure, for it does little more than to surpress the creative communication skills of people in the discipline.

Of course the over-riding pressures and expectations created by the Research Assessment Exercise (RAE) in the UK and similar systems elsewhere does not help with any of this. With the pressure put on the university system for output, so our ways of doing research is directly affected. There is a switch from the notion of long-term scholarship to short bursts of activity leading to the annual crop of refereed journal articles. One day it will change and the priorities will be different as the values of what is really important are reassessed. Until then we are left with what has been going on in micro and small business research in terms of the methodologies being used. This is the concern of the next section.

METHODOLOGICAL APPROACHES IN MICRO AND SMALL BUSINESS RESEARCH[1]

How then can methodology help us to unlock the secrets of the entrepreneurial small firm and its interaction with marketing? Day (1998) observed that in respect of methodology most researchers at the marketing-entrepreneurship interface are working with small samples sizes of less than 100. Within the papers presented at the UIC/AMA–MEIG symposiums most data is cross-sectional (63.1% of 236 papers observed compared to 8.5% time series or 3.8% using a longitudinal approach) using national data. Methodologies were described as varied and often used in combination. There was some evidence at the time of writing, when the US sample was compared to the UK, that European researchers had a preference for case study and qualitative methodologies. A later study by Gilmore and Coviello (1999) based on much the same data (352 conference papers at MEI 1987–98) also identified similar patterns.

As interest in entrepreneurial micro and small firms has grown many researchers have been drawn in from a variety of discipline backgrounds. They have brought with them the range of methodological tools which they were familiar with in their original disciplines. Thus, from management and the social science disciplines including economics, psychology and sociology researchers came along with their associated attachment to positivistic, single reality philosophical orientations which manifested themselves in the use of quantitative approaches. In a very simple way these researchers largely perpetuate their way of doing research to the next generation of researcher within the business disciplines. As their own careers advance they in turn become responsible for scrutinizing research proposals for funding bodies and in all likelihood become drawn to the familiar in terms of research methodology. Thus, the popular perception is that quantitative studies achieve research funding more easily than qualitative-based methodologies. This is in line with Gummesson's (2002) comment on the lack of creativity and qualitative input into new marketing theory generation via the research process.

Many of the research papers have identified that the small firm is different from other firms and therefore a new paradigm is needed to guide the research into explaining the phenomena. It is at this point that the qualitative approach begins to come into its own as it is gradually adopted by researchers, especially within the UK and to some extend in Europe more generally. It is probably fair to say that the qualitative approach is less well received in the US conferences circuit and journals. If you look at a typical issue of the *Journal of Marketing* it can be quite daunting in terms of the number of papers devoted to a heavy quantitative methodology. While technically the approach is fine, it begs the question about the perceived outcome from the study; is it really getting in close enough to the subject to unlock the subject under study rather than being caught up in replication and using statistics for statistics sake? The qualitative approach makes a case for a less structured (but no less robust), creative exploration using a range of techniques.

It is argued here that a qualitative approach gets you 'up close and personal'. The underlying principle of this approach are that people view the world differently. The only reality is that constructed by individuals involved in any research situation. Thus multiple realities exist in any given situation namely, those of the researcher, the individuals being researched and those of the reader or audience. Qualitative researchers at the interface embrace the notion of multiple realities and accept that each entrepreneur constructs their own reality as they interpret and perceive the world. To represent this world the researcher must represent or reconstruct the world as seen by others.

Throughout the research process the researcher must be aware of the nature of the relationship between themselves and the subject(s) of the research. The researcher will interact closely with the subject and the distance between the two will be minimized. This is probably the point where the qualitative approach is most at odds with the positivist approach because researchers are deliberately trying to get in close to their subject. Instead of viewing subjectivity as a problem, qualitative researchers use it as a strength/competency. No one is saying that the approach has to be neat and tidy. This approach admits, recognizes and embraces the value-laden nature of the constructivist paradigm. These values have to be taken into account by the researcher and reported in order that the reader can detect any biases. The language of the reporting does not have to be in the third person but can be more direct and personal. Indeed, there is an opportunity to move away from the relatively rigid academic paper and find new ways of expressing the outcomes of research which just might be more accessible, more fun to read and better grounded on a lived reality.

One of the great attractions of the interface in attempting to unlock this lived reality is the variety of methodologies which can be applied ranging from, for example, case studies, action research to grounded theory (Creswell, 1994). It is this diversity of approach that is the key to unlocking some of the interesting features of marketing-entrepreneurship interface research. Tesch (1990) lists some 20 qualitative methods. Catterall (1998) refers to attempts by researchers outside the management disciplines to classify the variety in qualitative research but with limited success (Guba and Lincoln, 1994; Jacob, 1987). Given the plurality of philosophies and theories that can underpin qualitative work it is hardly surprising that the methods do not lend themselves to easy categorization. Atkinson (1995) sees them 'at best a collection of assumptions, methods and kinds of data that share some broad family resemblances'. In a sense this is a positive approach. It should not be necessary to limit the development of qualitative approach as if they were static. Instead new developments, eg debates in qualitative sociology on new realism (Catterall, 1998), may open up new ways of seeing which could in turn be grafted into the interface by researchers.

One useful guide as to how to approach methodology at the interface comes from Hill and McGowan (1998) who advocate a 'menu' of methods based on the constructivists view that there are multiple realities, and that distances between the observed and the observer are minimized and value laden. They describe a 'syncretized qualitative methodology for research into SMEs' which, they argue, allows a 'holistic' picture to emerge from the data.

Hill and McGowan (1998) favour a longitudinal data gathering exercize until patterns emerge. This can take the form of frequent interviews with entrepreneurs and making use of secondary information which exists in the business. Observation techniques can also be applied, for example sitting in on meetings and observing the interactions. Obviously this suggests a long period of immersion with the business in order to get attuned to the patterns of behaviour. As the picture builds up it is possible to 'analyse on the hoof' until saturation occurs. By this we mean that patterns will become established and after a point it will become clear that the perceived explanation is consistent. From this point on how robust the explanation is can be evaluated by the researcher prior to writing up. Within the syncretized qualitative methodology menu there are many possibilities available, eg case studies, participant observation, focus groups, ethnographic interviewing, grounded theory, in-depth interviewing, archival data and ethnography. This can be carried through to analysis and interpretation where suggested approaches include post-data analysis, analysis as you go, frameworks for analysis, introspection, indwelling, reduction and interpretation, marketing narrative and the comparative method. This concept of the potpourri (earlier referred to by Hari Das, 1983) helps as an analogy in the sense that the blending of different scents of the dried petals reveals a structure beyond the superficial and obvious colour/smell of the flower. In this way the qualitative researcher at the interface can literally 'smell the roses'!

The final outcome of the analysis is a construction of the entrepreneurs experiences and the meanings attached to them. This enables the researcher to vicariously experience the challenges small firms meet in relation to their business environment. The clarity of the qualitative approach is to provide a lens through which to view the world of the entrepreneur.

Often the charge that the results of qualitative research cannot be generalized is levied, and it is often assumed that the findings are only relevant to the particular context within which the data were collected and therefore limited by time and space. However at this level so too are the outcomes from quantitative data as they are also true for the sample at a particular point in time. Even with the most perfect representative sample (which itself is pretty difficult to achieve) the influence of time and space cannot be removed. From the qualitative point of view the general resides in the particular. Elements of the truth the researcher seeks is embodied in the specific case under study and this can be looked for in other cases. Thus, while positivistic criteria of internal and external validity, reliability and objectivity may not be appropriate tests, it is argued that credibility, confirmability for authenticating the outcomes of qualitative research is possible. In part this does not have to wait until the end of the process as triangulation can be undertaken by cross-checking data from others involved in the firm during the research and data regarding one phenomenon can be compared across different phases of the fieldwork by looking at what the participants are saying and how consistent it is. In doing this the researcher is 'getting in deeper' and creating the potential for valuable insights to be drawn. Thus, the quality checking process leads, by its nature, to improved assurance.

It can be seen that qualitative methods provide an 'array of interpretative techniques which seek to describe, decode, translate and otherwise come to terms with the meaning, not the frequency' of certain more or less naturally occurring phenomena in the social world (Maanen, 1979). Work by Fillis (2003) and Herman and Fillis (2003) promotes the adoption of

biographical methodology to unlock the marketing entrepreneurship interface. Gilmore and Carson (2000) argue strongly for integrative qualitative
research and suggest that an integrative study could include in-depth
interviews with owner-managers, observations of marketing activity of a
specific company, data comparison of competitive activity and analysis of
appropriate company records. The use of qualitative techniques in this way
can be linked to the concept of creating a 'stream of research' as discussed
by Davies et al. (1985). Over time the conclusions drawn from the previous
stage can be used to inform the next stage and interpretations and managerial implications can be drawn in relation to the findings at that stage of
the study.

This approach allows the research process to have that 'lived in look'; it
grows from the experience of the researcher and is then represented by them
in textual form. Unfortunately it is at this stage of the research process
where the majority of researchers start to conform to the expectations of the
journal editors and a conventional line of presentation. It is easy to see why
this happens but it seems that to have taken the road less travelled, it would
be healthy to be more adventurous with the writing-up of the results. There
tends to be more of a sense of adventure at conferences, either because that
is the tone of the conference itself (eg Marketing Illuminations series at the
University of Ulster with Stephen Brown) or because there is more freedom
generally at the conference stage for exploration (eg examining the link
between marketing and art in order to inform contemporary marking
theory).

From the discussion of methodological approaches the theme which
emerges is one of innovation and open-mindedness. Success in unlocking
the interface will ultimately depend on researchers being prepared to 'think
out of the box' and by placing conventional and unconventional methodologies side by side until a more detailed understanding is reached.

WHERE DO WE GO FROM HERE?

The previous section has shown that researchers working at the marketing-
entrepreneurship interface have adopted flexibility in their approach to
methodology. This flexibility is born of the attraction of researchers from
a variety of discipline backgrounds, which gives rise to new opportunities
in our 'ways of seeing'. The question then becomes one of how can other
areas of Marketing be persuaded to be more open? A starting point for this
methodological shift could quite simply be: 'Tell me a story'.

In many cultures the story telling method has had a powerful influence
on the transmission of knowledge between the generations. Work by

Caulkins (1988) provided an insight into how an anthropological frame-work could be used as a framework for research on the social structure and culture of small business. Other disciplines too have used this method to focus their enquiry. For example one method of historical enquiry (adapted from Harris, 1971) follows four points:

1. Primary concern is with the particular.
2. Explanation may take into account the thoughts of relevant individuals.
3. Explanation may use general laws.
4. Explanation relies heavily on the reflective judgement of individuals.

Other workers researching within the marketing-entrepreneurship interface have also made useful contributions based on the ethnographic approach involving micro level inquiry, for example, Anderson (1997), Ennis and Ali (1997), Jack and Bower (1997).

This very much reflects my recent work on small companies within the Scottish arts and crafts sector. It is apparent that a holistic approach is necessary to advance the understanding of these micro businesses other-wise only a partial picture would be achieved. Thus, having the story of the company related is the key way of achieving understanding. It is clear that an understanding of the individual entrepreneur is crucial to the understanding of the firm. For example growth is as much an internal per-sonal (psychological) development of the entrepreneur as it is an external 'visible' development of the company.

Within this approach we can construct a figure to illustrate the interrela-tionships between data collection, data display and the task of under-standing the data which enables us to draw conclusions (Figure 3.1). This, of course, is an iterative process and the conclusions drawn may lead to new demands for data collection. Over time our ideas are clarified and refined but as the environment is constantly changing our state of knowledge and understanding should, perhaps, be viewed as partial, and fluid rather than stone. Central to any degree of understanding in this process is the intuitive involvement of the researcher as the subjective judge of the state of know-ledge on the topic.

While story telling can be a mainstay of data collection in the study of small firms other methodological adaptations will also help in the study of internationalization. These include the use of longitudinal rather than snapshot approaches; studies which involve cross-cultural comparisons; and studies where the balance between the complementary strengths of the quantitative and qualitative perspectives is better achieved. A paper by Coviello and McAuley (1999) highlights the importance of triangulation

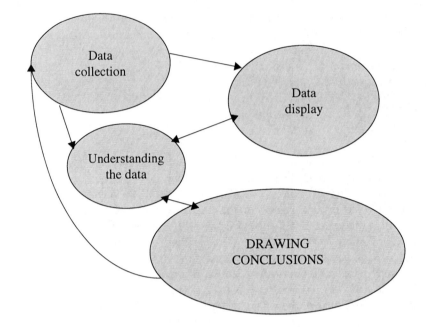

Source: Adapted from Miles and Huberman, 1984.

Figure 3.1   The iterative research process

between the three main theories of SME internationalization. Shaping our research should be a focus on the outcomes rather than our current fixation with method. The key question should be what are we trying to achieve with our research and the method is only a tool to get there, not an end in itself.

It should be possible to take all these improvements and blend them into an approach to Micro-Marketing Inquiry (with apologies to Brookfield, 1964). This follows three stages: (1) general statement about areal patterns and interrelationships; (2) detailed local inquiries about processes; and (3) synthesis of the general and local material to produce explanatory generalizations. This is simple, accessible, straightforward and achievable.

CONCLUSION

By starting afresh, research in marketing could learn from what has been going on in micro and small business research. Future debate should encourage the adoption of unconventional approaches in order to feed into new theory construction. Carson and Coviello (1996) remark that the firm should be investigated within the context of its individual setting (Morris and Stenberg, 1991). Investigation of any firm using qualitative approaches enables free flowing thought and interpretation of core issues. Carson and Coviello (1996) note that owner-managers do not carry out research activities in the way described in marketing textbooks: 'Instead, they take a naturalistic, even artistic approach to gathering marketing information'. This being the case, then the notion that the researcher embraces similar creative, artistic thinking can be conveyed in marketing research. Brown (1996) draws from the work of Eisner in identifying the merits of following an artistic approach to the research process. This involves the use of evocative statements and looks to persuade, illuminate, penetrate and generate insight, rather than be overly concerned with validity constructs and issues of bias. The use of case studies and extraordinary events are used to illustrate thinking. Generalizability comes from understanding individuality, rather than from a broad-based 'scientific' survey. Non standard interpretations and solutions are encouraged, rather than replications in the pro forma standard. Subjectivity, imagination and self-expression are central to the artistic research process, rather than continuation of study replication of scientific 'facts'. The ultimate aim of the approach is to create meaning and generate understanding, something that is often lacking in positivistic marketing research, which is too often caught up in statistics for statistics sake. Carson and Coviello (1996) summarize this approach: 'This is not an impossible notion: after all, "art" may be based on forms and structures, and on perspectives and views, but the individual outcomes are still essentially singularly creative with unique circumstances in mind'.

Finally, there are many analogies which the qualitative researcher can draw on in order to convey the meaning wrapped up in what is being studied. These can be taken from the arts; for example, we can think of the colours in a painting blending together to give form and shape to the subject, or think of the colours and tones within a singer's voice which expresses so much about the meaning of the song. The words alone are vital, as is the music, but together they transcend the ordinary and climb to new heights of expression which clarifies the intention. This is not to say it is perfect. No qualitative methodology may well explain everything but neither does principal components analysis with many factor loadings leaving much unexplained. The argument here is that the best research gets pretty close to the lived reality and how it is perceived and which as researchers we seek to explain. So different methodologies can be thought of as an orchestra with the researcher acting as conductor to blend and mix the cacophony of sound into an ordered whole. Yes there is minimized distance, multiple realities, value laden judgements and the rest but it is richer, far, far richer and more fundamental than the blinkered quantitative researcher could describe.

Having indulged myself in these thoughts which I have shared with you I hope that you will be moved to address more directly the issues raised by methodology in your own research. All is not gloom and doom. Despite the despair there are, at times, glimpses of the 'Delectable Mountains' – with some people being brave enough to buck the trend for respectable methodologies and tell it like it is. The basis of this approach, particularly in relation to smaller firms, could more often be story telling or case-studies more akin to anthropological approaches. This ethnographic approach, while popular with younger researchers, still finds resistance from reactionary reviewers. Time itself will solve this problem but we all could do more now to help. There is no one way up the mountain; we need a multiplicity of approaches woven together if we are to shine some light on the world and make some sense of it. There is hope but there is a pressing need to re-evaluate this game we play with methodologies and how we present our knowledge.

NOTE

1   The ideas in the section are partly derived from an unpublished working paper by Andrew McAuley and Ian Fillis – 'Up Close and Personal: Methodologies to Unlock the Interface'.

REFERENCES

Aaby, N.E. and S.F. Slater (1989), 'Management influences on export performance: a review of the empirical literature 1978–1988', *International Marketing Review*, **6**(4), pp. 7–26.

Anderson, A.R. (1997), 'Entrepreneurial marketing patterns in a rural environment', paper presented to the AM/AMA/UIC Symposium on the Marketing Entrepreneurship Interface, Dublin, January.

Atkinson, P. (1995), 'Some perils of paradigms', *Qualitative Health in Research*, **5**(1), pp. 117–24.

BBC (1996), 'Do not stand at my grave and weep', *The Nation's Favourite Poems*, London: BBC Books, p. 7.

Berger, J. (1972), *Ways of Seeing*, BBC broadcast and London: Penguin Books.

Brookfield, H.C. (1964), 'Questions on the human frontiers of geography', *Economic Geography*, pp. 283–303.

Brown, S. (1996), 'Art or science? Fifty years of marketing debate', *Journal of Marketing Management*, **12**(4), pp. 243–68.

Carson, D. and N. Coviello (1996), 'Qualitative research issues at the marketing/entrepreneurship interface', *Marketing Intelligence and Planning*, **14**(6), pp. 51–58.

Carson, D., A. Gilmore, C. Perry, and K. Gronhaug (2001), *Qualitative Marketing Research*, London: Sage.

Catterall, M. (1998), 'Academics, practitioners and qualitative market research', *Qualitative Market Research: an International Journal*, **1**(2), pp. 69–76.

Caulkins, D. (1988), 'Networks and narratives: an anthropological perspective for small business research', SEF Occasional Paper Series 01/88, Stirling: Scottish Enterprise Foundation, University of Stirling.

Coviello, N.E. and A. McAuley (1999), 'The internationalization process and the smaller firm: a review of contemporary empirical research', *Management International Review*, **39**(3), pp. 223–56.

Creswell, J.W. (1994), *Research Design: Qualitative and Quantatative Approaches*, London: Sage.

Davies, C.D., G.E. Hills and R.W. LaForge (1985), 'The marketing/small enterprise paradox: a research agenda', *International Small Business Journal*, **3**(3), pp. 31–42.

Day, J. (1998), 'Defining the interface: a useful framework?', in B. Hulbert, J. Day, and E. Shaw (1998), *Proceedings of the Academy of Marketing UIC/MEIG-AMA Symposia on the Marketing and Entrepreneurship Interface 1996–1998*, Northampton: Nene University College.

Ennis, S. and Ali, M. (1997), 'Opportunities and obstacles to small business development in a developing economy: the case of Multan in Pakistan', paper presented to the AM/AMA/UIC Symposium on the Marketing Entrepreneurship Interface, Dublin, January.

Fillis, I. (2003), 'A plea for biographical research as insight into smaller firm marketing theory generation', *Journal of Enterprising Culture*, **11**(1), pp. 25–46.

Gilmore, A. and D. Carson (2000), 'The demonstration of a methodology for assessing SME decision making', *Journal of Research in Marketing & Entrepreneurship*, **2**(2), pp. 108–24.

Gilmore, A. and N. Coviello (1999), 'Methodologies for research at the marketing/entrepreneurship interface', *Journal of Research in Marketing Entrepreneurship*, **1**(1), pp. 41–53.

Guba, E.G. and Y.S. Lincoln (1994), 'Competing Paradigms in Qualitative Research' in N.K. Denzin and Y.S. Lincoln (eds), *Handbook of Qualitative Research*, Thousand Oaks, CA: Sage, pp. 105–17.

Gummesson, E. (2002), 'Practical value of adequate marketing management theory', *European Journal of Marketing*, **36**(3), pp. 325–49.

Hari Das, T. (1983), 'Qualitative research in organisational behaviour', *Journal of Management Studies*, **20**(3), pp. 301–14.

Harris, R.C. (1971), 'Theory and synthesis in historical geography', *The Canadian Geographer*, **15**, pp. 157–72.

Herman, R. and I. Fillis (2003), 'A biographical study of Isambard Kingdom Brunel as insight into entrepreneurial marketing endeavour', 8th Annual Academy of Marketing Symposium on the Marketing/Entrepreneurship Interface, Cheltenham: University of Gloucestershire, January 8–10.

Hill, J. and McGowan, P. (1998), 'Small business and enterprise development: questions about research methodology', in B. Hulbert, J. Day and E. Shaw (1998), *Proceedings of the Academy of Marketing UIC/MEIG-AMA Symposia on the Marketing and Entrepreneurship Interface 1996–1998*, Northampton: Nene University College.

Jack, S.L. and D.J. Bower (1997), 'Entrepreneurship in the periphery: some examples from Scotland', paper presented to the AM/AMA/UIC Symposium on the Marketing Entrepreneurship Interface, Dublin, January.

Keane, F. (1996), *Letter to Daniel: Dispatches from the Heart*, London: Penguin, pp. 35–38.

Maanen, Van L. (1979), 'Reclaiming qualitative methods for organisational research: a preface', *Administrative Science Quarterly*, **24** (December), 520–26.

McAuley, A. et al. (1984), 'Relevance revisited?', *Area 16*, **1**, 68–9.

McAuley, A. (1995), 'An assessment of research into the internationalization process' in G.E. Hills et al., *Research at the Marketing/Entrepreneurship Interface*, University of Illinois at Chicago, pp. 331–42.

McAuley, A. and I. Fillis (2003), 'Up close and personal: methodologies to unlock the interface', unpublished working paper, Department of Marketing, University of Stirling.

Miesenbock, K.J. (1988), 'Small businesses and exporting: a literature review', *International Small Business Journal*, **6**(2), 42–61.

Miles, M.B. and A.M. Huberman (1984), *Qualitative Data Analysis: a Sourcebook of New Methods*, Beverley Hills, CA: Sage.

Morris, L.J. and L. Stenberg (1991), 'Entrepreneurship research: methodological issues in marketing strategy studies', in G.E. Hills and R.W. LaForge (eds), *Research at the Marketing/Entrepreneurship Interface*, Chicago: University of Illinois at Chicago, pp. 185–201.

Seale, C., G. Gobo, J.F. Gubrium and D. Silverman (eds) (2004), *Qualitative Research in Practice*, London: Sage.

Tesch, R. (1990), *Qualitative Research: Anaylsis Types and Software Tools*, London: Falmer Press.

4. Qualitative methodologies for enterprise research*

Audrey Gilmore and David Carson

INTRODUCTION

Enterprise research is concerned with exploring and understanding how entrepreneurs or owner managers perceive and undertake marketing management in the context of doing business, usually in the specific context of small and medium-sized enterprises (SMEs).

Small and medium-size enterprise characteristics are widely discussed in the literature, however many studies do not explicitly incorporate contextual influences into their research design. Rather than the firm, the unit of analysis is often the entrepreneur/owner/manager, so any research method should take cognisance of the individual's characteristics and how these impact upon decision making and behaviours. (The term entrepreneur will be used throughout to refer to the entrepreneur owner and/or manager of an SME). The difficulties of penetrating entrepreneurs' thought processes in order to fully understand how they think when making decisions is well documented (Hills and LaForge, 1992). Indeed it is the 'process' behind decisions and actions, how and why decisions are made and behaviours occur, that needs to be understood. Therefore it is imperative that the methodologies employed in enterprise research allow for penetration of such issues, in some depth.

This chapter reviews the scope and parameters of qualitative research methodologies and emphasizes how they are important to enterprise research. The use of a combination of qualitative methods adapted for researching enterprises and entrepreneurs is described and an illustration of 'experiential research' using academics, consultants and entrepreneurs is provided. An emphasis is given to the need for in-depth understanding and how each methodology can provide meaningful insights into understanding enterprises and their decision making.

GATHERING INFORMATION

Entrepreneurs' intuitively gather information. They use a variety of apparently unconnected approaches to piece together a picture of market information that serves as a foundation for decision-making and action. It could be argued that entrepreneurs' mode of gathering information is a natural or common sense way of making sense of market and human behaviour. For example they may start with a 'hunch', react to an idea or event, or an anecdote that raises their interest in a particular issue, new idea or market. This may lead to the entrepreneur beginning to look for confirmation or contradiction of the developing hunch, so s/he may begin to observe the market place, activities and interactions, or talk to others in the social or work environment. S/he will have a 'feel' for the value or usefulness of information and its source and will intuitively accept or reject information as it is gathered. In this way entrepreneurs' often do their own marketing research, that is they do it intuitively and would not call it 'market research'. Instead it could be described as information gathering and much of this activity may well be subconscious on the entrepreneurs' behalf.

Clearly this will present some difficulties for researchers trying to penetrate entrepreneurs' thought processes. These cognitive processes are important to understand and therefore research methodologies need to allow for identification and penetration of issues related to the research process. Thus it is important to consider how research methods can be used to suit the practitioners needs, allow for convenience and/or expediency, and yet also provide meaningful information of high quality for academic research purposes.

CONTEXTUAL INFLUENCES ON ENTERPRISE RESEARCH

Entrepreneurs tend not to take decisions along functional frameworks (Gartner et al., 1992; Carson, 1993). Instead, any management decisions are likely to be intertwined and embedded in decisions concerning the holistic running of the enterprise (Gilmore and Carson, 1999) in the context of doing business and the overall priorities of that business. Therefore any attempt by researchers to reach some depth of understanding of how entrepreneurs operate will require research methods that take account of the specific characteristics of enterprises, and should recognize that the research will be influenced by the relatively dynamic business environment in which they exist (Carson et al., 2001). Such research needs to recognize the importance of gaining an understanding of the phenomena and to adopt methods that will take account of the holistic, contextual dimensions of the environment in which these managers operate. That is, understanding the 'process' behind the actual decisions and the characteristics of the entrepreneur.

Therefore, research methodologies employed should be appropriate for penetrating phenomenon in some depth and allow for specific issues to be studied over both long and short time periods if necessary.

THE SCOPE OF QUALITATIVE RESEARCH METHODOLOGIES

This section explores different methodologies that have been 'adapted' to suit the nature of enterprises and entrepreneurs for use in enterprise research. The research methodologies build on the strengths of qualitative methods, particularly their flexibility and ability to explore the complex and interrelated nature of entrepreneurial decision making in the context of enterprise characteristics. Qualitative methods can be combined to carry out research that gets much closer to the phenomenon and adapted to suit the specific context of enterprises under study. Firstly qualitative interviewing and using a stream of research is described and later an illustration of 'experiential research' is given to demonstrate how researchers can work very closely with entrepreneurs in order to gain an in-depth understanding of how they perceive their business and its environment.

Initially it is useful for researchers to understand management decision-making processes in enterprises. Such understanding is unlikely to stem from research administered from a distance, since it has been advocated that small firms should not be stripped of their context (Aldrich, 1992; Borch and Arthur, 1995; Brown and Butler, 1995). In addition, the level of understanding required is unlikely to be achieved through a highly structured and orderly research approach such as the traditional survey methodology. Bygrave (1989) contends that entrepreneurship is not a smooth, continuous linear process and as such should not be studied using methods that were designed for such processes. Instead research should try to mirror enterprise decision-making processes which are in themselves unlikely to be orderly and structured.

In-depth understanding of the influences upon the series of processes involved in SME managerial decision making and activity benefits from a research approach that allows the phenomenon to be studied closely (Gilmore and Carson, 1996; Carson et al., 2002), longitudinally (Hornaday and Churchill, 1987; Bygrave, 1989), taking cognisance of an 'insider' perspective. Thus it is unlikely that conventional quantitative research will reach the required level of penetration (Daft and Weick, 1983). Studying SME entrepreneurs will not be about testing variables, nor about testing techniques since isolating and manipulating variables will create an artificial environment and will remove the opportunity to understand the change processes inherently involved in human action and behaviour (Patton, 1987; Easterby-Smith et al., 1991). Obviously, the 'closer' the research and the researcher can get to the actual decision-making process, the greater the richness of findings in providing a genuine understanding from the enterprise entrepreneur's perspective.

The variability and flexibility of qualitative methods contribute to their suitability for adaptation in enterprise research. For example, methods can be readily adapted to take account of specific industry and business contexts, individual owner-managers viewpoints and idiosyncrasies, organizational circumstance and the development of situations over time. Indeed, the use of a variety of techniques will achieve a wider and more in-depth understanding of the complex and often vague processes and outcomes of managerial decision making in the context of wider business activities. They will permit the study of the interactive and performance dimensions of decision-making within a natural setting over a longitudinal time period. This allows recognition of a dynamic or change environment.

The basic underpinning techniques of qualitative methods that are particularly useful for studying business enterprises and entrepreneurs are qualitative interviewing, using a combination of methods as outlined below and creating a stream of research. These can be adapted and developed to fit the particular enterprise research context.

QUALITATIVE INTERVIEWING

When carrying out fieldwork for enterprises, specific consideration must be given to the nature of the environment in which data gathering will take place; and perhaps more importantly, the characteristics of the individuals involved in the phenomena under study. In a longitudinal study it will be advantageous to prepare for at least two visits to the key informants.

The first part of a study will involve face-to-face in-depth interviews with entrepreneurs, allowing for follow-up interviews at a later date if necessary. These interviews should be audio-taped with the respondent's consent. The objective of such interviews is to allow entrepreneurs to describe their views in relation to what they do, how, why, when and where. Therefore a suitable interview approach is one that takes account of the entrepreneur's characteristics and individuality. In-depth interviews following a relatively unstructured pattern using the 'tell me about . . .' (Carson et al.,

1998) approach for investigating business decision-making activity, allows respondents to describe opinions and views in relation to what they do, how, when, where and why, in their own words. These in-depth interviews can then provide an open, flexible, experiential and illuminating way to study complex, dynamic interactive situations, such as management decision-making and business activities. Such an interview technique provides all the advantages of in-depth interviewing:

- covering a wide area of interest, allowing the researcher to become familiar with the areas of interest as the research progresses;
- identification and exploration of the key issues as they are revealed due to the open-ended nature of the interview protocol;
- allowing opportunity for further probing and examining until mutual understanding is reached.

It is also critical to consider the language used for researching entrepreneurs. The language used by the interviewer should deliberately exclude marketing and business terminology but focus instead on what the informant does in relation to various aspects of business. This is a vital prerequisite for understanding the entrepreneur's motivations behind decision-making and various behaviours. Previous studies have shown that entrepreneurs will adapt the mode of the recipient to their views (Hills and Muzyka, 1993). This is particularly so if the entrepreneur has had technology transfer or prior knowledge in an area of business. Other entrepreneurial characteristics contribute to a situation where the entrepreneur will quickly respond to an interviewer in terms s/he thinks the interviewer will expect. For example, a need to be perceived to be in control of the business, guiding it's direction and in charge of his/her own destiny. As a consequence of this, the entrepreneur will answer questions in the language in which they are put. For example, if a question refers to marketing strategy the answer will be given using appropriate marketing strategy 'jargon'. Analysis of previous empirical data shows a significant correlation between the language of the question and the language of the reply (Hills and Muzyka, 1993). In avoiding such a circumstance questions should completely avoid the use of business terminology.

Question variations and extensions used in such a study should encourage the interviewee to use his/her own language and terminology and expand on descriptions of business activities. For example, the first question in each interview may be deliberately open and general allowing the interviewee to describe business activities in his/her own way. Thus the opening question might be: 'How do you do business?' The ensuing description of business activities and evolution of these activities may be investigated by the use of some probing questions as and when necessary. Throughout the interview the following guidelines are suggested:

- care should be taken not to interrupt the flow of the interviewee's response regardless of relevance;
- if the entrepreneur uses jargon, this should be ignored if possible and non-jargon language used;
- remain silent as much as possible when the entrepreneur is talking;
- avoid engaging in conversations of agreement or disagreement;
- remain detached but receptive, for example, by nodding frequently;
- maintain eye contact as often as possible;
- where possible, use encouraging phrases such as: 'can you tell me more about . . .' and means of clarification such as: 'tell me what you mean by . . .'.

As qualitative research aims to achieve in-depth understanding, raw data should be recorded and transcribed verbatim. Specific criteria for analysis can be developed and used to 'organize' and 'group' the new data into manageable frameworks.

A COMBINATION OF METHODS

There are many advantages of using a combination of research methods to understand enterprises and how they do business. A significant feature of using a combination of techniques is that data can be collected and analysed holistically. It allows the researcher to take account of the specific characteristics of the firm and decision-makers in question; and enables research to be carried out within a relatively dynamic business environment. Thus, a combination of methods will provide a useful means of studying the complex, interactive, and personal nature of entrepreneurial decision-making. Some of the most commonly used qualitative methods include focus groups discussions, surveys, observations studies, ethnographies, conversational analysis, content analysis and in-depth interviews (for further reading see Carson et al., 2001, Chapters 6–11). The use of a combination of two of more of these allows a variety of data to be gathered, for example, verbal reports, observed occurrences, written reports, prior documentation, and data involving researcher experience within a specific context.

Overall, a combined approach can accommodate flexibility, variety and a 'pot-pourri of interpretative techniques' (Das, 1983, p. 301). Variability and flexibility will contribute to adaptation for business and managerial situations. In particular, qualitative methods can be readily adapted for research in entrepreneurial contexts and marketing situations to take account of specific industry and business contexts, individual owner-managers' viewpoints and idiosyncrasies and organizational circumstances.

The use of a combination of techniques help to achieve a wider and more in-depth understanding of the complex, often vague processes and outcomes of managerial decision-making in the context of wider business activities. They permit the study of the interactive and performance dimensions of decision-making activities studied within a natural setting over a longitudinal time period, which incorporates recognition of a dynamic or 'change' environment. A combination of methods can be chosen to suit the purpose of the research, and to build on and develop understanding as the research time progresses.

Clearly, the choice of a variety of methods is important whereby each one contributes some understanding about specific aspects of decision-making and behaviours of enterprises, and should allow the next research stage to build and develop on previous learning and understanding. In this way a combination of methods used can provide a rich portrait of phenomena under study. This allows the researcher to learn about the 'inputs and outcomes but also gain an understanding of the texture, activities and processes' (Belk et al., 1988, p. 449) occurring in the day to day operations and activities and the impact of these occurrences on enterprise activity. It also permits further experiential understanding of the worst and best scenarios in relation to the phenomenon under study.

The number of methods used can be expanded and adapted as appropriate for the specific research topic to allow researchers to develop the 'best' possible methodologies for specific research problems or issues. To illustrate how this might be used in practice, for example, a study could include:

- a survey of entrepreneurs/owner/managers in a particularly industry context;
- in-depth interviews with 'key informant' owner-managers;
- observations of the business activity of a specific company;
- data comparison of competitive activity;
- analysis of appropriate company records.

This borrows from case research where a combination of methods are used to study a small number of companies or situations but this combination of methods is more focused on the specific issues relevant to how enterprises do business and takes account of the wider environmental context and circumstance.

A STREAM OF RESEARCH

A further extension of the use of a combination of methods can be developed from the idea that 'individual method studies should be carefully designed to build upon what has been learned in previous studies' (Davies et al., 1985, p. 31). A stage by stage process of data collection and interpretation can aid development in the understanding of the entrepreneur's decision making and behaviours. This is particularly relevant in the context of individual organizations operating within a specific industry context, where the longitudinal 'stream' approach allows each part or 'stage' of the research to build on what had been learned in a previous 'stage'. At the end of each stage, specific interpretations and managerial implications can be drawn in relation to the findings of that stage of study (Gilmore and Carson, 1996). Thus the longitudinal dimension is important in taking cognisance of the 'holistic' dimension of entrepreneurial, decision-making practices, and how time impacts on business decisions and activities. This is illustrated in Figure 4.1 (from Gilmore and Carson, 1996).

These research approaches, qualitative interviewing, combining methods and using a stream of research can be adapted for the research context of enterprises and their entrepreneur's characteristics. An example of 'experiential research' is described below.

EXPERIENTIAL RESEARCH

In the search for an appropriate methodology for studying enterprises the characteristics of entrepreneurs are considered because of their significance and impact upon researching this domain. Such is this significance and impact that academic researchers often find it difficult to achieve meaningful understanding of enterprises and entrepreneurial phenomena. Understanding is often more easily reached through practitioners who are entrepreneurs or who are working with entrepreneurs. A research approach that takes account of both academic and practitioner perspectives and the contributions that both of these bring to researching entrepreneurs can help to achieve a more in-depth understanding and allow closeness to the research phenomena.

Academic Researchers with Experience of Researching Entrepreneurs

If 'closeness' is crucial to greater understanding of SME marketing decision making, then how close can an academic researcher hope to get to entrepreneurs? The research methodology literature tells us that some form

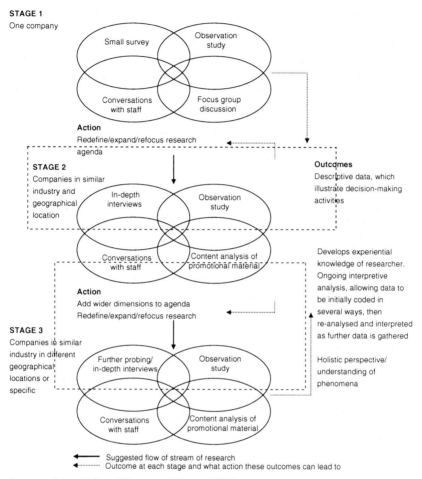

STAGE 1
One company

Action
Redefine/expand/refocus research agenda

STAGE 2
Companies in similar industry and geographical location

Outcomes
Descriptive data, which illustrate decision-making activities

Action
Add wider dimensions to agenda
Redefine/expand/refocus research

Develops experiential knowledge of researcher. Ongoing interpretive analysis, allowing data to be initially coded in several ways, then re-analysed and interpreted as further data is gathered

STAGE 3
Companies in similar industry in different geographical locations or specific

Holistic perspective/ understanding of phenomena

Small survey
Observation study
Conversations with staff
Focus group discussion

In-depth interviews
Observation study
Conversations with staff
Content analysis of promotional material

Further probing/ in-depth interviews
Observation study
Conversations with staff
Content analysis of promotional material

Suggested flow of stream of research
Outcome at each stage and what action these outcomes can lead to

Source: Adapted from Gilmore and Carson (1996).

Figure 4.1   Stream of research

of ethnographic approach offers the best opportunity for academic research to get 'close' to a phenomenon (Bott, 1955; Becker, 1958; Cohen, 1968). Indeed in small firm research, calls have been made for more grounded data that can be collected using ethnographic techniques (Curran, 1987; Curran and Burrows, 1987; Bygrave, 1989). This is where academic researchers will engage in such studies by 'immersing' themselves in the activities of an enterprise, at least as far as an entrepreneur will allow (Rosen, 1991). Such studies invariably require a longitudinal dimension and are time and resource intensive (Easterby-Smith et al., 1991). A crucial enhancement towards 'closeness' of such a research approach is 'experiential learning' whereby the researcher experiences the entrepreneurial way of doing business and develops an understanding of how entrepreneurs and SMEs take marketing decisions (Gilmore and Carson, 1996). Such experiential learning is rare, chiefly because the research is unlikely to lead to or assume responsibility for any decision making. The 'experience' therefore is likely to be 'experience by examples'. This can contribute to some learning experience but it is weak compared to actual experiential learning and subsequent knowledge.

It is difficult, if not impossible for academic researchers to get close enough to entrepreneurs to glean in-depth knowledge of a particular phenomenon within an individual enterprise without total immersion over an extended time period. Over several years academics may accumulate contacts with entrepreneurs, develop some experiential knowledge of these phenomena and in this way become an 'expert' assessor of the phenomena. However, the problem of getting as close as possible to the phenomena in any specific research study remains. Is there an alternative approach to the conventional ethnographic methodological approaches normally associated with achieving 'closeness' to data? A research framework that illustrates that a greater closeness is possible is illustrated in Figure 4.2, 'Researchers Characteristics and Strengths' (from Grant et al., 2001).

This figure illustrates how different 'players' can contribute to an in-depth research study of SME entrepreneurs decision making. Academic researchers (upper left box and circle) can bring a meaningful contribution by providing a broad multi-dimensional perspective of SMEs and enterprise research in terms of theory and conceptualization. In addition, they provide a research rigour founded upon academic principles. Further, they will draw on prior experiential knowledge of research in the field and will have an ability to articulate issues of importance.

SME Consultant Researchers

Of course, the earlier debate about limited closeness still applies to such academics and the research phenomena. Thus, this model includes another dimension that provides both different and greater closeness, that of SME consultant researchers, who work closely with enterprises (upper right box and circle). It is widely recognized that entrepreneurs will often seek knowledge and experience from outside their own sphere of competence (Dubini and Aldrich, 1991; Tjosvold and Weicker, 1993; Donckels and Lambrecht, 1995). The main providers of such external competence (outside of the entrepreneurs own network of personal contacts that will have been exploited before considering 'buying-in' competence), are specialist business

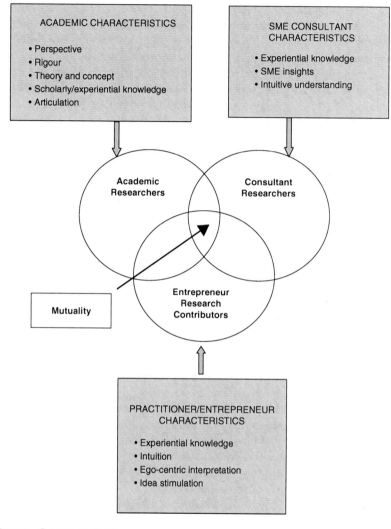

Source: Grant et al. (2001).

Figure 4.2   Researcher's characteristics and strengths

consultants. Such consultants will have accumulated considerable experiential knowledge of small businesses and as such will have acquired meaningful insights into SME activities and operations. They will also possess an intuitive understanding of entrepreneur behaviour and the characteristics of enterprises. Since such consultants will normally work longitudinally with entrepreneurs they become greatly immersed in the enterprise. Such immersion is greater than an academic researcher could hope to gain because the consultant has responsibility for achieving expected outcomes. Thus the experiential knowledge is 'real' as opposed to being experience by 'example'.

A further dimension is added if such consultants proactively use their experiential knowledge and seek greater understanding that, in turn, will contribute to their own expertize in future consultancies. In such a circumstance these consultants can be classified as 'Consultant Researchers'.

Entrepreneurial Characteristics

The third component of the model is the entrepreneur him/herself (the bottom box and circle). Research methodologies such as case study research; delphi methods and focus group discussions will often incorporate respondents in a final check, clarification and authentication of research interpretations and data descriptions. Such methods do this to ensure transparent verification, application and interpretation. However, in researching entrepreneurs and small businesses it is possible to go further. By using entrepreneurs as part of the research process, not only as respondents but also as interpreters of findings, the research will have substantially greater meaning and value. Entrepreneurs' inherent characteristics of experiential learning and intuition, coupled with an egocentric perspective of business issues allow for insightful contributions within a research study. Furthermore, the entrepreneurial characteristics of vision and creativity will often stimulate ideas for further research.

These three components: academic researchers with experience of researching entrepreneurs; small firm consultants who have a genuine interest in knowing about their clients; and entrepreneurs who are interested in and stimulated by their involvement in such research provide a strong 'mutuality' and incentive for research understanding of outcomes (Grant et al., 2001). This mutuality is further considered in terms of the entrepreneur's naturalistic way of doing business and academic and consultants mutual compatibility.

MUTUALITY OF RESEARCHERS

The mutual compatibility of both academics and consultant practitioners can make a significant contribution to enterprise research. Academic researchers have an experiential knowledge that is based upon rigour and construct. They tend to have a wide perspective over a variety of business, commercial and marketing activities. They do not often become directly involved in marketing practice except as observers or advisors, neither of which requires personal implementation and therefore responsibility for the actual marketing activity. However, their experiential knowledge enables them to compare and contrast various scenarios. They have the inherent or at least learned ability to build theory and to conceptualize around general concepts and frameworks that they will then seek to test or confirm in practice. In addition, because of their teaching and learning focus academics develop an ability to articulate perspectives, theories and concepts.

In contrast, consulting practitioners' expertize stem from their closeness to entrepreneurial enterprises. As a consequence they glean significant insights into the characteristics of enterprises, and those of the entrepreneurs. They tend to develop an innate intuitive understanding of the decision-making processes and stimuli of entrepreneurs. Their experiential knowledge enables them to be highly focused and personal in relation to individual enterprises. They view enterprise issues and problems in the 'singular/unique' rather than in the general context.

Therefore it is reasonable to say that academics view enterprises from the 'outside', bringing a wider environmental perspective to the phenomenon, whereas consultant practitioners deal with enterprises from 'inside', helping to guide individual enterprises through their problems. The combination of both perspectives allows these researchers to perform a wider and deeper analysis and evaluation of enterprise phenomena.

RESEARCHERS' EXPERIENCE

There are two significant influences that enterprise research can acknowledge, these are the influence that the researchers' experience can bring to bear and the need to understand the approaches, often different, that the entrepreneur takes in doing business. Gibb and Davies (1990) recognize these influences when they state: 'the influences of the values of the researcher in designing methods of data collection and failure to recognise that owner/manager respondents have different approaches to providing information than professional managers'.

It is important to recognize the influence and value of a researcher's experiential learning in evaluating data and phenomena. The researcher needs to have a 'feeling' for and understanding of the context in which entrepreneurs operate. Qualitative research permits the research to evolve, develop and build on earlier pre-understanding (Gilmore and Carson, 1996). It allows researchers to directly experience the world of informants and all of its variations. Living through the 'highs' and 'lows' of their lives allows the researcher to know the phenomenon under investigation in a way that few other methodologies permit (Hill, 1993). Van Maanen (1979) illustrates this advantage further when he compares qualitative and quantitative methods:

> Qualitative research focuses on the unfolding of the process rather than social structures that are often the focus of quantitative researchers. Qualitative researchers in contrast to their quantitative colleagues claim forcefully to know relatively little about what a given piece of observed behaviour means until they have developed a description of the context in which the behaviour takes place and attempted to see that behaviour from the position of its originator (p. 521).

The experiential nature of qualitative research, combined with the experiential learning of the researcher allows understanding throughout the research to evolve and build on previous stages of the research and contribute to a deep and meaningful understanding both of the relevant phenomena and the context in which the phenomena occurs. This is of particular value in studies of how business is carried out and how entrepreneurs make decisions in the context of the organizational and business environment. For example, it is difficult to isolate specific 'variables' in a business context, where many issues impact on each other; and where there are many external and internal influences on managerial and business activities.

DESIGNING A SPECIFIC RESEARCH METHODOLOGY FOR STUDYING SMEs

The discussion so far has presented a conceptual model framework that draws on the compatible strengths of each of it constituents. It has argued that these constituents embody different aspects of research experience, and have had some experiential learning regarding the phenomena. This conceptualization is now applied to an empirical study.

Using researchers from different perspectives (three academics and two practitioner/consultants) the focus of an empirical study was to seek greater understanding of the way entrepreneurs take decisions, and the context of how they do business in general. The aim was to reach an 'interpretative understanding of action' (O'Shaughnessy, 1987), where phenomena are considered within a specific context, taking account of the subject's view and their understanding and meaning of the situation. Some key considerations to be taken into account or acknowledged were the character of the entrepreneur and the inherent flexibility and informalities of small business enterprises. Due to these considerations, it was useful for the researchers to define their own criteria for researching business performance in enterprises.

Research Process

The criteria for selecting companies was based on each firm being established for at least five years and having exhibited growth. The rationale for selecting enterprises that had been established for 5 years was so that they could be deemed to have 'come through' the early turbulent years (Barkham et al., 1996). This was to ensure that they had grown out of the dynamic turmoil of the early establishment years; where many small firms exist in an oscillating cycle of rapid environmental changes involving threats and opportunities from one year to the next. Also these firms employed more than 10 people so they were not deemed to be 'self-employed', 'ma and pop' enterprises. More importantly, they were established for a period of 'doing business', which had led to established practices and customs of decision making. Therefore business decision making becomes 'established' in that they know what 'works' for them and are unwilling to experiment with new techniques except as part of a controlled development of the business.

Members of the research team (three academics and two consultant researchers) identified potential companies for participation. These companies were either previously known by the team, or referred to the team. A collective decision on the selection of each company was made based on how well the entrepreneur was likely to meet the established criteria and participate in the study. Before the interviews took place the entrepreneurs were approached to obtain their commitment to participate in this study. It was explained to each potential participant that the project involved a longitudinal study that could extend over several years.

Research Design

The nature of the qualitative approach enabled the 'research team', the academics and practitioner/consultants, to gather insights and to analyse and interpret SME owner-managers' rationale for the decisions made in the overall context of their business environment. The research design built upon the key strengths and advantages of the conceptual model and significant characteristics highlighted so far in this discussion. While this research adheres to the requirements of academic research it does 'step out' of the confines of research done solely by academics. The distinctive feature of this research design is the tripartite combination of research instigators and contributors; the research 'team' in this research design consisting of three academics; two consultant practitioners; and 15 SME entrepreneurs. Each of the contributors brought their own unique strengths to the research as described in Figure 4.2 above. The combination of these strengths created an inherently positive and complimentary research team.

This study recognized the importance of using a holistic variety of research methods for gathering data, as emphasized by Hofer and Bygrave (1992). Figure 4.2 illustrates how the triumvirate research team employed a variety of research methods to achieve an integrated research approach. The sequential essence of the research approach was to use a series of in-depth interviews, case studies, longitudinal ethnographic consultations and focus group evaluations to build an understanding of each enterprise's decision-making processes.

Stage 1 – interviews with entrepreneurs

At Stage 1 initial in-depth interviews were carried out with selected entrepreneurs at an appointed time, often in the early evening to suit entrepreneurs. Each interview lasted between one and two hours and was carried out by an academic or a consultant. All interviews were tape-recorded. Entrepreneurs were encouraged to talk openly and were assured of confidentiality.

The research followed an interview protocol designed from a comprehensive search of the literature combined with the experiential learning of the research team involved in the project. Riley (1996) states that when eliciting socially constructed knowledge, formally structured questions should be minimized; and that any subsequent interventions should take the form of prompts and probes, based on the words of the informant. Therefore the questions were open-ended and designed to encourage the interviewee to 'volunteer' information. Specifically, the language used by the interviewers deliberately excluded marketing terminology, and focused instead on what the entrepreneur did in relation to various aspects of his/her business. The reason for this was to avoid leading questions that could influence responses by the interviewee. Previous studies (for example, Hills and LaForge, 1992) have shown that entrepreneurs will adopt the mode of the recipient to their views, particularly if they have had technology transfer or prior knowledge in an area of discussion. Instead the approach was to allow the interviewee to volunteer information regarding the decisions s/he makes and to investigate the rationale for those decisions.

Interviews began with the question: how do you do business? Some prompts were used when necessary. These included questions relating to how the business developed over time, such as: 'once the business was established – how did you do business?' Also, 'what is different today from how you did this 3/6/12 months ago?'

The analysis was carried out as follows. Each interview transcript was analysed by an academic and a consultant separately and then findings and researcher understandings and interpretations were discussed. After this, the key findings were written up. A summary of the key issues, together with illustrative quotes from the transcripts was used to prepare a short presentation for the participant entrepreneurs in the study.

Stage 2 – focus group discussions

All 15 entrepreneurs who participated in the in-depth interview were invited to a central location to attend a presentation of the study's findings. The experiential knowledge gleaned from interview participation and a variety of informal conversations about the research was exploited by involving the entrepreneur further in focus group evaluations. These focus group discussions led to the development and refinement of outcomes. Most significantly, they produced new research phenomena/outcomes that elongated the longitudinal ongoing dimension of the research programme.

At these focus group meetings one or more academic researcher would present the key findings to *all* the research team. That is, in addition to the three academics and two consultant researchers, the focus group consisted of at least six of the entrepreneur participants who were hearing the 'collective' interpretation of findings for the first time. The implications and interpretation of these findings were then discussed. During these 'focus group' discussions the interpretation of the findings were debated further, refined and confirmed in more detail and made more context specific by all participants. The entrepreneurs responded with queries, clarifications and additions. The ensuing discussions were then tape-recorded for further analysis. Further interviews and focus groups were carried out to consider new research issues and new insights from the findings of previous interviews. This research developed over a longitudinal time period of three years. During this time, all participants identified research issues. Most significantly they produced new research insights and outcomes that elongated the research programme.

OUTCOMES OF RESEARCH APPROACH

This study led to many new topics being identified as part of SME entrepreneur decision making and how they do business. Table 4.1 summarizes the benefits of using academics, consultants and entrepreneurs in a mutual research approach in relation to data gathering, data analysis, and inputs and outputs of the research process (Grant et al., 2001).

More significantly, the study identified aspects of new understanding and insights into SME entrepreneurial decision making. From the research team's perspective, and perhaps most significantly in the wider context, the qualitative research approach adopted for the study has contributed to the bridging of the gap between academic marketing theory and the day-to-day decision-making processes of SMEs. It has demonstrated that academics, consultants and entrepreneurs can work together in reaching greater insights and understanding of the world in which all are concerned. To illustrate, some of the findings are briefly outlined here.

Table 4.1   The benefits of academics, consultants and entrepreneurs in a 'mutual research' approach

	Input processes	Outcomes
Data gathering	• Selection of appropriate interviewees, with no refusals • Up-front creditability of the researchers • Up-front commitment by the interviewees to collaborate in a long-term process	• Ability to probe potentially relevant or ambiguous areas in greater depth • Resulted in more open discussion • Search in more depth the meaning of question responses
Data analysis	• Provide an appreciation and interpretation of the broader commercial context of the responses • Improve the quality of the analysis by providing the commercial experience that enables a better understanding of responses	• Assist with the linking of the responses with the theory • Conclusions were based on the consensus of the researchers. Given their differing perspectives, this gives more robust outcomes from a small sample

Source: Grant et al. (2001).

Key finding 1   Findings led to an understanding of how entrepreneurs use networking as an inherent tool of marketing and that this networking activity is very compatible with how entrepreneurs do business. The study also led to many insights about the purpose and process of entrepreneurial marketing by networking and how entrepreneurs relied heavily on their networking activities for everyday business management.

Key finding 2   The study also contributed to an understanding and interpretation of how SME entrepreneurs add value to their marketing activities. Entrepreneurs focus on achieving competitive advantage through added value marketing approaches and they do so as an inherently natural way of doing business. For example value is added through the firm's product offering, its pricing approaches, delivery, sales activities, promotional campaigns and customer service provision. Although entrepreneurs engage in many aspects of added-value marketing they do not consider this as anything exceptional, but as normal day-to-day business activities to pursue customer satisfaction and ultimately competitive advantage.

Key finding 3   Findings illustrated that in addition to the well documented scope of innovative marketing (reactive and market-led, profit-driven, continuous and incremental, based on existing ideas and encompassing all marketing activity), entrepreneurs can expand this scope of innovative activity by being opportunistic, using networking activities, flexible offerings and developing their competencies.

Key finding 4   The study also provided some insights on how entrepreneurs develop competencies for doing business. Over time, entrepreneurs' existing competencies can combine to create experiential knowledge by developing experiential learning. Where some entrepreneurs bring technical competence to their own business, many will have had little prior marketing management decision-making experience and therefore will need more immediate development. The study emphasized how entrepreneurs make a concerted effort to improve their decision-making by building on their existing competencies and by actively developing experiential knowledge over time.

CONCLUSION

Given the history of research in relation to enterprises and entrepreneurial activity thus far, and the relative newness of the research area, research at the interface should not be 'method bound'. Instead, research should be designed to suit the purpose and context of SMEs, especially given the developmental and interactive nature of enterprises.

This chapter has advocated the merits of qualitative methodologies and analysis for researching small to medium-sized enterprises. Qualitative methods are flexible, adaptable and penetrative and can aid the researcher in identifying important issues that are inherent in how entrepreneurs do business. The actual research design for individual studies can be 'unique' to the specific situation of each research project. Such refinement can reflect the characteristics of the enterprise or entrepreneur.

An 'experiential research' design illustrated how academics, consultants and entrepreneurs could work together in a 'mutual' way to achieve an in-depth research approach, allowing researchers to get close to the phenomena under study and contributing to a rich understanding of enterprises and how entrepreneurs do business.

NOTE

*   This chapter is based on the following articles, with special thanks to Nicole Coviello, Ken Grant, Richard Laney and Bill Pickett: Grant, K., A. Gilmore, D. Carson, R. Laney and B. Pickett (2001), ' "Experiential" research methodology: An integrated academic-practitioner team approach', *Qualitative Market Research: An International Journal*, **4**(2), pp. 66–74; Gilmore, A. and N. Coviello (1999), 'Methodologies for research at the marketing/entrepreneurship interface', *Journal of Research in Marketing and Entrepreneurship*, **1**(1), pp. 39–51 and Gilmore, A. and D. Carson (2000), 'Demonstration of a Methodology for assessing SME decision making', *Journal of Research in Marketing and Entrepreneurship*, **2**(2), pp. 108–24.

REFERENCES

Aldrich, H.E. (1992), 'Methods in our madness? Trends in entrepreneurship research', in D.L. Sexton and J.D. Kasarda (eds), *The State of the Art of Entrepreneurship Research*, Boston, MA, Kent, PWS, pp. 191–213.

Barkham, R., G. Gudgin, M. Hart, and E. Hanvey (1996), *The Determinants of Small Firm Growth: An Inter-Regional Study in the United Kingdom 1986–1990*, London: Jessica Kingsley Publishers Ltd.

Becker, H.S. (1958), 'Problems of inference and proof in participant observation', *American Sociological Review*, **23** (December), 652–60.

Belk, R., M. Wallendorf and J. Sherry (1988), 'A naturalistic enquiry into buyer behaviour at a swap meet', *Journal of Consumer Research*, **14**(4), 449–71.

Borch, O.J. and M.B. Arthur (1995), 'Strategic networks among small firms: implications for strategy research methodology', *Journal of Management Studies*, **32**(4), 419–41.

Bott, E. (1955), 'Urban families: conjugal roles and social networks', *Human Relations*, **8**, 345–84.

Brown, B. and J.E. Butler (1995), 'Competitors as allies: a study of entrepreneurial networks in the US wine industry', *Journal of Small Business Management*, **33**(3), 57–65.

Bygrave, W.D. (1989), 'The entrepreneurship paradigm (I): a philosophical look at its research methodologies', *Entrepreneurship: Theory & Practice*, **14**(1), 7–26.

Carson, D. (1993), 'A philosophy for marketing education in small firms', *Journal of Marketing Management*, **9**(2), 189–204.

Carson, D., A. Gilmore, D. Cummins, A. O'Donnell and K. Grant (1998), 'Price setting in SMEs: some empirical findings', *Pricing Strategy and Practice*, **7**(1), 74–86.

Carson, D., A. Gilmore, C. Perry and K. Gronhaug (2001), *Qualitative Marketing Research*, London: Sage.

Carson, D., M. Enright, A. Tregear, P. Copley, A. Gilmore, D. Stokes, C. Hardesty and J.H. Deacon (2002), 'Contextual marketing', paper presented to The Academy of Marketing/AMA/UIC Special Interest Group on the Marketing and Entrepreneurship Interface, University of Hertfordshire, January.

Cohen, Y.A. (1968), 'Macroethnology: large scale comparative studies', in Clifton, J.A., *Introduction to Cultural Anthropology, Essays in the Scope and Methods of the Science of Man*. Boston, MA: Houghton Mifflin.

Curran, J. (1987), 'Starting and surviving: some small firms in the 1980s', presentation to the 10th National UK Small Firms Policy and Research Conference, Cranfield School of Management.

Curran, J. and R. Burrows (1987), 'Ethnographic approaches to the study of the small business sector' in K. O'Neill, R. Bhambri, T. Faulkner and T. Cannon. *Small Business Development: Some Current Issues.* Avebury: Gower.

Daft, R. and K. Weick (1983), 'Toward a model of organisations as interpretation systems', *Academy of Management Review*, **8**, 284–95.

Hari Das, T. (1983), 'Qualitative research in organisational behaviour', *Journal of Management Studies*, **20**(3), 301–14.

Davies, C.D., G.E. Hills and R.W. LaForge (1985), 'The marketing/small enterprise paradox: a research agenda', *International Small Business Journal*, **3**(3), 31–42.

Donckels, R. and J. Lambrecht (1995), 'Networks and small business growth: an explanatory model', *Small Business Economics*, **7**(4), 273–89.

Dubini, P. and H. Aldrich (1991), 'Personal and extended networks are central to the entrepreneurial process', *Journal of Business Venturing*, **6**, 305–13.

Easterby-Smith, M., R. Thorpe and A. Low (1991), *Management Research: An Introduction*, London: Sage.

Gartner, William B., Barbara J. Bird and Jennifer A. Starr (1992), 'Acting as if: differentiating entrepreneurial from organisational behaviour', *Entrepreneurship: Theory and Practice*, **16**(3), 13–31.

Gibb, A. and L. Davies (1990), 'In pursuit of frameworks for the development of growth models of the small business', *International Small Business Journal*, **9**(1), (Oct–Dec), 15–31.

Gilmore, A. and D. Carson (1996), '"Integrative' qualitative methods in a services context', *Marketing Intelligence and Planning*, **14**(6), 21–6.

Gilmore, A. and D. Carson (1999), 'Entrepreneurial marketing by networking', *New England Journal of Entrepreneuriship*, **2**(2), 31–8

Grant, K., A. Gilmore, D. Carson, R. Laney and B. Pickett (2001), '"Experiential" research methodology: an integrated academic-practitioner team approach', *Qualitative Market Research: An International Journal*, **4**(2), 66–74.

Hill, R. (1993), 'Ethnography and marketing research: a postmodern perspective', *American Marketing Association Conference Proceedings*, Summer, 257–60.

Hills, G. and R. LaForge (1992), 'Research at the marketing interface to advance entrepreneurship theory', *Entrepreneurship: Theory and Practice*, **16**(3), 33–59.

Hills, G.E. and D.F. Muzyka (1993), 'Introduction', in G.E. Hills, D.F. Muzyka, G.S. Omura and G.A. Knight (eds), *Proceedings of the UIC Symposium on Marketing and Entrepreneurship Interface*, Chicago: The University of Illinois, pp. vii–xv.

Hofer, Charles W. and William D. Bygrave (1992, 'Researching entrepreneurship', *Entrepreneurship Theory and Practice*, **3**(16), 91–100.

Hornaday, J.A. and N.C. Churchill (1987), 'Current trends in entrepreneurial research.' in *Frontiers of Entrepreneurship Research*, N.C. Churchill, J.A. Hornaday, B.A. Kirchhoff, O.J. Krasner and K.H. Vesper, Wellesley, MA: Babson College, 1–21.

O'Shaughnessy, J. (1987), *Explanation in Buyer Behaviour, Central Concepts and Issues*, New York: Columbia University.

Patton, M.Q. (1987), *How to Use Qualitative Methods in Evaluation*, London: Sage.

Riley, R. (1996), 'Revealing socially constructed knowledge through quasi-structured interviews and grounded theory analysis', *Journal of Travel and Tourism Marketing*, **15**(2), 21–40.

Rosen, M. (1991), 'Coming to terms with the field: understanding and doing organisational ethnography', *Journal of Management Studies*, **28**(1), 1–24.

Tjosvold, D. and D. Weicker (1993), 'Cooperative and competitive networking by entrepreneurs: a critical incident study', *Journal of Small Business Management*, **31**(1), 11–21.

Van Maanen, J. (1979), 'Reclaiming qualitative methods for organisational research', *Administrative Science Quarterly*, **24**, 520–26.

5. Quantitative methodological considerations

**Robert G. Schwartz, Nancy J. Birch
and Richard D. Teach**

INTRODUCTION

Entrepreneurship researchers must seek the 'truth' in their data analyses. Utilizing appropriate methodology is not only the right path to the truth, but also the duty of each researcher. The 'truth' also accompanies the interpretations that accompany the analyses. There is a difference between statistically significant and 'practically significant'. An adjusted r square that has a value of 2 per cent, with significance at the 0.000 level, provides little information about the real world. An analysis that is conducted utilizing point-in-time samples of firms provides only results for that time and those firms studied, not for all time and or all firms. Thus, while social scientists struggle to provide generalized results of agglomerated and in the most part, anonymous data, little is learned about specific firm types.

As strategies are multivariate constructs, the use of multivariate techniques to explain strategic relationships is a critical methodological issue. Focusing on particular firm types, rather than on all firms, and over time, allows researchers to better understand firm behaviour and the linkage to performance. As entrepreneurial firms and their environments change over time, a series of point-in-time studies of similar firms or longitudinal studies are then efficacious. Thus, researchers can contribute to a body of knowledge and an increasing level of understanding about a variety of firm types serving to enhance the education of students, practitioners, and researchers alike.

The chapter concludes with examples of two known but rarely used methodologies: factor structure comparisons utilizing interpoint distance calculations and survival analysis for predicting and understanding factors related to firm failure.

THE 1970s

In the late 1970s, a small number of researchers began to explore small firms and their strategies and their entrepreneurs. Entrepreneurship in the United States (US) had a small research following and Schumpeter's 1933 definition (paraphrased) of 'doing something not obvious to one skilled in the particular business art' was what entrepreneurship and subsequently incubators were focused on. An incubator in the late 1970s was a Fortune 500 or other large research oriented firms or organizations that spun off early stage firms. The 'opportunities' were then important to the creation of new firms and new jobs for the communities in which the large firms and organizations were located.

Computers

Related to what continues to serve as both the historical impetus and a powerful tool for the proliferation and production of entrepreneurship and general business research, in 1967 the first IBM 360 remote terminal main frame was installed at Iowa State University, thus allowing for the first remote access of computers by users. In the 1970s, for most, access to the computer continued to be boxes of cards or streams of tapes, diligently punched using card or tape punches. Turn around for data could be as much as 'days' at a time, meaning that researchers had time to both think about what was being 'run' and also about the desired outcomes. With the invention of the personal computer (PC) followed in 1984 by the development of PC based software packages, statistical software has reduced the time needed to analyse data. Perhaps then it has become too easy to analyse data leading to less thoughtful analyses.

2005

In 1980, in universities around the world there were only a small number of entrepreneurship courses taught. By 2005, there were over 225 entrepreneurship Chairs in the US and likely another 100 or more world-wide; well over 1,000 universities teaching entrepreneurship courses; the Global Entrepreneurship Monitor was active and utilized in 33 countries (see www.gemconsortium.org); the National Business Incubation Association had over 800 members worldwide (see www.nbia.org); and in spite of a world-wide stock market depression suffered in 2000–03, due in part to the entrepreneurial dot.coms and their failures, there has been an expanding world-wide interest in entrepreneurship. Concomitant with this world-wide growth in interest, the number of entrepreneurship professors, students, research papers, and conferences has greatly proliferated. With this increase in research output, methodological lapses have occurred.

Over the past 20 years an increasing number of researchers have studied entrepreneurship, its strategies, financing and environments. Traditional, multivariate regression: factor, discriminant and cluster analyses have been used to elucidate a diversity of entrepreneurial strategies. The vast majority of these studies use one point-in-time data, from anonymous firms, from diverse industries, resulting in generalized conclusions. Furthermore, many researchers have assumed that firm strategies remain relatively constant over time. Such conclusions have resulted in generalizations that conflict from study to study (Schwartz and Teach, 2001).

Perhaps three seminal papers most eloquently elucidate the challenges associated with the use of 'appropriate' methodology. Howard Stevenson (Stevenson and Harmeling, 1991), one of the early participant/founders of the Babson College Conference on Entrepreneurship Research, suggested that firms evolved in a chaotic world. This world is not that of a myriad of management studies that assume states of near equilibrium, with only small changes occurring over long periods of time. He suggested that in real life there is evidence of minor changes that have profound influences on firms. He also suggested that the ability to analyse valid observations and to provide valid prescriptive advice depended upon the nature of the industry the firm operated in and its stability. As there is no long-term equilibrium in nature, the only constancy is the constancy of change. Business events are more stochastic in nature, rather than repetitive and predictable. Certain truths (typologies) may not be consistent over time (Stevenson and Harmeling, 1991), (Schwartz et al., 2005a).

Bygrave (1989a, 1989b) suggested that advanced mathematics and statistics will likely not yield precise (business) models that can be verified with precise empirical data, but the use of them will help us form and sharpen philosophy and methodology. However, sophisticated models and equations of state are too complex and difficult to both define and to solve, although appealing in the Laplacian view, ie, a series of equations which explain the state of the firm and allow for prediction are desired. However, if too difficult to justify the end result, what should researchers do to modify their present techniques in order to produce results that can more validly portray 'the real world' (Bygrave, 1989a, 1989b)? Suggested responses to the above 'inquiries' follow.

STRATEGY AND STUDIES OVER TIME

Ansoff (1967) recognized that firms' strategies changed over time. Based on the opportunistic model of organizational adaptation, researchers should expect to find that firms, particularly in turbulent industries, would seek new opportunities and not remain stable in their strategic focus. Further, these firms should be expected to evidence complex (and different) behaviours (Miller et al., 1996).

Mintzberg (1987) suggested that strategy is a pattern of activities evolving over long periods of time (adaptive view). However, 'every match at a given point-in-time between the environment and organizational form can be considered on average, as random' (Boone and van Witteloostuijn, 1995). Thus, temporal and longitudinal studies are indicated as being efficacious in the study of entrepreneurial firms and firms in turbulent industries. Furthermore, studies in single industries or industry segments are also then indicated (Schwartz and Teach, 2001).

SINGLE INDUSTRY STUDIES

In the mid-1980s Teach, Tarpley and Schwartz (1985) conducted one of the first microelectronics firm surveys and noticed that when variables were analysed across predominately software firms versus predominantly hardware firms there were statistically significant differences ($<.100$) among variables among the firm types.

FACTOR ANALYSIS AND INTERPOINT DISTANCE CALCULATIONS

Prior statistical studies in psychology identified a technique that can be utilized for multivariate analyses. Over 200 papers were published from 1968 to 1996 covering factor analysis of marketing data (Rothman, 1996). Factor analysis has utility for data reduction in order to better understand underlying management and marketing processes, but naming these factors can be a questionable technique (Rothman, 1968) and utilizing a statistical technique to compare factor structures may be more efficacious (Schwartz and Teach, 2001).

The psychology literature suggests a robust methodology to compare strategies (Poor and Wherry, 1976). The methodology is appropriate to use in cases where two or more multidimensional subsamples can be compared. Examples of sub-samples could be fast versus slow growing firms, or new versus established firms. The 'interpoint distance methodology' has utility (Maa et al., 1996; Poor and Wherry, 1976) to directly compare factor structures and the invariance of the underlying strategies (Schwartz and Teach, 1999; Teach and Schwartz, 2000a and b; Schwartz and Teach, 2001).

Until recently this methodology has not been applied to data analyses in entrepreneurship research (Schwartz and Teach, 1999; Teach and Schwartz, 2000a and b; Schwartz et al., 2005a).

Factor analysis creates an n-dimensional (one dimension for each factor) configuration where each co-ordinate point on each factor in the configuration represents each observation. The distance between any two points, i and j, would be defined to be the interpoint distance, D_{ij}. The interpoint distances between all possible pairs of points in this n dimensional space represents all the information contained in the original data set. Thus a correlation of '1' would indicate that two factor structures contain the same information. A correlation of less than one would indicate that the data structures were different. The degree of difference would be indicated by the size of the correlation coefficient; the smaller the correlation coefficient the greater the difference. Finally, the interpoint distances identify the large outliers, 'good' information for the analyst.

SURVIVAL ANALYSIS

Survival analysis is a group of statistical techniques used to model the time it takes for an event to occur (death, failure, etc). Often the actual time to failure is unknown; that is, the event has not yet occurred when the study ends; these observations are referred to as censored. Tabachnick and Fidell (2001) present an excellent and thorough discussion of survival analysis which includes the use of a variety of statistical programs. Kauffman and Wang (2001) have also suggested the use of the technique for analysis of success and failure of dot.coms. The present authors have also applied the technique (Schwartz et al., 2005b).

The survival distribution function is the cumulative proportion of firms surviving to the beginning of i + 1st interval. That is, the proportion of firms surviving to i + 1st interval is the proportion of firms who survived to the start of ith interval times the probability of surviving to the end of the ith interval. Plotting the estimated survival curves for the two types of firms, business to business and business to consumer (B2B and B2C) is a useful initial procedure for comparing the survival experience of the two types of firms. More formally the difference in survival experience can be tested with the log-rank test. Figure 5.1 displays the survival curves and life table survival estimates for B2B and B2C firms.

The log-rank test for a difference in the survival curves of the two types of firms, B2B and B2C, was not significant, $\chi^2_1 = 1.3295, p = 0.2489$. This result suggests that there is no difference in the survival experience between B2B and B2C firms, that is, the survival curves were propor-

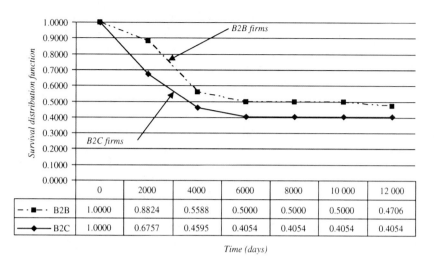

	0	2000	4000	6000	8000	10 000	12 000
- · ■- · B2B	1.0000	0.8824	0.5588	0.5000	0.5000	0.5000	0.4706
——◆—— B2C	1.0000	0.6757	0.4595	0.4054	0.4054	0.4054	0.4054

Time (days)

Source: Schwartz et al. (2005b).

Figure 5.1   Survival curves for B2B and B2C firms

tional. However, as Figure 5.1 indicates, the B2C firms began to fail earlier than did B2B firms.

Another set of survival analysis procedures can be used to determine how independent variables are related to the dependent variable, time to failure. Similar to logistic regression the analysis uses a log-linear model and results in the output of odds ratios. However, unlike logistic regression, survival analysis is able to handle censored cases. Thus, survival analysis appears to be useful when the goal is to describe the survival times at various time intervals and/or to understand what independent variables may influence the time to failure of firms.

CONCLUSIONS

Since 1985, with advances in computer hardware and statistical software, the use of statistical analyses of data and the sophistication of the analyses have increased dramatically. However, the usefulness of the analyses remains dependent on the quality of the data and the appropriate use of the statistical techniques. Data sets often include at least one of the following types of errors: sampling frame, response, measurement, non-response, or administrative errors.

As an example, a review of the literature in the relationship between strategy and firm performance will lead the young (and old alike) researcher to the conclusion that there is a positive, neutral or negative relationship between strategy and firm performance. The truth of that conclusion is that all three are true because of the nature of the data sets and the specifics of the reported studies. Researchers should compare similar data analysed utilizing similar techniques at similar points in time.

Perhaps much of the confusion regarding the 'technical' study of entrepreneurship results from researchers comparing results that utilized different data sets collected under different conditions at different times. Researchers also have begun to assume that all SMEs are entrepreneurial and firm types play no role in the analyses. The authors of this chapter suggest 'Mom and Pop' lifestyle shops are not similar to the high growth software/technology driven start-ups. Making these fundamental errors in comparing research outcomes has caused much of the confusion in the literature. Authors need to be aware that finding significant relationships between or among variables does not imply causation.

Thus, similar firms ought to be analysed over time and results compared over time. Entrepreneurial firms ought to be compared to similar entrepreneurial firms and SMEs to similar SMEs.

Outliers in small data sets can alter the variables that enter into highly significant equations and the removal of outliers from the analyses should be explained with the rationale for inclusion or exclusion.

Finally the choice of variables and how they are measured often predetermines multivariate relationships and thus the interpretation of strategies hinges upon the data collection and analyses, not the result of entrepreneurial practice.

Perhaps another 20 years of study may be needed to better elucidate relationships and the use of 'proper' research and statistical techniques. In the 'old' days, when analysis was technically difficult, complicated statistical analyses were performed by statisticians. Perhaps entrepreneurial researchers ought to go back to the past.

REFERENCES

Ansoff, H. Igor (1967), 'Strategies for diversification', *Harvard Business Review*, September–October.
Boone, C. and A. van Witteloostuijn (1995), 'Industrial organization and organizational ecology: the potentials for cross-fertilization', *Organization Studies*, 16(2), 265–98.
Bygrave, W.D. (1989a), 'The entrepreneurship paradigm (I): a philosophical look at its research methodologies', *Entrepreneurship: Theory and Practice*, 14(1), 7–26.
Bygrave, W.D. (1989b), 'The entrepreneurship paradigm (II): chaos and catastrophes among quantum jumps?', *Entrepreneurship Theory and Practice*, 14(2), 7–30.

Kauffman, R.J. and B. Wang (2001), 'The success and failure of dot coms: a multi-method survival analysis', accessed 5 November, 2005 at www.coba.panam.edu/faculty/wang/Research/KW_CIST2001_092501.pdf.

Maa, J., D.K. Pearl and R. Bartoszynski (1996), 'Reducing multidimensional two-sample data to one-dimensional interpoint comparisons', *Annals of Statistics*, **24**(3), 1069–74.

Miller, D., T.K. Lant, F.J. Milliken and H.J. Kom (1996), 'The evolution of strategic simplicity: exploring the two models of organizational adaption', *Journal of Management*, **22**(6), 863–87.

Mintzberg, H. (1987), 'The strategy concept I: five Ps for strategy', *California Management Review*, Fall, 11–32.

Nunnally, J. (1962), 'The analysis of profile data', *Psychological Bulletin*, **59**(4), 311–19.

Poor, D.D. and R.J. Wherry (1976), 'Invariance of multidimensional configurations', *British Journal of Mathematical & Statistical Psychology*, **29**(1), 114–25.

Rothman, J. (1968), 'Some considerations affecting the use of factor analysis in market research', *Journal of the Market Research Society*, **10**(3), 208–19.

Rothman, J. (1996), 'Some considerations affecting the use of factor analysis in market research', *Journal of the Market Research Society*, **38**(4), 369–82.

Schwartz, R.G. and R.D. Teach (1999), 'A model of opportunity recognition and exploitation: an empirical study of incubator firms', in *2000 Proceedings of the AMA/UIC Research at the Marketing/Entrepreneurship Interface*, pp. 72–87.

Schwartz, R.G. and R.D. Teach (2000), 'Entrepreneurship research: an empirical perspective', *Entrepreneurship Theory and Practice*, **8**(3), 32–40.

Schwartz R.G. and R.D. Teach (2001), 'Temporal issues related to marketing at the entrepreneurship interface: the high technology case', *Journal of Research in Marketing & Entrepreneurship*, 3(2), 82–96.

Schwartz, R.G., R.D. Teach and N.J. Birch (2005a), 'A longitudinal study of firms' opportunity recognition and product development management strategies: implications by firm types', *International Journal of Entrepreneurial Behaviour and Research*, forthcoming.

Schwartz, R.G., R.D. Teach and N.J. Birch (2005b), 'Techniques of analysis: strategy and performance of dot.coms 1999–2003', *Frontiers of Research*, Summary of the Babson College Conference on Entrepreneurship Research, forthcoming.

Stevenson, Howard and S. Harmeling (1991), 'Entrepreneurial management's need for a more "chaotic" theory', *Journal of Business Venturing*, **5**, 1–14.

Tabachnick, B.G. and F.S. Fidell (2001), *Using Multivariate Statistics*, 4th edn, Needham Heights, MA: Allyn and Bacon.

Teach, R.D., R.A. Tarpley and R.G. Schwartz (1985), 'Who are the microcomputer software entrepreneurs?-1985', in *Frontiers of Research*, findings of the Babson College Conference on Entrepreneurial Research, pp. 435–51.

Teach, R.D. and R.G. Schwartz (2000a), 'Opportunity recognition and exploitation and the entrepreneurial firm: firm size differences', *2000 AMA/UIC research at the Marketing/Entrepreneurship Interface Conference Proceedings (Scotland)*, accessed at www.ewu.edu/academyofmarketing.

Teach, R.D. and R.G. Schwartz (2000b), 'A temporal study of the product development management strategies in entrepreneurial technology-based firms', in *Frontiers of Entrepreneurship Research*, findings of the 2000 Babson College Conference on Entrepreneurship Research, p. 574.

6. Integrating qualitative and quantitative techniques in entrepreneurship research: an illustration of network analysis*

Nicole Coviello and Hugh Munro

INTRODUCTION

In recent years, a number of scholars have argued that qualitative methodologies for data collection and analysis are particularly well suited for researching entrepreneurship network behaviour. This chapter suggests that while the inductive collection of qualitative data can significantly enhance our understanding of entrepreneurial behaviour, data analysis can benefit from the application of what we refer to as a bifocal lens. That is, where data is interpreted with two lenses: (1) qualitative and (2) quantitative. To illustrate this methodological approach, the dynamics of an entrepreneurial firm's network structure and interactions are analysed by combining the interpretation of qualitative data with statistical analysis of that data. Specifically, the data generated through case research is examined using content analysis, event analysis and the application of UCINET 6, a software package used in social network analysis.

As a preface to introducing and illustrating this method, it is useful to first understand the nature of, and current approaches to, researching entrepreneurial networks. The context of networks, more specifically those for new ventures, is introduced and implications for research methodology are highlighted. The chapter then proceeds to a discussion of methodological perspectives in network research and introduces the bifocal approach in an applied case context. Implementation of the methodology and its results are discussed in detail, and the chapter concludes with a review of methodological contributions, limitations and implications.

THE NATURE OF ENTREPRENEURIAL NETWORKS AND IMPLICATIONS FOR RESEARCH METHODOLOGY

As evidenced in recent years, research on networks has become a topic of interest in disciplines ranging from sociology to marketing, and entrepreneurship to international business. Network research is multi-dimensional in that it can involve analysis of network size and structure, the interactional processes by which network structures are created, network influences, networking behaviours, networking skills, etc.

Research suggests that to enhance our understanding of entrepreneurial networks the following dimensions should be addressed:

- the evolutionary and dynamic nature of networks (eg Davidsson and Honig, 2003; Hite and Hesterly, 2001);
- the structural characteristics of a network – including network density, cohesion and extent of structural holes (eg Hite and Hesterly, 2001; Mitchell, 1969);
- network size, particularly its reflection of the extent of resources that might be accessed by the entrepreneurial firm (eg Hoang and Antoncic, 2003);
- the nature of interactions within the network in terms of the content or meaning of a relationship, reciprocity/mutuality, frequency, direction of initiation (inward or outward), and duration of interactions (eg Larson and Starr, 1993; Mitchell, 1969);
- power and position within a network as evident in the firm's ease of access or contact within the network (eg Mitchell, 1969).

From the above it is argued that ideally, any research method applied to network analysis should be time sensitive in order to be able to assess the evolutionary processes and dynamic character of a network. Related to this, if the research is focused on new ventures, the method should also be able to incorporate the earliest stages of the firm's life cycle. Finally, a method enabling empirical assessment of both the structure of the network and the nature of the interactions/relationships between network actors is required, incorporating the assessment of power, position, and resource access. What then, is the appropriate method by which to conduct such an analysis? To address this question, we turn to a discussion of how to assess network structure and interactions over time by applying a bifocal analytic lens to the research method.

NETWORK ANALYSIS – TOWARDS AN APPROPRIATE METHODOLOGY

There is general criticism in the literature that typically, network research has demonstrated an over-reliance on cross-sectional survey methods (Johannisson, 1997; O'Donnell and Cummins, 1999; O'Donnell et al., 2001) with Greve and Salaff (2003) commenting that this approach can not capture the dynamics of change both within and between a firm's stages of development. Therefore, if researchers are to understand how networks evolve over time, the adoption of a phenomenological paradigm (as argued for by O'Donnell and Cummins, 1999; Hines, 2000) and a focus on social process seems relevant to help explain the network phenomenon. Indeed, as outlined by Larson and Starr (1993), Hill et al. (1999), Shaw (1999), O'Donnell et al. (2001) and Hoang and Antoncic (2003), research on the dynamics and processes of entrepreneurial firm networks requires a holistic and humanist approach, including observation and in-depth interviewing of entrepreneurs within their own environments and over a period of time.

As previously noted however, networks possess both interactional and structural qualities (Mitchell, 1969; Johannisson, 1987; O'Donnell et al., 2001; Hoang and Antoncic, 2003). This therefore increases the complexity of the investigative process since both 'soft' and 'hard' data are necessary for a complete network analysis. Typically, when faced with this challenge, researchers argue for multiple data collection methods whereby methods are combined as and when deemed appropriate (Hofer and Bygrave, 1992; Carson and Coviello, 1996; Gilmore and Carson, 1996). However, we follow O'Donnell and Cummins (1999) in arguing that to understand network relationships and their dynamics over time, a qualitative approach to data collection is most relevant. This is for the simple reason that the qualitative data generated through inductive phenomenological research is particularly appropriate when rich, deep, process-based network information is required. Furthermore, while quantitative data is uni-dimensional, qualitative data is unique in that it can be analysed and interpreted both qualitatively and quantitatively. This is a critical advantage for qualitative data and means that network analysis can be conducted by applying what we refer to as a 'bifocal lens'. That is, an approach that integrates the interpretation of qualitative data with statistical analysis of that data. This is essentially, a modified form of the rapprochement solution offered by Borch and Arthur (1995).

As described by Borch and Arthur (1995), the original rapprochement solution involves using case study methodology as a mediator between the subjectivist and objectivist schools of thought, whereby researchers are able to include quantitative analytic methods within qualitative research (eg in the form of structured content analysis of cases). Like Borch and Arthur (1995), we believe that the case study approach is particularly suited to network research in that it helps generate insight into social dynamics and the operations of both the firm and the owner-managers over time (Anderson et al., 1994; Coviello and Munro, 1995; Ennis, 1999; Shaw, 1999). We argue however, that it is appropriate to extend Borch and Arthur's (1995) notion of rapprochement by expanding analysis of the case data beyond the use of descriptive tables, written case presentation and illustrative quotes aided by frequency counts. Specifically, we believe that the richness of the case data is able to be considerably enhanced by the application of specialized software that allows for sophisticated statistical analysis and comparisons of network characteristics over time.[1]

In applying the bifocal approach to network analysis (and thus, combining qualitative and quantitative techniques), the classic problems with the objectivist approach to network research outlined by Borch and Arthur (1995) can be overcome. That is, the modified rapprochement solution allows the researcher to: (1) trace the deeper aspects of the network in its social context; (2) address the organization system or network as a whole; (3) capture important dynamic dimensions of the network and (4) encompass both interactional (soft) and structural (hard) network dimensions.

The specific focus of this chapter is, therefore, to illustrate how the dynamics of a network can be effectively analysed with a bifocal lens. The research method is described in detail, using a single case site as an illustrative example: FLUX Glassworks International, a start-up glass studio and gallery. The following section outlines the bifocal approach and delineates three specific steps in the research process: data collection, data preparation and data analysis. This is followed by a discussion of the findings and observations regarding the research method employed. The chapter concludes with a review of the method's limitations and future research opportunities.

ANALYSIS OF NETWORK DYNAMICS USING THE BIFOCAL APPROACH

FLUX is a family-owned business founded and managed by Brian Hall and his parents, Wendy and David. The three owners/founders of the case firm were the sole informants for this research. They were all directly involved with firm start-up and growth, and were able to draw on rich personal experience to inform the case research process. Importantly, the case site and the founders had an organizational history traceable through concept development, commercialization and early growth.

Data Collection Process

Data collection involved the use of inductive in-depth interviews following case research procedures outlined by Eisenhardt (1989), Yin (1989) and Bergmann Lichtenstein and Brush (2001). This approach allowed the investigator to probe and explore issues in context, as they rose through the discussion process. The focal unit of analysis was the overall network relevant to FLUX within a specific time frame, as defined by the three focal actors: the co-founders. As suggested by Anderson et al. (1994), the focal actor's views of the overall network defined the network horizon. The part of the network that they considered relevant was the network context.

The personal interview protocol followed a predefined set of seven open-ended questions:

1. How did the idea for your business come about?
2. When did this happen?
3. Why did it happen?
4. Who was involved?
5. Why were they involved?
6. What specific impact did they have on your business?
7. What happened next?

These questions were repeated as necessary, allowing for iterative and circular questioning/discussion over a number of interviews, and ongoing clarification and verification of information. The overall process involved generating the 'life story' of the firm, including chronological events in the context of the firm's business activities. It also followed O'Donnell and Cummins (1999) and Grant et al. (2001) whereby the informants were given every opportunity to articulate and explain their personal views, and questions deliberately excluded marketing and network terminology. All interviews took place at the FLUX studio/gallery or in the informant's family home during normal working hours, thus allowing the informants to relax and participate in familiar surroundings.

It is also worth noting that although O'Donnell and Cummins (1999) argue for a longitudinal multi-stage research design this approach is not always feasible. Thus, while a truly longitudinal data collection process would be ideal, this research took a retrospective approach, relying on informant recollection of the firm's life story since start-up. While the limitations of relying on memory are recognized, using multiple (three) primary informants allowed for triangulation in the interview process. In addition, the time frame in question was limited to a 4-year period, thus enabling recall.

Data Preparation Process

Similar to Coviello and Munro (1995) and Hill et al. (1999), data was audio-taped and transcribed verbatim, allowing for a full case study to be written. From the full case, an excerpt of the life story of the firm was prepared along with a preliminary chronology of events and relationships. The case transcripts were then re-visited in order to ensure the accuracy of the life story and chronology. While there are a variety of stage models in the literature, a particularly useful model is that offered by Kazanjian (1988). This model is comprised of four stages: Stage I (concept generation, resource acquisition and technological development), Stage II (production-related start-up and commercialization), Stage III (sales growth and organizational issues), and Stage IV (stability and profitability). Although developed for technology-based new ventures, this model is also appropriate for new ventures with internally-generated growth, a focus on initial growth within a single product-technology base and in a market with non-limited demand conditions. As such, it was appropriate for assessment of a new venture such as FLUX. Importantly, the Kazanjian (1988) model is also recognized as a contextual framework relevant to the analysis of entrepreneurial evolution, and as noted by Hite and Hesterly (2001), is a more useful mechanism for identifying the boundaries of the entrepreneurial process than are specific time frames.

In this study, the chronology reflected Stages I, II and III, ie pre-emergence, emergence and early growth (see Table 6.1a). The tie descriptions include information on which actors were involved and how each tie occurred. Table 6.1a also includes summary information on the interactional dimensions of network ties as analysed in this study.

Using the chronology as a base, a complete network map was created for FLUX, capturing each actor and tie, as well as actor/tie content, direction and sequence of occurrence (see Figure 6.1). This particular method of portraying network data seems only to be found in the Coviello (1994) and Coviello and Munro (1995) studies of small and medium-sized enterprise (SME) internationalization, and reflects McEvily and Zaheer's (1999) suggestion that it would be useful for management to map the social capital ties that are relevant to the various tasks the organization faces. Given that any understanding about how the world is organized tends to rely on causal associations, and decisions involve causal evaluation (Ennis, 1999), the mapping technique as depicted in Figure 6.1 and summarized in Table 6.1a enables an understanding of how, why and when ties developed for the start-up.

The network map was revised as necessary until the optimal representation of the firm's history was captured in that it was considered by the

Table 6.1a   *Chronology, direction, content and durability of FLUX ties across Stage I evolution (concept and development, early–mid 1997)*

Order	Tie Actors and Description	Tie Direction		Tie Content			Tie Durability[1]		
		In	Out	Family/friend	Business	Both	Short-term (one-off)	Medium-term	Long-term (ongoing)
0[2]	David and Wendy Hall own/operate ProSolve Consulting (family business)	N/A		N/A				N/A	
1	FLUX concept born when Brian Hall approaches Wendy (mom) and David (dad) and says 'I want to blow glass'		✓	✓					✓
2	Hall family finds and leases FLUX studio/gallery site in Canmore strip-mall		✓		✓				✓
3	Brian approaches ACAD for equipment suppliers (through his contacts as a recent graduate of ACAD)		✓			✓			✓
4	FLUX approaches furnace equipment manufacturer, identified through ACAD contact		✓		✓		✓		

		18%	82%	18%	55%	27%	45.5%	9%	45.5%
5a	David approaches long-time friend Merv for advice and contacts to trades and suppliers		✓	✓					✓
5b	Merv contracts part-time with FLUX as project manager for studio set-up	✓				✓	✓		
6	Merv approaches strip-mall landlord to identify local contractors		✓		✓		✓		
7a	David and Wendy approach ProSolve's banker for FLUX financing		✓		✓		✓		
7b	Bank finances FLUX	✓			✓				✓
8	FLUX approaches Louise to join as glass artist and help set up studio (Brian's classmate at ACAD)		✓			✓		✓	
9	FLUX sends brochure to printer (identified through ProSolve)		✓		✓		✓		
	Ties created in Stage 1: 11	18%	82%	18%	55%	27%	45.5%	9%	45.5%

Notes:
[1] Tie durability is considered in terms of the intent and history of the relationship; eg Brian's relationship with ACAD is long-term and ongoing (tie 3), whereas Louise's relationship with FLUX was medium term in intent and duration (tie 8).
[2] The chronological reference of '0' reflects an event/relationship generated prior to concept generation of FLUX. As such it is not included in the tie analyses.

69

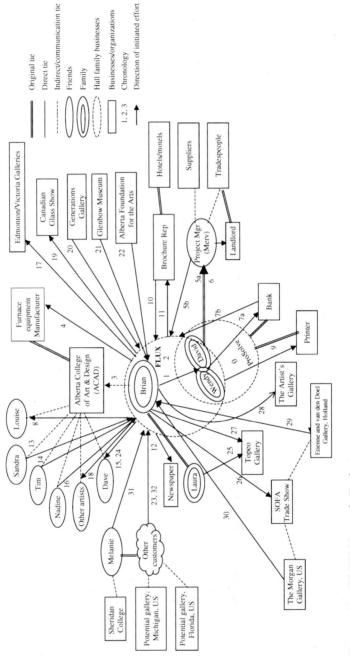

Figure 6.1   FLUX Network Evolution map

informants to be comprehensive, detailed and accurate. This enhanced the credibility and therefore validity of the case, chronology and map, allowing for confidence in data analysis. As discussed by Hines (2000), the process of iterative interviewing and map building is both live and participative, thus enriching the data collection experience for all parties. Indeed, Hines (2000) specifically refers to the 'gizmo effect' whereby the map (in his case, a cognitive rather than network map) creates a spontaneous 'wow factor' for the informants. This was also the experience in this research.

Given the interest in examining network dynamics over time, the initial map was then transformed into a set of three network matrices reflecting the FLUX network at each of the three stages of growth used in this study. Like the chronological summaries presented in Table 6.1a, each matrix incorporated the various developments, catalytic events and key relationships as appropriate to FLUX's stage of development. Each matrix can also be represented as a map reflecting the network at the three different stages.

To build the network matrices, simple spreadsheets were created using UCINET 6 software, a social network analysis tool (Borgatti et al., 2002). Following Hanneman (2001), each matrix was comprised of all actors for the relevant stage, with ties coded as absent (0) or present (1). Thus the resultant matrices and maps were binary and 'directed' in that the data reflected who initiated or directed the tie toward whom. This means the matrices were asymmetric as each row represented the source of a directed tie and each column the target. Finally, the matrices were simplex in nature, in that rather than distinguish between multiple different types of ties, they described only one type of tie: a tie relevant to the development of FLUX. To understand the multiplex character of the network over time, we relied on tie content information from Table 6.1a.

Data Analysis Process

The chronologies were first content analysed along the interactional dimensions relevant to this research. Only three of Mitchell's (1969) interactional dimensions were analysed since tie frequency and intensity are perhaps more relevant to research on (eg) advice networks rather than organizational evolution. Thus, the focus was on tie content, direction and durability. Tie content reflects the meaning of a relationship to the actor. Capturing tie direction enables an understanding of the extent to which a network is path dependent or intentionally managed (as per Hite and Hesterly, 2001), and assessing tie durability allows for an understanding of the dynamics of relationships and the stability of the overall network (Gadde and Mattsson, 1987; Iacobucci and Hopkins, 1992).

To facilitate content analysis, the data in Table 6.1a was coded to reflect the content or nature of each tie (friendship/social, business/economic or both). Importantly, rather than dichotomize relationships into either friendship or business ties (as is often found in the literature), the coding followed O'Donnell et al. (2001) by recognizing that the same two people can share a business relationship and a friendship relationship. As such, ties encompassing 'both' needed to be accounted for. Subsequently, each tie was analysed for direction, identifying if the tie was initiated by the focal firm/actor (noted as 'out') or initiated by an external party (noted as 'in'). Finally, each tie was examined for its durability in terms of the intent and actual duration of the relationship. These ties were coded as short-term (one-off), medium term, or long-term (ongoing). From this base, identification and analysis of interaction patterns within and between each stage of FLUX's development could be conducted.

In parallel with the analysis of interactions, the three staged network matrices were examined using UCINET 6 software. Analysis focused on the key structural dimensions of the network and patterns of structural change. Although Mitchell (1969) suggests that it is important to define the focus of analysis (ie at the level of personal or business relationships), the lines of distinction between personal and inter-organizational networks are multiplex (Larson and Starr, 1993; Hoang and Antoncic, 2003). Thus, the position taken in this research is that the entrepreneurial network includes ties between individuals, and between individuals and organizations. We did however distinguish between the analysis of the overall network (encompassing all actors) and that of individual egonets (eg Brian Hall's network). In examining the structure of the overall network, we measured density and overall cohesion, as well as the average distance between ties, where distance refers to the number of steps connecting actors.

At the level of the individual egonets, UCINET 6 was used to compute individual egonet density, as well as egonet size and reachability for each actor. For the latter dimension, each actor's 'outward reach' was assessed as this helped identify individuals who were well positioned to reach many others within a few steps (Hanneman, 2001). We also assessed 'betweenness centrality' or the number of times the actor fell between two others, thus creating opportunities for information dissemination and control. Finally, given the arguments of Hite and Hesterly (2001), our interest in structure was extended beyond Mitchell (1969) and Hoang and Antoncic (2003) to assess Burt's (1992) notion of structural holes. However, rather than relying on the common proxy measures of density and diversity, Borgatti et al. (1998) were followed to assess the effective size and constraints of the ego network. Of note, in this study, the structural characteristic of diversity was captured through analysis of tie content (an interactional dimension) since diversity/heterogeneity measures require attribute data not included in the UCINET matrices created here.

Overall, in assessing network structure by transforming qualitative data into quantitative measures, we were able to create frames for the analysis of the origins and outcomes of network processes, as described by Johannisson (1997). Furthermore, while the primary unit of analysis was the overall network within which FLUX operated, the UCINET 6 software allowed for analysis of all the various actors comprising the total network. As such, we were able trace the evolution of individual egonets such as those of a founder (eg Brian) or the firm itself within the broader network. In the context of an entrepreneurial start-up, this can provide insight as to the changing power structure within the network over time. The approach also recognizes Adler and Kwon's (2002) observations that when studying organizational emergence, there are challenges in distinguishing between social capital at the firm and individual level.

RESULTS OF THE BIFOCAL ANALYSIS

Beginning with network structure, Table 6.1b shows that the overall network (comprised of all actors) decreased in density over time. Importantly, even in Stage I (when density was at its peak) the network showed a large variation in ties, with only 25 per cent of all possible ties present and a high standard deviation. While lower density scores generally reflect a non-redundant or sparse network (assumed to be a positive influence on the firm if it is accepted that a firm with a central position in a sparse network has greater potential for success). The results in Table 6.1b suggest an extremely sparse network to the point of being disconnected and potentially, difficult to manage. This is also suggested by the cohesion measures which decreased over time, ultimately resulting in a low cohesion level of 0.30 or conversely, a high fragmentation level (0.70). At the same time, the average distance between network actors remained relatively stable through each stage (average path of 2.34 steps), indicating that there were at least two steps between each actor. This suggests that in spite of decreasing cohesion, actors were still able to access resources and transfer information over a relatively short path.

As noted previously, the structural characteristics of individual egonets can also be assessed using UCINET 6, and different egonets can be compared. Table 6.1c focuses on the FLUX egonet by stage of development, showing that its size (both actual and effective) increased over time. Thus, the number of actors that FLUX was directly connected to increased, creating opportunities for resource access and control. Importantly, the constraint measure also decreased over time, indicating greater opportunities

Table 6.1b   Chronology, direction, content and durability of FLUX ties across Stage II evolution (commercialization, mid-2000–early 2000)

Order	Tie Actors and Description	Tie Direction		Tie Content			Tie Durability		
		In	Out	Family/friend	Business	Both	Short-term (one-off)	Medium-term	Long-term (ongoing)
10	Brochure representative (Rep) approaches FLUX on cold-call for tourism magazine advertising	✓			✓		✓		
11	FLUX distributes brochures through the Rep to all hotels, motels, restaurants and petrol stations in the region		✓		✓				✓
12	FLUX promotes opening to community via self-initiated newspaper article		✓		✓		✓		
13	Sandra approaches FLUX as glass artist and gallery support (Brian's classmate at ACAD, based in Canmore)	✓				✓			✓
14	Tim approaches FLUX as glass artist (Brian's classmate at ACAD)	✓				✓		✓	
15	FLUX approaches Dave to teach new techniques (identified through ACAD contacts)		✓		✓			✓	

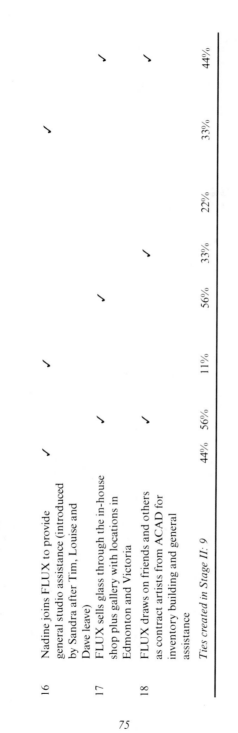

16 Nadine joins FLUX to provide general studio assistance (introduced by Sandra after Tim, Louise and Dave leave)

17 FLUX sells glass through the in-house shop plus gallery with locations in Edmonton and Victoria

18 FLUX draws on friends and others as contract artists from ACAD for inventory building and general assistance

Ties created in Stage II: 9

44% 56% 11% 56% 33% 22% 33% 44%

Table 6.1c   Chronology, direction, content and durability of FLUX ties across Stage III evolution (early growth, early 2000–early 2001)

Order	Tie Actors and Description	Tie Direction		Tie Content			Tie Durability		
		In	Out	Family/friend	Business	Both	Short-term (one-off)	Medium-term	Long-term (ongoing)
19	FLUX exhibits in Canadian Glass Show		✓		✓		✓		
20	FLUX asked to exhibit in Generations Gallery	✓			✓		✓		
21	Brian asked to speak at Glenbow Museum	✓			✓		✓		
22	Brian's piece purchased by Alberta Foundation for the Arts	✓			✓		✓		
23	Walk-in customers approach	✓			✓		✓		
	FLUX with potential employee (daughter Melanie – student at Sheridan College)								
24	FLUX approaches Dave to support Brian with general production (based on previous tie) (15)		✓		✓				✓
25	Laura (Brian's fiancé) approaches Topeo Gallery, US		✓		✓		✓		

		57%	43%	0	93%	7%	71%	0	29%
26	Brian attends SOFA in Chicago, representing himself as 'Hall'		✓		✓		✓		
27	Brian follows-up with Topeo Gallery, US (as 'Hall')		✓		✓		✓		
28	Brian approaches The Artist's Gallery, US (for 'Hall')		✓		✓		✓		
29	Etienne and van den Doel Gallery (Holland) approaches Brian (contact made through SOFA)	✓			✓				✓
30	The Morgan Gallery (US) approaches Brian (contact made through SOFA)	✓			✓				✓
31	Melanie joins FLUX as glass artist (see tie 23), after Nadine leaves	✓			✓		✓		✓
32	Long-term customer approaches FLUX about two US opportunities	✓				✓	✓		
	Ties created in Stage III: 14	57%	43%	0	93%	7%	71%	0	29%

for action given fewer of FLUX's relationship investments directly or indirectly involved only a single actor.

In terms of how FLUX was positioned within the overall network, Table 6.1c shows it had the highest outward reach of all actors in Stage I (0.82), declining to 0.54 by Stage III. Further analysis shows that FLUX could reach 62 per cent of actors within one step in Stage I, 46 per cent in Stage II and 37 per cent in Stage III. Comparing this egonet to all others, FLUX was the best-positioned actor in the overall (sparse) network, in that it could reach more actors than could others. At the same time, the FLUX reach decreased over time as evidenced by both the outward reach and betweenness centrality measures.

To understand shifts in centrality among network actors, Table 6.2 presents a comparison of certain actors by stage, using normalized measures of Freeman Betweenness Centrality and overall rank within the broader network. As above, while FLUX remained the most central actor through each stage (indicating it was more likely to link otherwise unconnected actors), its power decreased over time. In contrast, Brian's power first decreased and then increased until the bulk of the power in Stage III was shared by FLUX and Brian. To examine this more fully, it is helpful to view Table 6.2 by stage rather than actor. In doing so, we see that in Stage I, power was essentially spread among six actors: FLUX, Merv, Brian, David, ProSolve and the Alberta College of Art and Design (ACAD). By Stage II, Merv had left the network after completing the FLUX set-up and the ACAD had substantially increased its power base reflecting its role in providing the labour pool for FLUX. David's power had also decreased substantially. By Stage III, ACAD's role had diminished, and the network was essentially controlled by FLUX and Brian. Overall, Brian's power measures reflect an inverted-U shape, indicating a shift in the FLUX organizational base and suggesting that by early growth, his personal opportunities for exploitation of information and control benefits were enhanced. Indeed, by Stage III, Brian's outward reach measure of 0.57 (not reported in Tables 6.1c or 6.2) was greater than that of FLUX (0.54).

*Table 6.2   Structural characteristics of the overall network by stage
(all actors)*

Characteristic	. . . in Stage I	. . . by Stage II	. . . by Stage III
Density (sd)	0.25 (0.43)	0.17 (0.38)	0.08 (0.28)
Average distance	2.33	2.28	2.41
Distance-based cohesion	0.54	0.43	0.30

Given these patterns, the question then becomes: why? For the sake of simplicity, the focus is on Brian's changing position in the network and insight is provided by interpreting the qualitative data found in the case. For example, as revealed in the depth interviews, Brian's personal contacts with ACAD were important in Stage I but by Stage II, he was focused heavily on operations, ie glass production. During Stage II, concerns were expressed by Wendy (mother/accountant) as to the viability of FLUX, and Brian began to consider the possibility of shutting the gallery to focus on himself as an independent artist (rather than FLUX as a business). After a period of soul-searching, the Hall family decided to remain committed to FLUX but with an important difference: their emphasis would be on art glass and developing Brian as a leading glass artist. As a result, by Stage III, there had been a shift in the emphasis of both FLUX and Brian, with David commenting that: '[Brian] is selling Brian Hall now and FLUX just happens to be the studio where he works'. In line with this, all Stage III ties initiated by Brian were on behalf of himself (as the artist 'Hall'), rather than FLUX. This is reflected in the changing patterns of the overall network. Interestingly, in spite of the family's strategic decision to focus on developing Brian's profile and Wendy acknowledging that 'Brian will go along with what David is saying to a point, but if he doesn't agree, he will jump in', she also felt that there was (and should be) a certain amount of 'deference to dad and dad is the source of financing'. Thus, while the network power roles were shifting, this was not necessarily acknowledged by the Hall family with regard to their business relationships.

Further understanding of network evolution comes with the analysis of tie direction, content and durability: the interactional characteristics of a network examined in this study. For example, Table 6.1a shows that in Stage I, 82 per cent of ties were outward-oriented, but this proportion decreased on a stage by stage basis (to 56 per cent in Stage II and 43 per cent in Stage III). At an aggregate level, this resulted in an overall network characterized by a relatively balanced set of ties at early growth: 41 inward/59 outward (see Table 6.3). Thus, it appears that over time, FLUX began to attract rather than seek network contacts.

As regards tie content, Table 6.1a shows that the FLUX network consistently developed instrumental business ties (ranging from 55–56 per cent of ties in the first two stages, to 93 per cent in Stage III). Thus, although social ties or ties comprised of both a social and economic component were evident in the early stages of firm development, 71 per cent of the total network was made up of business ties by Stage III (see Table 6.3). While this pattern is perhaps tempered by the fact that the core founders of the business were three family members possessing complementary skills (thus minimizing the need to draw on other family or friends to any great extent)

Table 6.3   Structural characteristics of the FLUX ego net by stage

Characteristic	. . . in Stage I	. . . by Stage II	. . . by Stage III
Size of ego net	100.00	15.00	19.00
Structural holes			
• Effective size of ego net	7.60	13.13	17.48
• Constraints	0.31	0.19	0.13
Reachability			
• Ego's outward reach centrality (normalized)	0.82	0.68	0.54
• Betweenness centrality (normalized)	40.71	38.97	35.99

Table 6.4   Comparing actor power by stage

using normalized measures of Freeman Betweenness Centrality and overall rank.

Actor	. . . in Stage I	. . . by Stage II	. . . by Stage III
FLUX	40.71 (1)	38.97 (1)	35.99 (1)
Merv	27.89 (2)	0	0
Brian	23.63 (3)	18.06 (3)	29.09 (2)
David	18.12 (4)	1.84 (9)	0.97 (11)
Prosolve	16.67 (5)	10.29 (4)	2.70 (6)
ACAD	8.65 (6)	28.35 (2)	6.83 (3)
Total no. of actors	13	19	31

and the labour pool of artists were, by convenience, Brian's ex-classmates, it also reflects the nature of a niche business. That is, to sell glass, FLUX needed to aggressively develop business ties to generate sales opportunities.

Finally, Table 6.3 shows that the overall balance in short, medium and long-term ties remained generally consistent over time. However, if tie duration is analysed by individual stage (from Table 6.1a), 45 per cent of ties were short-term in Stage I, dropping to 22 per cent in Stage II and then increasing to 71 per cent in Stage III. This pattern likely reflects the processes inherent to each stage in that a moderate number of short-term ties were established (and ended) to start the business (eg build the facility, print brochures), a fewer number of short-term ties were then created to promote the business, and finally, a relatively large number of short-term ties were generated through early and rapid growth. Importantly, the longer-term ties were comprised of both family/friends and business relationships, with the latter essen-

Table 6.5   *Comparing FLUX network interactions over time*
            (% of total ties)

Interaction	. . . in Stage I (ties = 11)	. . . by Stage II (ties = 20)	. . . by Stage III (ties = 34)
Tie direction			
• Inward	18%	30%	41%
• Outward	82%	70%	59%
Tie content			
• Family/friend	18%	15%	9%
• Business	55%	55%	71%
• Both	27%	30%	20%
Duration			
• Short-term (one-off)	45%	35%	50%
• Medium term	9%	20%	12%
• Longer term (ongoing)	45%	45%	38%

tial to FLUX operations (eg the landlord, bank, brochure representative and galleries). Medium-term ties represented the FLUX labour pool.

Beyond the analysis of network structure and interactions over time, further analysis of the qualitative data would help identify other patterns that could be matched to the network's characteristics, by stage. For example, patterns associated specifically with entrepreneurial learning and performance can be identified, as well as family dynamics in terms of organizational role, power and decision-making processes. While not discussed in this chapter, matching these various patterns back to the network analysis could provide further insight to the dynamic interplay between the entrepreneur(s), the firm and its network.

METHODOLOGICAL CONCLUSIONS AND IMPLICATIONS

The research method and bifocal analytic approach outlined in this chapter allows for a richer understanding of entrepreneurial behaviour in the context of networks. As evidenced here, humanistic approaches to understanding networks using inductively generated case data can be meaningfully examined with a bifocal lens that integrates both qualitative and quantitative analytic techniques. While this study shows that a qualitative approach to data collection remains most relevant to understand network relationships and dynamics, the qualitative data lends itself well to a (complementary) quantitative analysis using UCINET 6. The latter approach provides crisper insights into the structure and nature of entrepreneurial networks while the former enlightens as to why such network phenomena are being observed.

The combination of UCINET 6 analysis with more classic qualitative approaches allows for time-based examination of whole systems of organizations. It also incorporates scrutiny of a range of dimensions pertaining to both: (1) network structure and (2) the interactions and relationships between individual network actors. Interestingly, of the various existing applications of UCINET 6, only Spencer (2003) uses the software to assess network structure over time, and none of the previous studies applying UCINET 6 have focused on the dynamics of the entrepreneurial firm as it moves from start-up through to growth. Thus, utilizing UCINET 6 for analysis in the current study is an additional contribution. The methodology also shows that important insight is offered when the start-up venture is tracked from conception (ie before formation as a legal entity and commercialization). Finally, analysis of network structure and interactions over time, facilitated with the modified rapprochement solution illustrated here, overcomes the weakness of cross-sectional comparisons of different ventures at varying stages of development as noted by Larson and Starr (1993) and Johannisson (1997).

In spite of the strengths inherent in the approach outlined here, there are of course, limitations to consider. First, the use of a single case site limits case representativeness. However, relying on a single case is considered acceptable for this study as the purpose was to simply illustrate the contribution of applying a bifocal lens to the analysis of case data. Secondly, while not truly longitudinal in nature, the collection of data in a retrospective manner is practical. Furthermore, it allows for retrospective analysis by the informants and in doing so provides a base for future strategic decisions. Thirdly, this example focused on ego-centric network data and thus relied on the accuracy of reports from the focal actors as regards the firm's network. This means that the views of other network actors were not captured. This is acceptable in this study as it was the focal net that was of interest, with the network parameters defined by the focal actors (the venture founders).

Finally, if not careful, the researcher can fall into the trap of static analysis and oversimplification by relying solely on the statistics generated by UCINET 6. Thus, the optimal use of this tool, in the context of understanding network dynamics, is best achieved when the structural patterns generated by UCINET 6 are used to provide a framework for discussion.

In doing so, the structural patterns become just one piece of the story of a firm's network, and are balanced by qualitative interpretation of the interactional dimensions of that network on a longitudinal and comparative basis. Indeed, without the richness of understanding created by the interpretive process of preparing the qualitative data for UCINET analysis, the statistical analysis provides only a limited amount of information.

Overall, we believe application of the bifocal lens facilitates a richer and more meaningful approach to network analysis. The analytic approach lends itself to comparative assessments, and as such, future research could involve multiple case studies and cross-network analysis. Multi-site network analyses would allow for investigation of whether or not firms are embedded in networks in idiosyncratic ways as suggested by McEvily and Zaheer (1999). Such research could also seek to capture additional data on the extent to which the various actors in the network are connected beyond the focal net. Moving from a firm-level analysis to that focused on the individual entrepreneur, future research could examine the networks of lead entrepreneurs in comparison to each other, over time. Overall, this approach would support Anderson et al.'s (1994, p. 12) comments that: 'to develop our knowledge, detailed case studies of development processes within different types of networks are needed'.

Interestingly, analysis of multiple networks with software such as UCINET 6 would also allow for an assessment of propositions such as those generated by Hite and Hesterly (2001) in their theoretical discussion of the evolution of firm networks. While some might well argue that case research is inappropriate for theory testing, the use of a small and purposively selected set of sites allows for researchers to get much closer to the unit of analysis than does survey research. This provides a better opportunity for a rich understanding of any propositions in question and further theory refinement. Finally, given the patterns identified in this study, future research should allow for mapping and analysis of network expansion, consolidation and contraction, and encompass the very early stages of the firm's lifecycle.

NOTES

*   This chapter is an excerpt of a paper by Nicole Coviello entitled 'Integrating qualitative and quantitative techniques in network analysis', appearing in *Qualitative Market Research: an International Journal*, 2005, **8**(1) (in press).

1.   In recent years, a number of researchers have illustrated the use of various software tools to aid the analysis of qualitative data. For example, Hill et al. (1999) use META-MORPH to help develop a theoretical model of small firm entrepreneurial network evolution and Hines (2000) and Ennis (1999) use cognitive mapping software (COPE) to study entrepreneurial decision-making. Perren (2002) applies NUDIST to qualitative

data to plot entrepreneurial networks, however, his maps do not reflect network evolution. All of these studies use the software tools for pattern identification rather than statistical analysis.

REFERENCES

Adler, P.S. and S.-W. Kwon (2002), 'Social capital: prospects for a new concept', *Academy of Management Review*, **27**(1), 17–40.

Anderson, J.C., H. Håkansson and J. Johanson (1994), 'Dyadic business relationships within a business network context', *Journal of Marketing*, **58**(4), 1–15.

Bergmann Lichtenstein, B.M. and C.G. Brush (2001), 'How do "resource bundles" develop and change in new ventures? A dynamic model and longitudinal exploration', *Entrepreneurship Theory and Practice*, **25**(3), 37–58.

Borch, O.J. and M.B. Arthur (1995), 'Strategic networks among small firms: implications for strategy research methodology', *Journal of Management Studies*, **32**(4), 419–41.

Borgatti, S.P., C. Jones and M.G. Everett (1998), 'Network measures of social capital', *Connections*, **21**(2), 27–36.

Borgatti, S.P., M.G. Everett and L.C. Freeman (2002), *UCINET 6 for Windows: Software for Social Network Analysis*, Cambridge, MA: Harvard University. Analytic Technologies.

Burt, R.S. (1992), *Structural Holes*, Cambridge MA: Harvard University.

Carson, D. and N. Coviello (1996), 'Qualitative research issues at the marketing/entrepreneurship interface', *Marketing Intelligence and Planning*, **14**(6), 51–7.

Coviello, N.E. (1994), 'Internationalising the entrepreneurial high technology knowledge-intensive firm', unpublished doctoral dissertation, prepared for The University of Auckland.

Coviello, N.E. and H.J. Munro (1995), 'Growing the entrepreneurial firm: networking for international market development', *European Journal of Marketing*, **29**(7), 49–61.

Davidsson, P. and B. Honig (2003), 'The role of social and human capital among nascent entrepreneurs', *Journal of Business Venturing*, **18**, 301–31.

Eisenhardt, K.M. (1989), 'Building theories from case study research', *Academy of Management Review*, **14**(4), 532–50.

Ennis, S. (1999), 'Growth and the small firm: using causal mapping to assess the decision-making process – a case study', *Qualitative Market Research: an International Journal*, **2**(2), 147–60.

Gadde, L.-E. and L.-G. Mattsson (1987), 'Stability and change in network relationships', *International Journal of Research in Marketing*, **4**, 29–41.

Gilmore, A. and D. Carson (1996), 'Integrative qualitative methods in a services context', *Marketing Intelligence and Planning*, **14**(6), 21–26.

Grant, K., A. Gilmore, D. Carson, R. Laney and B. Pickett (2001), 'Experiential research methodology: an integrated academic practitioner "team" approach', *Qualitative Market Research: an International Journal*, **4**(2), 66–74.

Greve, A. and J.W. Salaff (2003), 'Social networks and entrepreneurship', *Entrepreneurship Theory and Practice*, **28**(1), 1–22.

Hanneman, R.A. (2001), *Introduction to Social Network Methods*, Riverside, CA: University of California, Riverside Department of Sociology.

Hill, J., P. McGowan and P. Drummond (1999), 'The development and application of a qualitative approach to researching the marketing networks of small firm entrepreneurs', *Qualitative Market Research: an International Journal*, **2**(2), 71–81.

Hines, T. (2000), 'An evaluation of two qualitative methods (focus group interviews and cognitive maps) for conducting research into entrepreneurial decision making', *Qualitative Market Research: an International Journal*, **3**(1), 7–16.

Hite, J.M. and W.S. Hesterly (2001), 'The evolution of firm networks: from emergence to early growth of the firm', *Strategic Management Journal*, **22**(3), 275–86.

Hoang, H. and B. Antoncic (2003), 'Network-based research in entrepreneurship: a critical review', *Journal of Business Venturing*, **18**, 165–87.

Hofer, C. and W. Bygrave (1992), 'Researching entrepreneurship', *Entrepreneurship Theory and Practice*, **16**(3), 91–100.

Iacobucci, D. and N. Hopkins (1992), 'Modelling dyadic interactions and networks in marketing', *Journal of Marketing Research*, **29**, 5–17.

Johannisson, B. (1997), 'Contextualizing entrepreneurial networking', *International Studies of Management and Organization*, **27**(3), 109–36.

Kazanjian, R.K. (1988), 'Relation of dominant problems to stages of growth in technology-based new ventures', *Academy of Management Journal*, **31**(2), 259–79.

Larson, A. and J.A. Starr (1993), 'A network model of organization formation', *Entrepreneurship Theory and Practice*, Winter, 5–15.

McEvily, B. and A. Zaheer (1999), 'Bridging ties: a source of firm heterogeneity in competitive capabilities', *Strategic Management Journal*, **20**, 1133–56.

Mitchell, J.C. (1969), 'The concept and use of social networks,' in J.C. Mitchell (ed.), *Social Networks in Urban Situations*, Manchester: Manchester University Press, 1–50.

O'Donnell, A. and D. Cummins (1999), 'The use of qualitative methods to research networking in SMEs', *Qualitative Market Research: an International Journal*, **2**(2), 82–91.

O'Donnell, A., A. Gilmore, D. Cummins and D. Carson (2001), 'The network construct in entrepreneurship research: a review and critique', *Management Decision*, **39**(9), 749–60.

Perren, L. (2002), 'The entrepreneurial process of network development in small biotechnology firms: the case of Destiny Pharma Ltd.', *International Journal of Entrepreneurship and Innovation Management*, **2**(4/5), 390–405.

Shaw, E. (1999), 'A guide to the qualitative research process: evidence from a small firm study', *Qualitative Market Research: an International Journal*, **2**(2), 59–70.

Spencer, J.W. (2003), 'Global gatekeeping, representation and network structure: a longitudinal analysis of regional and global knowledge diffusion networks', *Journal of International Business Studies*, **34**, 428–42.

Yin, R.K. (1989), *Case Study Research: Design and Methods*, Beverly Hills, CA: Sage.

7. Convergent interviewing: a starting methodology for enterprise research programs*

Sally Rao and Chad Perry

INTRODUCTION

Some enterprise researchers can find themselves researching an area about which so little is known that they are uncertain how to begin a research project. This situation may occur in enterprise research because it often involves entrepreneurial activities that are new by definition. In contrast, other enterprise researchers may be so overwhelmed by previous researchers' articles that they are uncertain about where and how a new contribution can be made. This chapter aims to show how the relatively new, qualitative methodology of convergent interviewing can address issues in these under-researched or confusing areas. We demonstrate that its careful analysis of practitioners' experience can efficiently and effectively clarify researchers' ideas in the early stage of an enterprise research program. Our contribution is a comprehensive treatment of the use of convergent interviewing in enterprise research, building on the introductions to convergent interviewing in Carson et al. (2001) and Rao and Perry (2003).

The chapter has five parts. First, it describes the essentials of the convergent interviewing methodology and compares it with other qualitative methods. Then its strengths and limitations are noted. The third part shows how the methodology's validity and reliability can be enhanced, and how it is actually implemented in a series of steps. Finally, the two outcomes of a convergent interviewing project are described.

THE QUALITATIVE, THEORY-BUILDING METHODOLOGY OF CONVERGENT INTERVIEWING

This section describes and justifies the choice of convergent interviewing from among other qualitative research methods, with illustrations from

our research about the emerging role of Internet marketing in entrepreneurial enterprises (described in more detail in Rao and Perry (2003)).
Convergent interviewing is an in-depth interview technique with a structured data analysis process – a technique used to collect, analyse and
interpret qualitative information about a person's knowledge, opinions,
experiences, attitudes and beliefs through using a number of interviews
which converge on important issues (Dick, 1990; Nair and Riege, 1995).
That is, the process in itself is very structured but the content of each
interview only gradually becomes more structured to allow flexible
exploration of the subject matter without determining the answers (Nair
and Riege, 1995). In this process, more is learned about the issues involved
(Dick, 1990).

In more detail, convergent interviewing is a series of in-depth interviews
with experts that allow the researcher to refine the questions after each
interview, to converge on the issues in a topic area. In each interview after
the first one, the researchers ask questions about issues raised in previous
interviews, to find agreements between the interviewees, or disagreements
between them with explanations for those disagreements. That is, probe
questions about important information are developed after each interview,
so that agreements and disagreements among the interviewees are examined in the next interview. The flexibility of convergent interviewing arises
out of this continuous refinement of content and process. The interviews
stop when stability is reached, that is, when agreement among interviewees
is achieved and disagreement among them is explained (by their different
industry backgrounds, for example), on all the issues (Nair and Riege,
1995). Table 7.1 shows this process, including the end point of stability on
all issues.

In the early stages of theory building, little is known about the topic area
and several qualitative methods may be used to refine research issues and
reduce uncertainty about a research topic (King, 1996). This section compares convergent interviewing with the more often used methods of in-
depth interview, case research and focus groups, to explain why convergent
interviewing was chosen in our theory-building research project. The major
characteristics and differences of convergent interviews, in-depth interviews, case research and focus group studies are illustrated in Table 7.2 and
form the basis for this discussion. Essentially, convergent interviewing was
more appropriate for our Internet research than the other methods because
it provides:

- a way of quickly converging on key issues in an emerging area;
- an efficient mechanism for data analysis after each interview; and
- a way of deciding when to stop collecting data.

Table 7.1   A diagram of agreements and disagreements about issues in a series of convergent interviews

Issue / Interviewee	1	2	3	4	5	6
A	yes	raise	–	–	–	–
B	agree	disagree	raise	raise	–	–
C	agree	disagree	agree	agree	raise	agree
D	agree	disagree	agree	agree	agree	agree

Notes: This diagram is a hypothetical one and is not a diagram of our illustrative example of Internet/relationship research. In Table 7.1, interviewee A confirmed one issue (1) suggested in the literature and raised another (2) – new issues are shown as 'raise'. In the next interview, interviewee B agreed about one of these but disagreed with the other. She then raised issues 3 and 4 and so they were probed for agreement or disagreement in later interviews. Note that in the final interview with D, no new issues were raised and so stability was reached.

Source: Carson et al., 2001.

In-depth Interview vs Convergent Interview

In-depth interviews were not used for our research primarily because convergent interviewing has a more structured way of processing interviews and analysing data (row 4 of Table 7.2). That is, convergent interviews were considered more efficient than in-depth interviews for this exploratory research. The advantage of convergent interviewing over in-depth interviewing lies in its progression over several interviews that enables the research to refine content and process of the interview continuously to narrow down broad research issues (Dick, 1990) into more focused ones at the end of the research program (row 1 of Table 7.2).

This progressive nature of convergent interviewing develops a series of 'successive approximations' (Dick, 1990, p. 3) arising from a continuous refinement of process (such as details of the interviewing techniques and sample composition) and content (such as the interview questions and the evolving understanding of the subject matter of the research). This research began with a broad field of possible topics and ended with a focused one. In brief, convergent interviewing was more suitable than in-depth interviews because it is 'a series of tasks which lead to the progressive reduction of uncertainty' (Philips and Pugh, 1987, p. 72). These advantages of convergent interviewing over other interviewing methods of progressive exploration and data analysis, and identification of an ending point, are also advantages over the other methods to be discussed next.

Table 7.2   Differences between convergent interviews, in-depth interviews and case research

Qualitative method / Characteristics	In-depth interviews	Convergent interviews	Case research	Focus groups
(1) Main objective	To obtain rich and detailed information	Narrow down research focus	Mainly theory building/confirming	Group interaction
(2) Level of prior theory requirement	Low	Low	Medium to high	To obtain insights and various ideas
(3) Process	Flexible – unstructured to structured refinement	Structured process with continuous	Structured and standard procedures	Flexible – unstructured to structured
(4) Content	Unstructured to structured	Unstructured	Somewhat structured	Unstructured
(5) Strengths	Replication	Progressive	Replication effect in a group setting	Synergistic
(6) Weaknesses	Results may be biased and are not for theory testing knowledge and not sufficient on its own	Potential interviewer bias, requirement of interviewer's	Requirement of sufficient prior theory	Conforming effects in a group setting

Source: Developed from Carson et al., 2001 and Yin, 1994.

Case Research vs Convergent Interview

The case research method was not used in this research mainly because there was insufficient prior theory about the research problems of using case research. Admittedly, case research can be used to investigate a new research area or contemporary phenomenon within a dynamically changing, real life context (Yin, 1994; Eisenhardt, 1989; Carson et al., 2001). However, some researchers emphasize the importance of entering case research with prior theory or 'pre-structure' (Miles and Huberman, 1984, p. 17; Yin, 1994). Although three initial interview questions were developed from the parent literature about Internet marketing for our research, this prior theory was inadequate for developing the many questions for a case interviewer's guide that has to be standard across all the interviews in case research. That is, a mix of induction and deduction may be required for a research program involving case research (Perry, 2001), while this research was primarily induction. The blending of induction and deduction can be achieved by incorporating convergent interviews in the first stage of a project to provide the prior theory for the development of the interviewer's guide in the second, case research stage.

Focus Groups vs Convergent Interviews

Finally, focus groups were not used for the first stage of this research mainly because of the type of data this first stage aims at obtaining. Focus groups are appropriate when research need to uses group interaction to produce data and insights that would be less accessible without the interaction within a group (Morgan, 1993). That is, focus groups are most useful and appropriate in exploratory and developmental phases of a research where little is known about a somewhat subjective phenomenon (Morgan and Krueger, 1993; Stewart and Shamdasani, 1990; Cox, Higginbotham and Burton, 1989; Crimmons, 1988; Calder, 1980; Goldman, 1962). However, the information for our research could be obtained without the synergistic effect of a group setting offered by focus groups (Morgan, 1993). Indeed, business people in a focus group were unlikely to divulge their business innovations to others within the group who might be their competitors. In brief, convergent interviewing seemed to be the most appropriate methodology for the example research.

STRENGTHS AND LIMITATIONS OF THE CONVERGENT INTERVIEWING TECHNIQUE

Convergent interviewing offers three main strengths. Firstly, convergent interviewing is useful for the exploration of areas lacking an established theoretical base, as was the case for this research. That is, the flexibility provided by the convergent interviewing method allows for the refinement of research issues throughout the course of the interviews, resulting in the consolidation of the existing body of knowledge and a more precisely defined research problem (Dick, 1990). Secondly, it provides a flexible instrument to allow all issues related to the research problem to be identified and explored. This flexibility of convergent interviewing allows researchers to use a funneling process in which they control the flow of the type of information being sought (Riege, 2003).

The final strength of convergent interviewing is that the subjectivity inherent in qualitative data is largely overcome by the interviewer attempting to always explain answers after each interview, that is, to 'disprove the emerging explanation of the data' (Dick, 1990, p. 11). That is, subjective data is refined through the use of convergence and discrepancy that adds objective methods to the refining of subjective data (Dick, 1990).

Despite these strengths, there are limitations associated with the convergent interviewing technique (Woodward, 1996). First, convergent interviewing may allow potential interviewer bias to occur (Dick, 1990), like most qualitative methods. To guard against this bias, the interviewers need to be not only skilful and experienced, but also to have sufficient knowledge about the subject matter and be able to maintain data quality when recording and analysing the data obtained from the interviews (Aaker and Day, 1990). For example, in this research, the researcher had previous qualitative research training, and had begun to review the literature about broader literatures of Internet marketing and relationship marketing.

Secondly, the convergent interviewing method requires the interviewee to be knowledgeable about the research subject matter and so be able to contribute meaningful information to the exploratory research. Using the snowballing technique (Aaker and Day, 1990), we were able to access practitioner experts about the Internet who could provide their information and experience about the research topic. After each interview, the interviewee was sufficiently familiar with the aims of the research to refer the researcher to other experts. It is advisable to ask each interviewee for more than one other expert, at the end of an interview, to reduce the chances of a snowballing research project being locked into a mindset of just one network. For example, probe an interviewee for experts from other industries or for experts that the interviewee has rarely or not met.

Finally, convergent interviewing may affect the validity of the research because it is not sufficient on its own (Gummesson, 2000) to provide results that can be generalized to the wider population, like most other qualitative research (Marshall and Rossman, 1995; Maykut and Morehouse, 1994). However, this limitation was overcome in the Internet research because the aim was merely to build a theory for later testing; indeed, quantitative research was used later to validate the theory building stage of convergent interviewing (Rao, 2004). On balance, then, the strengths of convergent interviewing outweigh its limitations.

ESTABLISHING THE VALIDITY AND RELIABILITY OF THE CONVERGENT INTERVIEWING RESEARCH

This next section examines the issues of achieving validity and reliability in convergent interviews (Riege, 2003). Validity and reliability in qualitative

Table 7.3   Tests for validity and reliability of qualitative research such as convergent interviewing

Test	Research design	Phase of research
Construct validity	• data collected from multiple sources (convergent interviews) provide multiple measures of the same phenomenon	research design and data analysis
	• establishment of triangulation of interview questions	research design and data analysis
	• in-built negative case analysis	data analysis
	• flexibility of the proposed theoretical framework	research design and data collection
Internal validity	• sample selection for information richness	research design
External validity	• sample selection for theoretical replication	research design
Reliability	• interview guide developed for the collection of data	data collection and analysis
	• structured process for administration and interpretation of convergent interviews	data collection
	• use of a steering committee	research design data collection and analysis

Source: Developed from Yin, 1994.

research can be achieved through forms of cross-checking. These in-built checks and controls for qualitative research can be summarized under four tests of the research design, being construct validity, internal validity, external validity and reliability (Yin, 1994) and are summarized in Table 7.3.

Construct validity refers to the formation of suitable operational measures for the concepts being investigated (Emory and Cooper, 1991). Our convergent interviewing achieved construct validity through three tactics. First, triangulation of interview questions was established in the research design stage through two or more carefully worded questions that looked at Internet-facilitated relationship constructs from different angles. Secondly, the convergent interview method contained an in-built negative case analysis where, in each interview and before the next, the technique explicitly requires that the interviewer attempt to disprove emerging explanations interpreted in the data (Dick, 1990). Finally, the flexibility of the mode allowed the interviewer to re-evaluate and re-design both the content and process of the interview program, thus establishing content validity.

Internal validity refers to causal relationships and the validity of the influence of one variable on other variables (Zikmund, 2000). Internal validity in the convergent interviews in the Internet research was achieved through purposeful sample selection on the basis of 'information richness' (Patton 1990, p. 181), and is described in some detail below.

External validity concerns the ability of the research findings to be generalized beyond the immediate study (Emory and Cooper, 1991; Sekaran, 2000). In this research, some external validity was achieved through theoretical replication in the interviewee selection described below. That is, experts were selected to ensure that a cross-section of opinions was provided.

Reliability refers to how consistently a technique measures the concepts it is supposed to measure, enabling other researchers to repeat the study and attain similar findings (Sekaran, 2000). Our qualitative research secured reliability through five tactics. First, reliability was attained through the structured process of convergent interviews. Secondly, reliability was achieved through organizing a structured process for recording, writing and interpreting data.

Thirdly, the other procedure recommended by Dick (1990) in which at least two interviewers conduct the interviews and that they work individually but in parallel with each other, was adopted in this research whenever the co-researcher was available. In addition, research reliability was achieved through comparing this research's findings with those of other, albeit few, researchers in the literature. Finally, the use of a steering committee to assist in the design and administration of the interview program is another way that reliability can be achieved (Guba and Lincoln, 1994). If a number of the members of the committee agree about a phenomenon, then their collective judgment is relatively objective. Thus, reliability was addressed as best it could be. In brief, four tests of validity and reliability were applied to the second stage of this research.

IMPLEMENTING THE CONVERGENT INTERVIEWING TECHNIQUE

This section gives more details about how the convergent interviewing method was implemented. The amount of information and prior theory required is defined, the selection of the sample to be interviewed is discussed, and the planning and execution of the interviews is described.

Defining the Information Required

The first step of planning the interview is to define the information required and the nature of the problem that has given rise to the research to provide an early focus for the planning (Dick, 1990). Defining information is accompanied by having prior theory (Perry, 1998). An 'enfolding' approach for the prior theory in the literature (Eisenhardt, 1989, p. 25) was applied in our research. That is, the literature was reviewed while the convergent interviews were being done. In this enfolding process, the researcher began with a few preliminary propositions and then allowed the data and enfolding literature to suggest new directions for shaping the body of knowledge as the interviews proceeded. After conducting the first two interviews, new insights led to a more focused review of the sparse literature. More interviews were conducted and provided new insights to re-examine the literature and helped the development of an initial conceptual framework.

Deciding Sample Size

Selecting the optimal sample size for the interviews depends on what is to be found and why, and how the findings are to be applied (Patton, 1990). Research has suggested different sample sizes for the convergent interviewing method. Dick (1990) suggested that the sample size should be one per cent of a target population of up to 200 and as a minimum the sample size should not be less than 12 people. Others have argued that sample size is determined when stability is reached, that is, when agreement among interviewees is achieved and disagreement among them is explained (by their different industry backgrounds, for example), on all the issues raised (Naire and Riege, 1995), as noted above. For example, Naire and Riege (1995) found stability can occur after only six interviews, and Woodward (1996) found convergence occurred after only five interviews. In our research, this stability occurred after ten interviews.

Deciding the Sampling Method

In qualitative research, the sampling method is purposeful rather than random (Patton, 1990). The Internet research initially selected a small and diverse sample of knowledgeable people who did not know each other, and after each interview the interviewees were then asked to recommend other people who should be interviewed. Such a snowball sampling technique is appropriate when research is concerned with a small, specialized population of people who are knowledgeable about the topics (Aaker and Day, 1990; Neuman, 2000; Patton, 1990). Another part of the sampling process is the careful selection of the first interviewee as the first snowball (Nair and Riege, 1995). That is, the first interviewee must be able to direct the researcher to others who are familiar with the area of the research, as well as be an expert. In this research, identifying these key industry figures was done with the assistance of the National Office for Information Economy. Seven of the interviewees were marketing managers with considerable experience of Internet marketing. The other three interviewees were business/marketing consultants who had been in this field for considerable periods of time.

Conducting the Interviews

In a qualitative interviewing process the interviewer acts as the instrument and so care must be taken in both the planning and management of the interviews. The following discussion examines the planning and management issues relating to convergent interviewing and is based mainly on steps recommended by Dick (1990, pp. 12–14).

Step 1: contacting the respondent   Initial contact with potential participants was established through email or telephone calls. Where the initial contact was by email, a telephone call followed. After being given an overview of the research and the purpose of the interview, the respondents were asked to participate in the interviews. When they agreed, the venue and time were decided (Carson et al., 2001).

Step 2: time and setting   In this research, interviewees were informed that the length of the interview would be 30 minutes to an hour. Later interviews became longer as the number of probe questions increased. All interviews were carried out face-to-face at the respondents' place of work, because it was easier to establish rapport and to capture interviewees' body language. All interview times were fixed at the initial contact and confirmed a few days prior to the interview.

Step 3: establishing rapport and neutrality   Clarification of a number of preliminary issues at the start of the interview was made to encourage rapport and cooperation during the interview (Carson et al., 2001). The researcher introduced herself and gave a brief explanation of the purpose of the research. Interviewees were also informed of the confidentiality of the interviews and asked for permission to tape record the interview.

Step 4: opening question   The opening question needs to be framed in such a manner as to encourage the interviewees to reveal their attitudes about the research topic without placing boundaries on the responses (Dick, 1990). That is, the objective of the opening question is to provide a broad starting point that may lead to further probe questions (Nair and Reige, 1995) and to define the nature of the topic without implying any constraints on the nature of the response. The opening question used in this research was, 'Can you please tell me a story of your experience of dealing with another business using the Internet?' (Nair and Riege, 1995; Perry, 1998). This question did not put pressure on the respondents to think about any specific issues, that is, the interviewees did not have to intellectualize or justify their responses. Rather, the interviewee merely shared his or her experience with the researcher in a relaxing manner and this assisted the interviewee in organizing his or her thoughts.

Step 5: probe questions   Probe questions follow the opening question and help to keep interviewees talking and the interview focused. In convergent interviews, probe questions are also the mechanism through which the sim-ilarities and dissimilarities from previous interviews are explored. For this research, probe questions were developed before each interview after the first one, based on the proceeding interview. They were printed out in an interview guide and given to the interviewee at the start of the interview. As well, questions such as 'Can you give me an example for this?' and 'Can you elaborate a little?' were used in the course of the interviews. This proce-dure helped to focus the interview and keep the interview within time constraints.

Step 6: inviting a summary   When it is apparent that little more informa-tion will be secured, a researcher can start closure by inviting the respon-dent to pick out the key points from what has been so far discussed, perhaps also indicating their relative priority (Dick, 1990). For this research, the question to invite summary was 'Of all the issues you have mentioned what are the most and least important issues?' and then questions were asked about, priority, such as 'Could you please prioritize them in order of importance?'

Step 7: concluding the interview   When the interviewee could no longer add information, the interviewer summarized the interview to ensure that all questions planned were investigated and to confirm interviewees' responses. Then the interviewee was thanked for his or her cooperation and a copy of the data analysis was offered. The interviewee was again assured that the information obtained during the interview would remain confidential and anonymous, unless otherwise agreed to.

THE TWO OUTCOMES OF THE CONVERGENT INTERVIEWS

The penultimate outcome of the convergent interviewing process is a list of themes progressively raised and investigated in the interviews, along the lines of Table 7.1 above. This table is constructed by progressive content analysis of the interview transcripts and usually fits the themes into three to five 'chunks' of ideas called research issues. The table shows how the number of issues involved in the topic area increased as each interviewee in turn added their insights to what had been said before, until the final interview added no new issues. Agreements between interviewees are shown, as are disagreements that could be explained. For example, some of the entries in our Internet research table about the final 'chunk' of themes uncovered in the interviews were:

Issue 3: Internet usage is perceived to be positively associated with business performance.

- The use of the Internet has a positive effect on sales and market share.
- The use of the Internet has a positive effect on long-term profits but not on short-term profits.
- The use of the Internet has a positive effect on return on assets.

This table is the first outcome of convergent interviewing and is a stepping-stone towards the next outcome of a conceptual framework. That is, from a close examination of the quotations about the issues summarized in the table, and from the scant literature, a new conceptual framework about the research project's objectives can be developed. This stepping from a first, exploratory outcome to a final outcome is common in qualitative research (Miles and Huberman, 1994). Early versions of a model of this framework were presented to the interviewees at the end of each interview, for their comments and ideas about revisions.

In our experience, this model could not have been developed before the convergent interviews began because there was no previous research about the variables involved and, in particular, the complex interrelationships among the variables could not have been unearthed without the flexible, in-depth processes of convergent interviewing. Incidentally, after the analytic generalization (Yin, 1994) summarized in the model is finalized, some researchers use case research for further analytic generalization, that is, to confirm or disconfirm the model. However, in our research, we moved directly to statistical generalization because several of the variables identified in the convergent interviews had already been investigated in previous research. That is, we used structural equation modelling of survey data to test the model. Most of the model's variables and relationships were shown to be valid.

CONCLUSIONS AND IMPLICATIONS

In summary, this chapter provided a comprehensive description of the convergent interviewing method, compared convergent interviewing with other qualitative methods, showed how its validity and reliability can be enhanced, reviewed its strengths and limitations and finally noted how it can be implemented. The two outcomes of a convergent interviewing research project were identified. In conclusion, we argue that convergent interviewing is more appropriate than in-depth interviews, case research and focus groups in under-researched areas where there are few experts because it provides a way of quickly converging on key issues in the area, an efficient mechanism for data analysis after each interview, and a way of deciding when to stop collecting data. It is often an ideal way to begin a program of enterprise research.

NOTE

* This chapter is an adaptation for enterprise research of core ideas in the psychology book by convergent interviewing's developer, Bob Dick (1990) and incorporates ideas and words of reports by several others who have refined the process for marketing research, for example, Drs Gerry Batonda, Godwin Nair, Andi Riege and Tracy Woodward. We thank them for their pioneering work. This chapter is adapted from Rao and Perry (2003) and Carson et al. (2001).

REFERENCES

Aaker, D.A. and G.S. Day (1990), *Marketing Research*, 4th edn, New York: John Wiley and Sons.

Calder, B.J. (1980), 'Focus group interview and qualitative research in organisations', in E.E. Lawler, D.A. Nadler and C. Cammann (eds), *Organisational Assessment*, New York: John Wiley and Sons.

Carson, D., A. Gilmore, K. Gronhaug and C. Perry (2001), *Qualitative Research in Marketing*, London: Sage.

Cox, K.K., J.B. Higginbotham and J. Burton (1989), 'Applications of focus group interviews in marketing', in T.J. Hayes and C.B. Tathum (eds), *Focus Group Interviews: a Reader*, Chicago: American Marketing Association.

Crimmons, J. (1988), 'More truth and more consequences', *Applied Marketing Research*, **28**(2), 44–49.

Dick, B. (1990), *Convergent Interviewing*, Brisbane: Interchange.

Eisenhardt, K. (1989), 'Building theory from case study research', *Academy of Management Review*, **14**(4), 532–50.

Emory, C.W. and D.R. Cooper (1991), *Business Research Methods*, Homewood: Irwin.

Goldman, A.E. (1962), 'The group depth interview', *Journal of Marketing*, **26**(2), 61–68.

Guba, E.G. and Y.S. Lincoln (1994), 'Competing paradigms in qualitative research', in N.K. Denzin and Y.S. Lincoln (eds), *Handbook of Qualitative Research*, London: Sage.

Gummesson, E. (2000), *Qualitative Methods in Management Research*, 2nd edn, Thousand Oaks, CA: Sage.

King, E. (1996), 'The use of self in qualitative research', in J. Richardson (ed.), *Handbook of Qualitative Research Methods for Psychology and Social Sciences*, Leicester: BPS Books.

Marshall, C. and G.B. Rossman (1995), *Designing Qualitative Research*, 2nd edn, Newbury Park: Sage.

Maykut, P. and R. Morehouse (1994), *Beginning Qualitative Research: A Philosophical and Practical Guide*, London and Washington, DC: Falmer Press.

Miles, M.B. and A.M. Huberman (1994), *An Expanded Sourcebook: Qualitative Data Analysis*, Thousand Oaks, CA: Sage.

Morgan, D.L. (1993), *Successful Focus Groups: Advance the State of Art*, Thousand Oaks, CA: Sage.

Morgan, D.L. and R.A. Krueger (1993), 'When to use focus groups and why', in D.L. Morgan (ed.), *Successful Focus Groups*, London: Sage.

Nair, G.S. and A.M. Riege (1995), 'Using convergent interviewing to develop the research problem of a postgraduate thesis', *Proceedings of Marketing Education and Researchers International Conference*, Gold Coast.

Neuman, W.L. (2000), *Social Research Methods: Qualitative and Quantitative Approaches*, 4th edn, Boston: Allyn and Bacon.

Patton, M.Q. (1990), *Qualitative Evaluation and Research Methods*, Newbury Park: Sage.

Perry, C. (1998), 'Processes of a case study methodology for postgraduate research in marketing', *European Journal of Marketing*, **32**(9/10), 785–802.

Perry, C. (2001), 'Case research in marketing', *The Marketing Review*, **1**(1), 303–23.

Phillips, E.M. and D.S. Pugh (1987), *How to Get a PhD*, Buckingham and Philadelphia, PA: Open University Press.

Rao, S. (2004), 'The internet and business-to-business relational bonds: perspectives from an Australian service industry', *International Journal of Internet and Advertising*, **1**(4), 12–29.

Rao, S. and C. Perry (2003), 'Convergent interviewing to build a theory in under-researched areas: principles and an example investigation of internet usage in inter-firm relationships', *Qualitative Market Research: an International Journal*, **6**(4), 236–47.

Riege, A.M. (2003), 'Validity and reliability tests in case study research: a literature review with "hands-on" applications for each research phase', *Qualitative Market Research: an International Journal*, **6**(2), 75–86.

Sekaran, U. (2000), *Research Method for Business: a Skill Building Approach*, New York: John Wiley and Sons.

Steward, D.W. and P.N. Shamdasani (1990), *Focus Groups: Theory and Practice*, California: Sage.

Woodward, T. (1996), 'Identifying the measuring customer-based brand equity and its elements for a service industry', PhD thesis, prepared for Queensland University of Technology, Queensland.

Yin, R.K. (1994), *Case Study Research: Design and Methods*, Beverley Hills: Sage.

Zikmund, W.G. (2000), *Business Research Methods*, 6th edn, Chicago: The Dryden Press.

8. Case and iCase: facilitating case survey methods for creating research and teaching synergies in innovation and enterprise

Lars Bengtsson, Rikard Larsson, Andrew Griffiths and Damian Hine

INTRODUCTION

It is hard to argue against the desirability of synergies between research and teaching. However, the realization of such synergy potentials has been rather difficult. The research utilization of semi-captured convenience samples of students have become increasingly questioned as the 'science of the sophomores' with limited scientific as well as pedagogic value. If the students are more consciously involved in the research effort, they may learn more at the expense of possible sample contamination. Another example of apparent negative synergies between research and teaching is the common occurrence of academic recruitments and evaluation being mainly research-based to the frustration of students who prefer more pedagogic skills.

Case studies have the potential for bridging the gap between research and teaching. Lessons learned from case studies enhance managerial decision-making regarding the development of innovative products, processes or services. Irrespective of discipline, results of case study analysis can highlight the key elements for sustaining existing industries or technologies, and provide an understanding of the essential elements in the innovative process for the commercialization of emerging technologies. They have mainly been used for teaching purposes in the United States (US), while Europeans have used them more for qualitative research. Even though Europeans are also increasingly adopting case teaching, a key remaining barrier to more fully realizing research-teaching synergy potentials is the limited statistical generalizability and comparability of single or a small number of case studies.

The case survey method is an under-utilized research approach to combine the respective strengths of ideographic case studies and nomothetic surveys (Yin and Heald, 1975; Bullock and Tubbs, 1987; Larsson, 1993; Larsson and Bengtsson, 1993). It consists of (1) selecting a sample of existing case studies relevant to chosen research questions; (2) developing a coding scheme for systematic conversion of the qualitative case descriptions into quantified variables; (3) having multiple raters coding the cases and measuring their interrater reliability; and (4) statistically analysing the coded data.

The ability of the case survey method to quantitatively analyse qualitative case studies is not limited to research. The case survey method also has great potential to bridge between research and teaching. The structured comparative analysis of cases can help students to understand both individual cases and patterns across cases at the same time as their case codings can generate research case survey samples with interrater reliability as well as data on individual decision-making and group processes.

What is proposed in this chapter is a methodology for better utilizing case studies in both research and teaching. This chapter combines two distinct initiatives designed to enhance case study research. To facilitate the expanded exploitation of the case survey technique, a case study capture and storage system known as iCase is explained. Improved use of case studies, developed through case study sampling requires access to a repository of case studies, preferably held in electronic format for ease of access and enhancement. Both the case survey method and its partner technique iCase are explored in this chapter. The 'i' in iCase refers to innovation. This is the first area of application of this electronic case study capture technique. Innovation and entrepreneurship research and teaching complement each other and are the most dynamic area of enterprise research.

CONFLICTING DEMANDS OF RESEARCH AND TEACHING

There are a number of reasons why synergies between research and teaching fail to be realized: (1) The merit system in academia generally recognizes research activities more than teaching activities. Thus, for most academic teachers it seems logical to focus their main efforts on research instead of teaching. For the individual teacher it seldom pays off to plan for and carry out activities that will realize synergies between teaching and research; (2) quantitative research often requires random and representative sampling, while teaching mostly involves a narrow demographic range of students (thus students often make up an unrepresentative sample);

(3) qualitative research often involves studying longitudinal processes and context, while teaching mostly involves short-term, context-free student participation; (4) in qualitative research it is often difficult to design data collection for both research and teaching purposes at the same time; (5) management research in general deals with empirical data from managerial practice; (6) using more interactive teaching methods may actually reduce their research value by being contaminated by inappropriate research hypotheses, thus research when applied to students becomes a poor pedagogic tool in teaching; (7) even the rare individuals who master both teaching and research find it difficult to do both well simultaneously. They rather do research first and then tell about it afterwards in class, or develop research ideas in class that are subsequently investigated, but not joint research and teaching. However, the above list indicates that there is a clear divide between research and teaching, particularly in applied areas such as entrepreneurship and innovation.

STRENGTHS AND WEAKNESSES OF THE CASE SURVEY METHOD

The case survey constitutes an inexpensive and potentially powerful method to identify and statistically test patterns across existing studies (Lucas, 1974). It is particularly suitable in areas where case studies dominate (Yin and Heald, 1975), the organization is the unit of analysis, the researcher is interested in incorporating a broad range of conditions (Jauch et al., 1980), and experimental design is impossible or otherwise fails to capture situations relevant to managerial practice (Bullock and Tubbs, 1987).

Larsson (1993) and Larsson and Bengtsson (1993) have previously summarized the strengths of the case survey method. It taps prior research efforts reported in a vast number of idiographic case studies with managerially relevant data from the case study method's greater reliance on what Argyris (1970) calls organic, action-oriented research (rather than mechanistic, rigorous laboratory experiments).

The case survey method capitalizes on the idiographic richness of case studies to enable the study of more complex phenomena and contexts than more superficial nomothetic surveys (cf. Tsoukas, 1989). Organizational processes and multiple stakeholder perspectives are better captured through the typically longitudinal and multi-source data collection in case studies (cf. Walton, 1972). The case survey method can be utilized for both theory-building through, for example, theoretical sampling of cases (cf. Glaser and Strauss, 1967; Yin, 1984) and theory-testing through statistical sampling of cases.

Case surveys can overcome major drawbacks of single case studies, namely the inability to examine cross-sectional patterns and to generalize about larger populations. This is done by pooling relevant case studies into sufficient samples for statistical testing to utilize the cross-sectional and generalization strengths of nomothetic research.

Case surveys can be replicated, since both the coding scheme and the case study reports are available to other researchers. The coding scheme can also be applied to other case studies to cross-validate or extend the original findings. Furthermore, the reliability of the case codings can be readily measured through multiple independent raters coding the same cases and assessing to what extent they agree. All this reduces the risks associated with the idiosyncratic art of reviewing research, such as ignored information and sample biases (cf. Cook and Leviton, 1980; Hunter et al., 1982).

The case survey method avoids premature exclusion of studies based on a priori judgements of their specific research design (eg, different perspectives, amounts, and methods of data collection), publication status, and age – all of which often plague research reviews. Instead, the aim of case surveys is to include initially most studies relevant to the research questions and test to what extent different research designs, publication status, and time affect the findings of the case studies. Such a broad inclusion enables the researcher to identify possible effects of different study characteristics by treating them as empirical questions rather than succumbing to premature exclusion based on prejudice or convenience. If significant differences are found, it is easier to distinguish between the case findings that result from the phenomena studied and the findings that emanate from the study characteristics and it is thereby possible to make more informed choices regarding possible exclusion of unduly biased cases. If no significant differences are found, it suggests that the findings are robust for different study characteristics. None of these conclusions would have been possible if a priori exclusion had been done.

The inclusion of case studies from different time periods also enables the analysis of patterns of complex phenomena over time in order to detect, for example, possible effects of organizational learning (cf. Lucas, 1974). Case studies benefit from longitudinal analysis of certain organizational processes whereas cross-sectional surveys at one point in time do not. However, case studies are limited to the longitudinal study of the focal process situated in one time period. Case surveys can be used to compare organizational processes as they occur in different time periods to explore or test the impact of different phases of the business cycle, organizational learning over time, and so on. Furthermore, even if a longitudinal case study spans several turns of the business cycle, the singularity of the observed process makes it difficult to distinguish the influence of the business cycle from other factors. The nomothetic benefit of statistical control of these other factors can be utilized in case surveys. The methodology permits more interactive research processes with examining rich ideographic data, inductive and deductive theorizing, nomothetic testing, re-examination of readily available case data for theoretical elaboration, and so forth.

In the broader perspective, the case survey method provides a valuable bridge over not only the gap between the nomothetic and idiographic approaches, but also other traditional research gaps, such as quantitative versus qualitative methods. This is accomplished by quantifying the primarily qualitative case studies to enable statistical hypothesis-testing of interpretive data. While the triangulation of quantitative and qualitative methods is advocated by several social scientists, actual accomplishment of substantially integrated fieldwork and survey methods have been rare (Jick, 1979). Case surveys can contribute to this triangulation, which 'heightens qualitative methods to their deserved prominence and, at the same time, demonstrates that quantitative methods can and should be utilized in complementary fashion' (Jick, 1979, p. 610). Similarly, it follows the strategy of the multi-method approach to 'attack a research problem with an arsenal of methods that have non-overlapping weaknesses in addition to their complementary strengths' (Brewer and Hunter, 1989, p. 17).

Hence, the strengths of the case survey emanate from drawing on the benefits of both the idiographic and nomothetic approaches to overcome their respective weaknesses. A single case study forfeits the opportunity of cross-case pattern analysis that is advantageous for generating theory (Eisenhardt, 1989) as well as theoretical generalization (Yin, 1984). Multiple case studies can achieve this opportunity, but the resource-consuming, intensive research typically limits the sample sizes below what is needed to utilize the nomothetic benefits of advanced statistical cross-case analysis and generalization (eg Gersick, 1988). The number of case studies that can be done within a certain resource limitation can be increased through standardized designs, but here we arrive at a major problem of the trade-off between idiographic and nomothetic research. Such standardization sacrifices the in-depth nature of the case data as well as further exposing the numerous case studies to such nomothetic weaknesses as common method variance (eg Podsakopf and Organ, 1986) where the use of the same researcher and design can create artifactual covariance. The case survey method attempts to solve this trade-off problem not only by extending resource limitations through the utilization of already existing cases, but also by drawing on their in-depthness, different researchers and designs (to overcome the problem of common method variance), as well as nomothetic cross-case analysis and statistical generalization.

However, case surveys can suffer from a number of weaknesses (Bullock and Tubbs, 1987; Yin, 1981; Yin and Heald, 1975). They are limited by the number of available case studies that are relevant to the specific research questions. It is often easy to believe that not enough case studies have been done on a certain subject of interest to collect a sufficiently large sample. Yet, it is our experience that a surprising number of cases can be found through the use of multiple search strategies and sources.

Yin (1984) states that the selection of case studies is beyond the control of the secondary investigator, and therefore, case surveys are unlikely to achieve theoretical and statistical generalization. This view disregards, however, that case survey researchers can control the secondary selection of cases to include in the sample. The early recommendation of Lucas (1974) to utilize sampling parameters and bias analysis actually suggests a way to accomplish this control through stratified case selection.

Case study reports restrict the available information for case surveys by tending to leave out much of the collected data due to space limitations. The involvement of at least a subsample of the case authors can, however, provide access to all their primary data. The quality of the case survey is no better than the quality of the case studies it analyses. Still, both the effects of different research designs and the validity of case codings can be tested even though the literature has so far given little and fragmented attention to these issues.

The coding procedure of assigning numbers can unduly simplify complex phenomena under investigation. This coding simplification is a key issue in case survey methodology since it constitutes the bridge from idiographic richness to nomothetic generality. While the coding procedure necessarily simplifies the information contained in the case studies, the central question is rather if this information loss can be compensated for by the benefits of quantitative analysis across a larger case sample. When designing a study, it seems reasonable to expect diminishing marginal utility of making an already extensive nomothetic survey even more extensive (eg adding one more observation to a large sample) and an already intensive idiographic study even more intensive (eg adding one more aspect to a multi-aspect case). Diminishing marginal utility favours designs with a more balanced mix of nomothetic and idiographic approaches.

The design of the case survey method seeks to reduce the inherent weaknesses of case study approaches and enhance the strengths. As has been described in other chapters in this book, quantitative and qualitative research should not be seen as a dichotomy for researchers to choose between. They are steps along a research continuum. Case survey methods offer not only a bridge between teaching and research but also a bridge between qualitative and quantitative research.

However, as with quantitative research generally, there is a need in the case survey method to collect a considerable number of cases in order to conduct the type and level of analysis that will provide research results which completes the theory building and commences the theory testing process. The collection of cases in numbers for analysis is problematic.

THE PURPOSE OF iCASE

The development of an online repository of cases submitted from a range of sources including researchers, industry partners and representatives and students, provides a partial solution to the problematic goal of providing the large number of case studies required to competently and confidently undertake the case survey method. In this section we elaborate on the development, mechanics and structure of iCase.

iCase is an interactive online innovation case study network designed to provide an electronic, integrated case infrastructure for industry and academia, enhancing the collection and diffusion of knowledge on innovation and entrepreneurship.

iCase can create a facilitative infrastructure for dynamic links between industry and academia, which will provide the number and variety of cases required to be successful. Through this process iCase stimulates international collaboration on innovation by providing a rich resource for applied research. It also offers its own innovations through the development of database applications for new forms of electronically based archival material, such as Gantt Charts, meeting minutes and electronic communications such as email and web sites. It is planned that iCase ultimately will be a tool for industry as much as it is a tool for researchers, which can help build corporate capacity for organizational memory through knowledge creation in partner organizations.

The focus of iCase is on innovation and entrepreneurship. Globally, these two interlinked areas have become the competitive imperative for organizational and industrial success. To sustain growth, competitiveness, and industrial advantage, innovation knowledge must be captured and utilized. iCase provides the infrastructure for the management and generation of innovation knowledge created for and by researchers and industry practitioners. Knowledge in the form of cases, stories, critical incidents, anecdotes, observations, and histories are the cornerstone of iCase.

Currently there exist a number of internationally-based case clearing houses – Harvard Business School, Stanford Graduate School of Business and the European Case Clearing House. They provide teaching cases to academics and industry on a cost recovery basis, but do not address

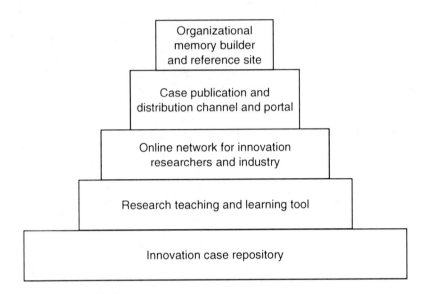

Figure 8.1   The building blocks of iCase

broader learning and knowledge sharing issues. iCase differs significantly from the traditional case clearing house approach. iCase, like the case clearing houses, provides access to cases online. However, an important difference is that these cases will be research as opposed to teaching focused. iCase also provides researchers and industry with access to online case study methodologies to enable these groups to construct their own research case studies. In the case of organizations, this will lead to the generation of organizational memory tools. Finally, iCase acts as a conduit to collect industry case study material and case research.

The objectives of iCase are diverse. It is designed to provide researchers and managers in innovation with an online tool that enables them to access high quality case studies for studying all aspects of the innovation process. The area of innovation research is cross disciplinary, as effective innovation required the interaction of diverse disciplines across diverse industries. The development of iCase will draw on the strengths across areas such as Engineering, Science, Management, IT, R&D, Health, Arts and others, while enabling researchers from within each area to cross fertilize and utilize diverse case material.

iCase is also designed to encourage the diffusion of innovation in firms through outreach by providing a source of interactive and browsable case studies and vignettes demonstrating both successful and unsuccessful examples of innovation in industry. The aim is to enhance cross industry innovation. This will occur through quick access for the diffusion of know-ledge that enhances the competitiveness of firms through: (a) advanced forms of innovation benchmarking; (b) provision of exemplar cases of best practice; and (c) the linking of industry managers to researchers by encour-aging managers to not only be information gatherers (users of innovation-based case material) but also to be information givers (by commenting online on the quality of case material and leaving examples of case mater-ial online).

iCase will also provide innovation researchers with a readily available, online tool that enables them to create high quality research case studies by using and developing online case study materials and methodologies in order to enhance their research outcomes. Although books and journal articles are available, currently there exists no online interactive tools that enhance the ability of researchers to refine their case study methodologies and enhance their ability to undertake case study research. iCase provides a unique opportunity to enhance the research skills and knowledge outputs of managers. For instance, both researchers and managers will be able to construct multiple case studies using individual or partial cases from within this facility, and augmented by further empirical work will provide for stronger research studies and enhance their international research reputa-tion through publishable outcomes. The research training role of iCase will provide a methodological focus to augment the content focus of cases to ensure rigour. Each new case is then added to the repository after a quality check and editing. This builds not only the case study database, but a com-munity of researchers and users of this facility.

THE ESSENTIAL COMPONENTS OF iCASE

iCase is an online repository of peer reviewed exemplar case studies on innovation. These case studies are compiled by both academics and indus-try. Cases are distinguished by their depth and rigour. As a result there are two different levels of cases: peer reviewed, and general submissions and postings. Furthermore, there is a wide variety of case study styles allowable so as to meet the needs of a broad audience. This variety of case study styles includes: stories; vignettes; teaching cases; research cases; critical incidents; exemplar cases and snapshot cases. iCase provides a mechanism for gathering case materials and data through: conversations and stories; ethnographic approaches; participant observation; interviews (including in-depth interviews); historical – primary, secondary – archival material.

A number of demographic fields are available for all cases to identify and group them. From this, geographical maps of innovation and a topical category map of innovation are available. Defining criteria include country data, business size, industry sector, level of management, as well as whether the case relates largely to content or process. The fields discussed in the paragraphs above form the basis of the knowledge management database on innovation and entrepreneurship which can be accessed by a keywords search that can be used for theory building and organizational learning.

While iCase is still in the early stages of development, as the case supply to iCase builds, a grid matrix of methodologies will be instituted with units of analysis defined – including individual, group, project, organization, industry, country, cross-national. Each is a digital dynamic case, that is one which grows in an interactive sense as participants add more information. This creates an online digital and interactive case facility with a participating organization by having stakeholders able to upload comments at any point in time and by having key stakeholders being sent a structured data collection instrument that they have to fill in and then submit – this will be on the basis of structured – (open ended/closed) questions. Aligned with this input approach is the output of material through 'Quote Bank', in which anecdotes and statements from cases are available under searchable fields.

The establishment of iCase has required a substantial supporting infrastructure to be established, including:

- Dedicated proprietary software – Windows-based software development, build around case method and case collection, supported by encryption and security functions;
- A Project Manager/IT Support Manager;
- Web design – website – with multi-site accessibility including UQ, Cranfield and Cranfield Clearinghouse;
- A peer review panel;
- Stakeholder pilot commitment with industry and university partners;
- The selection of a pivotal partner to extend industry networks in the first instance;
- Infrastructure/technology and backup facilities – server and associated peripherals;
- Extensive research assistance;
- Recruitment of a technical expert to join the lead group;
- A policy on membership access and subscription base – including membership concessions for contributors, institutional/organizational and individual memberships.

The broadest operational objectives are set out in three stages and will take three years to reach fruition. The first stage was run as a pilot

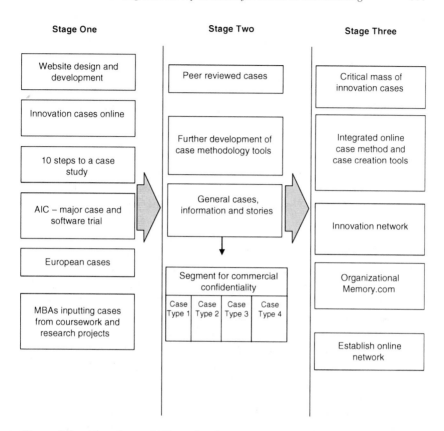

Figure 8.2   Flowchart of iCase development

project for one year. The second stage requires the constitution of a Beta testing stakeholder group to fast track the development of the overall product package and to facilitate innovation in the design process. The third stage is the expansion of iCase to an international commercial joint venture, linking the major markets: Asia-Pacific, Europe and North America.

CASE SURVEY STEPS TO COMBINE TEACHING AND RESEARCH BENEFITS

iCase provides the opportunity to confidently commence the case survey method. Its facultative role is essential as it is critical that the number and variety of cases be assured prior to the selection of case survey method as a viable enterprise research technique in both teaching and in research. iCase can provide this assurance.

We have so far only seen the case survey method being used for research purposes, with the exception of Mintzberg, Raisinghani, and Theoret's (1976) famous study 'The structure of "unstructured" decision processes'. While they made no such methodological point, their study actually fulfills the basic case survey steps of investigating research questions through a coding scheme applied to a set of cases. These cases were created by students. Out of a total of 48 cases, the authors selected the 25 most detailed case descriptions of 'unstructured decision processes' for their analysis, which rendered them a widely cited publication in *Administrative Science Quarterly*.

To assist in building a critical mass of case material, iCase utilizes post-graduate students' case material developed within their coursework, with appropriate recognition given. Having students collect primary data and write up cases that then is surveyed is thus one way of combining research and teaching benefits of the case survey method. In this chapter, we propose that even the students can benefit from making use of previous research efforts by others with a different case survey teaching design. Rather than having to create own cases of possible doubtful scientific quality, the students can become 'co-case surveyors' by collecting, coding and comparing existing cases of often more established quality than their own student cases.

Using Larsson's (1993) 12 step case survey research design, we will present how a teacher and a class of students can jointly create research and teaching synergies by not only using analysis of separate cases, but also systematically compare them and even test hypotheses about patterns across the cases.

SELECTION OF RELEVANT CASE SAMPLE

1.   Research Questions

Research questions are the obvious starting-point for case surveys. They preferably focus on complex organizational processes, and can be theory-driven testing of hypotheses as well as exploratory surveys of 'what the literature says'. When applied to teaching, the research question of a case-survey-based class should correspond to a key issue of the particular topic of the class. Thus, the students as well as the teacher are given an overall class assignment of investigating this key research question. This assignment is to be accomplished by mainly small student groups of 2–3 persons finding, analysing, coding, and comparing, and finally testing hypotheses across a set of case studies.

2.   Case Selection Criteria

Case selection criteria should be made explicit and based on the theoretical domain given by the developed research questions (Bullock and Tubbs, 1987). Further specified exclusion rules are stated to explicitly delineate which cases (a) belong to this theoretical domain, and (b) have at least the minimum amount of reported information about the domain to be meaningfully included in the case sample. The less admissible research design, publication status, and time criteria should be used as variables to analyse possible effects of case differences in these regards, as discussed earlier. Thus, it is the extent of reported data on an empirical occurrence of the theoretical domain that determines if the case should be initially included rather than how, when, or where it was reported. In the teaching situation, the case selection criteria become the guideline for both the teacher and students collection of cases.

3.   Case Study Collection

The collection of case studies involves several substeps: (A) The teacher can provide a certain set of pre-collected cases to get the student groups started with, for example, a suitable opening teaching case and one case per student group. (B) As many different search strategies (eg, bibliographies, computer search, experts, and reference lists) as possible should be employed to both minimize biases due to certain strategies research-wise and enable the students to learn various ways of gathering secondary data. (C) The search strategies should cover as many sources (eg, research publications, dissertations, conference papers, teaching cases, business literature, and unpublished sources) as possible to minimize source-specific biases. (D) Explicit screening procedures are needed to inspect the collected case references and exclude the cases that appear to have too little information or constitute an overly resource-demanding sample (cf. Osborn et al., 1981). The target number of cases for each student group to collect can vary with both the time allotted to the case survey activities and the expected availability of relevant cases. (E) Initial comparisons between sample characteristics and existing population or larger sample statistics can indicate sample biases and the possible need for stratified sampling. Even if available resources or cases do not allow for stratified sampling to improve the representativeness of the case sample, it is still important to make these comparisons for a more informed discussion of the findings and their limitations.

4.   Coding Scheme Design

The Coding Scheme is the core of case surveys. It documents and guides the conversion of qualitative case study data into quantified variables that operationalize the research questions. The design of the coding scheme revolves around the basic trade-off between resource-saving, reliable simplicity versus information rich complexity. Even though more complex coding schemes with extended ranges of alternative positions for each variable require more work, they can capture more information than simple yes–no categories. However, the more alternative positions and the finer the distinctions, the greater the risk that lower interrater reliability can undermine the value of the extra work.

The main argument for more complex coding schemes is that they enable the maximization of information extraction, since unreliable scales can be collapsed so that reliable distinctions can be made (eg, from a seven to a five-point Likert scale). In contrast, simple scales cannot subsequently be expanded since the information contained in the more detailed distinctions has already been lost. While high interrater reliability is generally seen as favourable for research measurement purposes, here it can be a sign that more information could have been extracted. Manimala's (1992, p. 491) case survey, for instance, reported very high interrater reliability (>.9 correlation) and yet he concluded that the study was limited by 'its inability to have finer measurements than the three-point scale'. This alleged inability cannot be known without empirically testing if more detailed scales yield significantly worse interrater reliability, which was not reported.

Bullock and Tubbs (1987, pp. 195, 189) note the limitations of simple coding schemes and that 'the pursuit of high reliability could become a dysfunctional end in itself', but still they recommend that 'simpler is better'. Their recommendation initially maximizes interrater reliability at the expense of the information that may be extracted with adequate reliability when a more complex scheme is used. The complex alternative corresponds to Ashby's (1960) law of requisite variety where a system needs a variety of responses to control the variety of disturbances it faces. Raters need enough coding variety in response to the rich variety of the case studies to avoid unnecessary coding simplification of the idiographic data. Complex schemes give the coders at least the opportunity to prove that their judgement can yield more information than mechanical reading.

The limit of how much information a case survey can capture from the case studies is indicated by the point at which interrater reliability becomes unacceptably low due to an overly detailed coding scheme. The only way to determine the level at which this occurs is to start with an overly detailed coding scheme and gradually simplify it until adequate reliability is reached. An initially reliable, simple scheme may have yielded more reliable information that cannot be extracted without recoding all the cases. By aiming at a coding scheme that is slightly too complex with somewhat low reliability, maximum information with adequate reliability can then be achieved through minor simplification without too much extra work due to excessive complexity.

There are several teaching reasons for the teacher to have pre-designed at least the core of the coding scheme. Since all of the cases collected and coded by the student groups are to be eventually pooled, the case coding scheme needs to be the same for all student groups. It is also typically quite difficult for students to develop a good coding scheme from scratch. The coding scheme will also structure most of the students' case analyses during the class, so the teacher should also make sure that key variables are included for both teaching and research purposes. Finally, having a pre-designed core coding scheme enables it to be reused in subsequent classes to further accumulate a larger case survey sample over time. For example, each class can focus on cases of certain industries and this focus can then be changed from class to class to get an increasingly industry-wide case survey database over time. It is still possible to supplement the pre-designed scheme with questions suggested by the student groups to allow for greater participation and creativity. If each of, let's say, 20 groups is asked to contribute one self-developed question to be added to the pre-designed core of 30 questions, the specific case coding scheme for that whole class will consist of a total of 50 questions. The most useful of the student-generated questions can then be included in the pre-designed scheme for the next class.

5.   Multiple Coding and Inter-rater Reliability

The Case Coding can be broken down to several substeps: (A) All students of the whole class should code the opening teaching case individually to actively familiarize themselves with the coding scheme and compare codings for calibration purposes. (B) All students within each group should code each of that group's collected cases individually. That is, it is import-ant that the groups do not start coding the cases collectively, since inde-pendent individual case codings are required first to establish interrater reliability for both research and teaching purposes. If the group size is two students, the collective number of cases of the whole class is maximized. In contrast, if there are three students in each group, three raters per case improve the information extraction through elimination of mistakes and single-minded interpretations as well as enable majority considerations and more learning discussions when resolving discrepancies. (C) The teacher can participate as a rater of, for example, one of each student group's cases to interact with the students and increase the quality of the case codings. (D) Both the teacher and the students should not voice their respective ideas for hypotheses to test on the whole class' case survey sample to ensure that the majority of the raters are blind to the theoretical hypotheses to safeguard against undue coding influence by the coders themselves. (E) To facilitate the subsequent discrepancy resolution, raters should note passages in the text that they view as important for their codings as well as suggestions for possible coding scheme changes.

6.   Author Participation

Author Participation provides an excellent extra rater of their own cases. Thus, the students can contact and ask the authors of each of the cases that they have collected to code their own case and judging from our experience, there is a good chance that one out of two or three case authors agrees to this. More complex designs will especially benefit from the additional information that the authors can bring to bear on the codings and the secondary validation by the primary researchers' first-hand knowledge of the cases. Idiographic case studies involve many aspects that are subsequently not reported in condensed write-ups with a specific purpose. The comprehensive data collection makes case studies more malleable to meta-analyses with somewhat different purposes than the original studies if the non-reported data can be accessed through author participation. On the other hand, author participation actually invites lower interrater reliability by having raters with different information code the cases. This conflict between information and reliability considerations needs to be solved by distinguishing between intentional discrepancies to improve the information value and discrepancies from lack of clarity in case reports and coding schemes. The following steps will address this issue.

7.   Inter-rater Reliability

Interrater Reliability is a crucial measure of coding quality even though its overzealous pursuit has often been shown to have dysfunctional effects. The literature on interrater reliability is relatively diverse as illustrated by Jones,

Johnson, Butler and Main (1983). Bullock and Tubbs (1987) discuss extensively its application in case surveys and conclude that per cent agreement (simple percentage of cases where all raters coded a variable identically) should be used as the primary reliability index especially for categorical variables. Larsson (1993) focuses on how the often contradictory reliability and information considerations can be reconciled through the following development.

Per cent absolute agreement

The per cent absolute agreement discriminates against the use of three (or more) raters since the risk that at least one rater will code a variable differently increases with the number of raters. Nor does it capture whether all three (or more) raters disagree with one another or if only one rater disagrees with the others. This can be solved by calculating Larsson's average pairwise per cent agreement (APPA):

$$\text{Larsson's APPA} = \frac{\text{number of pairwise identical codes}}{\text{total number of pair comparisons}}$$

Larsson's APPA is a measurement of interrater reliability that is neutral to the number of raters since it captures partial agreements missed by absolute per cent agreement. Thus, it does not discriminate against the information-enhancing use of more than two raters per case. It provides a comparable measure across case surveys with different number of raters as well as across cases that for some reason have different number of raters within the same case survey. The comparative advantage of APPA can be illustrated by the example of three raters coding a variable five, five, and four for the same case. The absolute per cent agreement is 0 per cent while APPA is 33 per cent. If only two of these raters had been used the absolute per cent agreement would have been either 0 per cent or 100 per cent depending which of the two raters were used. In one out of three situations, this would result in higher reliability from merely reducing the number of raters.

To avoid discriminating against the author participation, which intentionally creates discrepancies to add more information, a second and more 'true' interrater reliability should be computed for only raters with equal information.

Per cent identical agreement

Per cent identical agreement discriminates against the use of more detailed scales by: (a) not adjusting for increased probability of chance agreements with fewer categories; and (b) ignoring different discrepancy magnitudes for ordinal, interval, and ratio scales. This was compensated for by Miller and Friesen (1977) who computed their interrater reliability based on similar agreements (+/− one point) on their seven-point scales. Bullock and Tubbs' (1987) consensus resolution approach (see next paragraph) provides a preferable solution by allowing for the subsequent collapsing of scales until reliable distinctions can be made. Furthermore, this approach offers the information-enhancing feature of detecting and correcting coding mistakes (ie, clerical errors, unintentional omissions, and simple misreadings of text and scheme).

Normally, coding mistakes are prevented by simplifying the coding scheme but this solution has negative information effects. Neither of these features of the consensus resolution approach is reflected in the initial and equal interrater reliability measures in spite of the fact that both features substantially improve the quality of the coded data. Thus, a final 'corrected' interrater reliability measure, after the deduction of identified mistakes and coding scheme changes, needs to be computed to adequately reflect the reliability of the resolved data set to be analysed. These three stepwise APPA measures provide a more complete account of the whole coding process and do not motivate dysfunctional maximization of reliability at the expense of information extraction.

The interrater reliability analysis is also good for teaching purposes, since it will clearly uncover issues of subjective versus intersubjective interpretation of cases. This will thereby provide a structured basis for group discus-sions regarding the case analyses.

8.   Discrepancy Resolution

The Discrepancy Resolution has been effectively discussed by Bullock and Tubbs (1987, pp. 202–03). They list four techniques for resolving discrepant codings through the use of: (1) the codings of one designated (expert) rater; (2) the modal score; (3) the average score; and (4) developed consensus ratings. They stated: 'All [four] techniques meet reliability standards, but they differ in validity and reproducibility, which we believe are more important than reliability in case meta-analysis. Though average, modal, or single expert ratings are frequently used, we recommend the consensus approach because the data are readily available to improve the potential validity and reliability'. The consensus approach utilizes multiple raters through meetings where discrepant codings are discussed relative to the case reports to jointly arrive at the most correct codes. This is a superior way to correct coding mistakes (eg clerical and omission errors), since it eliminates the influence of the least correct codings. Even obvious mistakes would affect the average score and there is no need for majority interpretations to always be correct.

The consensus resolution is superior to alternative resolution approaches also from a teaching perspective, since it will generate discussions and problem-solving processes in each of the student groups.

STATISTICAL ANALYSIS

9. Validity Analysis

The Validity Analysis is accomplished in two major ways: First, the use of the secondary data constituted by the case reports can be validated against the authors' primary case data. If the resolution analysis above indicates that very few of the authors' initial codes were changed in favour of other interpretations, the final codings of cases with participating authors can be seen as representative of the primary data. Then these cases can be compared with those that lack author participation, and if no systematic differences are found, it constitutes a secondary validation of the whole case sample. Secondly, other data sources that are external to the case study can be used for primary validation of the final case codings. Primary respondents in the case organizations and/or outside experts can be asked to make their own estimations of a subset of the coded variables for agreement or correlation analysis (cf. Miller and Friesen's (1980) hybrid design opposed to their 1977 study that validated the case reports but not their codings). Archival accounting and stock market data can be used to validate coded performance variables. The more data sources and methods to tap them, the more convincing the support of the primary validity of the final data set.

The ideal situation would be to have some of the main variables entirely measured through data independent of the case study to avoid possible problems with common method variance (Kemery and Dunlap, 1986). This is often difficult to do for the whole case sample due to the commonly suppressed identities of case studies and the lack of databases that include all the selected cases. Still, the case survey method is better for safeguarding against common method variance than self-report studies (cf. Podsakoff and Organ, 1986). The typically longitudinal, multi-source data collection of case studies are less subject to post-rationalization and social desirability than individual self-reports (Miller and Friesen, 1977). Furthermore, multiple raters and consensus resolution make the case interpretations a collective rather than a subjective endeavour. The primary and secondary validation procedures are the strongest safeguard since they bring independent primary data and several different researcher purposes, perspectives, frameworks, and methods to bear on the case codings. The validity analysis also enables students to learn about the importance of finding additional sources of information to evaluate the quality of interpretations.

10. Empirical Analysis

The Analysis of Case Collection, Research Design, Publication, and Time empirically investigates to what extent and how the case codings are affected by differences in these case study characteristics. While at least parts of the previous validity analysis is made by the separate student groups, the author-based secondary validation and most other statistical analyses in this and the next steps are best done collectively on the whole case survey sample with all student groups' cases pooled together. The search strategy generating the case should be noted and included as a variable in the data base. The coding scheme should include variables representing: (i) different aspects of the research design of the case studies such as the extent and types of data collection, main perspective, and validation procedures; (ii) the publication status such as academic journals, research books, dissertation, conference papers, business press, and unpublished working papers; and (iii) the year(s) of the studied phenomena. If significant relationships are found to indicate systematic influences of the search strategies, research design or publication status (eg the lower the status the more favourable the reported performance), then informed judgements can be made regarding methodological control variables and possible exclusion of cases that suffer from undue influence.

11. Data Analysis

The Data Analysis can be done through conventional statistics (depending on the types of scales). Bullock and Tubbs (1987) recommend only bivariate statistics for research questions in undeveloped theoretical areas. While this may be appropriate in their area of organization development, some recent case surveys have shown the usefulness of multivariate statistics. LISREL appears especially relevant for researching the complex interrelationships typically found in case studies. Podsakoff and Organ (1986) also suggest LISREL as a means for dealing with common method variance as illustrated by Glick, Jenkins and Gupta (1986). For teaching purposes, simpler statistics are advisable. The teacher as well as each student group can test hypotheses that they have developed regarding the key research question(s) stated at the start of the course.

12.   Reporting

The Reporting of these 11 steps presents a practical trade-off problem between adequate documentation and space limitations. Previous research case surveys have often solved this through book publications and additional methodological articles. Still, the viablility of the case survey method depends on the establishment of a condensed reporting system that enables case surveys to be adequately documented in single articles. Such a system should include: (1) a divided or 'asterisked' reference list with (a) included cases, (b) excluded cases, and (c) other references; and (2) a small print appendix with the coding scheme. The two case reference lists can utilize general footnotes to indicate the type of search strategy that generated the case in question and which exclusion rules were applied for the excluded cases. The frequencies, mean, and standard deviation of each variable can be included in the coding scheme appendix in conjunction to its operationalization. A general reference can be made in the text to the coding scheme for the definition of each variable to avoid having to define them in the text. For teaching purposes, students can have a paper where they write up their literature review, hypotheses, and results as their final examination and the teacher can encourage the best ones to submit them for publication reviews in minor, more practically oriented journals.

CONCLUSION AND TEACHING AND RESEARCH SYNERGIES

The case survey method requires access to substantial numbers of cases for analysis through statistical techniques, expanding the generalizability of those cases when analysed in aggregate. iCase provides the solution to the compilation of cases in innovation and entrepreneurship as a facilitator of the case survey method. The benefits derived from the combination of iCase and the case survey method can be gained in both teaching, through the data gathering and analysis in undergraduate and particularly postgraduate entrepreneurship programmes, and in research. Students can be both a source and application of the data and the results available through the case survey method.

In fact there are clearly a number of synergies between research and teaching using the Case Survey Method. From a research perspective we find the following possible benefits of teaching with the Case Survey Method: (1) it is possible to find more relevant case studies as part of the students' task; (2) students can perform multiple codings of x number of cases; (3) interrater reliability analysis becomes more robust when using different raters of the same cases; (4) you may perform methodological as well as substantive comparisons between different individual's coding decisions; (5) you may perform consensus resolution of coding discrepancies by student groups as part of collective case analysis and discussion; (6) you may test the methodological impact of different case study designs; and finally (7) it may provide additional motivation for author participation.

From a teaching perspective there are the following possible benefits to using the Case Survey Method: (1) analysis of individual cases may become more structured; (2) you may perform a structured comparison with an author coded 'teaching manual'; (3) you may perform structured comparisons of several cases; (4) it is easier to perform inter-person comparisons of case analysis; (5) groups experience processes of resolving coding discrepancies; (6) it may facilitate inter-class cooperation to generate comparative case databases among school networks and over time, and (6) it stimulates research participation to collect data (rather than being collected data from).

If the development of a methodological awareness of how different perspectives, designs, and time periods influence research results through the material offered in this chapter, then there is a clear benefit to both students and researchers. This may also stimulate and facilitate more interactive teaching, promoting a more dynamic and rewarding learning situation.

REFERENCES

Argyris, C. (1970), *Intervention Theory and Method: A Behavioral Science View*, Boston, MA: Addison-Wesley.

Ashby, W.R. (1960), *Design for a Brain*, Chapman and Hall.

Brewer, I. and A. Hunter (1989), *Multimethod Research: a Synthesis of Styles*, Sage.

Bullock, R.J. and M.E. Tubbs (1987), 'The case meta-analysis for OD', *Research in Organizational Change and Development*, 171–228.

Cook, T.D. and L.C. Leviton (1980), 'Reviewing the literature: a comparison of traditional methods with meta-analysis', *Journal of Personality*, 449–72.

Eisenhardt, K.M. (1989), 'Building theories from case study research', *Academy of Management Review*, 532–50.

Gersick, C. (1988), 'Time and transition in work teams: toward a new model of group development', *Academy of Management Journal*, 9–41.

Glaser, B.G. and A.L. Strauss (1967), *The Discovery of Grounded Theory: Strategies for Qualitative Research*, Aldine.

Glass, G.V., B. McGaw and M.L. Smith (1981), *Meta-analysis in Social Research*, Sage.

Glick, W.H., G.D. Jenkins and N. Gupta (1986), 'Method versus substance: How strong are underlying relationships between job characteristics and attitudinal outcomes?', *Academy of Management Journal*, 441–64.

Hunter, J.H., F.L. Schmidt and G.B. Jackson (1982), *Meta-analysis: Cumulating Research Findings Across Studies*, Sage.

Jauch, L.R., R.N. Osborn and T.N. Martin (1980), 'Structured content analysis of cases: a complementary method for organizational research', *Academy of Management Review*, 517–25.

Jick, T.D. (1979), 'Mixing qualitative and quantitative methods: triangulation in action', *Administrative Science Quarterly*, 602–11.

Jones, A.P., L.A. Johnson, M.C. Butler and D.S. Main (1983), 'Apples and oranges: an empirical comparison of commonly used indices of interraters agreement', *Academy of Management Journal*, 507–19.

Kemery, E.R. and W.P. Dunlap (1986), 'Partialling factor scores does not control method variance: a reply to Podsakoff and Todor', *Journal of Management*, 525–30.

Larsson, R. (1993), 'Case survey methodology: quantitative analysis across case studies', *Academy of Management Journal*, 1515–46.

Larsson, R. (1989), *Organizational Integration of Mergers and Acquisitions: a Case Survey of Realization of Synergy Potentials*, Sweden: Lund Studies in Economics and Management.

Larsson, R. and L. Bengtsson (1993), *Integrating Method and Substance in Strategic Research: a Case Survey of Individual versus Collective Organizational Learning*, presentation to the Strategic Management Society's Annual International Conference, Chicago, September.

Larsson, R. and S. Finkelstein (1999), 'Integrating strategic, organizational, and human resource perspectives on mergers and acquisitions: a case survey of synergy realization', *Organization Science*, 1–26.

Lucas, W.A. (1974), *The Case Survey Method: Aggregating Case Experience*, Rand Corp.

Manimala, M.J. (1992), 'Entrepreneurial heuristics: a comparison between high PI (pioneering-innovative) and low PI ventures', *Journal of Business Venturing*, 477–504.

Miller, D. and P.H. Friesen (1977), 'Strategy-making in context: ten empirical archetypes', *Journal of Management Studies*, 253–80.

Miller, D. and P. Friesen (1980), 'Archetypes of organizational transition', *Administrative Science Quarterly*, 268–92.

Mintzberg, H., D. Raisinghani and A. Theoret (1976), 'The structure of "unstructured" decision processes', *Administrative Science Quarterly*, 246–75.

Osborn, R.N., L.R. Jauch, Martin and W.F. Glueck (1981), 'The event of CEO succession, performance, and environmental conditions', *Academy of Management Journal*, 183–91.

Podsakoff, P.M. and D.W. Organ (1986), 'Self-reports in organizational research: problems and prospects', *Journal of Management*, 531–44.

Tsoukas, H. (1989), 'The validity of idiographic research explanations', *Academy of Management Review*, 551–61.

Walton, R.E. (1972), 'Advantages and attributes of the case study', *Journal of Applied Behavioral Science*, 73–8.

Yin, R.K. (1981), 'The case study crisis: some answers', *Administrative Science Quarterly*, 58–65.

Yin, R.K. (1984), *Case Study Research: Design and Methods*, Sage.

Yin, R.K. and K.A. Heald (1975), 'Using the case survey method to analyze policy studies', *Administrative Science Quarterly*, 371–81.

Yin, R.K. and D. Yates (1974), *Street-level Governments: Assessing Decentralization and Urban Services*, Rand Corp.

9.   Action research for enterprise research

Chad Perry and Sally Rao

INTRODUCTION

Action research has been found to be a practical research methodology in business and management research. It has been effective in solving business problems in the areas of marketing (for example, Vignali and Zundel, 2003), manufacturing, engineering and operations management (for example, Coghlan and Coghlan, 2002; Kwok, 2002), organizational change and transformation (Kotnour, 2001; Kotnour et al., 1998), information systems and e-commerce (Goh, 2002; McKay and Marshall, 2001; Stirling, Petty and Travis, 2002; Chiasson and Dexter, 2001, Yoong and Gallupe, 2001) and accounting (Kaplan, 1998).

That is, action research develops human, social and professional competencies within a business organization. However, can it satisfy the more theoretical concerns of academics too? On the one hand, managers are generally action and result oriented and they want tangible outcomes of their action research projects. On the other hand, academics are interested in making a contribution to a body of knowledge from an action research project. Thus an academic researcher involved in action research faces two goals or 'imperatives' (McKay and Marshall (2001, p. 46). One goal is to solve a practical problem within an organization, and the second is to generate new knowledge and understanding.

How to address both these goals has been rarely addressed in the literature (Perry and Zuber-Skerritt, 1994; Carson et al., 2001) so that there is 'little direct guidance on "how to do" it' (McKay and Marshall, 2001, p. 49). That is, action research usually ignores analytic generalization (Yin, 1994) – how the findings from one situation can be applied in other situations or firms or industries. It is this generalization that readers of academic articles and theses are interested in, and explains why one of the most common criticisms of published action research is that 'it lacks theory' (Coghlan and Brannick, 2001, p. 115).

Thus the aim of this chapter is to present procedures for academic researchers involved in action research to solve practical enterprise problems and to also develop a new theory for academic purposes. The chapter has three sections. First, action research is defined. Then a review of scientific research paradigms establishes that action research fits within two paradigms. This is followed by a description of how those two paradigms can be straddled in the two reports of action research. The chapter's contribution is its foundation of scientific paradigms and complements earlier treatments in Carson et al. (2001), Coghlan and Brannick (2001), Perry and Zuber-Skerritt (1992), and Zuber-Skerritt and Perry (2002).

DEFINITION OF ACTION RESEARCH

Before discussing action research, it needs to be defined. In its purest form, action research emphasizes three aspects of action research (Zuber-Skerritt, 2001):

- a group of people at work together,
- involved in the cycle of planning, acting, observing and reflecting on their work as shown in Figure 9.1, more deliberately and systematically than usual; and
- a public report of that experience (such as a report to an organization's board).

Essentially, the methodology is used by a group of people who work together to improve their work processes, that is, a community of practitioners or co-researchers (Lewin, 1946; Altrichter et al., 2000). That is, action research is process-oriented in one work situation that is changing. It looks at action to bring about change of one workgroup's processes, by adding to the workgroup's understanding of those processes. Action research is also problem-focused, context-specific and future-oriented and integrates thought and action. It allows practitioners to research their own professional activities by critically examining their own beliefs and practices. It helps managers to be multidisciplinary and work across technical, cultural and functional boundaries to improve practice at the workplace.

When could this form of action research be an appropriate methodology within an academic program of enterprise research? There are three justifications for an academic researcher using action research rather than some other methodology of data collection (adapting Yin's (1994) justifications for case research in general and for research about a single case in particular):

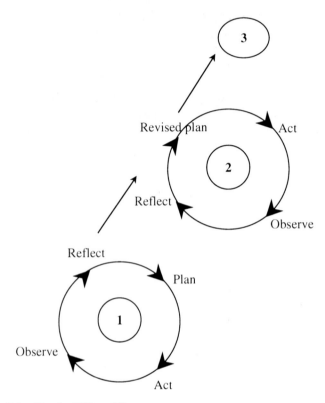

Source: Zuber-Skerritt (2001, p. 15).

Figure 9.1   The spiral of action research cycles

- little is known about the research problem – it is within a 'pre-paradigmatic' body of knowledge and so an inductive, theory-building methodology is needed;
- context and phenomenon are not clearly distinct – the research is about the in-depth 'how' or 'why' of a complex social science phenomena (rather than the more shallow 'what' or 'how much' of other methodologies such as a survey) – it is an investigation of the changing processes with which people work together;
- the phenomena is rarely accessible to academic researchers and the research provides a window on to a critical part of the phenomena.

Note that this definition of action research distinguishes action research from action learning. Action research necessarily focuses on a workgroup within an organization or community, all of whom are involved in the cycles of planning/acting/observing/reflecting shown in Figure 9.1. In contrast, action learning emphasizes individual learning and so should be placed within the constructivism paradigm. Admittedly, the set of associates or 'comrades in adversity' (Revans, 1982, p. 23) in action learning is a group, but each individual within that group learns from separate experiences that do not necessarily involve other associates, and the separate experiences may not even involve workgroups. Action research involves action learning, but not vice versa, because action research is more deliberate, systematic, critical, emancipatory and rigorous.

RESEARCH PARADIGMS

As a beginning to exploring the different audiences of reports about action research – practitioners and academics – consider what a research paradigm is. Essentially, scientific research paradigms are overall conceptual frameworks within which some researchers work, that is, a paradigm is a worldview or 'a set of linked assumptions about the world which is shared by a community of scientists investigating the world' (Deshpande, 1983, p. 101). More specifically, beliefs about the nature of reality (ontology) within the paradigm drive how knowledge about that reality is sought (epistemology). In turn, those beliefs then drive the research techniques (methodology) chosen for the research.

In essence, a paradigm reflects a researcher's understanding of the nature of existence that is beyond 'logical' debate because each paradigm is 'rational' within it's own constructed logic (Lincoln and Guba, 1985). That is, there is no 'objective' ground for choosing a paradigm. All that one can do is work within a paradigm that is consistent with your own ultimate presumptions as a researcher, presumptions that cannot be tested on any empirical or logical grounds. Thus assumptions behind some paradigms need to be discussed first, to try to determine how closely or not they 'fit' the perceived values and needs of the stakeholders of the two different research 'projects' that were described above. A comprehensive classification of scientific paradigms (Lincoln and Guba, 1994) is summarized in Table 9.1 below, and will guide this discussion. It describes four paradigms:

- positivism (in which 'reality is reality, full stop');
- constructivism and critical theory (in which 'perception is reality'); and
- realism (in which perceptions are 'windows on to reality') (Perry, Riege and Brown, 1999).

Table 9.1   Four scientific paradigms

Element	Paradigm			
	Positivism	Constructivism	Critical theory	Realism
Ontology	Reality is real and apprehensible	Multiple local and specific 'constructed' realities	'Virtual' reality shaped by social, economic, ethnic, political, cultural, and gender values, and crystallized over time	Reality is 'real' but only imperfectly and probabilistically apprehensible; and so triangulation from many sources is required to try to know it
Epistemology	Findings true – researcher is objective by viewing reality through a 'one-way mirror'	Created findings – researcher is a 'passionate participant' within the world being investigated	Value mediated findings – researcher is a 'transformative intellectual' who changes the social world within which participants live	Findings probably true – researcher is value-aware and needs to triangulate any perceptions he/ she is collecting
Common methodologies	Mostly concerned with a testing of theory. Thus, mainly quantitative methods such as survey, experiments, and verification of hypotheses	In-depth unstructured interviews, participant observation, action research, and grounded theory research	Action research and participant observation	Mainly qualitative methods such as case studies and convergent interviews

Note: Essentially, ontology is 'reality', epistemology is the relationship between that reality and the researcher and methodology is the technique used by the researcher to discover that reality.

Source: Based on Perry, Riege and Brown (1999), which itself was based on Guba and Lincoln (1994) from which the quotations come.

The first, positivism paradigm is the most widely used paradigm for business school research (Orlikowski and Baroudi, 1991) and assumes implicitly or explicitly that reality can be measured by viewing it through a one way, value-free mirror. Positivism assumes that only observable occurrences can be researched, for it asserts that science can ascertain the exact nature of reality (Easterby-Smith et al., 1991). Positivism does not usually allow the researcher to work with dynamic phenomena. It makes no allowances for the contribution of relatively unobservable realities that are present in a management environment, like a follower's belief in a leader. Moreover, it is primarily deductive, exploring direct cause and effect outcomes.

Historically, there has been a heavy emphasis on positivism. This 'received view' (Guba and Lincoln, 1994, p. 106) of science has dominated the formal discourse in the physical and social science for some 400 years (Guba and Lincoln, 1994). However, the positivism paradigm has both internal and external critiques, such as its exclusion of the discovery dimensions in inquiry and the under-determination of theory (Deshpande, 1983; Guba and Lincoln, 1994). For example, the assumptions of positivism noted above are appropriate in a natural science such as zoology, but are inappropriate when approaching a complex social science phenomenon which involves reflective humans. Indeed, a review of 30 year's research into a complex social science phenomena like organizational culture concluded that the research had uncovered little because most of it was positivist (Redding, 1993). Moreover, positivists separate themselves from the world they study (Perry, Riege and Brown, 1999) while involvement is required to uncover data in many social science situations (Carson and Coviello, 1996).

Major alternatives to positivism in the social sciences are constructivism and critical theory. Essentially, these paradigms argue that the world is 'constructed' by people and that these constructions should be the driving forces investigated in social science research. For example, some people perceive Levi jeans are the best jeans and worth buying, even though tests done within a positivism framework by consumer magazines show their cloth, stitching and buttoning is not as well-constructed as other brands' jeans. That is, a core of these two paradigms is that each person's constructed reality is so powerful an influence on their behaviour that any external reality is relatively unimportant and, moreover, there is no way of comparing the multiple constructed realities of different people. The critical theory paradigm is the implicit or explicit paradigm behind action research because it focuses on a group's constructed learnings.

However, relativism is at the heart of these two paradigms and this makes the two paradigms a cul de sac for many academic researchers. For example, Hunt (1991, p. 318) asks how these paradigms can help in trying to research whether the social science phenomenon of the holocaust occurred to Jews in the 1940s – some people perceive that it occurred and some that it did not, and these differences cannot be compared within the two paradigms of constructivism and critical theory:

It is indeed true that one of the 'multiple realities' that some people hold is that the Holocaust never occurred. An alternative 'multiple reality' is that the Holocaust did in fact occur. Which 'multiple reality' is correct? Sincere advocates of reality relativism must stand mute when confronted with this question.

In particular, constructivism and critical theory are not especially relevant in enterprise research about an organization having to survive within a market, because marketing managers have to deal with a world that is external, that is out there and that does not particularly care about the perceptions of an individual manager (Gummesson, 2000).

The final paradigm, of realism, consists of abstract things that are born of people's minds but exist independently of any one person, it 'is largely autonomous, though created by us' (Magee, 1985, p. 61). A person's perceptions are a window on to that blurry, external reality. Realism is about mechanisms of structures within a social context that do exist 'out there' (Easton, 1998; Pawson and Tilley, 1997), and is summarized in the right hand column of Table 9.1. That world of mechanisms and their contexts is not as straightforward as the world that physical scientists like engineers work within. An engineer knows that too much weight upon a bridge will definitely cause the bridge to fall. However, social science realists work with causal tendencies rather than causal certainties – A may cause B sometimes but not always or even mostly. The imprecision of these causal tendencies is exacerbated by the ability of people to change their behaviour after reflecting upon it. This is the paradigm within which much academic theorising about enterprises is done.

ACTION RESEARCH AS A BLEND OF TWO PARADIGMS

Upon this foundation of paradigms, consider how an academic researcher involved in action research has to somehow blend the critical theory and the realism paradigms of practitioners and academics respectively. The definition of action research above highlights the critical theory paradigm underlying practitioner action research by noting that it involves a group of people who are transforming how they construct their perceived work 'reality'. Of course, the action researchers' spirals are testing out their perceptions of reality against reality, but the emphasis is on the perceptions because they drive behaviour within one organization in a way that perceptions of one person or a small group cannot drive a school of academic thought.

An example of such pure action research is James' project. He was a human resource manager in a small firm that was introducing a new information system in a project involving contracted information systems consultants. He arranged 1½-hour meetings each fortnight with two other staff who were involved in the project, and two consultants. He facilitated the meetings and focused the reflection discussion on the processes they were using in the project. They wrote a report of their deliberations for the owner/manager with conclusions about later IT system development.

However, James' practitioner report about his own organization did not include the theory building about other organizations that constitutes the analytic generalization that academics are interested in. Thus a 'two project' approach is needed. That is, an action research can be divided into a core action research project to provide a report for managers, and an academic project to provide 'general' action research results for academics. These two projects are 'integrated, but they are not the same' (Cohglan and Brannick, 2001, p. 21).

The first, core action research project consists of the normal spirals within a workgroup that produces reflection data in the form of journals, memorandums, minutes of meetings and so on. These spirals will normally conclude with a report to senior management of that organization. In turn, the second, academic project takes that data from the first project and uses it in its own, normal thesis or article processes of literature review, data collection and analysis, and conclusions that provide analytic generalization from the findings of the first project. The thesis or article will finish with a newly built theory about a phenomenon that exists in several situations.

Figure 9.2 shows these two projects and how they are linked at the point of data developed during the reflection processes of the first project. The data collection parts of the thesis or article will cover methodological issues covered in all academic reports such the steps/spirals taken and their justification, and how issues of validity and reliability were covered (for

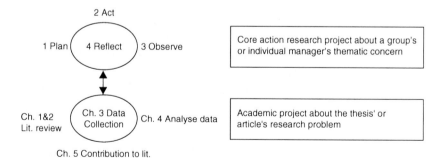

Note: The numbers in the thesis project refer to the 'standard' chapters of a thesis (Perry, 1998), but they could also be parts of an article.

Figure 9.2   General action research uses two 'projects': core and academic

example, through a discussion of the five points of these being construct validity, neutrality/confirmability, truth value/credibility, applicability/transferability, and consistency/dependability based on a synthesis of Lincoln and Guba (1985) for critical theory, and Healy and Perry (2001) for realism, as justified and demonstrated in Thompson and Perry (2004).

Consider an example of how these two projects can be carried out. Jean had a consulting project to develop a strategic plan for the managers of an innovative architectural practice. She conducted in-depth interviews with the two most senior professionals and then facilitated a strategic planning retreat with all five professionals. These were spirals 1 and 2 of the core action research project. She then developed a five-year plan that incorporated the professionals' visions for change, which was spiral 3. The senior professionals accepted this report.

After this first project had finished, she had time to start her second project. She wrote a dissertation about the processes she had used, relating concepts in the literature like Porter's generic strategies and forces of competitive advantage to a professional practice (about which little had been written). Also, she justified why she had done things the ways she had, in particular why she did them differently from the way they were normally done in a large, private firm. Her thesis data was collected from the minutes, reports and journals she had written during the action research project. Not all of this data was relevant to the thesis project's research problem, but much of it was and that part was content analysed for patterns about the thesis' research problem. She then said how the findings could be fitted into the literature about strategic planning and used in other types of professional practice and possibly in other organizations, summarized in new theory being built. The first report and the dissertation were both submitted for her degree.

Consider a more detailed example of an academic researcher's thesis. The five chapters of the thesis were:

1. Research problem: How can the entrepreneurial competencies of indigenous staff be developed in large Australian firms?
2. Definition of 'entrepreneurial potential' and then a review of the literature about entrepreneurship and indigenous management development, to lead into the core research issues/objectives of the thesis project.
3. Action research methodology: the methodology is justified because the thesis concerns a complex social situation about which little is known, as noted above; the thematic concern is how we as senior managers can develop indigenous staff in my firm, using three plan-act-observe-reflect cycles described in detail; the paradigmatic issues are discussed, as is validity and reliability, and ethical issues.

4. Analysis of the reflection data from the three cycles of the thesis.
5. Analytical generalization of the analysed data to other organizations in Australia and overseas, to build a new theory about the research problem.

In brief, it is possible to write a report of an action research project that has been done within the critical theory paradigm, that will interest readers of journal articles and theses who operate within the realism paradigm. Each paradigm has its own, self-evident worldview, but they can be bridged where the practitioners' reflection data feeds into the academic report.

This two-project approach for academic researchers involved in action research makes the differences between the two underlying paradigms clear. The aim of the first project is the 'thematic concern' of the workgroup (Kemmis and McTaggart, 1988, p. 9) and the aim of the second project is to fill a gap in the literature that interests readers of academic journals and theses. Similarly, while the methodology chapter of a thesis may use the person 'I' to reflect its critical theory worldview, the other chapters will follow normal academic conventions to reflect their realism worldview. This two-project structure provides equal importance to both paradigms, whereas other action research structures place overwhelming emphasis upon the critical theory paradigm (ie, Dick, 1999; McNiff et al., 1999). For example, they do not differentiate between the two different goals of the action research and the academic research. Furthermore, they require a story of what took place and self-reflection by the action researcher. However, these are relegated to an appendix in our thesis project's structure or not even written up at all, because they occur in all academic research and will have to be included in a thesis or article at the expense of theory-building issues. Note, too, that the story of how fuzzy methods and answers becomes clearer – the essence of the spirals of action research (Gummesson, 2000) – is only described in the context of workgroup activities and not in terms of how the thesis or article was written. After all, all academic research and writing are exercises in 'gradually reducing uncertainty' as they are progressively narrowed and refined (Phillips and Pugh, 1987, p. 37), and there is no need to say this once again in an article or thesis.

CONCLUSION

This chapter aimed to show how academic enterprise researchers involved in an action research action research can meet the needs of the two audiences of their report. To begin, action research was defined and then the scientific paradigms underlying action research and other management research were distinguished. Next, focusing on the critical theory and realism paradigms in particular, a two-paradigm, two-project approach to using action research in management research was presented. One project is based on the customary action research cycles, and the other project is based on the more common outcomes of academic research like a journal article or a thesis. The chapter detailed how to integrate and implement the two projects and gave examples of their use by postgraduate students. In conclusion, action research can enhance learning by practitioners within an organization, as well as make a contribution to a body of knowledge that interests academics.

REFERENCES

Alrichter, H., S. Kemmis, R. McTaggart and O. Zuber-Skerrit (2000), 'The concept of action research', in Action Research Unit (ed.), *Action Learning, Action Research and Process Management: Theory, Practice, Praxis*, Brisbane, Australia: Faculty of Education, Griffith University.

Carson, D. and N. Coviello (1996), 'Qualitative research issues at the marketing/entrepreneurship interface', *Marketing Intelligence and Planning*, **14**(6), 51–8.

Carson, D., A. Gilmore, K. Gronhaug and C. Perry (2001), *Qualitative Research in Marketing*, London: Sage.

Chiasson, M. and A.S. Dexter (2001), 'System development conflict during the use of an information systems prototyping method of Action Research: implication for practice and research', *Information Technology and People*, **14**(1), 91–108.

Coghlan, D. and T. Brannick (2001), *Doing Action Research in Your Own Organisation*, London: Sage.

Coghlan, P. and D. Coghlan (2002), 'Action research for operations management', *International Journal of Operations and Production Management*, **22**(2), 220–40.

Deshpande, R. (1983), 'Paradigms Lost: on theory and method in research in marketing', *Journal of Marketing*, **47**(4), 101–10.

Dick, B. (1999), 'You want to do an action research thesis?', accessed 5 March at http://www.scu.edu.au/schools/sawd/arr/arth/arthesis.html.

Easterby-Smith, M., R. Thorpe and A. Lowe (1991), *Management Research: an Introduction*, London: Sage.

Easton, G. (1998), 'Case research as a methodology for industrial networks: a realist apologia', in P. Naude and P.W. Turnbull (eds), *Network Dynamics in International Marketing*, Oxford: Pergamon, pp. 73–87.

Goh, M.H. (2002), 'Implementing business continuity planning in an international bank using action research', in S. Sankaran, B. Dick, R. Passfield and P. Swepson (eds), *Effective Change Management Using Action Learning and Action Research: Concepts, Frameworks, Processes and Applications*, Lismore, NSW: SCU Press.

Guba, E.G. and Y.S. Lincoln (1994), 'Competing paradigms in qualitative research', in N.K. Denzin, and Y.S. Lincoln (eds), *Handbook of Qualitative Research*, Thousand Oaks, CA: Sage Publications, pp. 105–17.

Gummesson, E. (2000), *Qualitative Methods in Management Research*, London: Sage.

Healy, M. and C. Perry (2000), 'Comprehensive criteria to judge the validity and reliability of qualitative research within the realism paradigm', *Qualitative Market Research – an International Journal*, **3**(3), 118–26.

Hunt, S. (1991), *Modern Marketing Theory: Critical Issues in the Philosophy of Marketing Science*, Cincinnati, OH: South-Western.

Kaplan, R.S. (1998), 'Innovation action research: creating a new management theory and practice', *Journal of Management Accounting Research*, **10**, 89–118.

Kemmis, S. and R. McTaggart (1988), *The Action Research Planner*, 3rd edn, Melbourne: Deakin University Press.

Kotnour, T., S. Barton, J. Jenning and R.D. Bridges Jr (1998), 'Understanding and leading large-scale change at the Kennedy Space Center', *Engineering Management Journal*, **10**(2), 17–21.

Kotnour, T. (2001), 'Building knowledge for and about large-scale organisational transformations', *International Journal of Operations and Production Management*, **21**(8), 1053–75.

Kwok, R. (2002), 'An action learning experience in an engineering organisation', in S. Sankaran, B. Dick, R. Passfield and P. Swepson (eds), *Effective Change Management Using Action Learning and Action Research: Concepts, Frameworks, Processes and Applications*, Lismore, CA: SCU Press, pp. 247–57.

Lewin, K. (1946), 'Action research and minority problems', *Journal of Social Science Issues*, **2**, 34–36.

Lincoln, Y. and E. Guba (1985), *Naturalistic Inquiry*, Newbury Park: Sage.

Magee, B. (1985), *Popper*, 3rd edn, London: Fontana.

McKay, J. and P. Marshall (2001), 'The dual imperatives of action research', *Information Technology and People*, **14**(1), 45–59.

Mcniff, J., P. Lomax and J. Whitehead (1996), *You and Your Action Research Project*, London: Routledge.

Orlikowski, W.J. and J. Baroudi (1991), 'Studying information technology in organisations: research approaches and assumptions', *Information Systems Research*, **2**(1), 1–14.

Pawson, R. and N. Tilley (1997), *Realistic Evaluation*, London: Sage.

Perry, C. (1998), 'A structured approach for presenting PhDs: notes for candidates and their supervisors', *Australasian Marketing Journal*, **6**(1), 63–85.

Perry, C. and O. Zuber-Skerritt (1992), 'Action research in graduate management research programs', *Higher Education*, **23**(2), 195–208.

Perry, C. and O. Zuber-Skerritt (1994), 'Doctorates by action research for senior practising managers', *Management Learning*, **25**(2), 341–64.

Perry, C., A. Riege and L. Brown (1999), 'Realism's role among scientific paradigms in marketing research', *Irish Marketing Review*, **12**(2), 16–23.

Phillips, E.M. and D.S. Pugh (1987), *How to Get a PhD*, Milton Keynes: Open University Press.

Redding, S.G. (1993), 'The comparative management theory zoo: getting the elephants and dinosaurs from the jungle into the iron cage', paper presented at the Conference on Perspective's on International Business Theory, Research and Institutional Arrangements, University of South Carolina Centre for International Business Research.

Revans, R. (1982), *The Origins and Growth of Action Learning*, Bromley: Chartwell-Bratt.

Stirling, M., D. Petty and L. Travis (2002), 'A methodology for developing integrated information systems based on ERP packages', *Business Process Management Journal*, **8**(5), 430–46.

Thompson, F. and C. Perry (2004), 'Generalising results of an action research project in one work place to other situations: principles and practice', *European Journal of Marketing*, **38**, 401–17.

Vignali, C. and M. Zundel (2003), 'The marketing management process and heuristic devices: an action research investigation', *Marketing Intelligence and Planning*, **2**(4), 205–29.

Yin, R.K. (1994), *Case Study Research Design and Methods*, Thousand Oaks, CA: Sage.

Yoong, P. and Gallupe, B. (2001), 'Action learning and groupware technologies: a case study in GSS research', *Information Technology and People*, **4**(1), 78–90.

Zuber-Skerritt, O. (2001), 'Action learning and action research: paradigm, praxis and programs', in S. Sankaran, B. Dick, R. Passfield and P. Swepson (eds), *Effective Change Management Using Action Research and Action Learning: Concepts, Frameworks, Processes and Applications*, Lismore: Southern Cross University Press, 1–20.

Zuber-Skerritt, O. and C. Perry (2002), 'Action research within organisations and university thesis writing', *Organisational Learning*, **9**(4), 171–79.

10. Case research about enterprises

Robyn Stokes and Chad Perry*

INTRODUCTION

Case studies are familiar to marketing educators and their students as stories used as teaching devices. For example, the Harvard Business School's cases are widely used so that students can be emotionally involved and learn action-related analysis of real, complex situations (Christenson and Hansen, 1987). However, case research is different from these case studies/stories for it is a research methodology that develops theory (Parkhe, 1993; Yin, 1993). Yet no journal of case research methods exists and the most common social science and evaluation research methods text-books 'hardly mention case studies' (Yin, 1993). Indeed, one survey of PhD dissertations in six fields concluded that case studies used in them were mere stories – eliminating them would be one way to rectify the 'mindless empiricism' of many doctoral dissertations (Adams and White, 1994).

However, case research has become more rigorous since the judgement was written. For example, reports of theory-building case research have been published in marketing journals, in Alam, 2002; Alam and Perry, 2002; Batonda and Perry, 2002; Beverland, 2004; Madden and Perry, 2003; Riege et al., 2001 and Riege and Perry, 2000. Essentially, these articles have a literature review that develops some research issues or objectives about an overall research problem. Then the case research methodology's data collection and analysis processes are described, along with a justification for its use. The data is then analysed, based on the research issues, and a final theory is built. Nevertheless, case research is not widespread or well understood in scholarly enterprise research, although it has been used in PhD programs in Sweden, Finland and Australia.

Thus the aim of this chapter is to show how case research can be done in enterprise research projects. We refer to the literature and use an example of research about entrepreneurial events tourism in Australia to illustrate the procedures. Although our focus is on case research about entrepreneurship, the principles are the same as those used, for example, in evaluating education programs (Patton, 1990) or other consulting work (Yin, 1994). The chapter is closely based on earlier treatments in Perry (1998, 2001) and

Carson, Gilmore, Perry and Gronhaug (Carson et al., 2001a) and the research about entrepreneurship in events tourism that illustrates many points in the chapter is from Stokes (2004).

The chapter has four parts. The first is about the realism research that will underlay much enterprise research. Then procedures of case research such as the number of cases and interviews are described. Next, how the quality of case research is maintained is explained. Finally, limitations of case research are presented.

The term 'case research' is used in this chapter to ensure that readers distinguish it from descriptive 'case studies'. In more detail, case research is defined here in a comprehensive way that synthesizes some of the literature; that is, case research is:

- an investigation of a contemporary, dynamic phenomena and its emerging (rather than paradigmatic) body of knowledge (Eisenhardt, 1989; Chetty, 1996; Gable, 1994; Romano, 1989; Yin, 1994);
- within the phenomenon's real-life context where the boundaries between the phenomenon and context under investigation are unclear (Bonoma, 1985; Chetty, 1996; Stake, 1995; Yin, 1994);
- when explanation of causal links are too complex for survey or experimental methods (Eisenhardt, 1989; McGuire, 1997) so that single, clear outcomes are not possible (McGuire, 1997);
- using interviews, observation and other multiple sources of data (Bonoma, 1985; Perry, 1998; Robson, 1993).

THE REALISM RESEARCH PARADIGM

Because case research is about an under-researched, complex phenomenon within its environment, the research area can be called pre-paradigmatic (Perry et al., 1998). Therefore, the choice of a research paradigm that supports theory development in an emergent field of enquiry is required (rather than the alternative positivism, constructivism and critical theory paradigms). In brief, the realist paradigm position is that explanatory knowledge is sought (Easton, 1998) of a real world that is independent of researchers (Perry et al., 1997; Naude and Turnbell, 1998). In other words, the research problem addressed in the research should be in the form of a 'how' or 'why' question rather than a 'what' or 'how much?' problem (Yin, 1994).

The realism paradigm is often appropriate for case research for several reasons (Yin, 1994). For example, for the events tourism research (Stokes, 2004), the social realities of the sets of inter-connected relationships of events agencies and events tourism strategy processes were complex. Also, the opportunity for further research of business networks and relationships had been emphasized by various authors (Greenhalgh, 2001; Healy, 2000; O'Donnell et al., 2001) including those in tourism (Greer, 2002; Tinsley and Lynch, 2001; Watkins and Bell, 2002). Thus an external reality remained to be discovered for this research project with opportunities to build theory (Easton, 1998). The research problem in the events tourism research might be: How do inter-organizational relationships of entrepreneurial events agencies impact upon their strategies for events tourism?

To address this problem, several research issues were identified from the literature and from preliminary convergent interviews. Examples of these issues are:

- How and why do the planning processes used by entrepreneurial events agencies impact upon their inter-organizational relationships?
- Why are entrepreneurial events agencies interested or disinterested in using inter-organizational relationships for their events tourism strategy making?

PROCEDURES OF CASE RESEARCH

A 'Case' in Case Research

As noted above, the research problem and issues that drive case research should be 'how' or 'why' questions. After deciding on the research problem and research issues, the next step is to decide on the unit of analysis, that is, what constitutes a case. Deciding this issue is related to the research problem. If the research is about what a person can do, then the unit of analysis is an individual. However, case research is often more appropriate for the more complex situations involving two or more people and/or their organizations. Thus case research can be done about the relationship between two businesses, about the relationship between two individuals, about decisions, about programs, about organizational change, about laws and about neighbourhoods. Deciding on the unit of analysis can sometimes be a confusing process, and often requires some long discussions with a colleague to finalize. For the events tourism research we have introduced, the unit of analysis was the 'inter-organizational relationships' of events development agencies in those Australian states and territories involved in the study. As the unit of analysis, these relationships were studied from the perspective of those agencies and organizations that might be expected to contribute to events tourism strategies in each location.

Sometimes researchers use small cases that are a part of a big case that is the unit of analysis for a study. For example, in a study of organizational change within the marketing departments of a corporation, it might be useful to analyse the individual marketing departments of each strategic business unit of a corporation. These parts or sub-cases are called embedded cases because they are embedded in the bigger unit of analysis (Yin, 1994). The important issue in embedded cases is that each of the embedded cases in each big case must be considered and compared with other embedded parts of the same big case, before the big cases can be compared. For example, the strategic business units within each corporation have to be analysed to find the pattern within each corporation, before several corporations can be compared. In brief, the research problem usually determines the unit of analysis in case research but sometimes embedded cases are included.

The Interviewer's Guide

The interviewer's guide is a central vehicle in the design and application of this qualitative research (Perry, 2001). In effect, it gives direction, structure and some flexibility to the investigation of the research issues and also enhances the reliability of the results (Burns, 1994; Yin, 1994). Through trials, we have found that the starting question in an interview should invite the interviewee to simply tell the story of their experience of whatever the research is about, ie, 'What is the story of your experiences or involvement in events tourism?' This question asks the interviewee to merely tell a story, it does not ask the interviewee to 'think' and so make them apprehensive about being on trial in the interview.

Although the interviews start in this general way as induction by the interviewee, the analysis of the interview data will be deduction or confirmation/ disconfirmation of prior theory by the interviewer/researcher. That is, the researcher/interviewer has some prior theoretical issues raised from some preliminary methodology such as convergent interviewing and from the literature. Thus some probe questions are asked after the initial question, about particular research issues. However, one hopes that the answers to the probe questions are provided in the free flowing answers to general questions, before the particular probe questions are put. The probe questions usually always start with 'How' and can definitely not be answered with 'yes' or 'no'. Care should be taken to phrase the probe questions with the words used by the interviewee – for example, 'links' rather than 'inter-organizational networks' – and to not show what answer is preferred by the interviewer. Other techniques for the interviews are noted in the chapter on interviewing in Carson et al., 2001b.

We have also found that an interviewer's guide could include Likert-scaled questions summarizing the overall perceptions of an interviewee toward the issue addressed in each question, to be answered by the interviewer (Yin, 1994, p. 69) during or after the interview. These Likert-scaled questions are asked after some broad questions have asked for the interviewee's own views about issues. These scales assist in writing up the data analysis chapter of a report. For example, a Likert scale from 'formal' to 'informal' can summarize the discursive answers about how strategic market planning is carried out, for each case. However, it must be clear that this is qualitative research about underlying reasons for phenomena occurring and so mere numbers from such Likert scales are indicative only, and should be referred to only within brackets of the report and not in the text of the report. To reiterate, it is the reasons for the relativity of case responses to each other that are of most interest in case research.

Number of Cases

Procedures for interviews for each case were discussed above, but how many cases are required, and how are they selected? Let us consider the issue of the number of cases first. There are no precise guides to the number of cases to be included – 'the literature recommending the use of case studies rarely specifies how many cases should be developed. This decision is left to the researcher' (Romano, 1989, p. 36). In a similar vein, (Eisenhardt, 1989) recommends that cases should be added until 'theoretical saturation' is reached and Lincoln and Guba (1985, p. 204) recommend sampling selection 'to the point of redundancy'. Patton (1990, p. 181) does not provide an exact number or range of cases that could serve as guidelines for researchers, claiming that 'there are no rules' for sample size in qualitative research. However, their views ignore the real constraints of time and funding in most research and so some guidelines about how many cases are required in case research are required.

For a start, consider research with just one case. Having only one case is unusual but can be justified if it meets at least one of these three criteria (Yin, 1994):

- the case is a critical one for confirming, challenging or extending a theory because it is the only one that meets all of the conditions of the theory;
- the case is rare or extreme and finding other cases is so unlikely that research about the situation could never be done if the single case was not investigated (for example, a clinical psychology case sometimes fits in this category);

- the case provides unusual access for academic research, and unless the case is investigated, an opportunity to investigate a significant social science problem may be lost. An example may be the access to his or her own firm provided to a researcher to show how strategic marketing planning is actually done in the real world (with all its confidential information, power politics and human weaknesses that usually prevent academic researchers from finding out the real story about it).

If you can justify just the use of one case for one or more of these reasons, it is also preferred that there are two or more theories to be tested on the information in the case (Yin, 1994, p. 16).

More than One Case

Consider the more usual situation where Yin's three single-case criteria do not apply. Other authorities on case design have attempted to recommend a range for the number of cases, such as between four and ten cases (ie Eisenhardt, 1989). However, there are somewhat different views. The usual view is that four cases is the minimum: 'in practice, four to six groups probably form a reasonable minimum for a serious project' (Hedges, 1985, pp. 76–77). For the maximum, Hedges (1985) sets an upper limit of 12 because of the high costs involved in qualitative interviews and the quantity of qualitative data which can be effectively assimilated. In the same vein, Miles and Huberman (1994, p. 30) suggest that more than 15 cases makes a study 'unwieldy'. In brief, the widest accepted range seems to fall between 2–4 as the minimum and 10, 12 or 15 as the maximum. Our own experience suggests that between 4–8 cases is usually appropriate.

For the events tourism research, a six-case research design was adopted to capture the picture of inter-organizational relationships for events tourism in Australia's states and territories. The use of multiple cases was justified because of the diversity of institutional settings, organizational structures and personnel involved in events tourism in Australia. In addition, not one of the justifications for the use of a single case study was applicable to this research (Yin, 1994). There was no one state or territory in Australia that represented an extreme or unique case, nor was there a critical case that could be used to test well-accepted theory or a case that was previously inaccessible to researchers. In brief, a number of cases were investigated that were suitable for consideration in this research.

Types of Cases to be included – Replication Logic

How should all the cases be selected? The principle underlying the answer to this question is replication. In other words, the several cases should be regarded as 'multiple experiments' and not 'multiple respondents in a survey', and so replication logic and not sampling logic should be used for multiple-case studies (Yin, 1994, pp. 45–50). Other researchers support this replication method of case selection and highlight the inappropriateness of random sampling – for example, Eisenhardt (1989, p. 537) states that the 'random selection of cases is neither necessary, nor even preferable'. Patton (1990) lists 15 strategies of 'purposeful sampling' (in contrast to 'random sampling'), which can be used to select cases. Of these, 'maximum variation' sampling is usually the most appropriate for our analytical and general purposes in enterprise research. Maximum variation sampling includes very extreme cases – for example, a researcher investigating company turnarounds found an outside-the-boundaries case which had continued to decline and had not turned around, providing valuable insights into the turnaround process.

Thus, relevance rather than representativeness is the criterion for case selection (Stake, 1995). Careful choice of cases should be made so that they either:

- produce similar results for predictable reasons, that is, literal replication; or
- produce contrary results for predictable reasons, that is, theoretical replication (Yin, 1994).

For the events tourism research, replication logic was derived from the institutional arrangements and lifecycle phase of events tourism development in each state/territory, that is, the context of the cases. The six states and territories displayed some similarities and differences on these criteria. To begin, the institutional arrangements for events tourism were compared and these were sometimes the same and sometimes different across the six states. For example, the states of Western Australia, South Australia and Victoria each had an events development division or company housed within the state tourism department but Victoria also had a government funded events development corporation. Therefore, sources of literal and theoretical replication were observed across the states and territories in terms of their institutional arrangements for events tourism.

Number of Interviews

Turning from the cases to the interviews used to collect data about the cases, our experience and anecdotal evidence suggests that 35 or so interviews are required to provide a credible picture in a reasonably sized research project like a PhD (Perry, 1998). Similarly, de Ruyter and Scholl (1998) say a qualitative research project has between 10–60 respondents, with about 40 in a large project. The interviews could involve about three interviews at different hierarchical levels within eight case organizations. However, more than one interview in a small business or in an Asian organization is difficult, so interviewees researching case studies in these organizations or locations would include additional interviews in the 'context' of case organizations such as industry associations, consultants and government advisers, to bolster the number of interviews.

In brief, a researcher should use the above guidelines for the number of cases and interviews as starting points for research design, and then possibly use this quotation from Patton (1990, p. 185) to justify their final choice: 'the validity, meaningfulness and insights generated from qualitative inquiry have more to do with the information-richness of the cases selected and the observational/analytical capabilities of the researcher than with sample size'.

In the events tourism research, seven or eight interviews were planned within each of the six case states/territories. When combined with the six interviews in the convergent interviewing stage of the research project, a total of 54 interviews were conducted across 26 organizations. These interviews produced a comprehensive body of data to address the research issues and complete both within-case and cross-case comparisons. Interviews were conducted with two to three senior managers within events agencies in each state/territory, two to three executives within tourism bodies, two managers of event organizations and one or two executives of other city or local government authorities. Within the tourism and event authorities or departments, more than one interview was usually conducted. In most cases, it was possible to interview executives at different levels within both the events and tourism organizations.

Approximately one and a half hours were allocated for each of these case study interviews. A combined use of audiotapes and note taking enhanced the quality and credibility of this implementation phase. In addition, mental observations were made by the researcher about the interviewee's tone, emphasis and interpersonal communication during the interview to add meaning to the data. Following the interviews, the transcription of interview data fulfilled a need for auditable evidence.

Analysis of Data

After selecting cases and conducting interviews, the researcher must analyse the data. It is customary for within-case analysis to always precede cross-case analysis (Patton, 1990; Miles and Huberman, 1994) because the within-case analysis provides the data for the cross-case analysis. Thus, a description of each case is near the beginning of the data analysis part of the report – it is often restricted to less than half a page per case, with other descriptive material relegated to appendices or the database. However, it is during the later cross-case analysis that the researcher can most clearly display his or her analytical capabilities and escape the 'mindless' description of many case study theses (Adams and White, 1994, p. 573). That is, in the cross-case analysis, the report emphasizes reasons why differences occur, with an explanation for them.

QUALITY OF CASE RESEARCH

An important requirement of all research is that it is trustworthy (Lincoln and Guba, 1999). For case research, this can be established through the use of rigorous methods of research design, data collection and management. Criteria for ensuring that the qualitative research is trustworthy are it's credibility/internal validity, transferability/external validity, dependability/reliability and confirmability/objectivity (Guba and Lincoln, 1994; Healy and Perry, 2000; Lincoln and Guba, 1999; Miles and Huberman, 1994; Sykes, 1990; Yin, 1994). If the researcher follows the procedures above, they will ensure that these criteria are met.

In relation to the reality being investigated, credibility/internal validity of the research can be established in a number of ways. Firstly, the research problem itself has to be suited to the realism paradigm so that its 'how' and 'why' questions are appropriate (Healy and Perry, 2000). Secondly, the use of both methodological and data source triangulation (Denzin and Lincoln, 1994; Hall and Rist, 1999; Jick, 1979; Oppermann, 2000; Perry, 1998; Stake, 1995; Yin, 1994) can provide a clearer window to the reality being investigated. For example, in the events tourism research, multiple sources of data were achieved with the inclusion of personnel from public sector events agencies, individual events, tourism departments and city marketing agencies. This triangulation served to create a 'family of answers' (Healy and Perry, 2000, p. 152) about inter-organizational relationships.

The credibility of the research can be enhanced through cross-case comparisons and the linkage of these findings to existing literature (Amaratunga and Baldry, 2001). This strategy helps to establish strong connections in the data, with an iterative process of examining cases against prior theory leading to a more valid reading of the findings (Sykes, 1990). Finally, a process of subject review or feedback on the credibility of the research findings should be adopted to corroborate the reported 'realities' among participants (Bloor, 1999).

Internal validity of the research, that is, the validity of the mechanisms and contexts being described in the research must also be considered (Carson et al., 2001a). This can be done through careful replication logic when selecting cases, as was described above. This replication logic assists in explaining 'why things happened' from the case interviews (Carson et al., 2001a; Yin, 1994). Clear descriptions of background variables (such as the history of events tourism involvement of participating states/territories and organizations within them) also assist in building internal validity.

In turn, the transferability/external validity of the case research depends on the researcher's ability to make analytic extrapolations based on a cogency of theoretical reasoning (Ward Schofield, 2000). Therefore, the researcher ensures that the initial process of identifying research issues from the literature and perhaps from a preliminary methodology like convergent interviewing, is comprehensive and rigorous (Perry, 2001). The researcher also ensures that a detailed description of the context, for example, the nature of inter-organizational relationships (Stokes, 2004), is provided. In addition to the use of prior theory, external validity can be enhanced by the maintenance of a readily accessible case study database and triangulation techniques (Healy and Perry, 2000). Computer transcriptions and audio recordings of data are therefore maintained to verify the procedures adopted in this investigation.

Triangulation also helps to improve construct validity. Triangulation is using several sources of information about a phenomenon, to try to get a clear picture of it through convergence. That is, case research depends on multiple perceptions of reality. These multiple perceptions usually involve triangulation of several data sources and types of sources, and of several peer researchers' interpretations of those triangulations. The basis of triangulation (Patton, 1990) can come from:

- several sources, for example, interviews with different managers in a case;
- several types of sources, for example, an interview and observations about a case;
- several analysts, for example, having colleagues re-code transcripts of interview; and,
- several perspectives, for example, qualitative and quantitative methods (although this often does not lead to convergence because the

perspectives provide pictures of very different aspects of the phenomenon rather than converging pictures of the same aspect of the phenomenon).

The dependability/reliability of the research should also be considered in the methodology or processes used by the researcher in the data collection and analysis phases of the case study research. For example, reliability can be enhanced by providing a clear trail of evidence for auditing, using coding schemes for data analysis and archiving the data for access at a later date (Yin, 1994; Lincoln and Guba, 1999; Lincoln and Guba, 1985; Healy and Perry, 2000; Halpern, 1983).

Finally, when considering the confirmability/objectivity of the research, the realism paradigm is seen to be neither value laden nor value free, but value aware (Healy and Perry, 2000; Perry, 1998). There are multiple perceptions of reality. Hence multiple interviews within an organization as well as multiple perspectives achieved through triangulation serve to enhance the value awareness of the research. The use of broad questions before probing, the maintenance of a self-critical perspective of the researcher's own values and the provision of findings for participant and peer review each contribute to more objectivity (Healy and Perry, 2000). In brief, the above criteria for maintaining the quality and trustworthiness of the research can assist in justifying the qualitative approaches that accompany the realism paradigm.

LIMITATIONS OF CASE RESEARCH

Criticisms have been directed towards the qualitative case methodology. One of these criticisms is that the method leads to overly complex theories and that it can result in narrow idiosyncratic theories (Eisenhardt, 1989; Parkhe, 1993). The use and development of prior theory and specific research questions to address issues within the theoretical framework are aspects of the research design that assist in minimizing the risk of complexity. In addition, it is important to view qualitative research as a process of theory development, and so, case research is not intended to provide final theory about the subject matter (Parkhe, 1993). The need for statistical generalization to test the theory that was built in a case research project must always be acknowledged.

Further criticisms of case research relate to issues of quality raised earlier in this chapter. Although the methodology has been criticized for its logistical and operational problems (Eisenhardt, 1989; Parkhe, 1993), the use of replication logic for case selection and the development of the interviewer's guide address these criticisms. Other criticisms of the case methodology related to external validity, research rigor and the ability to generalize have already been addressed above. In effect, the development of clear guidelines for the management of case study validity and reliability by the researcher ensure that the above criticisms are addressed. In brief, careful planning and execution of case research can ensure that its strengths are enhanced and its weaknesses are diminished.

CONCLUSION

This chapter described a case research methodology that operates from within the realism paradigm. The methodology emphasizes the building of theories but also incorporates prior theory. How to use the methodology was described, starting with the appropriate research problems through to the selection of cases and interviews, the analysis of interview and other data based on theoretical and literal replication of the cases. How to make the knowledge that the case research develops trustworthy was discussed under four types of quality. Finally, some limitations of the case research methodology were also discussed. In conclusion, case research is a rigorous and coherent research based on justified philosophical positions.

NOTE

*   This chapter is closely based on previous introductions to case research in Perry (1998, 2001) and Carson, Gilmore, Perry and Gronhaug (2001a). The authors thank all the researchers they have worked with in developing procedures for implementing case research such as Len Coote, Andi Riege, Godwin Nair, Gerry Batonda, Hoda Master, Kathy Hastings, Kym Madden and others.

REFERENCES

Adams, G. and J. White (1994), 'Dissertation research in public administration and cognate fields: an assessment of methods and quality', *Public Administration Review*, **54**(6), 565–76.

Alam, I. (2002), 'An exploratory investigation of user involvement in new service development', *Journal of the Academy of Marketing Science*, **30**(3), 250–61.

Alam, I. and C. Perry (2002), 'A customer-oriented new service development process', *Journal of Services Marketing*, **16**(6), 515–34.

Amaratunga, D. and D. Baldry (2001), 'Case study methodology as a means of theory building: performance measurement in facilities management organisations', *Work Study*, **50**(3), 95–104.

Batonda, G. and C. Perry (2002), 'Approaches to relationship development processes in inter-firm networks', *European Journal of Marketing*, **37**(10), 1457–84.

Beverland, M. (2004), 'Uncovering theories in use: building luxury wine brands', *European Journal of Marketing*, **38**(3/4), 446–66.

Bloor, M. (1999), 'On the analysis of observational data: a discussion of the worth and uses of inductive techniques and respondent validation', in A. Bryman and R. Burgess (eds), *On the Analysis of Observational Data: a Discussion of the Worth and Uses of Inductive Techniques and Respondent Validation*, London: Sage, pp. 447–65.

Bonoma, T.V. (1985), 'Case research in marketing: opportunities, problems and a process', *Journal of Marketing Research*, **XXII**(May), 199–208.

Burns, R.B. (1994), *Introduction to Research Methods*, Melbourne: Longman Cheshire.

Carson, D., A. Gilmore, C. Perry and K. Gronhaug (2001a), 'Case-based research', in *Case-based Research*, London: Sage.

Carson, D., A. Gilmore, C. Perry and K. Gronhaug (2001b), 'Indepth interviewing and convergent interviews', in *Indepth Interviewing and Convergent Interviews*, London: Sage.

Chetty, S. (1996), 'The case study method for research in small and medium sized firms', *International Small Business Journal*, **15**(1), 173–85.

Christenson, C. and A. Hansen (1987), *Teaching and the Case Method*, Boston: Harvard Business School.

de Ruyter, K. and N. Scholl (1998), 'Positioning qualitative research: reflections from theory and practice', *Qualitative Market Research: An International Journal*, **1**(1), 7–14.

Denzin, N.K. and Y.S. Lincoln (1994), *Handbook of Qualitative Research*, Thousand Oaks, CA: Sage.

Easton, G. (1998), 'Case research as a methodology for industrial networks: a realist apologia', in P. Turnbell and P. Naude (eds), *Case Research as a Methodology for Industrial Networks: a Realist Apologia*, Oxford: Elsevier Science, pp. 73–87.

Eisenhardt, K. (1989), 'Building theories from case study research', *Academy of Management Review*, **14**(4), 532–50.

Gable, G.G. (1994), 'Integrating case study and survey research methods: an example in information systems', *European Journal of Information Systems*, **3**(2), 112–26.

Greenhalgh, L. (2001), *Managing Strategic Relationships – the Key to Business Success*, New York: The Free Press.

Greer, J. (2002), 'Developing trans-jurisdictional tourism partnerships – insights from the Island of Ireland', *Tourism Management*, **23**(4), 355–66.

Guba, E.G. and Y.S. Lincoln (1994), 'Competing paradigms in qualitative research', in N.K. Denzin and Y.S. Lincoln (eds), *Competing Paradigms in Qualitative Research*, Thousand Oaks, CA: Sage, pp. 105–17.

Hall, A.L. and R.C. Rist (1999), 'Integrating multiple qualitative research methods (or avoiding the precariousness of a one legged stool)', *Psychology and Marketing*, **16**(4), 291–304.

Halpern, E. (1983), *Auditing Naturalistic Enquiries – the Development and Application of a Model*, Bloomington, IN: Indiana University.

Healy, M. (2000), 'Structures and processes of the international networks of Australian small businesses', Toowoomba, Queensland: University of Southern Queensland, p. 271.

Healy, M. and C. Perry (2000), 'Comprehensive criteria to judge validity and relia-
    bility of qualitative research within the realism paradigm', *Qualitative Market
    Research: an International Journal*, **3**(3), 118–26.
Hedges, A. (1985), 'Group interviewing', in R. Walker (ed.), *Group Interviewing*,
    Aldershot: Gower.
Jick, T.J. (1979), 'Mixing qualitative and quantitative methods: triangulation in
    action', *Administrative Science Quarterly*, **24**(1), 602–11.
Lincoln, Y.S. and E.G. Guba (1985), *Naturalistic Enquiry*, London: Sage.
Lincoln, Y.S. and E.C. Guba (1999), 'Establishing trustworthiness', in A. Bryman
    and R. Burgess (eds), *Establishing Trustworthiness*, London: Sage, pp.
    397–444.
Madden, K. and C. Perry (2003), 'How do customers of a financial services insti-
    tution judge its communications?', *Journal of Marketing Communications*.
McGuire, L. (1997), 'Case studies: story telling or scientific research method?', in
    Foster et al. (eds), *Case Studies: Story Telling or Scientific Research Method?*,
    Melbourne: Monash University.
Miles, M.B. and A.M. Huberman (1994), *Qualitative Data Analysis*, 2nd edn,
    Thousand Oaks, CA: Sage.
O'Donnell, A., A. Gilmore, D. Cummins and D. Carson (2001), 'The network con-
    struct in entrepreneurship research: a review and critique', *Management Decision*,
    39(9), 749–60.
Oppermann, M. (2000), 'Triangulation – a methodological discussion', *Inter-
    national Journal of Tourism Research*, **2**, 1–146.
Parkhe, A. (1993), ' "Messy" research, methodological predispositions, and theory
    development in international joint ventures', *Academy of Management Review*,
    18(2), 227–68.
Patton, M.Q. (1990), *Qualitative Evaluation and Research Methods*, 2nd edn,
    Newbury Park, CA: Sage.
Perry, C. (1998), 'Processes of a case study methodology for postgraduate research
    in marketing', *European Journal of Marketing*, **32**(9/10), 785–802.
Perry, C. (2001), 'Case research in marketing', *The Marketing Review*, **1**, 303–23.
Perry, C., Y. Alizadeh and A. Riege (1997), 'Qualitative methods in entrepreneur-
    ship research', in *Small Enterprise Association of Australia and New Zealand
    (SEAANZ) Conference*, Coffs Harbour, Australia: Southern Cross University,
    pp. 547–67.
Perry, C., A. Riege and L. Brown (1998), 'Realism rules OK: scientific paradigms
    in marketing research about networks', presentation to *Australian and New
    Zealand Marketing Academy Conference*, Dunedin, New Zealand.
Riege, A. and C. Perry (2000), 'National marketing strategies in international travel
    and tourism', *European Journal of Marketing*, **34**(11/12), 1290–1304.
Riege, A., C. Perry and F. Go (2001), 'Partnerships in international travel and
    tourism marketing: a systems-oriented approach between Australia, New
    Zealand, Germany and United Kingdom', *Journal of Travel and Tourism*, **11**(1),
    59–78.
Robson, C. (1993), *Real World Research: a Resource for Social Scientists and
    Practitioner-researchers*, Oxford, UK: Blackwell.
Romano, C. (1989), 'Research strategies for small business: a case study',
    International Small Business Journal, **7**(4), 35–43.
Stake, R.E. (1995), *The Art of Case Study Research*, Thousand Oaks, CA, Sage.
Stokes, R. (2004), 'Inter-organisational relationships for events tourism strategy

making in Australian states and territories', PhD thesis prepared for Griffith University, Brisbane, accessed at www.scholar.google.com.

Sykes, W. (1990), 'Validity and reliability in qualitative market research: a review of the literature', *Journal of the Market Research Society*, **32**(3), 289–328.

Tinsley, R. and P. Lynch (2001), 'Small tourism business networks and destination development', *International Journal of Hospitality Management*, **20**, 367–78.

Ward Schofield, J. (2000), Increasing the generalizability of qualitative research', in R. Gomm, et al. (eds), *Increasing the Generalizability of Qualitative Research*, London: Sage, pp. 69–97.

Watkins, M. and B. Bell (2002), 'The experience of forming business relationships in tourism', *International Journal of Tourism Research*, **4**(1), 15–28.

Yin, R.K. (1993), *Applications of Case Study Research*, revised edn, *Applied Social Research Methods Series*, vol 5, Newbury Park, CA: Sage.

Yin, R.K. (1994), 'Case study research: design and methods', 2nd edn, *Applied Social Research Methods Series*, vol 5, Thousand Oaks, CA: Sage.

11. Change in a dynamic climate: a single longitudinal case study in a high technology industry

Damian Hine

INTRODUCTION

Change and firm transition have been studied extensively over many years. Most of this focus has been on larger established firms. It would seem there is little new we can divulge to industry. Yet when we look back at the history of change studies, it soon becomes apparent that the study of this most dynamic of phenomena has been reliant on static studies. Most studies have been cross-sectional, snap-shot studies, from which interpretations of change have been extrapolated. There has been limited focus on the small firm, the impact of its environment on the internal environment of the firm, particularly from a temporal perspective.

Numerous exhortations exist for the use of longitudinal studies to be conducted to gain a true, dynamic picture of change in firms as well as in industry. Rarely has a longitudinal study, the most logical methodological device for examining corporate and industry change, been published. A cursory view of research papers and theses provide the usual explanation for selecting the inferior cross-sectional methodology – limited resources, particularly time.

This chapter does not dwell on the content literature of organizational change, entrepreneurship or small business management. The focus on this chapter is on the design of a research project which tracks the development of a single small entrepreneurial firm over time, in an industry sector in which change is dramatic and constant.

STAGES OF DEVELOPMENT OF A RESEARCH AREA

Using a single case is considered to be the first step on the road to theory building, leading inevitably to theory testing.

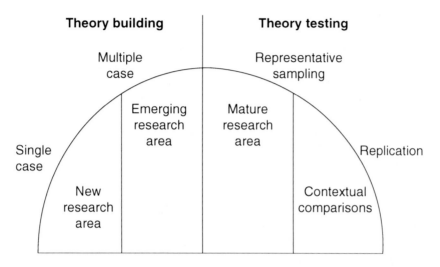

Figure 11.1   Stages of development of a research area

As an area of research begins, there is a need to build a body of know-ledge in the area which extends beyond conceptualization. In-depth obser-vation in a single case is often the first opportunity to analyse the phenomenon under investigation. Theories are established, yet need to be developed further through information rich data gathering. This tends to lead to multiple cases which can provide that information richness, while offering comparability and analysis of similarities and variances to add to the depth of the theoretical framework. While being able to extrapolate to a population, the multiple case approach permits expansion of the appli-cation of the concepts developed. Extrapolation is a logical next step in the development of the research area under investigation, leading inevitably to hypothetic-deductive representative sampling. At this point, it can be regarded that the theories have been established and now the hypotheses are stated to test the established theory in the population of interest. This can take a large variety of forms and employ many analytical techniques beyond the scope of analysis of this chapter. The final stage of development of a research area seems to be indicated by replication studies which accept that the theories have not only been established, but have been tested already. The replication selects a 'niche' to focus on to test the specific appli-cation of the established theory in a defined context, a sub-population if you like. These stages of development of a research area are tentatively offered in Figure 11.2 below.

LONGITUDINAL STUDIES

For investigations studying change processes, Monge (1990) strongly advocates longitudinal methods explaining that 'one reason why organisation science has made little progress in developing dynamic process theories is because its tool kit has largely been limited to verbal and linguistic analysis and correlational research at a single point in time'.

Ahuja (2000) and Ahuja and Katila (2001) used a longitudinal study to gauge the impact of strong ties, weak ties and structural holes on the network effectiveness of firms in the chemical industry. Midgley and Dowling (1993) used a longitudinal study to further expound their innovation diffusion among consumer models with the unit of analysis being the individual. Oszomer and Prussia (2000), employed longitudinal analysis of industry data to test causality from marketing strategy to marketing structure. Each of these, and many more studies, have used the longitudinal technique to track large data sets over time. Most have considered the influence of an independent variable on a dependent variable over time. Such quantitative approaches require the range of variables under consideration to be limited. A study which uses multiple units of analysis, thereby being highly embedded, can explore in greater depth phenomenon which not only vary over time, but whose cause or effect may vary over time. Few have undertaken in-depth case analysis of a single firm over time.

More typically, the longitudinal study is a T1–T2 study, which administers a survey instrument at two points in time (Vazzana, Elfrink and Bachmann, 2000). While longitudinal in essence, the results are more like that of combining two cross-sectional studies.

As with any methodological selection, the unit of analysis varies dramatically in longitudinal studies, from the individual, to groups and teams, to projects, to organizational units, to the firm, to networks, markets, industries, nations and continents. Furthermore, the concept of longitudinal can vary dramatically in terms of time and points of observation. Effectively, if there are two observation points separated by a time period, then the study can be considered to be longitudinal rather than cross-sectional.

This is not to say that such studies don't exist. One example of a quality study of a single organization over a four-year period is provided by Lawrence, Hardy and Phillips (2002) in their *Academy of Management Journal* paper entitled 'Institutional effects of interorganizational collaboration: the emergence of proto-institutions', which undertook a 4-year study of the collaborative activities of a small non-governmental organization in Palestine. Their findings that collaborations that are both highly embedded and have highly involved partners are the most likely to generate proto-institutions were important, both from the point of view of the content and the fact that the paper was published in such a prestigious journal.

Koza and Lewin (1999) conducted a single longitudinal case study of a professional service network in the public accounting industry. The study of a network is difficult to achieve. Many studies of networks have been partial analyses, necessitated by the inability to assess all variables, both internal and external that will impact the network. A single case study is the only realistic means of exploring and documenting the majority of variables, their relationships, both direct and indirect and the impact on dependent variables. The full extent of these relationships can only be understood when a temporal assessment is undertaken, particularly where the effect of the independent variable is not immediately apparent.

This is clearly the intent for Koza and Lewin (1999, p. 638) in their study, as they state in their abstract: 'Applying and extending a coevolutionary perspective (Koza and Lewin, 1998), the paper explores the antecedents and stimuli for the formation of the network, the network's morphology, the motivation of the network members, and the ways in which the network coevolves with its environment and with the adaptation practices of its members'.

More specific to the topic of the study focused on in this chapter is the study by von Gelderen, Frese and Thurik (2000) entitled 'Strategies, uncertainty and performance of small business startups'. While quantitative in nature, and limited in its variable analysis, as indicated in their statement 'These relations are controlled for characteristics of the environment of the firm', p. 169, a detailed confirmatory analysis is conducted which concludes: 'The results suggest a dynamic process between strategy and performance' (p. 178).

Majchrzak, Rice, Malhotra, King and Ba (2000), for example, concentrated on a single team, in a study which analysed how an inter-organizational virtual team, tasked with creating a highly innovative product over a 10-month period. Rice, Kelley, Peters and O'Connor (2001) reported on their longitudinal study of eight radical innovation projects in six large, multi-national, R&D-intensive firms in one paper and a six-year longitudinal study of 12 radical-innovation projects in 10 large, mature companies in another paper (Leifer, O'Connor and Rice, 2001). While the famous work of Alfred Chandler (1990), was an historical analysis of the major industrial firms in the United States (US) and Europe over a century (not of course observed in person over that time). Chandler's work compared companies, industry sectors, nations and continents.

DEFINING A CASE

A case study is defined as 'a research strategy that focuses on understanding the dynamics present within single settings' (Eisenhardt, 1989, p. 534). In contrast to these definitions that focus on description, Yin's (1994) definition of a case study emphasizes the actual processes and use of case studies as a research tool. A case study is: 'an empirical inquiry that investigates a contemporary phenomenon within its real-life context; when the boundaries between phenomenon and context are not clearly evident and; in which multiple sources of evidence are used; and should not only be looked upon as a data collection tactic or solely as a design feature, but also as part of a comprehensive research strategy' (Yin, 1994, p. 13).

That is, a case study has three major characteristics. It is:

- descriptive – it has richness and depth and is focused on contextual meaning;
- heuristic – it illuminates and raises the possibility of new perception; and
- inductive – hypotheses, relationships and understanding emerge from the data and immersion (Lewis and Grimes, 1999).

In summary, all these definitions contain themes applicable to the characteristics of case studies and the definition of case research used for this research is the combination of these definitions. For this research, the definition for case research developed by Lewis and Grimes (1999) is adopted because of its comprehensiveness and recency:

- an empirical investigation of a dynamic (Eisenhardt, 1989), contemporary, paradigmatic body of knowledge (Bonoma, 1985; Burns, 1994; Chetty, 1996; Dyer et al., 1991; Gable, 1994; Romano, 1989; Yin, 1994);
- that leads to theoretical generalization (Bonoma, 1985; Eisenhardt, 1989; Robson, 1993); by
- investigating a new research area or contemporary phenomenon within a real-life context (Eisenhardt, 1989; Merriam, 1988; Yin, 1994); to
- provide contextual richness and depth of information which describes an actual situation (Kaplan, 1986; Merriam, 1988; Robson, 1993); from
- clinical observation and examination using multiple sources (Bonoma, 1985; Robson, 1993; Yin, 1994).

Theory building from case study research is predominantly an inductive process. It is argued that case study research should be purely an inductive process, where theories are developed without considering prior theory in the literature. However, it is difficult to ignore prior theory already in the literature. Using a purely inductive approach does not allow cases to be compared with each other. Deductive research involves theory testing or confirming prior theory. This implies that a tight structure should be set up before interviews begin, with the posing of clear and precise questions and the use of theory and reviews of previous research to develop and test hypotheses.

THIS CASE

There are two types of logic underlying the selection of cases: sampling logic and replication logic. In contrast to the sampling logic, replication logic is a purposive selection. Replication logic and not sampling logic should be used for multiple case studies (Patton, 1990) because relevance rather than representativeness is the criterion for case selection (Stake, 1995). Eisendhardt (1989) indictes that random selection of cases is neither necessary, or even preferable.

Replication is carried out in multiple case research to achieve literal or theoretical replication. Literal replication is where cases are selected to predict similar results for predictable reasons (Eisenhardt, 1989; Perry, 1998). The idea of theoretical replication is the key to the selection of cases and the rigorous analysis of case study data (Perry and Coote, 1994). Logically, cases should be added because of differences and unique features that they have rather than similarities.

Selecting a Rapidly Changing Sector

The importance of the small business sector in Australia cannot be under-estimated, whether it be measured by weight of sheer numbers, or by its economic contribution. It is important to realize the role small business plays in job generation. However, not all small businesses contribute to this job-generating role. It is the entrepreneurial businesses, those that seek and find niche opportunities in new or emerging markets, in which they thrive and grow, which provide the basis for job generation. To do this they have to be innovative in their products, the way they produce those products and in the way they run their businesses. Entrepreneurial businesses are recognizable as those that are growing rapidly; they tend to be the pioneers in new and emerging markets, and therefore are innova-tors.

SELECTING THE CASE

Yin offers the three bases upon which cases should be selected:

1. the case is a critical one for confirming, challenging or extending a theory because it is the only one that meets all the conditions of the theory;
2. the case is rare or extreme and finding other cases is so unlikely that research about the situation could never be done if the single case was not investigated;
3. the case provides unusual access for academic research, and unless the case is investigated, an opportunity to investigate a significant problem, gap or issue may be lost (Yin, 1994).

For those studying change, few industries are considered more dynamic, turbulent and susceptible to external influences than the Information Technology (IT) industry. There is considerable evidence of a high mortality rate amongst firms starting up in this industry. Product life cycles are short, and some argue shortening, leading to an associated short organizational life cycle among industry participants.

BACKGROUND TO THE CASE

Clariti, is an IT analysis and consulting services firm, whose Chief Executive Officer (CEO) Kelvin Andrews virtually fell in to the establishment of this company in 1999. Founding the business with his brother Ian, after Ian won a contract for IT consulting services and called on Kelvin's assistance to complete the contract, the business quickly took off. Interestingly Kelvin's experience was in credit management. Within the first two years of its life, the company moved from being a Microsoft and Citrix LAN only software, hardware and service provider, to being a Unix/Linux and electronic security provider (the security area increased dramatically since September 11). In that time it even went through a major corporate restructure and a name change.

In the first two years of its existence, the company increased its staff from the two original founders to 30 employees. Turnover increased from some AUS \$4500 per month at birth to AUS \$250 000–AUS \$300 000 per month currently. So it is certainly a growing business.

Clariti was first among local firms to promote the service catch-cry 'on time and on budget'. Kelvin ensures the statement is backed up in practice by 'throwing free resources and people at a project if it looks like approaching deadline and budget'. This was an innovation in an industry where both deadlines and budgets were regularly overrun. Indicative of the success of this innovation is the adoption of this catch-cry by most major competitors systematically over the last year, to the point where it is virtually an industry standard. A dedication to internally generated research and development led to new directions for the company based on its expanded product range.

Clariti had a very recognizable organizational structure in place that includes a company board of directors that is chaired by Kevin Davies, a retired Director-General of the State Department of Public Works. Kevin's experience as a CEO is invaluable, as he passes on his knowledge to the key personnel in Clariti. Kevin's knowledge of both the tendering process and the public sector have created further opportunities for the company, as 85 per cent of their business came from public sector clients, with most of this work coming through the competitive tender process.

As with many fast growing entrepreneurial business, the future is always in the mind of the owners, exit strategies are always being considered. The initial idea enunciated by Kelvin was for an IPO (Initial Public Offering) within three years of the founding. The Dot.com crash put a dent in that plan. Yet an alternative was needed to facilitate the desired growth. The two traditional choices, debt and equity financing were considered, with the latter being the obvious choice, as it also allows for succession plans in senior management. Clariti gained venture capital funding with which to ensure the growth of the company. This did not come without some pain however. From that point, the venture capitalist held 50 per cent equity in the company.

The future for Clariti is as unpredictable as it is for all entrepreneurial companies. Strategy cannot be set in concrete as the market they operate in moves so quickly. To this point Clariti has achieved what many entrepreneurial companies aspire to – high growth, employing more staff, and offering an increasing product range through innovation.

RESEARCH DESIGN

The research design for the case investigations will be based upon a modified version of the analytical induction process (Denzin and Lincoln, 1978), that iteratively cycles through inductive theory building, enfolding literature and deductive theory testing (Eisenhardt, 1989; Wollin, 1996). The study was broken into four overlapping phases modified from Eisenhardt (1989): refining focus and procedures, data collection, data analysis, theory development, testing and dissemination:

1. Refining focus and procedures: despite the inductive nature of the study, it is important to have a clear focus for the study (Eisenhardt, 1989). This will lead to the design of case study and interview protocols.
2. Data collection: the need for multiple sources of data is well established.
3. Data analysis: exploration and refinement of constructs will primarily utilize the techniques of Strauss and Corbin (1990). Van de Ven and Poole's (1995) seven step process of tabulating and coding qualitative data into a chronological event sequence was employed.
4. Theory development, testing and dissemination: theory development and testing involving an iterative process of developing preliminary hypotheses from selected data, 'testing' against other data and enfolding literature (Eisenhardt, 1989).

CASE STUDY AND INTERVIEW PROTOCOLS

The case study protocol is an important aspect in achieving reliability. It provides guidance for another researcher who might attempt to repeat the case study (Burns, 1994; Emory and Cooper, 1991; Wimmer and Dominick, 1993; Yin, 1989). Case study protocol contains the data-gathering instrument as well as the procedures and general rules to be followed.

For the purpose of data triangulation, it is ill-advised to depend too heavily on one data source. Hence, two or more data sources should be used to compile the data required on a single case in order to verify statements with facts. In this case a number of data sources were available. The researcher attended all of the company's Board Meetings over a three-year period. Extensive notes were taken at each of these meetings by the researcher. After the second year an administrative assistant also took the minutes of the meetings, providing another point of comparison. This was supplemented by the material that was sent to all board meeting participants prior to each meeting, including financial data, new policies, strategies and public statements. Observational research was conducted with the researcher coming into the company the day of the board meeting every three months.

Being an IT company, major issues could be tracked through the company's website (these could be saved as offline as files for future reference). A structured interview protocol was developed early in the research project to be administered to the CEO at quarterly intervals. Of the data gathering techniques listed above, the last was the most critical in terms of design, as the interview protocol was the only data source which was open to researcher bias. It was important that consistency was achieved.

In this first session with the CEO a semi-structured interview protocol was used. This protocol was refined using further iterative reviews of the literature, archival and desktop research on the company and the interview responses. It was decided that for consistency to be achieved throughout the longitudinal research, a structured interview protocol had to be administered. This provided benchmark data which could be compared across the time intervals. Each of the questions had a temporal component, referring to past, current or future events and intent.

The standard questions below form the basis of the interview protocol. This of course was supplemented by the other data sources and data gathering techniques indicated above to ensure reliability and consistency of the data gathered. Standard questions of the CEO of Clariti:

- What would you see as the three most important developments this company has gone through since its inception?
- Who are your competitors now?
- Who are your collaborators now?
- Describe the company's network. Draw this if possible.
- Describe your own network. Draw this if possible.
- What do you see as the most important influences which will change the company over the next 12 months?
- Where will your growth come from over the next 12 months?
- Where does R&D and innovation stand within the company?
- What is your exit strategy?
- Who are the five most important people related to the company at this point in time?
- What problems do you see the company potentially facing over the next 12 months?

ANALYSING THE DATA

The analysis of the data gathered from the interview process forms the basis of theory building in case studies (Eisenhardt, 1989). However, unlike quantitative research techniques, there are no specific formulas to guide the researcher in analysing the data (Eisenhardt, 1989; Wimmer and Dominick, 1997; Yin, 1994). However, there are some guidelines and procedural suggestions that assist in analysing data (Patton, 1990). The aim of this section is to examine those guidelines and procedural suggestions and how they affected the analysis of the data in Chapter 4.

COMPARISONS WITH PRIOR THEORY

The final step in this analysis process was to build conceptual/theoretical coherence through comparisons with prior theory (Chapter 2) and considering instances where these research findings are capable of replications (Griggs, 1987; Miles et al., 1994) that are discussed in Chapter 5.

Coding establishes the link between the data and the prior theory developed in Chapter 2 (Bryman and Burgess, 1994; Carson et al., 2001). Coding refers to the tags and labels assigned to the word, phrases, paragraphs or information which allow the researcher to differentiate and combine the research data (Carson et al., 2001; Miles and Huberman, 1994). Thus it allows the researcher to sort and organize the data gathered into conceptual categories which creates ideas, themes or concepts (Griggs, 1987; Lincoln and Guba, 1985; Neuman, 1994; Pizam, 1994; Taylor and Bogdan, 1984). That is, 'these codes are retrieval and organising devices that allow the analyst to spot quickly, pull out, then cluster all the segments relating to a particular questions, hypothesis, concept, or theme' (Miles and Huberman, 1994, p. 56).

Coding categories were first developed by listing the themes, concepts, and interpretations in their transcripts to initially analyse their data (Taylor et al., 1984). The data was then coded and sorted into categories or subcategories and their relationship to a major topic of interest identified (Neuman, 1994; Taylor and Bogdan, 1984). In this research, all field notes, interview protocols, and interview transcripts and other materials were coded. Any remaining uncoded data was then fitted into existing categories, given new codes, or remain uncoded if the data was considered to be of no use for this research. Indeed, not all collected data should necessarily be used in every study (Taylor and Bogdan, 1984).

SOME OF THE RESULTS

It is not the purpose of this chapter to analyse in-depth the actual results of the study referred to. Nevertheless some idea of the responses and the changes which occurred over time can offer support for application of the longitudinal technique, which is the focus of this chapter.

In this first session a semi-structured interview protocol was used. This protocol was refined using further iterative reviews of the literature, archival and desktop research on the company and the interview responses. It was decided that for consistency to be achieved throughout the longitudinal research, that a structured interview protocol had to be administered. This provided benchmark data which could be compared across the time intervals. Each of the questions had a temporal component, referring to past, current or future events and intent.

Who are Your Competitors Now?

The responses to this question provide an indication of the extent of change in the competitive environment of the market that Clariti was operating in.

Who are Your Collaborators Now?

Not only does the competitive environment vary rapidly, but the list of collaborators showed even more variation, as Clariti sought to establish and test relationships, watched some collaborations whither on the vine, and had to observe whether one-off relationships could be extended beyond the initial contract into something more substantial.

Table 11.1   Who are your competitors now?

Time point	Competitor
Year 2, first quarter	Data #3 NetBridge – Bay Technologies
Year 2, third quarter	– Datec – Data 3 (public) – Comtech/Di Data – Powerlan (public – Sydney) – Volante (new Netcridge, AMH – public)
Year 2, final quarter	– Bay Technologies – Data 3 – Comtech – PowerLAN – Fujitsu (used to be Southmark)
Year 3, first quarter	Bay Technologies Powerlan Data #3 Volante
Year 3, final quarter	New Base Data #3 Fujitsu QCN

Table 11.2   Who are your collaborators now?

Time point	Response
Year 1, final quarter	1. ANCONS alliance partners – MOVs with them based on joint venture ideas. Don't go into partnership with anyone who treads across our toes – not direct competitors 2. Only work together in the grey area. Link with WAN on partner's side and link with LAN on ANCONS side – all this is MOV – very efficient involvement
Year 2, first quarter	1. Communications Design Management – 6 months 2. McDonald Phillips – 4 months
Year 2, third quarter	No-one, because whoever works with someone gets screwed – big enough now to stand on own two feet
Year 2, final quarter	1. GEtronics (used to be Wang) 2. Corporate Express 3. Pannaseer 4. NCR 5. Fiji group and all vendors: Express Data, Tech Pack
Year 3, first quarter	1. Tequinox (we are just starting to). We have before but had to stop due to bad debt. Work is starting to flow again now 2. Syzergy (we are just starting to)

Year 3, final quarter	We are more selective now:
	1. Pannaseer we work with – just partnering arrangement – low-key
	  • We shut down relationships with – Getronics (Wang), Corporate Express (just wanted to shift boxes, not services – wholesalers)
	  • Former collaborations haven't become competitors.
	  • We now have more focus on working with distributors and vendors
	  • We are now seeing leads come out of, eg distributors – (why?): Better relationships, longer relationships, proving don't let a lead go – act on it straight away.

Where will Your Growth Come from Over the Next 12 Months?

This question linked the previous question asked to the CEO: What do you see as the most important influences which will change the company over the next 12 months?, which focused the response on the external environ-

Table 11.3   Where will your growth come from over the next 12 months?

Time point	Response
Year 1, final quarter	No specific response to this – too early to tell.
Year 2, first quarter	Experience: getting known as having experience – industry riding on reference – more quotable references – work will increase – break down barriers facing till now: 1. Consultation in Microsoft, Citrix 2. Expect significant increase in hardware sales and licensing sales 3. Aiming to be 80/20 company: 80% services, 20% hardware 4. Now 57% services, 43% hardware 5. Expectation over 12 months 65% services, 35% hardware 6. Townsville – good lick of services: $80 000, software licensing: $200 000, hardware: $120 000–220 000 hardware servers. Can't separate them out – all in one price – can do conversions but doesn't work out that way – hardware much lower margins: 12% vs 24% for services – we want to up services – but started as a services company – services to product
Year 2, third quarter	Pacific geography – Product – Business Process Mapping

Year 2, final quarter	1. Geographically:
	  • Brisbane definitely,
	  • Fiji separate entity.
	2. Technology/Production:
	  • Security – need to move faster on security after September 11

Year 3, first quarter	Two places:
	  • Expansion in corporate market;
	  • Acquisition – know exactly (refer to emailed document – Executive summary how and why)

Year 3, final quarter	1. Increased services revenue – only way to significantly grow – need to increase reach to take in eg Townsville hunting further afield 2. Have Clariti Classroom – peer to peer seminars – 10–15 in each – run two to date – successful in generating business – key element of next year's growth 3. Have narrowed product base down and have settled on a mix happy with – six months ago had widened product mix beyond technical capability – now back to original – have been experimental

Innovative methodologies in enterprise research

Table 11.3   (continued)

Time point	Response
	4. We need to get vendors products, our own product has still not eventuated. We pretended to commit time to it, but we can't convince ourselves we have a winner, it's not R&D

ment, to how those changes will impact the firm, and how will the firm's strategy and future direction change as a response. The responses show a dramatic variation in focus between geographic, to product versus service mix, to its market orientation. Such variation underscores the sharp shifts in thinking which are driving the growth of the firm, the emergent nature of its strategies and the rapid changes in the external factors that are influencing the firm at any of these points in time. To this extent, a single response at a single point in time would be grossly inadequate in telling the true story of change for this firm.

CONCLUSION

While this was a single case study, the longitudinal nature of the study, providing rich information over a number of years, in a highly volatile industry, offered insights a cross-sectional study could not have. In fact the tables above indicate that the amount of variation in responses which occurred over this time period justifies the need to track companies over time as they proceed through their growth stages. While only a taste of the total data set has been made available for this chapter, the supporting archival research, company financial statistics, board meeting agenda and minutes, provide a depth to the analysis which could not be achieved through cross-sectional research. Areas available to analyse beyond what is presented in the tables above include: the external environment – global, national and local, as well as the turbulence in these environments; the changing face of the industry, particularly after a the major industry shock of the tech bubble bursting in 2000; start up structures of IT firms; an insight into changing and emergent strategies, as well as changing structure.

While it is a very resource intensive means of data gathering, especially in terms of time resources, it can be rigorous and rewarding. As for the company now – well it is still operating, now only growing marginally, with a new CEO and a dramatic change in ownership, changed location and constantly changing staff. The chair has left and the board configuration is vastly different to any time at which it was observed over the life of the study. So change never stops, and we can't afford to miss documenting these developments in the lives of young firms.

REFERENCES

Ahuja, G. (2000), 'Collaboration networks, structural holes, and innovation: a longitudinal study', *Administrative Science Quarterly*, **45**(3), 425–55.

Ahuja, G. and R. Katila (2001), 'Technological acquisitions and the innovation performance of acquiring firms: a longitudinal study', *Strategic Management Journal*, **22**(3), 197–220.

Bonoma, T.V. (1985), 'Case research in marketing: opportunities, problems and a process', *Journal of Marketing Research*, **XXII** (May), 199–208.

Bryman, A. and R. Burgess (eds) (1994), *Analyzing Qualitative Data*, London and New York: Routledge.

Burns, R.B. (1994), *Introduction to Research Methods*, Melbourne: Longman Cheshire.

Carson, D., A. Gilmore, C. Perry and G. Gronhaug (2001), *Qualitative Marketing Research*, London: Sage.

Chandler, A. (1990), *Scale and Scope: The Dynamics of Industrial Capitalism*, Cambridge, MA: Harvard University Press.

Chetty, S. (1996), 'The case study method for research in small and medium sized firms', *International Small Business Journal*, **15**(1), 173–85.

Denzin, N.K. and Y.S. Lincoln (1994), *Handbook of Qualitative Research*, Thousand Oaks, CA: Sage.

Dyer, W., A. Wilkins and K. Eisenhardt (1991), 'Better stories, not better constructs, to generate better theory: a rejoinder to Eisenhardt; better stories and better constructs: the case for rigor and comparative logic', *The Academy of Management Review*, **16**(3), 613–19.

Eisenhardt, K. (1989), 'Building theories from case study research', *Academy of Management Review*, **14**(4), 532–50.

Emory, C.W. and D.R. Cooper (1991), *Business Research Methods*, Irwin: Homewood.

Gable, G.G. (1994), 'Integrating case study and survey research methods: an example in information systems', *European Journal of Information Systems*, **3**(2), 112–26.

Griggs, S. (1987), 'Analyzing qualitative data', *Journal of the Market Research Society*, **29**(1), 15–34.

Kaplan, D. (ed.), *The Sage Handbook of Quantitative Methodology for the Social Sciences*, Thousand Oaks, CA: Sage, pp. 49–70.

Kaplan, R. and C. Tomkins (1986), 'The role for empirical research in management accounting/commentary', *Accounting, Organizations and Society*, **11**(4/5), 429–56.

Koza, M. and A. Lewin (1999), 'The coevolution of network alliances: a longitudinal analysis of an international professional', *Organization Science*, **10**(5), 638–53.

Lawrence, T., C. Hardy and N. Phillips (2002), 'Institutional effects of interorganizational collaboration: the emergence of proto-institutions', *Academy of Management Journal*, **45**(1), 281–90.

Leifer, R., G. O'Connor and M. Rice (2001), 'Implementing radical innovation in mature firms: the role of hubs, *Academy of Management Executive*, **15**(3), 102–13.

Lewis, M. and A. Grimes (1999), 'Metatriangulation: building theory from multiple paradigms', *Academy of Management Review*, **24**(4), 672–90.

Lincoln, Y.S. and E.G. Guba (1999), 'Establishing trustworthiness', in A. Bryman and R. Burgess (eds), *Establishing Trustworthiness*, London: Sage, pp. 397–444.

Majchrzak, A., R. Rice, A. Malhotra, N. King and S. Ba (2000), 'Technology adaptation: the case of a computer-supported inter-organizational virtual team', *MIS Quarterly*, **24**(4), 569–600.

Merriam, S. (1988), *Case Study Research in Education: A Qualitative Approach*, San Francisco: Jossey-Bass.

Midgley, D. and G. Dowling (1993), 'A longitudinal study of product form innovation – the interaction between predispositions and social messages', *Journal of Consumer Research*, **19**(4), 611–25.

Miles, M.B. and A.M. Huberman (1994), *Qualitative Data Analysis: A Expanded Sourcebook*, 2nd edn, Thousand Oaks, CA: Sage.

Monge, P.R. (1990), 'Theoretical and analytical issues in studying organizational processes', *Organization Science*, **1**(1), 406–30.

Neuman, W. (1994), *Social Research Methods: Qualitative and Quantitative Approaches*, Boston: Allyn and Bacon.

Ozsomer, A. and G. Prussia (2000), 'Competing perspectives in international marketing strategy: contingency and process models', *Journal of International Marketing*, **8**(1), 27–50.

Patton, M.Q. (1990), *Qualitative Evaluation and Research Methods*, Newbury Park: Sage.

Perry, C. (1998), 'Processes of a case study methodology for postgraduate research in marketing', *European Journal of Marketing*, **32**(9/10), 785–802.

Perry, C. and L. Coote (1994), 'Processes of a cases study research methodology tool for management development?', presentation to *Australia and New Zealand Association for Management Annual Conference*, New Zealand, Victoria University of Wellington.

Rice, M., D. Kelley, L. Peters and G. O'Connor (2001), 'Radical innovation: triggering initiation of opportunity recognition and evaluation', *R&D Management*, **31**(4), 409–20.

Robson, C. (1993), *Real World Research: A Resource for Social Scientists and Practitioner-Researchers*, Oxford: Blackwell.

Romano, C. (1989), 'Research strategies for small business: a case study', *International Small Business Journal*, **7**(4), 35–43.

Stake, R.E. (1995), *The Art of Case Study Research*, Thousand Oaks, CA: Sage.

Strauss, A.L. and J. Corbin (1990), 'Basics of qualitative research: grounded theory research: procedures, canons and evaluative criteria', *Qualitative Sociology*, **13**, 3–20.

Taylor, S. and R. Bogdan (1984), *Introduction to Qualitative Research Methods: The Search for Meanings*, New York and Chichester: Wiley.

Van de Ven, A. and M. Poole (1995), 'Explaining development and change in organisations', *Academy of Management Review*, **20**(3), 510–40.

Vazzana, G., J. Elfrink and D. Bachmann (2000), 'A longitudinal study of total quality management processes in business colleges', *Journal of Education for Business*, **76**(2), 69–74.

Von Gelderen, M., M. Frese and R. Thurik (2000), Strategies, uncertainty and performance of small business startups, *Small Business Economics*, **15**(3), 165–81.

Wimmer, R. and J. Dominick (1997), *Mass Media Research: An Introduction*, Belmont, CA: Wadsworth.

Wollin, A. (1996), 'Rigor in theory-building from cases', presentation to ANZAM Conference.

Yin, R.K. (1989), *Case Study Research: Design and Methods*, Beverly Hills, CA: Sage.

Yin, R.K. (1994), *Case Study Research: Design and Methods*, 2nd edn, Applied Social Research Methods Series, vol 5, Thousand Oaks, CA: Sage.

12. Issues in cross-national comparisons applied to building theory on informal innovation in SMEs

Asko Miettinen and Damian Hine

INTRODUCTION

The challenge of undertaking cross-national comparisons is driven by one of two factors. The need to explore a phenomenon for which there is an expectation of consistency across national borders and national cultures, or to explore the extent to which those national borders and national cultures impact the phenomenon under investigation. Under either condition, consideration must be made of the cultural, political, regulatory regimes which exist in each country. An in-depth consideration of these factors, while not solely dependent upon a thorough understanding of the contexts of these regimes in the countries under observation, is enhanced by an intimate knowledge of that context. It is far more resource efficient and may have an ameliorating impact on underlying assumptions about the phenomenon, for a resident of a country to actually undertake the study of a phenomenon in that country when cross-national comparisons are undertaken. An academic who is a resident of Finland will be far more attuned to the external environmental factors influencing small firms in Finland than will be a visitor to the land. This situation is underscored when language barriers are apparent.

This chapter elucidates on the process of cross-national studies as a collaboration between two researchers. It commences with an analysis of the issue of comparison between countries, and then focuses on a specific study being conducted by the two authors of this chapter.

Can 'x' be 'y' in another Context? The Price of Coca-Cola cans within the EU

From the beginning of 2002, a dozen EU countries moved to use a common currency, the Euro. This makes it possible to compare prices in these countries more easily than previously. Only a few days after January 1, Reuters announced a comparison of 'europrices' in 12 countries in a list including a set of the most popular products such as a CD disc, a Renault car and last but not least a can of Coca Cola. This comparison seemed to legitimate the title 'Pity for Finland'. The prices of CD discs and Coca Cola were highest in Finland in this particular comparison.

The Finnish media reacted immediately with big headlines. Several accusations, explanations and excuses were published, varying from high taxation to focusing on 'some less important special cases only'. The fact is, however, a can of Coca Cola costs 33 cents in Spain, in Germany 35 cents, in France 40 cents, in Italy 77 cents and in Finland 1 Euro and 18 cents.

One of the first people to appear in public to defend this differential was Ms Marketta Vehkametsä, the head of the information department for Coca Cola Finland Ltd who stated: 'The price is generally not that high. We think that the can has been purchased from a special place like a kiosk or some special shop'. The price was then split into its components by media. According to this analysis, the components are as follows: production, transportation, sales and marketing costs 76 cents, VAT 20 cents (17 per cent – among the highest in the EU), pawn (appreciated particularly among environmentally sensitive people) 15 cents, packing tax 5.5 cents and soft drink tax 1.7 cents (a unit tax). Another spokesperson explained that VAT in Denmark is even higher (25 per cent – applied also to foods) and that the 'gold medal' of highest food prices in the EU actually belongs to Denmark.

Further explanations and excuses were provided by the Finnish media and by Coca Cola Finland Ltd. The comparison made by Reuters was labelled to be, if not a lie, a distorted fact. It became clear that cans represent only 1.8 per cent of all Coca Cola sales in Finland. More than 60 per cent of Coca Cola users buy it in the 1.5 litre bottles.

WHY AND HOW TO COMPARE: A SERIOUS ISSUE

There are more serious concerns behind the Coca Cola can crisis, however. A great deal of empirical economic research involves comparison of some sort. Investigators use statistical methods to construct quantitative comparisons; they compare cases to each other and comparative cases to purely theoretically derived cases. Comparisons often provide a reasonable basis for making statements about empirical regularities and for evaluating and interpreting cases relative to substantive and theoretical criteria.

In a broad sense, virtually all economic research is comparative research. More especially, the term comparative method is typically used in a narrower sense to refer to a particular kind of comparison – the comparison of large macroeconomic units. The comparative method has been traditionally considered as the branch treating cross-economic differences and similarities.

Although this tradition has its evidence, there is substantial disagreement concerning the distinctiveness of comparative economic science in general and comparative method in particular. It is presumably most common to define comparative research as research that uses comparable data from at least two societies. This definition emphasizes the fact that the data of comparative economic science should be cross-societal.

Many researchers would probably find this definition too restrictive. Here we face perhaps the most distinctive aspect of comparative research: the wide chasm that seems to exist between quantitative and qualitative work. In the qualitative tradition, there seems to be a clear tendency to look at cases as wholes, and there is also the comparison of whole cases with each other. Even in the cases analysed in terms of variables, cases are viewed as configurations – as combinations of configurations. This holistic approach contradicts the rather narrow analytic tradition of most quantitative work.

The second characteristic of the qualitative approach is the tendency to be historically interpretative: it attempts to account for specific historical outcomes or sets of comparable outcomes or processes chosen for study, because of their significance in current institutional arrangements or social life in general (Ragin, 1987).

Other studies have tried to differentiate comparative economic science by emphasizing its multilevel character. Comparative work may proceed at two levels simultaneously: at the level of system (or the macroeconomic level) and at the within-system level. According to this argument, any analysis that is based only on macroeconomic similarities and differences (such as Gross National Product (GNP) per capita). Ideally, system level variables should be used to explain variation across systems in within-systems relationships.

The multilevel character of comparative economics relates to another issue of importance in most comparative studies: that of unit of analysis. It would possibly be misleading to conclude simply that comparativists differ from noncomparativists in terms of 'chosen unit of analysis'. An important source of confusion is that the term 'unit of analysis' is used to describe two different kinds of metatheoretical constructs. Sometimes, 'unit of analysis' is used in reference to data categories. At other times, however, the same term is used in reference to theoretical categories. This difference in use has created a great deal of confusion in the field of comparative studies: the analysis may proceed at one level (for instance the firm level) and the explanation at another level (usually the macro-economic level). It is thus necessary to distinguish between observational units and explanatory units. The term 'observational unit' refers to the unit used in data collection and data analysis; the term 'explanatory unit' refers to the unit that is used to account for the pattern of results obtained.

There are many practical problems associated with establishing cross-economic studies. Most of these practical problems concern the comparability of relative dissimilar societies. This concern for comparability derives ultimately from the fact that the cases (eg countries) have known histories and identities. That is, they are not anonymous, vacuum-based observations. Furthermore, it is often difficult to evaluate the explanatory statements of comparative studies because the number of relevant units available for such assessments is often limited by empirical constraints as well as theoretical criticism.

Considering that there are boundaries and limitations of this kind, it is quite understandable that many researchers in the field of comparative studies focus their interest on questions that are limited both substantively and historically. In many typical comparative studies, only a small set of cases may provide the basis for empirical generalization.

Comparative Studies in Action: dealing with Heterogeneity, Causality and Complexity

Many comparativists are interested in long range outcomes. That is why their explanations often address combinations of causal conditions and heterogeneity. The assessment of causal complexity, therefore, is of crucial importance in comparative studies. Yet studies tend to find a considerable amount of order in the complex phenomena they are exploring and feel that 'there must be method in this mess'. This sense of order-in-complexity has some history in comparative studies, stemming from the tradition of making sense of an individual case by drawing generalized parallels across a wide variety of cases. The real challenge comes in trying to 'make sense of the diversity across cases in a way that unites similarities and differences into a single, coherent framework', as Ragin (1987, p. 19) puts it. This emphasizes the difficulty of summarizing in a theoretically or substantively meaningful way the order that seems evident across diverse cases.

The search for order-in-complexity is manifested in two major forms: in the problem of constructing useful empirical typologies ('how to identify the types of cases in terms of setting boundaries on comparability'), and in the difficulty of assessing causal complexity, seen especially in 'multiple conjunctural causation'. Different combinations of conditions may obtain (or exist), for example, both within and between countries. There are usually two major approaches to this complexity: to simplify the complexity among combinations of characteristics of cases and then construct a model of the types that exist, or to simplify the complexity among combinations of an outcome (observable across a range of cases) and then construct a model of the causal combinations.

Another alternative, suitable in certain situations, is to register extreme values deserving detailed attention because these provide particularly pure examples of certain phenomena. For example, many anthropologists frequently justify their selection of cases on these grounds. The argument is that emergent cultural patterns that may seem strange or unusual in some way have important practical meaning and should therefore be understood in a wider context.

Causal complexity is not often encountered. The ideal, but rather rare, economic scientific comparison is identical in structure to the simple experiment, where the researcher compares an experimental group with a control group differing in only one respect – the experimental treatment, which is allowed to vary. Contrary to the case in the study of natural sciences, the investigator in economic sciences is able to manipulate causes directly to establish a basis for making comparisons. First, an outcome of interest to economic comparativists seldom has a single cause. Secondly, causes rarely operate in isolation. It is usually the combined effect of various conditions and their intersection in time and space, that produces a certain outcome. In other words, economic causation is often both multiple and conjunctural.

Thirdly, depending on the context, a specific cause may have diametrically opposed effects. Conditions having contradictory effects due to context naturally complicate the identification of empirical regularities. Unfortunately multiple conjunctural causation can be assessed directly only in experimental designs. It is obviously impossible to manipulate conditions affecting large masses of people. Comparativists are thus supposed to accept the challenge of studying naturally occurring ('non-experimental') data.

As alternatives to missing experimental designs, two strategies are traditionally used among scholars working in comparative studies. The first one is to exploit case-oriented methods, qualitative historical methods (Ragin and Zaret, 1983), the method of systematic comparative illustration (Smelser, 1976), and logical methods (Tesch, 1990; Punch, 1998) to mention only a few of the well-known labels used in the field.

Researchers can work with small, theoretically defined sets of cases. They may compare cases with each other as wholes to arrive at modest generalizations, concerning relatively narrow classes of phenomena. The outcomes can still be very beneficial through this 'small sample but big conclusions' approach.

Another approach is not typically concerned with accounting for historically defined phenomena, but rather formulating broad generalizations about economies and other large-scale institutions. Its roots stem from mainstream economic science methodology, especially quantitative methods. This research strategy is more concerned with variables and their relationships. It also attempts to approximate the rigor of experimental or quasi-experimental methods through statistical manipulation.

Cross-national Comparative Studies

So why undertake cross-national studies? Certainly it is to generalize beyond national boundaries, particularly in industry sectors which are global in their orientation. Researchers bring with them certain forms of cultural, disciplinary, and methodological baggage to their studies. This can be both a positive and a negative dependent upon the level of bias this has the potential to create, and the tolerance or acceptance of this bias built into the study. The study at the centre of this chapter seeks to understand the informal research and development practices of highly innovative small firms in a globalized high technology industry, information and communication technologies (ICT). As a global industry, it is expected that there will be many similarities between the firms studied in each country. However it is the variances which make the cross-national study valuable.

Informal Innovation in Small Firms – a Motivation for the Study

The dissatisfaction with the inadequacy of existing formal measures has spawned a quest for alternative measures of innovation, both for large and small firms. Early steps have been taken in seeking measures which are ideally suited to small firms and their circumstance. The concept of informal innovation and its measurement was raised by Romijn and Albaladejo (2002) in defining some new determinants of innovation capability in small electronics and software firms in southeast England. They refer to both formal and informal innovation support activities, such as staff training, informal technological efforts such as problem solving, informal research and development (R&D) such as learning on-the-job. They concede, however, that only estimates of such informal efforts can be made.

A study entitled 'Under-reporting of R&D in small firms: the impact on international R&D comparisons', emphasizes the point that under-estimation of innovation 'arises due to small firms' emphasis on developmental rather than fundamental research and because of this activity is often informally and organised' (Roper, 1999). Roper provides support for differentials between the small business sectors between countries in his study of German firms, indicating that 'international survey evidence suggests a greater degree of formality in the organisation of R&D in German small firms. This reduces the likely degree of underestimation of German small firms' R&D activity relative to that in the UK'.

Rigid measures have the tendency to promote rigid management techniques. This is alien to the innovative efforts of most innovative small firms. Creativity is the key (Foxall and Hackett, 1994) and it is supported by a flexible fluid organizational structure, little hierarchy and open communication systems both internally and externally. It would be detrimental to these firms to inflict formalization on them prematurely. Though in due course a small firm gets more mature; 'innovation must become less a personal and more an organisational characteristic', as Sebora et al. (1994) have noted.

Then there are the missing branches. Back in 1987, Kleinknecht stated that formal R&D measurements are sound for large firms' innovative activity only, but they failed to register informal innovative activities that are 'largely the province of small firms'. Inclusion of informal R&D data has raised questions (Brouwer, 1998) about the validity of the information collected, especially if the data is a function for receiving subsidies or rebates from governments. However Menkveld and Thurik (1999) in their reply to this criticism, aimed at their previous work in Van Dijk et al. (1997), argued that small firms do not have the capital or personnel to have a research department. Like Acs and Audretch (1988), Van Dijk et al. (1997) stated that taking a different approach in controlling data might lead to ambiguity, but it is a necessary step in the advancement of empirical studies of firm size and innovation activity.

Cross-national Comparison – Australia and Finland

With the increased interest and the burgeoning research agenda in innovation, there is an increasingly valuable body of international data available (OECD, 1997). This data provides the basis for comparing the innovativeness of the sectors across countries. The availability of such data can promote a more detailed analysis of the external environmental factors which impact these firms. At the Organisation for Economic Co-operation and Development's (OECD's) own admission (1997, p. 3). 'International comparability is still weak, however, due to divergent size-class definitions and sector classifications. To enable useful policy analysis, OECD governments need to improve their build-up of data, without creating additional obstacles for firms through the burden of excessive paper work'.

Unfortunately, given the 'partial measurement problem' a full cross-national analytical comparison is not currently achievable. Further specific cross-national research must be conducted, which will complete the portrait of innovativeness of the small firm sector in both Australia and Finland as a starting point.

The proposed study will be designed to develop alternative measures of innovativeness in small firms; more particularly, by accepting the informal nature of the research and development conducted by these firms to explore the independent and dependent variables associated with this broader form of innovation and innovativeness. By way of summary, there are a number of tasks a cross-national study between Australia and Finland can attempt:

- It can seek to improve the international comparability of data, a task deemed desirable by the OECD.
- It can seek to identify those roles, actions and activities which denote informal innovative efforts, thereby adding to the breadth of data on innovation.
- It can identify those informal innovation activities prominent in small businesses and to classify these on a formalization continuum.
- It can dovetail the new measures in with the existing measures.
- It can explore country specific aspects of the innovative effort in small firms.

THE STUDY

Drawing on a cross-national multiple-case study method, the authors investigate appropriateness of existing measures of innovation to small firms. The evidence of small firms' contribution to the innovative effort of nations is equivocal. There is still scope for many to question the centrality of small business to this innovative effort. The measurement techniques used internationally for gauging innovation concentrate largely on product innovation, patent counts, R&D data and bibliometric data. Each alludes to a formalized innovation process within the firm. Accordingly, the less formalized process that exist within many entrepreneurial small firms create the opportunity for innovation to occur, but don't offer comprehensive data on either the inputs or outputs of the innovation process to researchers, or national and international data collection bodies. In this era of flexibility, responsiveness and the acceptance of diversity, the traditional measures of innovation appear standardized, inflexible and limiting.

This study explores how small software firms innovate. It puts its emphasis on evaluating how innovative these firms are considered to be in different areas such as in creating new products and services to market, their innovation speed, investments in R&D, communication techniques in their internal management and management of external relationships, how they collaborate and what they see as the basis of their competitiveness.

Following an exploration of traditional and alternative measures of innovation in use currently, these measures are questioned in the context of small firm requirements and practices using data from a four case multiple case study of ICT firms from Finland and Australia. The findings indicate a need for alternative measurements of informal innovation and R&D for small firms. Measures of informal innovation are then proposed which better reflect the innovation processes occurring in smaller firms.

Sector Selection

The software industry is recognized as one of the most innovative (Gartner, 2005; OECD, 2004). The research and development pipelines are generally short compared to other high technology industries such as elaborately transformed manufactures and biotechnology. Product life cycles are correspondingly short.

The software industry has become one of the major growth industries over the past four decades. As Quinn et al. (1996) have indicated, software seems to be the primary element in most aspects of innovation – from basic research through to product innovation. Software provides the critical mechanism through which managers try to lower the costs, compress the time cycles, and increase the value of innovation. It is also at the heart of the learning and knowledge processes that give innovations their highest payoffs.

Software is also oftentimes the core element in process innovations or in creating the functionalities that make products valuable to customers. In others, software is actually the 'product' or 'service' the customer receives. Furthermore, software can provide the essential vehicle enabling inventor-user interactions, the fast distribution of products and market feedback that add most value to majority of innovations. Thus, software dominates today all innovation steps: it provides the enabling tools and infrastructure to ICT professionals in virtually all other industries (Nowak and Grantham, 2000). Given the changes within the information sector of the economy (typified by the shift in value added from hardware to software), there has been a significant rise in research interest in this area also.

In most advanced economies, the software industry has moved towards an internationalization of the sector occupying a key role in the development of the knowledge-based information economy. It is still characterized by a great number of small enterprises and a few large multinational companies. Another attribute of the sector is a large number of niche and small-scale market opportunity driven small firms due to rapid technological change and vertical integration. A great many firms appear to be relatively young, giving the evidence that the growth of the sector has continuously provided opportunities for new entrants.

The global volume of the software industry is estimated to be about €250 million. Its further expansion looks evident with an annual growth of 10–15 per cent, which is clearly above that of general industrial growth. The recent decline (2001–03) is expected to be of short duration and to reach the annual level of 10+ per cent again. An estimate for 2010 gives the global market volume of €450 billion. Although quite a few big merges took place (such as Oracle and PeopleSoft; Symantec and Veritas) in 2004, indicating an accelerating concentration tendency in the software industry, the market for small and mid-market businesses in this field is expected to be in the tens of billions in a year into the future.

The software sector in Finland started to develop quickly in the early 1990s. The turnover of this sector was €267 million in 1997, followed by a rapid growth in 1999–2001 and reaching the volume of €1,300 million during 2001 (out of which the proportion of exports was €408 million, or 31.4 per cent). In terms of personnel, there was also a fast growth from some 750 people in 1999 to 14,000 in 2001 working in more than 900 software companies, the majority of them being start-ups or in early growth stages. This is not a very high figure in the field: for example, Harrison et al. (2004) estimate that there are approximately 22,000 software small and medium-size enterprises (SMEs) across the United Kingdom (UK).

After the decline of 2002–03, the business cycles in the software sector have improved again. A recent survey (November 2004) indicated growing sales and an increase in the number of employees: two thirds of the respondents from software firms had recruited new personnel and considered the situation 'normal'. More accurately, 32 per cent expected to increase their sales in the near future, 68 per cent expected to maintain at the current level and 11 per cent estimated them to decrease (see Appendix).

The industry is a relatively new industrial sector characterized by a large number of small firms typically providing high-performance inputs into complex systems of production, of information processing and of product development. Technological accumulation takes place mainly through the design, build up and operational use of these specialized inputs. Specialized supplier firms benefit from the operating experience of advanced users, in the form of information, skills and identifications of possible modifications and improvements in this industry. Software-based firms oftentimes accumulate their skills to match advances in technology, with user requirements, which – given the cost, complexity and independence of production processes – put a premium on reliability and performance, rather than a price.

The main task of the innovation strategy of these firms is keeping up with users' needs, learning from advanced users and matching new technologies to users' needs. In terms of their technological trajectories, these firms belong to 'specialized suppliers' (Tidd et al., 2001). In this rapidly growing industry, entry barrier is relatively low – explaining the large proportion of small firms operating in this particular sector. Many small software developers are also potentially 'born global' making their 'opportunity window' very interesting.

Case selection and profiles
For this study four ICT companies were selected (two from Australia and two from Finland) as the case studies. The companies are identified as follows:

> F1 – Communication server and interfaces. Proprietary transmission control protocol/internet protocol (TCP/IP).
> F2 – Specialty is software implementation of digital signally process methods.
> A1 – Security software, data warehousing project outsourcing.
> A2 – Design and develop software for web content management and library automation.

Each of the respondents had established the business, and were still CEO at time of response. Hence they had appropriate knowledge of the company to respond effectively to the range of questions.

Of the four companies only one could be considered an established company with ages ranging between: F1 (four months), F2 (two years), A1 (two years) and A2 (15 years). The two measures of size are used, turnover and employee numbers. Each of the companies has shown growth in employee numbers. Of course the youngest companies have displayed the most dramatic growth. A2 is still growing despite being a 15-year-old company in an industry not recognized for its long-stayers.

Table 12.1   Company size by employee number and turnover

Company	F1	F2	A1	A2
Employees now	4	8	17	14
Employees 12 months ago	0	5	9	12
Turnover last 3 months (€)	40 000	90 000	427 824	133 695
Turnover same time last year (€)	Not established	35 000	207 970	<133 695

For each of the companies the majority of employees were technical/ trade people, with professional/senior management and marketing/sales people also represented in their ranks. The question on turnover relates to the last three months and asks the respondent to compare with the 3 months a year ago; this provides an assessment of their growth and takes account of the fact that one of the companies isn't a year old yet, so can't provide annual turnover as yet. The limitation of this question is the cyclical nature of turnover for these companies. For A1, December to February are lean times with regard to revenue. For both Australian companies June is usually a strong month. Only A2 was a major exporter (50 per cent of their products and services, all others were negligible.

To analyse the responses, both raw data presented in tabular form, and descriptive statistics are used, particularly means. The qualitative responses are summarized before being analysed. The findings are displayed under the four headings identified in the previous section.

Traditional measures of innovation
For traditional measures of innovation, questions relating to the accepted measures of major and incremental product innovation, process innovation and non-technological innovation were incorporated into the questionnaire.

Major product innovation With regard to major product innovation the following question was asked: 'How many new products and/or services has your company brought to market in the last 12 months?' The responses are provided in Table 12.2, with total product/service range in brackets.

The response for A2 is not surprising given, it is a 15-year-old company, that it is likely to concentrate more on incremental innovation if it has successful products, as it has.

Table 12.2   Major product innovation

Company	F1	F2	A1	A2
Major new products (frequency)	1 (1)	3 (3)	0 (0)	0 (2)
Major new services (frequency)	0 (1)	0 (0)	4 (5)	0 (2)
Improvements in existing products	0	3	0	2
Improvements in existing services	0	0	2	1
New production methods	2	3	0	1
New methods of service provision	0	0	6	1

Incremental product innovation   With regard to incremental product innovation the following question was asked: 'How many major improvements
have you made to your company's existing products and/or services in the
last 12 months?' (Incremental product innovation). F1 being the youngest
company, are reliant on their initial product for success and are yet to ini-
tiate the successive products which will create a product stream which can
sustain the business.

Process innovations   With regard to process innovations the question
was asked: 'How many new methods of production and/or service provision has your company implemented in the last 12 months?' In terms
of process innovations, each of the companies would be considered to
be somewhat innovative, with at least two innovations in the last 12 months.

Non-technological innovation   With regard to non-technological innovation, a set of three questions were asked. These questions follow the
organizational innovation questions used by the Australian Bureau of
Statistics in their 1995 and 1997 *Innovation Surveys* (ABS, 1997). The question was 'Have you implemented any of the following in the last 12 months?'
    Responses indicate that both the Australian companies would be consid-
ered innovative in the area of organizational innovation. The Finnish companies are not organizationally innovative. The limitations of these questions
are clear and the questions themselves are very open to interpretation. They
certainly need to be supported by further probing questions, which clarify
the organizational innovation situation in the individual company. This has
been less of a priority for institutions such as the OECD and national statistical bodies, with their focus on technological innovation and on aggregation to regional and national levels. The organizational innovation analysis
is more fine grained, though could still be aggregated to national level where
appropriate questions are asked which provide succinct responses.
    In combining the responses to all the innovation questions outlined
above, we can conclude that all the companies can be considered to be
innovative, though the basis of their innovativeness varies.
    None of the company responses indicated any bibliographic citations,

Table 12.3   Non-technological innovation

Company	F1	F2	A1	A2
Advanced management technique	No	No	Yes	Yes
Change in corporate structure	No	No	Yes	Yes
Change in corporate strategy	No	Yes	Yes	Yes

which is not surprising for small ICT companies. Also, none of the companies hold any current patents either, and none have any patent applications currently submitted – either domestic or international. This is despite considerable recognizable intellectual property in their products. For instance, A2's ProductX software is a truly international product being used as support for a major web design software used in online course development in Universities, schools and colleges around the world. A2 has copyright over the code for ProductX. It has also applied on a number of occasions for a Trademark, but has been denied on grounds of the generic nature of the name and on the size of the domestic market.

R&D

R&D personnel   The question was asked 'How many nominated Research and development personnel do you have currently employed in this company?' (eg R&D Manager, research scientist). F1 had three, F2 had six, A1 had none and A2 had three.

R&D expenditure   The question was asked 'On your Profit and Loss Statement for the last financial year, what proportion of your Expenditure is dedicated to R&D?' F1 had 0 per cent of expenditure dedicated to R&D, F2 also had 0 per cent, A1 had 1.1 per cent and A2 had a very sizable 48 per cent dedicated to R&D. A2 stands out here with a figure of 48 per cent. Financial staff did review this figure and confirmed the proportion. Two reasons can be given for this high figure – A2 does claim taxation concessions for its R&D expenditure. 'The share of R&D performed by SMEs (firms with fewer than 500 employees) is generally higher in smaller economies than in larger ones (with the exception of Korea and Sweden)' (OECD, 2002).

When asked: 'How long have you been calculating R&D expenditure in your financial statements?' F1 had for four months, F2 had never calculated R&D expenditure, A1 had been for a year and A2 had for two years.

Motivations for including R&D in financial statements varied on a country basis – the Australian companies gave external reasons for including R&D expenditure (tax reasons, R&D Start, R&D tax concession), while the Finnish companies indicated internal reasons (accountability and comparisons, expenditures are not dedicated to R&D). Australian governments are the fifth most generous amongst OECD nations in terms of R&D tax subsidies (with 11 cents for each US$1 spent on R&D), while Finland ranks fourteenth (at 0.9 of a cent per US$1) (OECD, 2001). So there is an external incentive evident motivating the Australian companies. A2 is also the oldest company, having been in operation for 14 years. It is not surprising then that the internal accounting system has assessed the R&D contribution more slowly. It is also a relatively slow process to be registered for the R&D Tax Concession in Australia. Research and development tax incentives are less generous in Finland, however other forms of public sector support are evident, such as for F1 to write a business plan and to fund market research in Europe. In all, R&D investments for 2004 were 3.5 per cent of GNP in Finland; firms account for 70 per cent of this and public sector 30 per cent.

Innovation speed

The CEO respondents were asked to list their three most successful products/ services identified in either Question 1 or 2. They were also asked, for each, how long it took their company to develop those products/services from inception to market (ie R&D cycle).

This provides an idea of the size and possible complexity of the product. Some of A1's developments have been undertaken by one or two people, while A2's ProductX was a team effort over two and a half years. Nevertheless, most of the R&D cycles are quite short when compared with products such as pharmaceuticals, medical equipment, computer hardware and even complex software such as SAP and Peoplesoft.

To incorporate an output measure of product innovation as a means of assessing the success of the product on the market, we asked the CEOs to estimate the proportion of their company's turnover being generated by the product innovations indicated. For this, F1 indicated that 10 per cent of their turnover came from product innovations; F2 earned 40 per cent; A1 earned 20 per cent and A2 earned 10 per cent. This measures the immediate impact of the product innovations developed. In a larger study, this can also be correlated with the number of innovations and the cycle times as indicated in questions such as the one above.

Table 12.4   Innovation speed

Company	F1	F2	A1	A2
Product/service	Communication server	Confidential	Security	Product Z
Months to develop	4	6	4	12
Product/service		Confidential	Storage	Product X
Months to develop		6	3	30
Product/service		Confidential	Unix*	
Months to develop		12	3	

Note: *Unix is an operating system used mainly for scientific and engineering work, as well as for servers running on the internet.

Informal Measures of Innovation

Many informal innovations explored in this study are impact indicators as we seek to gain a more in-depth picture of the involvement of staff and stakeholders in the innovation effort, as well as the impacts of innovation on individuals and associated groups. As a consequence, the impact indicators tend to be either internal or external. This has been identified with as many questions as possible.

Internal indicators   It is important in assessing the innovation effort to gain information on the extent of involvement of staff in the innovation process. Most innovation is dependent on a creative process. It is then useful to gather data on perceptions on the creativity of staff in the company.

Table 12.5 displays the answers to the question asked of the respondents, of estimating the proportion of staff in the company they would place in each of three levels of creativity.

The responses here are most interesting where the Australian CEOs don't see their staff as being nearly as creative as the Finnish CEOs, despite strong similarities between the companies. For instance, F2 and A2 would seem similar in their product profiles and the core competencies of their companies, but differ markedly in their response. A2 is the oldest, larger than the Finnish companies and is the most formal of the four firms. For new start-ups (such as F1 and F2) it seems quite natural to emphasize the creativity of their personnel. These firms also typically outsource services such as accounting, so as to keep their administrative staff as small as possible. Analysis of results such as this could take up a chapter on their own.

A more concrete and direct informal innovation question relates to the proportion of staff involved in the product, process and non-technological innovations. This is also an impact question. For this both F1 and F2 indicated 100 per cent of staff were involved in their innovations, while only 20 per cent of A1's staff and 90 per cent of A2's staff were involved in their innovation process.

The time staff actually spend on the innovation process is also an important impact indicator. We asked what proportion of employees' time is

Table 12.5   Percentage of creative staff

Company	F1	F2	A1	A2
Not creative	0	0	40	30
Reasonably creative	0	0	60	50
Very creative	100	100	10	20

spent on innovative activities. The responses varied widely with F1's staff spending 15 per cent of their time on innovation, F2's staff spending 100 per cent of their time, A1's staff spending only 10 per cent and A2's spending 50 per cent of their time on innovation. Again the results are consistent with the type of firms, with F2 and A2 as software developers requiring extensive involvement of staff in idea generation and product development. These questions provide a better assessment of staff involvement in the innovation process than nomination of R&D personnel or R&D expenditure for these smaller firms. This is not only because they are impact rather than just input questions, but that they more effectively piece together the innovation process jigsaw. For instance A1 has no R&D personnel nominated, but 20 per cent (more than three staff members) of staff are involved in the identified innovations, while A2 has three R&D personnel nominated, but 90 per cent (over 12 staff members) are involved in their innovations. A1 is a services, consulting and technical assistance-based company, while A2 is a software development company which relies on staff involvement in innovations and a level of creativity from them.

It should be clear that an amalgam of questions has been utilized in this study to help build a picture of the innovation process in the companies concerned. The next step was to break down involvement in the stages of the innovation/commercialization process. It was deemed valuable to also

Table 12.6   Number of staff involved in each stage of the innovation process

	Innovation	No. of people involved		
		Inception	Development	Market launch-commercialization
F1	1. Bearer interface	2	3	2
	2. Proprietary TCP/IP*	3	2	2
F2	1. Not disclosed	3	3	3
	2. Not disclosed	3	3	3
	3. Not disclosed	3	3	3
A1	1. Security	5	3	3
	2. Storage	5	3	3
	3. Unix	5	3	3
A2	1. Product Z	3	2	2
	2. Product X	2	4	5
	3. Training	2	5	–

Note: *Transmission control protocol/internet protocol.

ask the CEOs to select the three most important innovations achieved in the last 12 months and for each how many staff were involved in each stage of the innovation process.

It is of interest here that a modal response of three people was provided by the companies for most of the innovations, despite the difference in each company's employee numbers. This suggests there is a core group who 'case manage' the innovations from inception to market in each company. As small firms, functional distinctions are yet to emerge. As we will explore in more depth later in this chapter, the companies are largely project based, and it is the cross-functional project teams which would pre-dominate in the R&D process. So the personnel are not R&D, marketing or management personnel as such, they are fulfilling the multitude of roles that are required of staff in innovative small firms.

The IT industry, as with most high-technology industries, while it has somewhat less reliance on patents for maintaining intellectual property rights, relies heavily on the intellectual capital of its people. While the previous questions incorporated aspects of intellectual capital, the following question extends this probing into which skills are most critical to the innovative effort. Again, the Likert scales are designed for larger scale surveys than this exploratory study of four so it is included by way of example. This relates largely to *internal impact indicators* for the firm (with customer interaction the only item which could be argued lies across both internal and external camps). In this question we asked: 'How important is it for your staff to possess the following characteristics?'

The means and responses are provided here to indicate the variability of responses. For example A1's CEO indicated in an earlier question that only 10 per cent of his staff are very creative. The response in this question also indicates that he does not expect them to be creative, or entrepreneurial

Table 12.7   Staff possession of skills useful in innovation

Company	F1	F2	A1	A2	Means
Creativity	5	5	2	5	4.25
Entrepreneurial behaviour	5	3	2	5	3.75
Problem-solving ability	5	5	5	5	5.00
Independent action	4	3	4	5	4.00
Planning skills	4	3	4	4	3.75
Teamwork skills	4	4	5	5	4.50
Self-motivation	5	5	4	5	4.75
Technical skills	4	5	5	3.5	4.38
Customer interaction	3	4	5	5	4.25

(that's his job). Each of the items in this scale emanate from other skills studies conducted. One of the authors is conducting a Government funded national study on skills requirements in the Biotechnology industry using these categories (amongst others) in the questionnaire.

Communication techniques are very important in the internal management of a business when it comes to taking an idea through to fruition. The type of communication techniques used need to reflect the level of creativity, cooperation and fluidity necessary for innovations to emerge. This is particularly important for project-based companies such as these. It is not surprising then that on a five-point Likert scale of importance (5 = very important), face-to face was rated most highly (Mean = 4.88), electronic next (Mean = 4.38), telephone not as important (Mean = 3.38), tailing to meetings (Mean = 3.25) and paper (Mean = 2.25).

Incorporating Internal and External Indicators

Just as companies don't stand alone in their innovative efforts, innovation doesn't stand alone as an objective for any company. The purpose of innovation is profitability and achieving and maintaining a competitive position for the firm. It is then appropriate to question CEOs about the basis of their competitiveness as this will be linked strongly to the innovation processes within the firm. This creates also a nexus between the input and output. Accordingly the question was asked: 'What would you see as the basis of the competitiveness of this company?' The responses were indicated as: F1 – Innovativeness – entrepreneurship – communication skills – technological know-how; F2 – Technical skills – problem solving skills; A1 – Approachable, competent, customer-focused, quality and experience; A2 – Competencies built up over time through understanding of topic/area – size, agility, flexibility, quick reactions. The responses have a competency/skills focus, some internal, some external. The responses in this question also verify other quantitative questions as the one below, with regard to skills and core competencies in the firm.

External Indicators

More information can be gained about the innovation process when questioning respondents about where their innovations emerge from. In viewing the responses to this question, there is strong evidence of a market pull effect in the innovation process of each of the companies:

F1   Problem – boundary conditions analysis – research for existing solutions – initial suggestion – team session – new suggestion – refinement;

F2   They consider their innovation 'customer secrets';
A1   Market needs – current skills sets. Requirements normally filter from
        business development;
A2   80 per cent driven by market/customer feedback, 20 per cent inter-
        nally generated – generally extension of products/services.

Given this market-pull effect and the consequent importance of *external
relationships* in the market including customers, suppliers and collaborators, the picture is incomplete without questions relating to these relationships. A simple question: 'How many companies do you currently
collaborate with in developing/providing your products/services?' – was
then asked. This could be considered an impact question. Number of collaborators for F1 stood at three; for F2 it was five; for A1 it was three and
for A2 it was two.

The firms certainly don't operate in isolation according to this response.
However a simple question such as this needs to be backed up by further
probing questions to gain a more detailed understanding of the situation.
Hence, another more direct impact question was used to gain an indication of
the importance of various external relationships. This question enquired into
how important different relational forms are to the firm's innovation effort?

Customer involvement is obviously important in terms of involvement
and feedback. A more surprising result is the central tendency of the
importance of inter-firm collaboration. Partial explanation of this may
come from the age of the firms, with three of the four firms being very
young. New firms tend to concentrate more on their products and product
development, as they are seeking to establish in their market. An external
focus, including building networks is more likely when the firm is more
established in its market. This may also be a sectoral phenomenon, as the
IT industry is highly competitive, with low survival rates. Where products
can be developed in-house (as the low importance of ability to outsource

Table 12.8   The importance of relational forms to the innovation effort

Company	F1	F2	A1	A2	Means
Customer involvement	4	5	3	5	4.25
Customer feedback	5	5	4	5	4.75
Inter-firm collaboration	3	4	2	3	3.00
Relationships with Government	2	1	2	1.5	1.63
Arms-length negotiations	4	4	2	4.5	3.63
Ability to outsource	2	1	2	1	1.50

tends to indicate) the need to build relationships with other firms as part of the innovation effort is less ostensible.

Organizational Structure

Many of the questions asked have been structured ones. This is particularly important as the majority of studies on innovation are quantitative and we are seeking to enhance such studies whether they be independent studies or the myriad of national and international studies which feed into large databases such as those of the European Union (EU) and OECD. However, the final question included in this study, considered important by the researchers, required the respondents to draw their current organizational structure at present. This would be considered an input question as the organizational structure and innovation focus for a firm should have a close, possibly causal relationship. The diagrams are provided below.

It is evident from the diagrams above that these are project-based companies. This is the nature of the IT industry, reflected in the structure of many of the firms operating in the industry. The broad project focus is also indicative of an orientation towards economies of scope as the firms seek to extend their product range, in many cases through collaborations with other firms and facilitated by varying degrees of outsourcing of some of their non-core business processes.

DISCUSSION

The internal environment of the firm interacts constantly and unwaveringly with the external environment to influence the competitive position of the firm. The innovation process contributes to and is impacted by this interaction. In analysing the informal innovation process, beyond the traditional measures of innovation, those factors, which are attributable more to small innovative firms than larger ones, not only do input, output and impact factors need to be understood, but the influencing factors internal and external to the firm. This exploratory study, which will be followed by a more comprehensive quantitative cross-national study, has sought to identify the important internal and external factors which influence and support the innovative effort of small firms which are not captured in the traditional measures of innovation, particularly those identified by the OECD.

In terms of internal factors, Motwani et al. (1999) gave guidance on the need to create internal management systems and structures which themselves support the creation of a work environment that encourages individual initiative and entrepreneurial behaviour in a general work

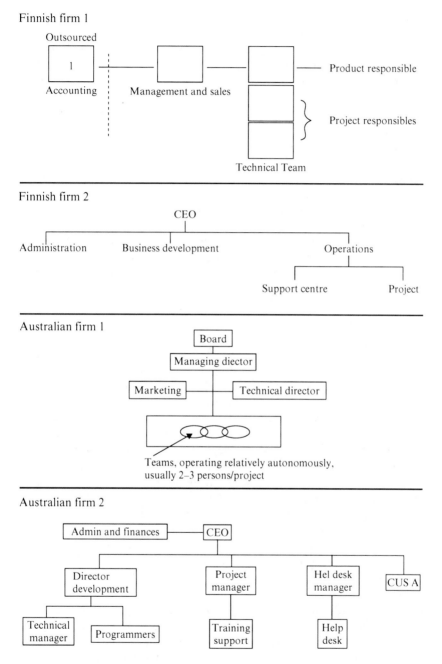

Figure 12.1   Organizational charts for each of the four cases

culture. So it was critical to incorporate measures of the level of creativity within the firm. This was measured by the proportion of staff involved in the product, process and non-technological innovations, as well as the time staff actually spend on the innovation process. Innovative firms such as software developers require extensive involvement of staff in idea generation and product development. These questions provide a better assessment of staff involvement in the innovation process than nomination of R&D personnel or R&D expenditure for these smaller firms.

Staff possession of skills useful in innovation relates largely to *internal impact indicators* for the firm (with customer interaction the only item which could be argued lies across both internal and external camps). It reflects the intellectual assets as well as the social and human capital available to the firm, incorporating diverse skills such as: creativity, entrepreneurial behaviour, problem solving ability, independent action, planning skills, teamwork skills, self motivation, technical skills, and customer interaction. The utilization of these skills is an important aspect of involvement in the stages of the innovation/commercialization process, and reflects the product development stages facing IT companies. This will vary by industry sector, with biotechnology and life sciences firms facing much longer and more complex pipelines (Hine and Kapeleris, 2006). In this study the stages are simplified to: innovation; inception; development; market launch-commercialization. This also differentiates the commercialization process from the innovation and product development process. For small firms also, their personnel are not R&D, marketing or management personnel as such. They are fulfilling the multitude of roles that are required of staff in innovative small firms.

Innovation speed (that is how long it takes to develop new products/ services from inception to market, the product development or R&D cycle), is critical to competitiveness and indicative of the firm's efficiency in bringing new ideas to fruition. In a Schumpeterian perspective, an innovation will only be recognized when it gets to market. It then needs to be novel when it arrives at market or else is not really an innovation as it will be unlikely to have any economic impact. Innovation speed also indicates the effectiveness of the informal innovation approach over formal innovation.

Success in terms of the outputs of the innovative process needs to be measured beyond the number of new products available on the market. The proportion of your company's turnover being generated by the product innovations indicated should also be measured. This measures the immediate impact of the product innovations developed. In a larger study, this can also be correlated with the number of innovations and the cycle times as indicated by the innovative speed questions. One additional suggestion to emanate from this study is to incorporate measures of what could be conceived to be failure. Innovation is a high risk strategy, with many ideas, prototype products, code, and entire programs either not reaching the market or failure upon release onto the market. Understanding the failure rates as well as the successes in the innovation process will inform us on efficiencies, resource utilization, corporate resilience, change and strategic direction of respondent firms. Failure can inform us as much as success, as the lessons of failure often lead to future success.

The second factor identified by Motwani et al. (1999) is the need for a structure for managing innovation. This adds formal structure to the creative effort with the purpose of bringing innovation to fruition. Idea generation is only a first step in the innovation process. The two fit together to create an innovative organization and an indicator of the elements internal to the innovative small firm that support the innovative effort.

In this study we looked at the organizational structure of the respondent firms. While the structure can be viewed as the basis of the internal workings of the firm, for innovative firms their structure will also be indicative of embeddedness in support networks of customers, suppliers and collaborating firms. The collaborations a firm is involved in also influence the organizational structure and design of that firm. The organizational structure is considered an input factor, as the organizational structure and innovation focus for a firm should have a close, possibly causal relationship. The structure, such as the project based structure evident in the four cases in this study, will provide insights into the management of the innovation process in these firms. Organizational structure is often reflective of existing relationships of firms. The organizational structure is often not formalized until the firm reaches a certain size, where scale requires a solution to communication and co-ordination problems.

The organizational boundaries of innovative small firms extend beyond their own employees. Customer, supplier and collaborator involvement in the innovation process, particularly of close to market developments as occur in the software development industry, are a source of innovation themselves. Where the traditional measures of innovation are internally focused, it is important to accept that the innovative small firm does not work in isolation. Hence knowing where innovations emerge from is fundamental to understanding the innovation, communication, network and idea generation processes in and of the firm. It is not surprising that there is strong evidence of a market pull effect in the innovation process, particularly in this market-oriented industry, with short product development cycles, customer involvement in the product development process and customer feedback on products (often beta products) seem to represent the most important relational form for these firms. Arms length negotiations with other industry players and inter-firm collaborations would seem to play a role, though their importance will be tested in further quantitative studies. The medium of communication, though again affected by the industry sector under observation can provide vital information on the channels through which collaborations are carried on.

Many informal innovation explored in this study are impact indicators as we seek to gain a more in-depth picture of the involvement of staff and stakeholders in the innovation effort, as well as the impacts of innovation on individuals and groups associated. As a consequence the impact indicators tend to be either internal or external. This has been identified with as many questions as possible.

In summary, the measures of informal innovation in innovative small firms could be categorized under the headings identified in the literature and in this study. Table 12.9 provides a structure to this categorization as a guide to future research, which is certainly needed in this area. The table also draws together factors and measures, all of which are in use currently in studies; however, to complete the jigsaw of the innovative process in innovative small firms these outcomes of each of these partial studies needs to be combined into a more comprehensive analysis applicable to this specific important sector of national economies.

There is certainly some overlap for a number of the measures, however this simply serves to underline the complexity of the innovative process and the supporting elements of this process.

The objectives of this study were; to highlight the inadequacies of the current innovation measurement approaches for small high-tech companies, and to consider and explore new techniques for assessing innovation in these firms. As an exploratory study using four cases, no hypothesis tests were undertaken and no proof given. However, the evidence is extensive that the traditional measures of innovation have limited application to these predominantly young, high-tech small companies. Their contribution to their sector and to national economies will be underestimated using these limited measurement tools.

The alternative assessments of their innovativeness offered tell a more extensive story with regard to their creativity, idea generation, relationships outside the company, communication techniques and organizational structure and design. Even in this exploratory study the responses to questions can be collated to paint a picture of innovation in the small firm, as well as extracting far more extensive information about the informal innovation occurring within these innovative small firms that would otherwise go unseen.

The extreme diversity of innovation processes at both industry and firm level suggests that a wider range of models, approaches and methodologies should be employed. The mainstream practice based on the idea that firms face only one problem of innovation, namely the scale and finance of R&D,

Table 12.9   *Measures to capture formal and informal innovation in entrepreneurial small firms*

	Internal management factors influencing innovation	External relationships influencing innovation
Input	• R&D Personnel • R&D Expenditure • Proportion of time staff actually spend on the innovation process • Staff possession of skills useful in innovation	• Relational forms used in the innovation effort (customer feedback, customer involvement etc)
Output	• Major new products/services • Improvements in existing products/services • New production/service methods • Number of new products over a time period • New products to initiated ideas • Proportion of firm's turnover from recently launched products/services	• Number of new customers and suppliers over a time period
Impact	• Advanced management techniques • Innovation speed (time for development at each stage) • Percentage of staff who are classified as creative • Proportion of staff involved in product/process/non-technological innovations • Major elements of organizational structure	• Communication techniques used (frequency/effectiveness) • Number, type, longevity and fruitfulness of collaborations • Where innovations emerge from • Mode of innovation generation (market pull or technology push) • Technology adoption and adaptation versus internal generation

is not a satisfactory starting point from the viewpoint of smaller firms. Research and development expenditure is important but measures only an input, which may have little to do with innovation outcomes. The varied nature of innovative activities and their sectoral specificity have been underlined in an extensive literature, which has confirmed the existence of a multiplicity of closely interdependent sources of innovation.

General statistics on innovation are certainly needed for policymaking, comparisons and societal planning, but more individualized, tailor-made metrics are needed in the case of smaller firms. At the policy level, a more proactive approach to encourage and support smaller companies in their innovative activities should be exercized – with the accent on relatively inexpensive and accessible information and advice. It is evident that in the case of smaller firms the principal barriers to important formal collaboration relate to lack of trust and the identification of suitable partners. In the face of such attitudinal constraints it is difficult to formulate meaningful policy measures.

Methodologically, in addition to standardized, quantitative metrics, qualitative and case-based research efforts are welcome in the diverse population of small businesses. Due to the variation of factors across the stages and nature of innovative activities, the measurement philosophy may be very different for large and small firms. Furthermore, because innovation is fundamentally uncertain and risky, its measurement will necessarily remain imperfect. Yet, by accepting the informal nature of the innovation activities conducted by small firms and by exploring the independent, dependent and moderating variables associated with these, the broader form of innovation and innovativeness as a management and research challenge will be recognized and appreciated.

The work undertaken in this small exploratory study, led the authors inevitably into the major study employing representative sampling. This study is beyond the brief of this chapter as it is more confirmatory in nature and design.

CONCLUSION

Clearly there are some advantages of cross-national comparisons and collaboration such as matching two data sets, comparing and contrasting contexts, analysis of variance, a truly international perspective – triangulation. There are also some disadvantages of cross-national comparisons and collaboration, such as co-ordinating communication, language barriers and varied interpretations, differing academic calendars, and building directly comparable data sets, to name but a few.

REFERENCES

Aces, Z. and B. Audrecht (1988), 'Innovation in large and small firms: an empirical analysis', *The American Economic Review*, **78** (September), 678–90.
Autere, Jussi (2005), 'The impact of referents on entrepreneurship – growth of small and medium-sized software companies in three Finnish regions', doctoral dissertation for the Helsinki University of Technology, Department of Industrial Management.

Banerjee, P. (2003), 'Some indicators of dynamic technological competencies: understanding of Indian software managers', *Technovation*, **23**(7), 593–602.

Brower, M. (1998), 'Firm efficiency in innovation: comment on van Dijk et al.', *Small Business Economics*, **11**, 391–93.

Crone, M. (2002), 'The Irish indigenous software industry: explaining the development of a knowledge-intensive industry cluster in a less favoured region', presentation to the 42nd Congress of the European Regional Science Association (ESRA 2002), Dortmund.

Foxall, G. and P. Hackett (1994), 'Styles of managerial creativity: a comparison of adaptation – innovation in the United Kingdom, Australia and the United States', *British Journal of Management*, **5**, 85–100.

Ganzach, Y. (1993), 'Theory and configurality in expert and layperson judgement', *Journal of Applied Psychology*, **79**, 439–48.

Harrison, R., C.M. Mason and P. Girling (2004), 'Financial bootstrapping and venture development in the software industry', *Entrepreneurship and Regional Development*, **16**, 307–33.

Helfat, C.E. and M.A. Peteraf (2003), 'The dynamic resource-based view: capability lifecycles', *Strategic Management Journal*, **24**, 997–1010.

Hietala, J., M. Maula, J. Autere, C. Lassenius, N. Kari and E. Autio (2002), *Finnish Software Product Business: Results from the National Software Industry Survey 2002*, Espoo: Centre for Expertise for Software Product Business, Helsinki University of Technology.

Hine, D. and A. Miettinen (2001), 'Informal innovation: measuring the hidden role of small business', presentation to the 46th World Small Business Conference, Brisbane, Queensland, Australia, July 2001.

Hine, D. and J. Kapeleris (2006), *Innovation and Entrepreneurship in Biotechnology: An International Perspective*, Cheltenham, UK, and Northampton, MA, USA: Edward Elgar.

Hoopes, D.G., T.L. Madsen and G. Walker (2003), 'Guest editors' introduction to the special issue: why is there a resource-based view? Toward a theory of competitive heterogeneity', *Strategic Management Journal*, **24**, 889–902.

Mathews, J.A. (2002), 'A resource-based view of Schumpeterian economics dynamics', *Journal of Evolutionary Economics*, **12**, 29–54.

McGrath, Rita G., I.C. MacMillan and Sari Scheinberg (1992), 'Elitists, risk-takers, and rugged individualists? An exploratory analysis of cultural differences between entrepreneurs and non-entrepreneurs', *Journal of Business Venturing*, **7**, 115–35.

Menkveld, A. and A. Thurik (1999), 'Firm size and efficiency in innovation: reply', *Small Business Economics*, **12**, 87–101.

Miettinen, A. (1998), 'Accuracy of self-rated business performance and its meaning', in Hans-Jobst Pleitner (Herausgegeber), *Renaissanceder KMU in einer globalisierten Wirtschaft*, Beiträge Zu den Rencontres de St-Gall.

Miettinen, A., R. Altpere and A. Lehtomaa (2000), 'Emerging Estonian entrepreneurship – a decade later', paper presented at the 11th Nordic Conference on Small Business Management, Århus, Denmark, June 2000.

Motwani, J., T. Danbridge, J. Jiang and K. Soderqvist (1999), 'Managing innovation in French small and medium-sized enterprises', *Journal of Small Business Management*, **37**(2), 106–14.

Nowak, M.J. and C.E. Grantham (2000), 'The virtual incubator: managing human capital in the software industry', *Research Policy*, **29**, 125–34.

Organisation for Economic Co-operation and Development (OECD) (1997), 'Report on Patents and Innovation in the international context', OECD/GO(97)210, Paris: OECD.

Podsakoff, P. and D. Organ (1986), 'Self reports in organizational research: problems and prospects', *Journal of Management*, **12**, 531–44.

Punch, K.F. (1998), *Introduction to Social Research*, London: Sage.

Quinn, J.B., J.J. Baruch and K.E. Zien (1996), 'Software-based innovation', *Sloan Management Review*, Summer, 11–24.

Ragin, C. (1987), *The Comparative Method: Moving Beyond Qualitative and Quantitative Strategies*, Berkeley, CA: University of California.

Ragin, C. and D. Zaret (1983), 'Theory and method in comparative research: two strategies', *Social Forces*, **61**, 731–54.

Rangone, A. (1999), 'A resource-based approach to strategy analysis in small-medium sized enterprises', *Small Business Economics*, **12**(3), 233–48.

Romijn, H. and M. Albaladejo (2002), 'Determinants of innovation capability in small electronics and software firms in South-east England', *Research Policy*, **31**(3), 1053–67.

Roper, S. (1999), 'Under-reporting of R&D in small firms: the impact on international R&D comparisons', *Small Business Economics*, **12**(12), 131–35.

Sebora, T., E. Hartman and C. Tower (1994), 'Innovative activity in small businesses: competitive context and organizational level', *Journal of Engineering and Technology Management*, **11**(1), 253–72.

Smelser, N. (1976), *Comparative Methods in the Social Sciences*, Englewood Cliffs, NJ: Prentice-Hall.

Sutcliffe, K.M. and G.P. Huber (1998), 'Firm and industry as determinants of executive perceptions of the environment', *Strategic Management Journal*, **19**, 793–817.

Tesch, R. (1990), *Qualitative Research: Analysis Types and Software Tools*, Basingstoke: Falmer.

Tidd, J., J. Bessant and K. Pavitt (2001), *Managing Innovation: Integrating Technological, Market and Organizational Change*, 2nd edn, Chicheaster: Wiley & Sons Ltd.

Tyrväinen, P., J. Warsta and V. Seppänen (2004), 'Toimialakehitys ohjelmistoteollisuuden vauhdit-tajana', 'Industry sector development speeding up software business', *Teknologiakatsaus 151/2004*, TEKES, Helsinki.

Wiklund, J. and D. Shepherd (2004), 'Knowledge-based resources, entrepreneurial orientation and the performance of small and medium-sized businesses', *Strategic Management Journal*, **24**, 1307–14.

Yammarino, F.J. and L.E. Atwater (1993), 'Understanding self-perception accuracy: implications for human resource management', *Human Resource Management*, **32**, 231–47.

APPENDIX 12.1   AUSTRALIAN QUESTIONNAIRE

Informal Innovations Questionnaire

1. How many *new products and/or services* has your company brought to market in the last 12 months? (Major product innovation)_____ Products/Services
2. How many *major improvements* have you made to your company's existing products and/or services in the last 12 months? (Incremental product innovation) _____ Products/Services
3. How many *new methods* of production and/or service provision has your company implemented in the last 12 months?
   _____ New production methods
   _____ New methods of service provision
4. Have you *implemented* any of the following in the last 12 months? (Tick box for yes)
   ☐ Advanced management technique
   ☐ Change in corporate structure
   ☐ Change in corporate strategy

Innovation Speed

5. List the three *most successful* of your products/services identified in either Question 1 or 2. For each, *how long* did it take your company to develop these products/services from inception to market? (R&D Cycle)
   1. Product/service _____ months to develop
   2. Product/service _____ months to develop
   3. Product/service _____ months to develop
6. Estimate the proportion of your company's *turnover being generated by the innovations* indicated in Questions 1 and 2 (% of company turnover).

Formal/traditional Innovation Measures

7. How many *patents* does your company currently hold?
   _____ Patents for Australia
   _____ Patents for Overseas
8. How many *patent applications* does your company currently have submitted?
   _____ Patents for Australia
   _____ Patents for Overseas

9.   How many *nominated Research and Development personnel* do you have currently employed in this company? (eg R&D Manager, research scientist)
10. On your Profit and Loss Statement for the last financial year, what proportion of your *Expenditure is dedicated to R&D*?
11. *How long* have you been calculating R&D expenditure in your financial statements?
     ____ Months
12. What was the *motivation* for including R&D in your financial statements?
13. Which *Government schemes* are you aware of which offer support for R&D and innovation?

Informal Measures

14. Estimate the proportion of staff in this company you would place in each of the following levels of *creativity*.
     A. Not creative B. Reasonably creative C. Very creative (% of staff)
15. What proportion of your staff have been *involved in the innovations* indicated in Questions 1, 2, 3 and 4
16. What proportion of these employees *time is spent on innovative activities* (on average)?
17. Select the three *most important innovations* (from your response in Questions 1, 2 and 3) you have achieved in the last 12 months. For each *how many* of your staff have been involved in each stage of the innovation process?
             Innovation   Inception   Development
             Market launch-commercialization
18. Give *examples* of how your innovations have emerged:

19. How important are each of the following communication techniques to the *internal management* of your business? (5-point Likert Scale questions)
     Face-to-face (1 on 1)
     Paper (eg memos)
     Electronic (eg email)

Telephone

Meetings

20. How important are each of the following communication techniques to the management of your *external relationships* such as customers, suppliers and collaborators? (5-point Likert Scale questions)

21. How important is it for your staff to possess the following *characteristics*? (5-point Likert Scale questions)

Creativity

Entrepreneurial behaviour

Problem-solving ability

Independent action

Planning skills

Teamwork skills

Self motivation

Technical skills

Customer interaction

22. What would you see as the *basis of the competitiveness* of this company?

23. How many companies do you currently *collaborate* with in developing/providing your products/services?

24. How important are each of the following in your *innovation effort*? (5-point Likert Scale questions)

Customer involvement

Customer feedback

Inter-firm collaboration

Relationships with Government

Arms length negotiations

Ability to outsource

Demographics and profile

25. How many employees do you have *currently* in this company?___
Employees

26. How many employees did you have *12 months ago*? ____ Employees

27. How long has this company been *operating*? ____ Years ____ Months

28. What was your *turnover* for the last 3 months? $____

29. What was your turnover for the same *3-month period 12 months ago*? $____

30. Did you? (Tick one box):
☐ Establish this company
☐ Take over from another owner
☐ Inherit the company
☐ Other Specify ____

31. What is the *main* product/service your company provides?

32. How many *different products and services* do you provide to the market?

_____ Products _____ Services

33. What proportion of your products/services do you *export*?

34. How many *full-time equivalent employees* do you have in each of the following categories in your company?

Professional/Senior Management

Technical/Trade

Financial/Accounting

Marketing/Sales

Administrative/Clerical

Unskilled

35. Could you please provide/or *draw your organizational structure* at present.

13. Marketing research for isolated SMEs

Mary F. Hazeldine and Morgan P. Miles

INTRODUCTION

This chapter illustrates the application of marketing research for small and medium-sized businesses (SMEs) in rural areas. We take the perspective of how SMEs might most effectively use simple marketing research techniques to more fully understand their customers' implicit and explicit needs to create more profitable marketing relationships (Gummesson, 2002). This enhanced understanding of the SME market, the associated consumer needs, and its competitors, is often a path for an SME to gain a competitive advantage. Marketing research is necessary for developing and promoting products and services to meet customer needs.

This chapter is organized as follows. Section one presents qualitative and quantitative research methods that may be useful. Section two suggests how to segment markets for better target marketing. Based on the first two sections, the last section provides insights into the development of e-commerce to expand market opportunities for rural SMEs. It is anticipated that this chapter can stimulate further interest in developing a richer understanding of the marketing issues that specifically impact rural SMEs.

MARKETING RESEARCH – OPPORTUNITIES AND LIMITATIONS

For all businesses the basic purpose of marketing research is to help manage the risk of marketing and strategic decision making. For SMEs facing resource constraints, the risks associated with a bad decision could be catastrophic. There is a growing body of research that suggests that firms that can effectively discover and leverage organizational and customer knowledge are more innovative and tend to perform better (Darroch and McNaughton, 2002, 2003). Simple, effective marketing research is a step towards an SME transforming itself into a knowledge management organization (Darroch, 2003).

Qualitative Research

Businesses can use qualitative research to gain insights into their customers' explicit and latent needs. Focus groups are a type of qualitative research that help businesses clarify and define problems that leads to exploration of possible solutions to those problems (Morgan, 1998; Malhotra, 2004). Focus group research is the most important type of qualitative research. Many researchers consider focus groups synonymous with qualitative research. Hundreds of research facilities around the world conduct focus groups. For some market research firms, focus group research is the only research service they provide (Malhotra, 2004).

Focus groups are composed of 8–12 customers led by a trained moderator, and tend to take an investment of one to two hours of time. If the business needs to find a moderator, contacting the local or regional University's business school, adult education programme, or government sponsored small business management development centre should enable the business to subcontract a skilled moderator. Table 13.1 shows the basic decisions that should be made before conducting focus groups (Moran and Krueger, 1998).

The first meeting with the moderator will focus on the business' main set of issues or objectives. Typical objectives may be to discover the explicit or latent needs of customers, to see how the business can improve its products/services offerings, to find out what product attributes are important to our customers, or to uncover any criticisms customers may have regarding the

Table 13.1   Basic decisions

---

1. Define the objectives of the project
2. Identify the role of the project's sponsor
3. Identify personnel and staffing resources
4. Develop the timeline for the project
5. Determine who the participants will be
6. Write the questions in for the discussion guide
7. Develop a participant recruitment plan
8. Set the location, date, and time for the focus group
9. Design the analysis plan
10. Specify the elements of the final report

Source: Moran and Krueger (1998).

business' products/services. The moderator should prepare a discussion guide. The business will be responsible for asking customers to participate. Other arrangements needed will include a tape recorder and/or video camera, a conference room, and refreshments. The business must also decide if the customers should be paid for their time. The moderator will transcribe the tape and prepare a report. Some limitations are that the interpretation of the findings of any focus group tends to be subjective and the moderator must be highly skilled to correctly interpret the findings. In addition, the selection of group members to interview is critical. It is very important to try to select participants that reflect the concerns, tastes and preferences of the target market.

Another type of qualitative research is using the snowball approach to conduct depth interviews. Like focus groups, depth interviews are an unstructured (or semi-structured), direct and highly interactive way to obtain information. Depth interviews are one-on-one chats with selected customers. As with focus groups, the moderator prepares a discussion guide. Snowballing is one method to facilitate depth interviews. Snow balling entails approaching one or two leading customers and ask each individually if they could spare 30 minutes for a discussion of some issues facing the business and could suggest one or two other businesses that would have similar needs that are not currently customers. This approach enriches the firm's knowledge base and often helps identify new prospects through the snowballing effect of having customers identify other potential customers. Offering discounts on the next order should enhance their interest in participation. The limitations of depth interviews are the same as for focus groups.

One place where focus groups and/or depth interviews can be performed is at a trade show. There are two kinds of trade shows: horizontal and vertical. The horizontal trade show contains companies from different industries, whereas the vertical trade show contains companies from the same industry. Chambers of Commerce in rural areas often tend to host horizontal business expos during the year to promote local SMEs. The Chamber can provide a list of expected attendees with their profiles, such as job titles. The small business should invite its customers to attend as well. A trade show is a good venue to boost sales for products, identify potential customers, conduct competitive intelligence, and conduct research. Expenses include the cost to participate, the cost of the exhibit, and pre-show advertising/direct mail. Asking customers to participate in a focus group during the trade show is an excellent use of time. In addition, for many SMEs it may be much more efficient to combine efforts with other firms to compile a database of mutually useful information about customers, suppliers, and other relevant stakeholders.

Quantitative Research

Survey research in the United States (US) is almost synonymous with quantitative research. According to Chakrapanie (1998), the steps needed to carry out survey research are:

- Define the project's objectives.
- Define the target population.
- Decide on the length and type of interview (in person, by mail, by telephone).
- Set the sample size (how many current/former customers, what margin of error will be allowed).
- Define the sample selection procedures (for example, stratify the sample into customer size and sample 100 from each category).
- Write the questionnaire (for example, a mail survey is different from a telephone survey). That may typically include:
  o respondents' demographics;
  o firm size;
  o critical decision factors;
  o what future issues are relevant to the firm and its customers.
- Administer and tabulate the findings.
- Interpret the findings.

The survey research limitation is that it requires specialized and technical knowledge to develop the survey instrument and the sampling design. If a business is not familiar with survey research procedures, it may contact a firm or a college department specializing in this technique.

There are other quantitative ways to help small businesses thrive. For example, SMEs should develop a database of its customers and their purchases. This database can be leveraged to target coupons towards specific customer segments. For example, a dry cleaning business with a customer database can track the types of clothing items each customer brings in for cleaning. The dry cleaner can then send a coupon, for example, to a household that mainly brings in pants and men's shirts. The customer will be delighted that the dry cleaner is paying attention to what he/she is bringing in. Targeting specific discount coupons to customers based on their buying habits is an excellent way to build customer loyalty.

Another area a small business can consider is customer comment cards. The business should ask its customers to fill out these cards so that the business can better understand and serve its customers. If the small business has a customer database, it could send out customer satisfaction surveys via email, fax or post. To entice customers to fill out surveys and measure response, the business should offer price discount coupons.

USING MARKETING RESEARCH IN SEGMENTATION, TARGETING AND POSITIONING

Much of the past studies in marketing have focused on the problems and issues of large corporations, with much less interest in understanding best business practices in the small and medium sized enterprise. Likewise, there has been limited research into the practice of segmentation, targeting and positioning by SMEs. For example, Kinsey's (1987, p. 24) survey of SME manufacturers in Scotland found that their marketing practices were not highly sophisticated, with 80 per cent of the SMEs having 'no formal planning process' and, more importantly, marketing was perceived by the SME executives as a strategic weakness in 14 per cent of the firms. However, Peterson (1991), in one of the very few empirical studies of segmentation and SMEs, surveyed Small Business Institute client firms in the US and found that 73.8 per cent of small manufactures utilized some form of segmentation and target marketing. In addition, he found that SMEs tend to use demographic and geographic customer variables to segment the market, rather than the more sophisticated use of attitude towards the product or lifestyle variables. Brooksbank's (1999) subsequent work in New Zealand on the implementation of marketing capabilities in SMEs suggests that segmentation and positioning is a critical task for marketing success by SMEs. These studies suggest that while the sophistication of marketing research and planning is typically not high in SMEs, the SME executives tend to feel that marketing is important to the success of their firm.

Segmentation is even more important for SMEs than larger firms, as SMEs are often niche marketers with critical resource constraints. This suggests that SMEs must be both effective and efficient in marketing strategy and implementation. Kotler (1994) describes market segmentation in terms of three distinct phases: (1) **Segmentation** of customers into clusters with homogenous tastes and preferences; (2) market **Targeting**; and (3) product **Positioning** (or the **STP** framework). While there have been more recent conceptualizations of segmentation theory, there is no more useful construct for SMEs than the STP framework. The remainder of this discussion will follow that framework.

Segmentation

Dickson and Ginter's (1987) *Journal of Marketing* article on market segmentation and product positioning is still the most useful description of what segmentation really is and how it can be used. Dickson and Ginter (1987, p. 5) define market segmentation 'as a state of demand hetero-geneity such that the total market demand can be disaggregated into seg-ments with distinct demand functions'. This suggests for an SME, that the market is not homogenous but heterogeneous in terms of consumer tastes and preferences, and is made up of the aggregation of each individual's unique demand function. If the SME does an effective job in segmentation, then the segments will conform to Peter and Donnelly's (1989) **3-M** crite-ria: (1) the variables used to segment the market are **Measurable**, (2) the seg-mentation variables are **Meaningful**; and (3) the resulting segments are **Marketable**, where the firm can create some type of competitive advantage. Isolated, rural SMEs must understand how markets work and the mechan-ics of how to leverage segmentation to gain competitive advantage. In fact, isolated SMEs would do well to adhere to Nathan Bedford Forest's phil-osophy by getting to under-served markets first with the most value.

Targeting

Target marketing occurs after the market has been segmented. Customers are segmented, markets targeted, and products positioned. Once the seg-ments have been identified (clusters of customers who have homogenous tastes and preferences with respect to that specific product), the SME manager must determine if there is a mass market or multi-segments that exist in the market. Typically, SMEs follow a market niche strategy, suggest-ing that the SME would seek un-served or under-served market segments to position their offerings towards where the SME would have a competitive advantage. Segments that are relatively large tend to be more attractive to larger corporations and tend to be less attractive due to scale issues to SMEs.

Positioning

Positioning products is the last step in segmentation for SMEs. Effective posi-tioning requires that the SME seek out market segments where it either has or can develop a competitive advantage. Typically, SMEs will not attempt mass market cost leadership strategy, but adopt a niche marketing strategy using a differentiation to gain competitive advantage. Kotler (1994) suggests that an SME can differentiate its market offering through product, service, personnel, channel and image differentiation. Most SMEs suffer resource constraints, and competitive situations that require them to leverage some combination of these differentiation tools to enhance value to the customer. For example, while few SMEs local retailers can compete with the low prices offered by online retailers, they can offer a much higher level of service and much more personal attention.

SME Sources of Information

Sources of information for aiding SMEs to develop better marketing research, business plans, and business strategy are the following:

- Entrepreneur Magazine's *Start Your Own Business* is a useful book developed through 24 years of covering how small businesses conduct business. The topics include evaluating a business idea, conducting marketing research, choosing a business structure, creating a business plan, finding financing, accounting and taxes, e-commerce, and starting a home-based business. The appendices are filled with business resource information.
- Brooksbank's (1999) article discusses the theory and practice of marketing planning for small businesses. It provides a framework for plan development.
- Kinsey's (1987) paper deals with a pilot survey of marketing and a small manufacturing firm in Scotland. Kinsey examined pricing, promotion, distribution, and product policy. The study found that the dimensions of design, quality, reliable service, flexibility, close customer contact, and price are strengths of small business marketing; however, these strengths need to be more fully developed.
- Peterson's (1991) article addresses how target marketing is used by small businesses. The article provides a useful table of segmentation methods.

Marketing research and creating a knowledge management organization is simply about making better and more strategic decisions. Small and medium-sized enterprises who ignore their markets, their environment, their stakeholders and their other relevant competitors tend not to be able to sustain profitability over the long term. We suggest that managers of all SMEs use simple, but effective marketing research tools to reduce the risk of bad decisions.

Promotion by Working with Local Newspapers

Once customers have been researched and identified and their needs and wants are understood, local SMEs normally turn to the local newspapers to promote products and services. For SMEs the local newspaper is the best source of advertising. Gee (2005), a 30-year veteran newspaper advertising executive located in a US SME, offers suggestions for SMEs advertising in newspapers. Based on Gee (2005) and the Newspaper Advertising Bureau (2005), the following principles and rules will be helpful to SMEs planning to promote business through the newspaper medium.

Consistency

A small advertiser using the local newspaper will use two types of advertising. The first is institutional or image advertising and the second is product advertising, which most retailers will use. In both cases consistency in advertising is most important. Regardless of the budget, consistency rules – repetition of the message and consistency of style and image are very important. Every time a message is seen it has been reinforced by preceding messages. The impact of a non targeted 'hit and miss' campaign is diminished if it is not reinforced in the public eye.

Budgeting

The local newspaper has representatives who call on the advertiser and provide services for the advertiser. Budgeting can be critical. A small advertiser may not know where to start. To make it easier, national retail magazines publish lists of business categories and the percentage of gross that each category of business averages. Retail business may spend an average 2–5 per cent of gross sales on advertising. Of course, these are averages and only a starting place. Telling the newspaper representative what the budget is in advance will help create an appropriate programme for the business. Hiding the budget from the media sales person may cost more in the long run. Specials and discounts can be used better if planned for.

Services

Most newspapers will do the layouts and write copy for the advertiser. The advertiser generally has to provide information and sometimes art work for the ads. If no product specific art is available, the newspaper has access to an art service for the advertiser. In larger newspapers there is a creative services department that can create custom ads from scratch with minimal input from the advertiser. Even an entire campaign can be developed, typically at a modest extra cost. If custom art is required this department can create it for an hourly fee. This can be costly for a small advertiser but may be worth it depending on the need. Many advertisers want to create advertisements on their own computer so they get exactly what they want. However, the newspaper may have restrictions on how they can receive the advertisement by email or by CD-ROM. This is due to the difference in programs and systems used to read them. A call ahead will put the advertiser and the newspaper on the same track.

The creation of an effective retail ad has a time honoured formula that has yet to be improved on. While any rule can be broken, these procedures give consistently good results. The following are rules an advertiser should follow:

- Use a benefit headline (answer the question 'What's in it for me?').
- The proposition is key.
- Use a dominant piece of art showing the product or service.
- Use descriptive copy that is direct and clear.
- Price the item – priced products consistently out-perform non-priced products without regard to how competitive the price is.
- Give complete information. Opening hours, address and phone number are minimum bits of information.

It is important to note that these rules apply to all products and services across all industries.

IMPACT OF E-COMMERCE

E-commerce is another avenue for SMEs, enabling companies to reach a wider audience. Gaining access to the growing net-worked economy starts with Opportunity Analysis – another area of marketing research.

Opportunity Analysis

Before building a website for e-commerce, a small business should evaluate the following criteria to determine the attractiveness of the opportunity:

- Competitive Intensity – measure the number and identity of competitors as well as their strengths and weaknesses, particularly in terms of delivering product/service benefits. Consider the competition's ease of duplicating e-commerce efforts.
- Customer Dynamics – determine how much unmet need exists in the marketplace; assess the likely rate of market growth.
- Technology Vulnerability – determine the customers' adoption of technology. Determine whether building a website will alter the attractiveness of the product/service.
- Microeconomics – determine the market size and the dollar amount of all sales generated in a specific market. Determine the profit margin that can be realized in the market.

Customer Interface

If the opportunity analysis shows a favourable market for e-commerce, the small business may need to hire a company or seek out the help of a local University's marketing programme to build a website. The customer interface is extremely important. Mohammad, et al. (2004) present a '7Cs' framework for developing the customer interface:

1. Context – aesthetics and functionality.
2. Content – text, video, audio, graphics, product/service information.
3. Community – message boards, chat rooms.
4. Customization – firm: tailoring; and for the user: personalization.
5. Communication – broadcast, interactive and hybrid.
6. Connection – links to sites, homesite background, outsourced content, homesite content, pathway of connection.
7. Commerce – registration, shopping cart, security, credit card approval, one-click shopping, orders through affiliates, configuration technology, order tracking, delivery options.

Website Development

Rayport and Jaworski (2004) present a six-step process for building a website. This process entails strategy formulation, user experience definition, architecture design process, implementation, test/fix, and launch.

1. Strategy Formulation – such as, a well defined set of business objectives, a definition of the market segments, project plan with checkpoints and milestones, a budget, and development resources.
2. User Experience Definition – how a user perceives and interprets a website.
3. Architecture Design Process – Site map and page schematics (layout for what each page on the site will look like).
4. Implementation – test the design and navigation system by building a functioning prototype.
5. Test/Fix – properly document the code and test the code, debug and resubmit for testing.
6. Launch – rollout to the servers' host environment, test as close to final version as possible. If tests meet expectations, go live with the website.

CONCLUSION

This chapter introduces marketing research, qualitative and quantitative, as an important step in the process to gather data for: (1) understanding customers, (2) implementing segmentation/targeting/positioning strategies, (3) using local newspapers for advertising, and (4) widening the marketplace through e-commerce. The use of customer focus groups, depth interviews and surveys sets the stage for strategy development and business planning.

REFERENCES

Brooksbank, R. (1999), 'The theory and practice of marketing planning in the smaller business', *Marketing Intelligence & Planning*, **17**(2), 78–90.

Chakrapani, Churck (1998), *How to Measure Service Quality and Customer Satisfaction*, Chicago: American Marketing Association.

Darroch, Jenny (2003), 'Developing a measure of knowledge management behaviors and practices', *Journal of Knowledge Management*, **7**(5), 41–45.

Darroch, Jenny and Rod McNaughton (2002), 'Examining the link between knowledge management practices and types of innovation', *Journal of Intellectual Capital*, **3**(3), 210–22.

Darroch, Jenny and Rod McNaughton (2003), 'Beyond market orientation: knowledge management and the innovativeness of New Zealand firms', *European Journal of Marketing*, **37**(3/4), 572–93.

Dickson, P.R. and J.L. Ginter (1987), 'Market segmentation, product differentiation, and marketing strategy', *Journal of Marketing*, **51**(2), 1–10.

Entrepreneur Magazine (various years), *Start Your Own Business*, accessed at www.entrepreneur.com/mag/0,4430,,00.html.

Gee, Larry E. (2005), personal Interview, January.

Gummesson, Evert (2002), *Total Relationship Marketing*, Oxford: Butterworth Heinemann.

Kinsey, J. (1987), 'Marketing and the small manufacturing firm in Scotland: findings of a pilot survey', *Journal of Small Business Management*, **25**(2), 18–25.

Kotler, P. (1994), *Marketing Management: Analysis, Planning, Implementation, and Control*, Englewood Cliffs, NJ: Prentice-Hall.

Malhotra, Naresh K. (2004), *Marketing Research: An Applied Orientation*, Englewood Cliffs, NJ: Prentice-Hall.

Mohammed, Rafi A., Robert J. Fisher, Bernard J. Jaworski and Gordon J. Paddison (2004), *Internet Marketing*, New York: McGraw-Hill/Irwin.

Morgan, David L. (1998), *The Focus Group Guidebook*, Thousand Oaks, CA: Sage.

Morgan, David L. and Richard A. Krueger (1998), *The Focus Group Kit*, Thousand Oaks, CA: Sage.

Newspaper Advertising Bureau (2005), accessed at www.nab.co.za.

Peter, J.P. and J.H. Donnelly (1989), *Marketing Management: Knowledge and Skills*, Homewood, IL: BPI/Irwin.

Peterson, R.T. (1991), 'Small business usage of target marketing', *Journal of Small Business Management*, **29**(4), 79–85.

Rayport, Jeffrey F. and Bernard J. Jaworski (2004), *Introduction to E-Commerce*, New York, NY: McGraw-Hill/Irwin.

14. Understanding small business enterprise networking: a qualitative case approach*

Steve Rocks, David Carson and Audrey Gilmore

INTRODUCTION

This chapter discusses the critical aspects of analysing qualitative data. It examines the data analysis process used in a longitudinal qualitative study of 12 small business (SB) enterprises within a distribution channel. The focus of this research was to gain an in-depth understanding of the marketing networking that occurs within the channel. However, the use of qualitative research methods using case study research, and the collection of data from multiple sources which allows an in-depth understanding of network activities to be achieved, is the focus and purpose of this chapter. The chapter explains how the data were analysed to produce meaningful findings within a specific context. This resulted in a marketing network theory that was grounded in the views of the practitioners, as well as previous research in related topic areas of networking in SB enterprises and marketing in SB enterprises.

The study illustrates that a case study methodology is an insightful alternative to the more conventional approaches of studying network theory. Data was collected using in-depth interviews with manufacturing, intermediary and retailer firm types, of small and medium-size. The case study database was examined and summarized through the identification and interpretation of core patterns and themes. While there is no singular way of analysing qualitative data, this chapter describes a process of data analysis that was continuous throughout the study in moving from data collection to data analysis, to data interpretation in a cyclical manner. The use of multiple cases allows cross-case comparison and replication and enables valuable insight into how firms interact within the distribution channel in both a horizontal and vertical dimension.

Criticism of qualitative research methods, in terms of lack of 'rigour' have arisen in the past by judging qualitative research by quantitative frameworks (Carson et al., 2001). Both validity and reliability must be considered in designing research methods irrespective of the philosophical standpoint (Dey, 1993). A qualitative research methodology is designed to ease the struggle between rigor and relevance by producing meaningful data that is both valid and reliable. The need for a structured approach to qualitative research is summarized by Silverman (1993): 'The worst thing that contemporary qualitative research can imply is that, in this post-modern age, anything goes. The trick is to produce intelligent, disciplined work on the very edge of the abyss' (p. 211).

It is generally agreed that there is no singular method for analysing qualitative data (Carson et al., 2001). The form of data to be collected determines how data may be analysed. However, it must not be forgotten that the task of data analysis and justification of validity and reliability of research findings applies to both qualitative and quantitative research.

The focus of this chapter is on case study analysis to enable in-depth understanding of the marketing network processes that occur within a distribution channel encompassing 12 SB enterprises; four manufacturers, four wholesalers and four retailers.

THE QUALITATIVE CASE STUDY RESEARCH CONTEXT

There are a number of justifications for using qualitative research in this context. It has been argued that marketing theory and network theory are both contemporary issues less suited to research using scientific methods, so qualitative research is more suited to their social nature and complexity (Gibb, 1990; Polonsky et al., 1999). In addition, as an under-researched area of research within SB enterprises, descriptive detail and insight are sought. In this chapter the focus is on analytic generalization as opposed to statistical generalization with the emphasis on theory building through explanation-building (Yin, 1994). This chapter discusses methodology from an interpretivist research position.

Qualitative research provides a useful way of fully understanding the complex patterns of ties involved in Marketing Network Processes and network analysis. It also allows a phenomenon to be examined within its real life context (Bonoma, 1985; Yin, 1994) due to the holistic view that case study methods provide (Gummesson, 1991; Hofer and Bygrave, 1992).

An interpretivist position is guided by both prior theory and prior knowledge of the researchers. This stance proposes reality in terms of multiple realities that are local and specific, and in this study meant analysing the views of different SB enterprise owner/managers. Thus knowledge is generated by researchers becoming passionate participants in the process (Guba and Lincoln, 1994). This interactive approach to the research is subjectivist, encompassing value judgements by the researchers and results in the findings being created between researcher and respondent as the research process proceeds.

In brief, the researchers' task in this process is to describe and analyse the processes relating to the complex and imperfectly understandable reality of marketing networks. The investigation of this marketing network study is the development of idiographic knowledge based upon natural and social experiences. The interpretivist view provides a means of understanding social phenomenon, explaining how and why Marketing Network Processes operate and sought that underlying reality. In an effort to get closer to contextual reality different views and perceptions are needed.

SMALL BUSINESS ENTERPRISES NETWORKING

This section defines the conceptual development for analysing the Marketing Network Processes (MNP) of SB enterprises in the context of a distribution channel. There are many ways to define networks. Given that this study is concerned with networks and networking within a distribution channel, three dimensions are presented and examined as key to networking within such a channel. Scholarly thought underpins these three dimensions, structure, relationship and usage, to better understand networking in SB enterprises within a marketing context. First, the structural dimension, defined in terms of sources used, focuses on the physical structure of each marketing network. Secondly, the relational dimension is defined in terms of network linkages, and measured in terms of the strength of the marketing network linkages that exist (Anderson et al., 1994). Finally, the third dimension of MNPs is the usage dimension that is defined in terms of the marketing activities of SB enterprises in relation to their network processes. The following sections examine each MNP dimension in turn.

The Structural Dimension of MNP

The focus to date on analysing networks in SB enterprises has been on describing the type of sources used. In the past, debate has focused on distinguishing between formal/business networks and informal/social networks in terms of the sources they use (Birley, 1985; Tjosvold and Weicker, 1993). A recurring theme is the use of both formal business networks, and informal networks consisting of a person's social/family network (Szarka, 1990).

This study focuses on each SB enterprise, to determine the network structure and therefore understand the structural dimension of each marketing network. By examining each firm individually, this study establishes who exactly is involved in marketing activities and who SB enterprise owner/managers talk to within the firm, and outside the firm, regarding those marketing activities. The structural dimension of each marketing network is defined in terms of structural components derived from and defined in the literature. Each structural component is defined and described below.

Network size is defined as the actual number of direct contacts used by the owner/manager in each SB enterprise, to help him/her do marketing. It is measured by counting the number of sources used within the firm and outside the firm to make marketing decisions or carry out marketing activities. It is accepted that SB enterprise networks are extensive (Butler and Hanson, 1991), and that SB enterprise owner/managers do, in fact, spend a considerable amount of time developing and maintaining network contacts.

Network formality is closely related to the concept of network diversity and is defined as the extent to which formal/business network contacts are used in doing marketing compared to informal/social network contacts. It is therefore measured by counting the number of strong network contacts that an SB enterprise owner/manager has of a formal/business nature and of an informal/social nature (Brown and Butler, 1993; Szarka, 1990; Brodie et al., 1997).

Network diversity is defined in terms of the variety of network sources used. It is measured by counting the number of different network sources that an SB enterprise owner/manager uses in doing marketing.

Network density is defined in terms of the connectedness, that is, the extent to which network members are linked to each other. As this study focuses on SB enterprises that operate within a distribution marketing channel, the most meaningful measure of density that can be examined is the connectedness that exists between the firms within the channel (Rylander et al., 1997). Therefore, network density is measured by determining the number of other firms within the channel with which each SB enterprise owner/manager is connected.

Network stability is defined as 'a condition in which inter-organisational relations in a bounded population remain the same over some specific time interval' (Aldrich, 1979, p. 332). More specifically, network stability is defined as the number of network linkages within the marketing network of an SB enterprise owner/manager that have existed for a minimum length of time. Network stability is measured by determining how many of these linkages between an SB enterprise owner/manager and his/her network sources have existed for a certain time, ie two years.

Network flexibility is closely related to network stability, but is a distinct feature of network structure. Network flexibility is defined as the number of network linkages formed and the number of network linkages broken within a specific period. It is measured by establishing the number of new and broken linkages within a specific time period, for example, the last 12 months. These structural dimensions of MNPs form part of a conceptual model, shown in Figure 14.1.

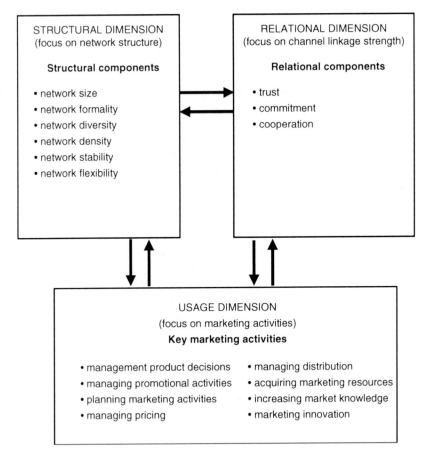

Source: Carson et al. (2004).

Figure 14.1   A conceptual model of SME marketing network processes

THE RELATIONAL DIMENSION OF MARKETING NETWORK PROCESSES

This section focuses on the second network dimension, namely the relational dimension, which considers the actual network linkages between an SB enterprise owner/manager and his/her network sources. More specifically, the relational dimension develops the concept of linkage strength.

The concept of networking can be further developed by studying the network linkages which exist within the marketing network of an SB enterprise owner/manager. The literature argues that formation and subsequent success of SB enterprise networks is largely determined by the owner/manager's efforts and skills to develop cooperative goals with network members (Tjosvold and Weicker, 1993). This introduces a relational aspect whereby marketing networks are considered in terms of the strength of the network linkages and the relational components which determine that strength, principally trust, commitment and cooperation.

The need to focus on network relationships is highlighted in the move from the traditional '4P' view of marketing to a relational view of marketing (Coviello et al., 1997). The relational dimension of network linkages is strongly argued and is based on relationships over time (Gilmore and Carson, 1999).

Network linkages are an important element of the network structure (Johannisson, 1990). There is a need to focus on the relational nature of networks to more fully understand them (Coviello and Brodie, 1991), since relational linkages are the essential building blocks of a network (Anderson et al., 1994). The network approach is a valuable means of examining this relational dimension because it shifts the focus from the SB enterprise itself, to the relationships the owner/manager has with other firms and people. The approach here, therefore, focuses on the strength of linkages between the SB enterprise owner/manager and his/her network members, since the development and maintenance of these linkages is a key SB enterprise strength (Butler and Hansen, 1991). The three relational components, trust, commitment and cooperation are now defined in turn.

There is an emphasis on the importance of trust in relation to network linkages (Aldrich et al., 1989), and the level of trust between an SB enterprise owner/manager and another firm can and will change over time (Johannisson, 1986). Trust is defined as 'a willingness to rely on an exchange partner in whom one has confidence' (Moorman et al., 1993, p. 82). Trust is measured in terms of the nature of the information shared and the confidence in advice received.

Since commitment is an important component in managing networking relations and indeed strengthening network relations, it is considered as a key relational component influencing the strength of marketing network linkages. Commitment is defined as the time and effort in maintaining network linkages. It is measured in terms of the frequency of communication between an SB enterprise owner/manager and each network member.

Cooperation is defined as the level of interdependence between an SB enterprise owner/manager and each marketing network member. It is measured in terms of the level of co-ordinated market activities, and the level of reciprocity and mutual compatibility regarding marketing goals between an SB enterprise owner/manager and his/her linkage partners.

The relational dimension focuses on the strong network linkages that exist between the SB enterprise owner/manager and other SB enterprises, and acknowledges the existence of strong and weak network linkages. It relates to the strong network linkages from the viewpoint of the focal person, each SB enterprise owner/manager and aims to build up a clear pattern of the existing marketing network. Indeed, there is evidence to suggest that there is a long-term nature to network relationships (Dubini and Aldrich, 1991).

Usage Dimension of Marketing Network Processes

Having considered MNPs in terms of network structure, and network linkage strength, the final dimension of MNPs to consider is the usage dimension of MNPs, focusing on SB enterprise marketing activities. In determining the propensity for SB enterprise owner/managers to use marketing networks in doing marketing (Carson, 1993) the role of MNPs is defined in terms of the usage dimension. This study aims to clearly establish the extent to which SB enterprises use their networks to do marketing.

This usage dimension focuses on marketing activities in terms of how MNPs influence or impact upon, the various marketing activities of SB enterprises. While there is a wide range of marketing activities that SB enterprises can draw upon, some key marketing activities are deemed to be most important, for example: managing product decisions; managing promotional activity; planning marketing activities; managing pricing; managing distribution; acquiring marketing resources; increasing market knowledge; marketing innovation.

In summary, Figure 14.1 above represents a framework to consider the key dimensions of marketing networks, namely the structural, relational and usage dimensions. The marketing activities identified by the literature are examined to gain a better understanding of why SB enterprise owner/managers network, and how network activities contribute to SB enterprise marketing.

THE STUDY

Theoretical frameworks regarding the structure, relational and usage dimensions, were developed prior to data collection. The theoretical propositions provided valuable guidance in the development of the interview protocol used in in-depth interview with owner/managers. Through multiple sources of data collection, a qualitative database was built up. The use of multiple sources of data evidence is a key characteristic of case study research (Yin, 1994) to provide sufficient depth of understanding and an opportunity for an holistic view of a process (Gummesson, 1991; Hofer and Bygrave, 1992). This research used multiple-cases in the form of 12 firms within a distribution channel; four manufacturers, four wholesalers and four retailers.

Case study research provides a platform for moving beyond the descriptive research process and addresses the underpinning research problems, particularly in trying to understand the complex patterns of linkages in network analysis. The holistic nature of this study allows SB enterprises to be studied within the context of their own environment and in addressing the research problem. That is to gain a better understanding of MNPs in SB enterprises within a distribution channel where MNPs are better understood through interpretation of the respondents' experiences and beliefs in their own terms (Gilmore and Carson, 1996).

This approach is also beneficial for gaining an understanding of dynamic contemporary events that occur in an environment where the researcher has little or no control (Bonoma, 1985; Yin, 1994). This research was carried out in a market that was experiencing dramatic change, where the SB enterprises were contending with significant and constant change. So the case study research design allowed this research to find out 'what's going on out there', through multiple case studies and using multiple sources of data collection.

RESEARCH DESIGN CRITERIA

Numerous articles have demonstrated the validity and reliability that can be achieved in qualitative research such as case study methodology (Lincoln and Guba, 1985; Yin, 1994). The commonly used qualitative research criteria include credibility, transferability, dependability and

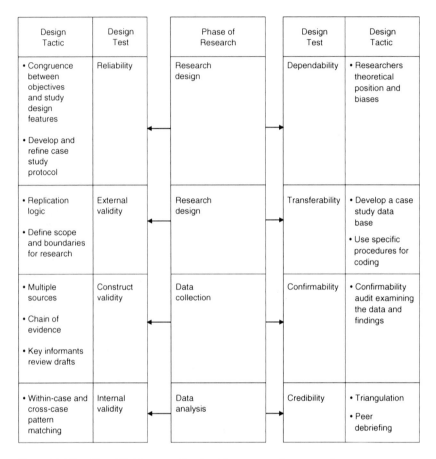

Design Tactic	Design Test	Phase of Research	Design Test	Design Tactic
• Congruence between objectives and study design features • Develop and refine case study protocol	Reliability	Research design	Dependability	• Researchers theoretical position and biases
• Replication logic • Define scope and boundaries for research	External validity	Research design	Transferability	• Develop a case study data base • Use specific procedures for coding
• Multiple sources • Chain of evidence • Key informants review drafts	Construct validity	Data collection	Confirmability	• Confirmability audit examining the data and findings
• Within-case and cross-case pattern matching	Internal validity	Data analysis	Credibility	• Triangulation • Peer debriefing

Figure 14.2   Establishing quality in this case study research

confirmability (Lincoln and Guba, 1985). These criteria were combined to ensure the reliability and validity of the data in this research. As the quality of qualitative data depends to a large extent on the skills of the researcher (Patton, 1987), the researchers' experiential knowledge in the industry is vital in developing this research design.

This study achieved quality by considering each design criteria, and implementing the necessary design tactics throughout the research process as outlined in Figure 14.2. This clearly shows the phase of the research process when the criteria for validity and reliability were used.

The blend of criteria developed underpins the validity and reliability of these research findings and the overall quality of this case study research.

RESEARCH IMPLEMENTATION

Data Collection Procedures

Multiple-case study research designs provide an opportunity for comparative analysis (Miles and Huberman, 1984; Perry, 1998). The use of multiple-case studies is recommended as a means of improving the quality of a research study (Bonoma, 1985; Patton, 1990; Yin, 1994), since analysing 12 cases offers a greater diversity of evidence than a single-case study research design. Secondly, multiple-case studies enables triangulation of data in comparing and contrasting the findings for each of the 12 cases, increasing the rigour of the research (Deshpande, 1983) by establishing credibility.

The process of theoretical sampling was used, whereby the cases were selected for theoretical reasons and not statistical ones (Handler, 1991). This process for selection is also known as purposive sampling, whereby SB enterprises were selected for this research on the basis of firm type and firm size. Consideration was also given to the value and quality of each case in contributing to theory development (Perry, 1998). This sampling decision then allows for extensive cross-case analysis in both a horizontal and vertical dimension. The four firms, at each level in the distribution channel, allows horizontal cross-case analysis of each firm type, and analysis between the three types of firm allows vertical cross-case analysis along the distribution channel.

This study consisted of two stages: first an initial research study; and secondly, the main research study. The initial stage was exploratory, consisting of four cases purposefully selected, and these findings helped to strengthen the validity of the conceptual frameworks as a basis for researching MNPs, and strengthen the reliability of the research design especially in relation to data collection for the main study. The main data collection was a three-phase process taking place over a 12-month period.

For this study, evidence was drawn mainly from in-depth interviews, documents and research observations. These multiple sources of data enabled research findings to be cross-checked and thus increase their validity. The use of multiple data sources allowed effective triangulation of data. Interview notes, observation study notes, and company documents, and keeping a diary record for the full duration of the data collection period (Carson et al., 2001), helped this process.

The Interview Process

Details of the steps involved in the interviews consisted of contacting the owner/managers directly by phone and explaining the purpose of the interview. The timing and location for each interview was agreed there and then, with each interview planned to last for approximately one hour, and taking place at the owner/managers place of work. In-depth interviews were used to provide a clear and accurate view of an owner/managers behavior or position on relevant issues (Ghauri et al., 1995). The interviews had a flexible, exploratory, open-ended format. The particular in-depth interview technique used in the initial study was the interview guide approach (Patton, 1987; Carson et al., 2001).

Care was taken in terms of the approach towards the owner/manager, how topics were raised, and the nature of the questions being asked. The opening question or topic was designed to begin the interview in a motivational way and allow the owner/manager an opportunity to discuss their present activities and experiences. So asking a truly open-ended question, in this case, 'talk to me about how you do business?' permitted the owner/manager to respond in his/her own terms.

Researcher behaviour was deliberately unobtrusive during the interview, with occasional use of pauses, encouraging noises and good eye contact. Interviewer bias was reduced by not interrupting, asking leading questions or introducing the researchers own ideas or opinions (Carson et al., 2001), thus establishing dependability. This resulted in a relaxed interview manner, at the end of which each owner/manager was thanked for their cooperation and asked for their permission to be contacted again with any follow-up questions or issues arising from analysis of the interview data.

The reaction at the end of each interview was very positive, with owner/managers comfortable with both the content and the manner of the interview process. The general comment of 'this has really made me think a lot more about the way I do business' was commonplace, and therefore increased owner/managers commitment to this research, increasing the quality of the data gathered. Each interview was followed up with a letter thanking the respondent for their time and their contribution to the study. Follow-up interviews were carried out at three-monthly intervals during the year of study to record any changes in the owner/managers focus and activities.

THE PROCESS OF DATA ANALYSIS

In the data analysis process, the continuous interplay between concepts, data, and categories developed through coding, allowed relationships between the categories to develop in producing more coherent theory (Araujo, 1995; Richards and Richards, 1995). Interviews were transcribed in full, to gain familiarization with the data and facilitate data analysis.

It is acknowledged that data analysis activities are not easily separated from data collection activities in qualitative research (Bryman and Burgess, 1994; Dey, 1993). In fact, qualitative data analysis is viewed as a continuous process, which starts during the data collection phase. A cyclical process of data collection and data analysis underpins the research methods used in this case study methodology. Case study analysis procedures establishing the principle of incorporating data analysis with data collection is a key feature of theory building research.

The process of building theory developed during the empirical data gathering and data analysis, and data interpretation phase in a cyclical process that was an integral part of the research process. In this study the cyclical process, incorporating feedback from SB enterprise owner/managers, allowed adjustments to be made to the data collection process to improve the quality of data collected (Carson et al., 2001). This facilitated the identification of core themes and the development of concepts. This is illustrated by the fact that the interview protocol used in the first phase interviews was revised for the second phase interviews.

Data Coding

The analytical technique of coding the collected data (with labels assigned to words, phrases, or information) allowed the researchers to differentiate and combine the research data (Miles and Huberman, 1984). This process links the data collected, with the frameworks or models developed for this study, and allows the data to be broken down into categories, as the first stage of conceptualizing the data (Bryman and Burgess, 1994). The coding of data was a means of ensuring it was managed, in that the researcher could access all the material (Johns and Lee-Ross, 1998). The coding or categorizing of data for analysis is based on the three conceptual categories, namely the structural, relational, and usage dimensions of MNPs.

Indeed, the theoretical propositions provided valuable guidance in the development of the interview protocol used and the subsequent data analysis process. Coding of data initially consisted of funnelling the data into the relevant dimension category for consideration. The coding categories were developed by recording the themes and concepts within each category during the analysis process, based on the composite model. Data reduction is similar to coding, whereby the emphasis is on organizing and managing the data, not on throwing away or ignoring data. This process is an effective means of analysing qualitative data, as it lays the conceptual foundations for analysis, and provides a basis for comparison (Dey, 1993).

In this research, all interview transcripts, interview notes, observation notes, and documents were coded by colour. This coding technique recorded all incidents within the data relating to each dimension in turn. This coding process allowed the researchers to focus strongly on each MNP dimension at a time (structural dimensions highlighted in yellow, relational dimensions highlighted in pink and usage dimensions highlighted in green). So each of the three topics were highlighted to allow the filtering of key statements relating to each marketing network dimension.

The data relating to each dimension were then sorted into sub-categories based on the theoretical frameworks developed previously. For example, in analysing the structural dimension of MNPs, there were six structural components derived, (Figure 14.1, top left), which constitute sub-categories. Since all data relating to the structural dimension were coloured yellow, all transcripts were read to consider all data highlighted in yellow in relation to structural components. So all transcripts and data were revisited a further six times, to extract data relating to each structural component. This process was repeated in relation to both the relational dimension and the usage dimension All transcripts and data was visited a further three times to examine each relational component (Figure 14.1, top right) derived from the literature, and a further eight times to consider each marketing activity derived from the literature (Figure 14.1, bottom).

The data analysis process for this research was very much a process of researcher immersion in the data, all interviews were transcribed and transcripts were repeatedly read over. A conscious decision was made not to 'paper and paste' the data by editing the transcripts under the three MNP dimension categories, and further under the MNPs component sub-categories. Instead, data relating to any aspect of this research was considered within the full transcripts to provide a more accurate and contextual view of the data or information available.

This study acknowledges that computer software packages can be used to facilitate the coding of data (Johns and Lee-Ross, 1998; Kelle, 1995). They were not used in this research because although computer programs are useful in dealing with the large volume of data generated by qualitative research, computer software does not provide the judgement needed to develop theories (Carson and Coviello, 1996; Lonkila, 1995). The task of data interpretation still depends on the skills of the researcher. Secondly, the data generated in this research was of a semi-structured form due to the use of the interview protocol, and not of a raw, unstructured nature which computer packages are potentially more useful in managing.

Data Displays

A key factor in determining the reliability of qualitative research findings is how well the entire process of analysis is made clear to the reader, and how clearly the findings are presented to the reader. Data displays provided an effective way of summarizing data. They helped this research by enabling data to be combined, compared, contrasted and visually reported. Bar charts, tables and diagrams helped to organize the data on a single page, and so help to illustrate and summarize the findings. They also help to visualize the possible relationships between categories or sub-categories, or the frequency of different issues. Data displays enhance data analysis by allowing the researcher to draw consistent interpretation of the findings. Quotations were also used to add qualitative insights and to provide support for data interpretation, thereby increasing the credibility of qualitative data analysis.

Data Interpretation

The final part of the data analysis process is the interpretation of the data through the drawing and verification of conclusions. Description and coding of data are not ends in themselves (Dey, 1993). Once the data is accessible and manageable, the focus must shift to interpretation of the data in terms of generating theories. Robson and Foster (1989) warn against an over-emphasis on coding, resulting in qualitative data being treated like quantitative data, instead of developing understanding and seeking patterns within the data (Stake, 1995).

The strategy of repetition was used to become familiar with the data. The opportunity to listen to the interview tapes extensively, allowed researchers to hear what the data had to say and utilize time well during the period of data gathering and analysis. The process of listening for key points/patterns helped to shape ideas, by comparing/contrasting them against the theoretical frameworks.

Consideration was given to the balance of this study: to get the right mix of descriptive and interpretive findings. While the findings contain a brief description of each case, the bulk of the findings were devoted to cross-case comparison in relation to the key research issues highlighted at the outset of this research. Verification of conclusions was also carried out by simply getting feedback from the SB enterprise owner/managers on the conclusions drawn (Miles and Huberman, 1984). This was done by arranging to meet an SB enterprise owner/manager informally, usually in a coffee shop setting, to talk through researcher interpretation of what they were saying and what issues they were facing.

Continuous Analysis

A summary document was produced to feed back key findings of the research to the SB enterprise owner/managers taking part in the research.

A Friday afternoon was set aside to formally present the key findings from the research contained in the summary document. A 45 minute presentation was then followed by a 90 minute open discussion with the 12 SB enterprise owner/managers in relation to the findings and issues arising. The rationale for this follow up discussion meeting combined:

- a thank-you/reward for each SB enterprise owner/manager participating in the research study in the form of a copy of the findings document and presentation slides;
- valuable feedback gained from the SB enterprise owner/managers in terms of confirming/verifying the conclusions drawn in the interpretation of data and presented back to them as findings;
- an opportunity to progress the research in terms of reviewing the findings and exploring new issues and challenges on a periodic basis in a workshop environment.

The case study methodology allowed theory to be developed using a data-driven method of building theory from the 'bottom up' (Richards and Richards, 1995), within a conceptual framework leading to theory development.

The longitudinal nature of the research, consisting of a 12-month data collection period, allowed the changes within the market-place to be more accurately reflected. This has also allowed the relational complexities and social interplay within the distribution channel to be better understood. In addition, the use of descriptive/non-mathematical data to study marketing network processes focused on both the structure and meaning, in comparison to the complex statistical models that dominate network research.

CONCLUSION

This study shows that a case study methodology is an insightful alternative to the more traditional positivist deductive approaches of studying network theory. Data was collected using in-depth interviews with manufacturing, intermediary and retailer firm types, of small and medium-size. The use of multiple cases allows cross-case comparison and replication, through the two dimensions of firm type and firm size. It provided valuable insight as to how firms interact within the distribution channel in both a horizontal and vertical dimension.

Despite the fact that the analysis process is more memorable for its moments of sheer despair in the face of the mass of data (Miles, 1979), the case study database was examined and summarized through the identification and interpretation of core patterns and themes. While there is no one correct way of analysing qualitative data, this chapter summarizes the fundamental basis upon which the data analysis process occurs. The process of data analysis was continuous during this research in moving from data collection to data analysis, to data interpretation in a cyclical manner.

Ultimately, each researcher has to develop his or her own analysis procedures, adapting the various methods and advice that is available in the literature. No doubt the quality of the data analysis and the validity of the consequent findings and conclusions will depend just as much on the creativity, imagination, intuition, and research interests of the researcher. Although the literature warns of qualitative data analysis being a labour intensive, time consuming, difficult and even dull process to carry out, a thorough and imaginative approach to the data analysis process raises the quality of research in terms of its findings and conclusions.

NOTE

* Further reading on the findings and insights of this study: Carson, D., A. Gilmore and S. Rocks (2004), 'SME marketing networking: a strategic approach', *Journal of Strategic Change* 13, pp. 369–82. Rocks, S., A. Gilmore and D. Carson (2005), 'Developing strategic marketing through the use of marketing networks', *Journal of Strategic Marketing* 13, June, pp. 81–92.

REFERENCES

Aldrich, H. (1979), *Organizations and Environments*, Englewood Cliffs, NJ: Prentice Hall, pp. 323–49.

Aldrich, H., P.R. Reese and P. Dubini (1989), 'Women on the verge of breakthrough: networking among entrepreneurs in the United States and Italy', *Entrepreneurship and Regional Development*, 1, 339–56.

Anderson, J.C., H. Hakansson and J. Johanson (1994), 'Dyadic business relationships within a business network context', *Journal of Marketing*, 58(4), 1–15.

Araujo, L. (1995), 'Designing and refining hierarchical coding frames', in U. Kelle (ed.), *Computer-aided Qualitative Data Analysis: Theory, Methods and Practice*, London: Sage, pp. 96–104.

Birley, S. (1985), 'The role of networks in the entrepreneurial process', *Journal of Business Venturing*, 1, 107–117.

Bonoma, T.V. (1985), 'Case research in marketing: opportunities, problems, and a process', *Journal of Marketing Research*, 22, May, 199–208.

Brodie, R.J., N.E. Coviello, R.W. Brookes and V. Little (1997), 'Towards a paradigm shift in marketing? An examination of current marketing practices', *Journal of Marketing Management*, 13(5), 383–406.

Bryman, A. and R.G. Burgess (1994), 'Developments in qualitative data analysis: an introduction', in A. Bryman and R.G. Burgess (eds), *Analysing Qualitative Data*, London: Routledge, pp. 1–17.

Brown, R.B. and J.E. Butler (1993), 'Networks and entrepreneurial development: the shadows of borders', *Entrepreneurship and Regional Development*, **5**(2), 101–16.

Butler, J.E. and G.S. Hansen (1991), 'Network evolution, entrepreneurial success, and regional development', *Entrepreneurship and Regional Development*, **3**, 1–16.

Carson, D. (1993), 'A philosophy for marketing education in small firms', *Journal of Marketing Management*, **9**(2), April, 189–204.

Carson, D. and N. Coviello (1996), 'Qualitative research issues at the marketing/entrepreneurship interface', *Marketing Intelligence and Planning*, **14**(6), 51–8.

Carson, D., A. Gilmore, C. Perry and K. Gronhaug (2001), *Qualitative Marketing Research*, London: Sage.

Carson, D., A. Gilmore and S. Rocks (2004), 'SME marketing networking: a strategic approach', *Strategic Change*, **13**, 369–82.

Coviello, N. and R.J. Brodie (1991), 'The role of marketing in the development and management of linkages for small technology-intensive firms: issues for research', *Proceedings of the 36th ICSB World Conference*, 24–26 June Vienna, pp. 95–101.

Coviello, N., R.J. Brodie and H. Munro (1997), 'Understanding contemporary marketing: development of a classification scheme', *Journal of Marketing Management*, **13**, 501–22.

Deshpande, R. (1983), 'Paradigms lost: on theory and method in research in marketing', *Journal of Marketing*, **47**, Fall, 101–10.

Dey, I. (1993), *Qualitative Data Analysis: a User-Friendly Guide for Social Scientists*, London: Routledge.

Dubini, P. and H. Aldrich (1991), 'Personal and extended networks are central to the entrepreneurial process', *Journal of Business Venturing*, **6**(5), 305–13.

Ghauri, P., K. Gronhaug and I. Kristianslund (1995), *Research Methods in Business Studies: A Practical Guide*, London: Prentice Hall.

Gibb, A. (1990), 'Organising small firms research to meet the needs of customers in the 21st century', paper presented at the 13th Small Firms Policy and Research Conference, Harrogate, 14–16 November.

Gilmore, A. and D. Carson (1996), ' "Integrative" qualitative methods in a services context', *Marketing Intelligence and Planning*, **14**(6), 21–6.

Gilmore, A. and D. Carson (1999), 'Entrepreneurial marketing by networking', *New England Journal of Entrepreneurship*, **2**(2), 31–38.

Guba, E.G. and Y.S. Lincoln (1994), 'Competing paradigms in qualitative research', in N.K. Denzin and Y.S. Lincoln (eds), *Handbook of Qualitative Research*, Newbury Park, CA: Sage, pp. 105–249.

Gummesson, E. (1991), *Qualitative Methods in Management Research*, revised edn, Newbury Park, CA: Sage.

Handler, W.C. (1991), 'Key interpersonal relationships of next-generation family members in family firms', *Journal of Small Business Management*, **29**(3), 21–32.

Hofer, C.W. and W.D. Bygrave (1992), 'Researching entrepreneurship', *Entrepreneurship Theory and Practice*, **16**(3), 91–100.

Johannison, B. (1986), 'Network strategies: management technology for entrepreneurship and change', *International Small Business Journal*, **5**(1), 19–30.

Johannisson, B. (1990), 'Community entrepreneurship – cases and concept', *Entrepreneurship and Regional Development*, **2**, 71–88.

Johns, N. and D. Lee-Ross (1998), *Research Methods in Service Industry Management*, London: Cassell.

Kelle, U. (1995), 'Introduction: an overview of computer-aided methods in qualitative research', in U. Kelle (ed.), *Computer-aided Qualitative Data Analysis: Theory, Methods and Practice*, London: Sage, pp. 1–17.

Lincoln, Y.S. and E.G. Guba (1985), *Naturalistic Inquiry*, Beverly Hills, CA: Sage.

Lonkila, M. (1995), 'Grounded theory as an emerging paradigm for computer-assisted qualitative data analysis', in U. Kelle (ed.), *Computer-aided Qualitative Data Analysis: Theory, Methods and Practice*, London: Sage, pp. 41–51.

Miles, M.B. (1979), 'Qualitative analysis as an attractive nuisance: the problems of analysis', *Administrative Science Quarterly*, **24**, December, 590–601.

Miles, M.B. and A.M. Huberman (1984), *Qualitative Data Analysis: A Sourcebook of New Methods*, Newbury Park, CA: Sage.

Moorman, C., R. Deshpande and G. Zaltman (1993), 'Factors affecting trust in market research relationships', *Journal of Marketing*, **57**(1), 81–101.

Patton, M.Q. (1987), *How to Use Qualitative Methods in Evaluation*, Newbury Park, CA: Sage.

Patton, M.Q. (1990), *Qualitative Evaluation and Research Methods*, Newbury Park, CA: Sage.

Perry, C. (1998), 'Processes of a case study methodology for postgraduate research in marketing', *European Journal of Marketing*, **32**(9/10), 785–802.

Polonsky, M.J., H.T. Suchard and D.R. Scott (1999), 'The incorporation of an interactive external environment: an extended model of marketing relationships', *Journal of Strategic Marketing*, **7**(1), 41–55.

Richards, T. and L. Richards (1995), 'Using hierarchical categories in qualitative data analysis', in U. Kelle (ed.), *Computer-aided Qualitative Data Analysis: Theory, Methods and Practice*, London: Sage, pp. 80–104.

Robson, S. and A. Foster (1989), 'The analysis and interpretation process', in S. Robson and A. Foster (eds), *Qualitative Research in Action*, London: Edward Arnold, pp. 85–99.

Rylander, D., D. Strutton and L.E. Pelton (1997), 'Toward a synthesized framework of relational committment: implications for the marketing channel theory and practice', *Journal of Marketing: Theory and Practice*, **5**(2), 58–71.

Silverman, D. (1993), *Interpreting Qualitative Data: Methods for Analysing Talk, Text and Interaction*, London: Sage.

Stake, R.E. (1995), *The Art of Case Study Research*, Thousand Oaks, CA: Sage.

Szarka, J. (1990), 'Networking and small firms', *International Small Business Journal*, **8**(2), 10–22.

Tjosvold, D. and D. Weicker (1993), 'Co-operative and competitive networking by entrepreneurs: a critical incident study', *Journal of Small Business Management*, **31**(1), 11–21.

Yin, R.K. (1994), *Case Study Research: Design and Methods*, Beverly Hills, CA: Sage.

15. The contextual stepwise approach to enterprise research and the use of undisguised stories and focus groups*

David A. Kirby

INTRODUCTION

This chapter argues that the traditional dichotomy between quantitative and qualitative research is erroneous and that in the context of entrepreneurship research a combined approach, based on the principles of the hermeneutic circle or spiral, is appropriate. It then goes on to outline the contextual stepwise approach that proceeds from pre-understanding to understanding, where step 1 furnishes pre-understanding for step 2 and so on. The chapter shows how the stepwise process may be operationalized using qualitative research (undisguized stories and focus groups) to explore the issues, quantitative research (questionnaire surveys) to identify the substantive context and then qualitative research (in-depth interviews and cases) to provide in-depth knowledge and understanding. While it recognizes that the process can be adapted to suit the research under investigation, the chapter concludes that such a stepwise model does appear to have relevance for most situations.

Carrying out good quality research is never easy. Carrying out good quality research in the enterprise field is particularly difficult. As Curran and Blackburn (2001, p. 5) have recognized, smaller enterprises are often more difficult to study than larger enterprises as they tend to lack clear structures and recording procedures, making it much more difficult to measure and test propositions. According to them it is this complexity of the subject that explains why small business research has had problems in 'achieving higher quality (and academic status) as well as greater influence on policy makers'. It could explain, also, why the field displays such a rich array of different approaches to research as researchers attempt to understand the phenomenon under study. In the process, though, rather than celebrate the diversity and complementarity of such different approaches, enterprise researchers are often divided into different 'warring' camps or Schools. In particular, there is the divide between the nomothetic and the positivistic approaches that tends to characterize the social sciences in general. This is clearly recognized by Ali and Birley (1999, p. 103) who, with reference to Henwood and Pidgeon, 1993), have suggested that:

> Opinions are divided amongst researchers as to what constitutes legitimate inquiry and warrantable knowledge in specific situations. Indeed, there appear to be two diametrically opposing views. On the one hand there is the 'experi-mentalist', 'hypothetico-deductive' or 'positivist' and on the other the 'natural-istic', 'contextual' or 'interpretative'.

Interestingly, this divide appears to be geographical. Traditionally European researchers have been more likely to emphasize qualitative research approaches, whereas those from the North American tradition have tended to adopt more quantitative methodologies. Thus Aldrich (2000, p. 17) concludes that though 'we can no longer draw a sharp con-trast between quantitative North American research and qualitative European research . . . we can say that a much larger proportion of European than North American researchers use fieldwork and other qualitative methods'.

The reasons for this dichotomy are unclear but they may reflect, as Gartner and Birley (2002, p. 392) have suggested, a question of 'timescales'. According to them, qualitative data take much longer to collect and analyse than do quantitative data, which does not always fit with the career pres-sures and timescales in United States (US) based universities. An alternative timescale explanation has been put forward by US researchers such as Aldrich (1992), Bygrave (1989), and Churchill and Lewis (1986), who have suggested that 'small firms research is at too "young" a stage in its develop-ment to benefit from a positivist research approach that encourages the use of quantitative methods of scientific inquiry' (Shaw, 1999, p. 59). This is an interesting observation, implying, as it does, that positivism is a sign of maturity in social science/enterprise research. It does not fit easily, however, with the fact that in Europe the main drive to positivism in the social sci-ences took place in the 1970s and early 1980s; since when social science researchers in general, and enterprise researchers in particular, have been adopting a more monothetic approach. This has been, at least in part, in response to the perceived shortcomings of positivism, particularly with respect to the complexity of the phenomenon under investigation, and the search for more accurate and deeper insights.

Whatever the reasons for this apparent dichotomy of approach between the two regions, it is often suggested that one approach is superior to the other and that quantitatively oriented entrepreneurship research lacks theory and is often descriptive, whereas 'qualitative research . . . goes beyond description to providing explanation'. (Gartner and Birley, 2002, p. 393). While the purpose of the grounded theory approach (Glaser and Strauss, 1967) is, indeed, to generate theory, in reality both approaches, if conducted correctly, can explain 'why' and help to generate theory. Indeed, this is purportedly the purpose of the positivist approach – to develop theories, laws and models – and there is no reason why quantitative research should confine itself solely to answering 'what', 'where', 'when' and 'how' questions. The point that needs to be recognized is that both approaches have their advantages and disadvantages. Rather than seeing them as alternatives, perhaps it is more appropriate to view them as complementary. Not only are different problems likely to be amenable to different approaches, but in the search for 'truth', different stages in the research process might also require different approaches. As pointed out elsewhere (Kirby, 1995), the debate should not be about adopting either a 'quantitative' or a 'qualitative' approach, but about developing a research design that is not just appropriate for the issue under investigation but which uses a 'battery' of research techniques in the search for explanation. This is the contextual stepwise approach.

THE CONTEXTUAL STEPWISE APPROACH

Possibly first formally propounded by Siu and Kirby (1999), the 'contextual stepwise' approach is not entirely new. In 1992, Gibb proposed a 'staged' approach to small business research in order: 'First to observe accurately and gain insight into the entrepreneur and small business. Second, to build better models of his/her behaviour which have a sound grounded base. Third, to use these to develop a better understanding of the process of small business development. Fourth, to offer clearer and more integrated explanations as to why certain things occur under certain conditions. And fifth, to retail this in such a way that it is clearly understood by a wide audience'. While he specified, clearly, the purpose of the staged approach he made little reference, however, to how it should be achieved, though the main thrust of his argument was a critique of the deductive quantitative approach to research and an argument for inductive, qualitative research. As he points out 'statements made by the process of inductive reasoning can give as many, if not more, insights as those based on deduction, particularly where the axioms on which the decision is based . . . are weakly grounded. There can be as much subjective bias in a structured survey questionnaire as there can be in a detailed intensive action research project, if not more' (op. cit., p. 132). Again, Davies, Hills and La Forge (1985) suggested the use of what they called a 'stream of research' approach, whereby research programmes are co-ordinated and each study builds upon what has been learned in previous studies in order to make an incremental contribution to the knowledge base. This, they suggested, might be achieved through the use of case studies or small-scale exploratory studies for example, followed by large-scale survey research methodologies and finally controlled field studies. This is probably closer to the contextual stepwise approach which proposes that 'a combination of research methods (preliminary research to explore the issue; follow-up quantitative research to identify the substantive context; and then qualitative research to provide in-depth knowledge) would be more appropriate to, and suitable for, small firm research' (Siu and Kirby, 1999, p. 136).

The whole purpose of the stepwise approach is to avoid the biases to which Gibb refers, with each stage of the process informing the next. Possible justification for this approach comes from the field of hermeneutics and, in particular, the work of Ricoeur (1981). Hermeneutics deals with the problems of interpreting texts and the extent to which interpretations presuppose other interpretations (ie a reading of a text will always be coloured by previous readings of other texts which, in turn, are interpreted in the light of other texts and so on). Ricour developed a methodology to address this, which he termed the 'hermeneutic arc'. His approach has two stages – first a move from the subjective to the objective, and second a move from the objective to the subjective, thereby preserving, as he recognizes, the benefits of both approaches. What this means in practical terms is that a research project moves 'from pre-understanding to understanding, where understanding from phase 1 furnishes the pre-understanding for phase 2, and so forth' (Gummesson, 2003, p. 484). Indeed, Gummesson suggests that the hermeneutic arc or circle might be better perceived as a spiral whereby data is interpreted and re-interpreted in order both to generate and test theory. Thus he perceives of research as a building. All research, he suggests, starts in the basement with the researcher's paradigm and pre-understanding, which is essentially interpretive, qualitative, subjective and intersubjective. It then moves into the middle floors where data is generated, analysed and interpreted and the approach is largely systematic and objective, but with elements of subjectivity and intersubjectivity, the data being conceptualized and compared to extant theory and other research in order to generate theory. Finally, the top floor is where the results are presented and the implications for theory and practice are considered. This stage, he suggests, is essentially interpretive, qualitative and subjective and concludes that the systematic and objective pursuit of the truth is a myth and that it is only:

a fraction of the research, albeit sometimes a pivotal fraction. Interpretive, subjective and qualitative elements are found throughout the research edifice. Whether research is labelled qualitative or quantitative is immaterial. There is no genuine conflict; we should use whatever tools are best suited to the job (op. cit., p. 487).

OPERATIONALIZING THE CONCEPT

In the following chapter (Chapter 16), Siu explores the application of the contextual stepwise approach to the study of small firm marketing, especially in a Chinese socio-cultural context. He does this by first analysing undisguized stories (or previously published cases) in order to observe accurately and gain insight. From this he is then able to construct a questionnaire and undertake a mail survey of Chinese small firms, in order to verify the insights gained from Stage one and to provide a clearer and more systematic picture of the phenomenon under investigation. Finally, in Stage three, he reverts back to qualitative research in order to triangulate the survey results, gain further insight and 'concretise' the findings. To do this, he carries out in-depth interviews with Chinese owner-managers in Hong Kong, China and Taiwan, and in this way he is completing what Kolb (1984) has termed the 'learning cycle'. This starts with observation and reflection, which results in the formation of abstract concepts and generalizations. Siu then tests these in new situations and finally embeds them in concrete experience. The whole stepwise process, then, is to 'build upon what had been learned previously in order to make an incremental contribution to the established knowledge base' (Siu and Kirby, 1999, p. 142) using research techniques that are 'fit for purpose' and appropriate for each stage of the research process.

Clearly in this operational model of the stepwise approach, a combination of tried and tested qualitative and quantitative research methods is used, together. In particular, questionnaire surveys are used in Stage two of the research to provide 'a clearer and more systematic picture of the phenomenon under investigation'. There is nothing new in questionnaire surveys. Whether undertaken face-to-face, by mail, telephone or email, they are the stuff of positivism and countless words have been written about them, including the early seminal work of British social scientists such as Moser (1958) and Oppenheim (1966). Despite this, questionnaire surveys are often poorly designed, frequently yielding data that have spurious degrees of accuracy. Probably the most common weaknesses surround the survey samples, which are often un-representative of the populations from which they are drawn, the fact that little, if any, attempt is made to check for non-respondent bias, and the inappropriate application of statistical tests to the data. However, there are other problems to do with question bias, as Gibb (1992) has pointed out, and the fact that 'the survey does not penetrate complex and ambiguous issues; it only touches some spots on the tip of the iceberg' (Gummesson, 2003, p. 487).

Nowhere is this more apparent, perhaps, than in the Global Entrepreneurship Monitor (GEM) (Acs, Arenius, Hay and Minniti, 2004). Launched in 1999, GEM is a collaborative project involving over 150 scholars from teams in 43 different countries. Its aim is to measure differences in the level of entrepreneurial activity between countries, uncover factors leading to appropriate levels of entrepreneurship and suggest policies that may enhance the national level of entrepreneurial activity. It is based on a randomly selected survey of adults in the participating countries plus standardized national data and up to 50 interviews with experts in each country. In order to measure the overall level of involvement in entrepreneurial activity it calculates what it calls 'the total entrepreneurial activity (TEA) index'. This is essentially the sum of nascent entrepreneurs (people in the sample in the process of starting a new business) and new businesses, expressed as a proportion of the 18–64 year olds in the participating country. Having thus calculated the TEA indices for each sample, the countries are then 'ranked' according to their score.

While recognizing the importance of GEM and its unique contribution, there are issues with the data and what it represents. First, there is concern over the representativeness of the samples and what they measure. Some of the samples are relatively small and the margins of error are wide. As a result, although the participating countries have been ranked, the results are not as definitive as appears to be the case as many actually have 'comparable levels of entrepreneurial activity' (op. cit., p. 18). Even though the researchers do point this out, the results of the survey give a spurious level of accuracy, and result in claims, for example, that 'The Global Entrepreneurship Monitor (GEM) places the UK ahead of rivals Germany, France and Italy when it comes to entrepreneurial activity' as was reported in the March 2004 *Monthly News Bulletin* of the Small Business Research portal (see http://www.smallbusinessportal.co.uk/views_news.php). Secondly, and perhaps of more importance, is the definition of entrepreneurial behaviour and the questions used to determine the total entrepreneurial activity (TEA). New venture creation is not the only indicator of entrepreneurial behaviour (Kirby, 2003). Apart from occurring in large as well as small organizations in the formal sector of an economy, it can also take place as much, if not more, in the informal sector and can manifest itself as social and civic enterprise rather than simply commercial, for profit activity. This is not recognized and hence the survey is simplifying or reducing the issues by asking questions solely about new venture creation. As Gibb has recognized, there is subjective bias in the questionnaire (ie the researchers are equating entrepreneurial activity solely with new venture creation), thereby making invalid the claim for the resultant TEA index that it measures the total entrepreneurial activity in a country. Only a small part of it is actually measured by the survey, in fact. Finally, and linked to this, GEM is largely descriptive, with only weak explanatory power – as is witnessed by such statements as 'one possible interpretation of . . . is that' (op. cit., p. 28) or 'this is probably because. . .' (op. cit., p. 36). To recall Gummesson (2003, p. 487) 'the survey does not penetrate complex and ambiguous issues' – necessarily. Clearly it may, but so often (as here), it does not.

Stages one and three in the contextual stepwise approach are intended to overcome the non-sampling issues associated with the survey process that the above example demonstrates. In particular, Stage three utilizes traditional qualitative techniques, such as in-depth, largely semi-structured interviews, to produce cases based on a sample of the respondents purposively selected. The intention here is both to illuminate (or 'concretise') different aspects of the findings and to triangulate for accuracy. This has two benefits. First, by purposively selecting from the main sample, it is possible to contextualize the cases and to overcome one of the criticisms of the traditional case study approach – namely that it is unclear how representative the cases are, or of what. By purposively selecting them, against a given set of criteria, it is possible to determine where they are drawn from within the 'big picture', and what part of it they represent. Thus the cases are contextualized. Secondly, the interviews provide important triangulation in order to help ascertain the accuracy of the findings. This is important. For example, in a study of the marketing practices of medium-sized manufacturing firms in the United Kingdom (UK), it was only after surveying a sample of the population that Brooksbank, Kirby and Wright (1992) discovered, through in-depth follow-up interviews with a sub-sample of Chief Marketing Executives, that there was not necessarily a uniform understanding of either the concepts or terminology of marketing, particularly with respect to the meaning of 'marketing orientation', 'formal marketing planning' and 'innovation'. Piloting had not picked up the problem, but such a problem is likely to have considerable implications for the survey findings. This is a problem typically encountered with questionnaire surveys, namely how to deal with 'technical' terminology in the questionnaire – the initiated will understand it, the uninitiated may not and vice versa. Thus how it is dealt with could affect the findings. If Stage one of the contextual stepwise model had been adopted though, it is possible that this difficulty could have been anticipated and dealt with successfully. Accordingly, the researchers conclude in a later work that 'the most appropriate form of research into small firm marketing involves a quantitative dimension that enables an examination of the strategy-performance relationship, plus a qualitative dimension that facilitates an investigation into the underlying implementation processes involved' (Brooksbank, Kirby, Thompson and Taylor, 2003, p. 270) and that 'a combination of these approaches has indeed proved valuable'.

This use of in-depth interviews and cases contradicts the traditional hierarchical view of research that suggests that cases should only be used for exploratory research (Platt, 1992), and that surveys are appropriate for description and experiments for explanation. As Yin (1994, pp. 3–4) has recognized 'each strategy [cases, surveys and experiments] can be used for all three purposes – exploratory, descriptive, or explanatory'. However, cases (undisguized stories) can be extremely powerful exploratory tools that can be used in Stage one of the contextual stepwise model as Siu and Kirby (1999) have demonstrated.

OPERATIONALIZING STEP 1

Step 1 is arguably the most critical in the process. Get it wrong and the error committed in this step may be transmitted or even compounded in the subsequent stages of the research. Hence it is critical to the success of the project that Step 1 provides the 'right' insights. That is the whole purpose of this step in the process – it is an inductive exercise intended to 'let reality tell its story on its own terms and not on the terms of received theory or accepted concepts' (Gummesson, 2003, p. 488). Possibly the best way of doing this is through an ethnographic investigation of the enterprise and the phenomenon under study, but the owners of small and medium-sized enterprises (SMEs) are notoriously reluctant to open their businesses to unknown researchers and, in any case, SMEs are not an homogeneous group, making selection of the (representative) enterprise(s) extremely difficult. Hence, two alternative approaches that may be used in Step 1 are undisguized stories (Manimala, 1999) and focus groups (Blackburn and Stokes, 2000). Neither approach is all that new, as will be shown, though their use in small firm research and as part of the contextual stepwise process is somewhat novel.

Undisguized Stories

Basically this involves analysing the content of published cases in order to identify pre-specified and pre-defined variables. The concept, which was first developed by the Rand Corporation in the early 1970s, requires the researcher to make judgements about the presence or absence of a phenomenon in the case. Clearly this is a subjective exercise and in order to check for and eliminate/reduce researcher bias, each story is normally content-analysed by two or more independent researchers. Indeed, Manimala (1999), in his research on the policies and strategies underlying managerial decisions in small firms, carried out a pilot study and used two researchers in addition to himself. As a check on his own personal biases resulting from his management training, only one of these was a trained management researcher. Once the reliability of the ratings has been established, using inter-rater agreement indices, the scores can be presented statistically and may be analysed using quantitative research measures with survey data. Further details on how undisguized stories may be analysed are provided by Marino, Castaldi and Dollinger (1989), Siu and Kirby (1999) and in Siu's contribution to this edition. However, a new technique, developed to analyse qualitative safety data and based on the principles of Ricouer's hermeneutic arc, is described in Wallace, Ross and Davies (2003). This, the Confidential Incident Reporting System, utilizes the NVivo computer software package to analyse the text and produce data that is then analysed statistically using SPSS (Statistical Package for the Social Sciences). The process includes six stages, namely:

1. initial review of the text;
2. breaking down the text into 'surface' elements (who, what, where, how, why);
3. reading through the whole text and building it up again;
4. breaking down the text into 'deeper' structures (frontline, supervisory and managerial level issues);
5. reading through the whole text again (to create a diagram of the issues and relationships);
6. breaking the text down into micro-elements within deeper structures (ie codes).

According to the authors, stages 2–5 are the hermeneutic circle, moving from the part to the whole text and they claim that not only does this process provide a method of analysis that can be shown to be reliable, but it 'is more rigorous and philosophically coherent than existing methodologies, and that it has implications for all areas of the social sciences where qualitative texts are analysed' (op. cit., p. 587).

However, there are problems with such a methodology and the generation of data from secondary sources. Clearly the material in the published cases usually has not been collected for the purpose for which it is now being used. The case writer will clearly only include what is relevant for his/her purpose and hence the case may not contain all of the required information. As a consequence the number of valid cases that can be used is often reduced. However, as Manimala (1999, p. 49) has recognized omissions 'may not be as serious a threat to validity as falsifications'. Although misreporting is unlikely in undisguized stories that are open to public scrutiny, it is not impossible, especially if the subject of the story has not had the opportunity to check it before it is published. In an attempt to counteract this, and check for accuracy, it is advisable to confirm the accuracy of at least a random sample of the stories, as appropriate, by author. Finally, the sample is likely to be biased as most published cases are of successful enterprises, rather than the unsuccessful ones, even though the latter could well be in the majority.

Against all of these difficulties, though, there are numerous advantages in using cases in this way, not least the fact that the owner-manager may find it more difficult to hide something from a case writer, studying an enterprise in detail, than from a remote researcher asking a series of questions. Hence, the cases can be expected to be free from deliberate falsification and misrepresentation and used to structure the investigation in Step 2, identifying hypotheses that require formulating and testing and the real issues that need to be addressed, as well as the questions that should be asked and the language to be used. The analysis of published, undisguized stories in this stage of the contextual stepwise approach is, therefore, to provide insight into the issues that need to be addressed and a platform from which to proceed to Step 2 of the investigation.

Focus Groups

Unfortunately, a supply of suitable published undisguized stories is not always readily available. In his study, Manimala (1999) had a supply of 138 stories, while Siu and Kirby (1999) drew on 110 reports in a study of small firms in Hong Kong, and elsewhere in this edition Siu is reporting on 319 undisguized stories in Hong Kong, China and Taiwan. In circumstances where such cases are not available, an alternative is required. This could be the focus group.

Although not widely used in research on entrepreneurship or SME management, focus groups do have very considerable potential as Blackburn and Stokes (2000) have demonstrated. The reasons why they have been shunned by academic researchers in general and enterprise researchers in particular is unclear. Possibly it has something to do with the fact that since their introduction in the 1940s (Merton and Kendall, 1946), their take-up has been greatest in an applied context, having become the technique in market research for product testing (Berg, 1998; Morgan, 1997). This situation seems to be changing, though, and focus groups appear to be achieving greater academic credibility as there appears to be emerging 'a reversal in the elitist attitude that focus group interviewing belongs to the somehow vulgar realm of marketing research' (Berg, 1998, p. 103). Certainly, as Denzin (1989) believes, they are particularly useful as an integral part of a more comprehensive research design in which they precede, supplement or triangulate results from other methods, and they can be used for generating hypotheses and for 'learning about participants' conceptualisations of particular phenomena and the language they use to describe them' (Stewart and Shamdasani, 1990, p. 15). These are precisely the roles required of the research undertaken as Step 1 of the contextual stepwise approach.

Essentially, a focus group is a discussion of a particular issue or concept in a group of approximately eight people (normally between 6–10) with the researcher or his/her representative acting as a facilitator or moderator. The rationale behind such groups is the fact that the group participants are likely to give candid, accurate answers because the focus is on the group rather than the individual, as well as more critical comments, and are more likely to come up with new ideas and explanations because of the interactions with other group members. The extent to which this can be achieved depends greatly on the skill of the facilitator who has to ensure that:

- no one individual, or group of individuals, dominates;
- all members of the group participate;
- all of the views of the group are aired and not just those the researchers wish to be aired;
- there are no pressures on the group members to conform.

Due to this, academic researchers have expressed considerable scepticism over the contribution that focus groups can make to academic research and this may well explain why there have been so few academic studies that have adopted this technique. It also explains why Blackburn and Stokes (2000) emphasize the need to undergo training on how to moderate focus groups in their 'tips' for the use of focus groups in small business research. Whatever, as in all good quality research, it is important to prepare well – to define the purpose for which the data is required and to consider, well in advance, the logistics of the whole exercise. At the same time, it is important to pay attention to detail, as Blackburn and Stokes recognize, and to transcribe notes or recordings of the discussion immediately after the session has taken place, summarizing the main points raised and including verbatim quotations to illustrate specific points. Once this has been done, the reports (or a summary of them) should be sent to the participants to ensure accurate reporting of the discussion. On verification, the reports are then content-analysed using techniques similar to those reported, above, for the undisguized stories.

As mentioned already, few studies of SMEs have been conducted using focus groups. A relatively early one is a study by MacMillan, Curran, Downing and Turner (1988) of how the UK government could establish and improve direct consultation with small businesses, while Curran and Blackburn (1994) undertook focus groups in a study of levels of local networking amongst small firms. In both cases, though, the focus groups were conducted after a main survey, with the same respondents, in an attempt to explain the results and provide validation and triangulation of them. In contrast, in a study of ethical behaviour in small firms, Vyakarnam, Bailey, Myers and Burnett (1997) report on the use of focus groups as a prelude to further research, as is being proposed here, while Kirby (1994) uses focus groups and case studies to explore the attitudes of smaller enterprises to customer service.

CONCLUSION

This chapter has argued for pluralism in enterprise research. This is not new but, as Grant and Perren (2002, p. 201) have recognized 'attempts at pluralism fall short of the sophisticated and explicit attempts at paradigmatic "rapprochement via bridge-building" '. The contextual stepwise approach to research is an attempt to overcome such criticisms and attempts have been made in this chapter to demonstrate how it might be applied in the enterprise field using traditional quantitative and qualitative research methods, respectively, in Steps 2 and 3 and more innovative, or less frequently used, qualitative techniques in Step 1. The basis of the process is the hermeneutic principle that each step or stage of the process builds upon the previous one in order to make an incremental contribution to the knowledge base. Thus, not only does the process have a sound grounding in the social sciences in general, and the hermeneutic concept in particular, but, as the research by Siu and Kirby (1999) and Siu elsewhere in this edition has demonstrated, it can contribute considerably to the development of insight and understanding.

The approach is not without its limitations, however. Clearly, research error in one step of the process can be transmitted or even compounded in the subsequent steps. Hence it is essential that in each step, the research is conducted rigorously and correctly to minimize research error – but that is true of any research project. Similarly, the methods used should be appropriate to the problem under investigation. This means that although a qualitative-quantitative-qualitative model has been developed here, the exact sequencing of the steps will depend on the precise phenomenon under investigation. However, a model that uses qualitative research (published undisguized stories and focus groups) to explore the issues, quantitative research (questionnaire surveys) to identify the substantive context and then qualitative research (in-depth interviews and cases) to provide in-depth knowledge and understanding, does seem to have relevance for most situations.

By using such a battery of research techniques in this way, it is possible to overcome the somewhat sterile debates on the benefits or otherwise of the quantitative and qualitative approaches to research, recognizing, instead, the specific contributions each can make in the ongoing search for truth. As Gummesson (2003, p. 486) has recognized 'by polarizing quantitative and qualitative research, a red herring is introduced and our attention is taken away from the real issue, namely the choice of research methodology and techniques that support access and validity'. By adopting the contextual stepwise approach it should be possible not just to integrate the two approaches, but to adopt techniques that are 'fit for purpose' and enable the researcher to access reality and produce results that accurately model it.

NOTE

*   This chapter is based on and extends, Siu, W.S. and D.A. Kirby (1999), 'Research into small firm marketing: a contextual stepwise approach', *Qualitative Market Research: An International Journal*, 2(2), pp. 135–46.

REFERENCES

Acs, Z., P. Arenius, M. Hay and M. Minniti (2004), *Global Entrepreneurship Monitor: 2004 Executive Report*, Boston, MA and London: Babson College and London Business School.

Aldrich, H.E. (1992), 'Methods in our madness? Trends in entrepreneurship research', in D.L. Sexton and J.D. Kasarda (eds), *The State of the Art of Entrepreneurship Research*, Kent, Boston: PWS.

Aldrich, H.E. (2000), 'Learning together: national differences in entrepreneurship research', in D.L. Sexton and H. Landstrom (eds), *The Blackwell Handbook of Entrepreneurship*, Oxford: Blackwell.

Ali, H. and S. Birley (1999), 'Integrating deductive and inductive approaches in a study of new ventures and customer perceived risk', *Qualitative Market Research: an International Journal*, **2**(2), 103–10.

Berg, B.L. (1998), *Qualitative Methods for the Social Sciences*, Boston, MA: Allyn and Bacon.

Blackburn, R. and D. Stokes (2000), 'Breaking down the barriers: using focus groups to research small and medium-sized enterprises', *International Small Business Journal*, **19**(1), 44–67.

Brooksbank, R., D.A. Kirby and G. Wright (1992), 'Marketing and company performance: an examination of medium-sized manufacturing firms in Britain', *Small Business Economics*, **4**, 221–36.

Brooksbank, R., D.A. Kirby, G. Thompson and D. Taylor (2003), 'Marketing as a determinant of long-run competitive success in medium-sized UK manufacturing firms', *Small Business Economics*, **20**, 259–72.

Bygrave, W. (1989), 'The entrepreneurship paradigm (1): a philosophical look at its research methodologies', *Entrepreneurship Theory and Practice*, **14**(1), 7–26.

Churchill, N.C. and V.L. Lewis (1986), 'Entrepreneurship research: directions and methods', in D.L. Sexton and R.L. Smilor (eds), *The Art and Science of Entrepreneurship*, Cambridge, MA: Ballinger.

Curran, J. and R.A. Blackburn (1994), *Small Firms and Local Economic Networks, the Death of the Local Economy?*, London: Paul Chapman.

Curran, J. and R.A. Blackburn (2001), *Researching the Small Enterprise*, London: Sage.

Davies, C.D., G.E. Hills and R.W. La Forge (1985), 'The marketing/small enterprise paradox', *International Small Business Journal*, **3**, Spring, 31–42.

Denzin, N.K. (1989), *The Research Act: A Theoretical Introduction of Sociological Methods*, Englewood Cliffs, NJ: Prentice Hall.

Gartner, W.B. and S. Birley (2002), 'Introduction to the special issue on qualitative methods in entrepreneurship research', *Journal of Business Venturing*, **17**, 387–95.

Gibb, A.A. (1992), 'Can academe achieve quality in small firm policy research?', *Entrepreneurship and Regional Development*, **4**, 127–44.

Glaser, B.G. and A.L. Strauss (1967), *The Discovery of Grounded Theory: Strategies for Qualitative Research*, Chicago: Aldine.

Grant, P. and L. Perren (2002), 'Small business and entrepreneurial research: meta-theories, paradigms and prejudices', *International Small Business Journal*, **20**(2), 185–212.

Gummesson, E. (2003), 'All research is interpretive', *Journal of Business and Industrial Marketing*, **18**(6/7), 482–92.

Henwood, K.L. and N.F. Pidgeon (1993), 'Qualitative research and psychological theorising', in M. Hammersley (ed.), *Social Research: Philosophy, Politics and Practice*, London: Sage.

Kirby, D.A. (1994), 'Customer service and the smaller business', *Customer Service Management*, **II** (March), 18–19.

Kirby, D.A. (1995), 'Marketing and entrepreneurship: post-symposium reflections', in G.E. Hills, D.F. Muzyka, G.S. Omura and G.A. Knight (eds), *Research at the Entrepreneurship/Marketing Interface*, Chicago: University of Illinois at Chicago.

Kirby, D.A. (2003), *Entrepreneurship*, Maidenhead: McGraw-Hill.

Kolb, D.A. (1984), *Experiential Learning*, Englewood-Cliffs NJ: Prentice Hall.

MacMillan, K., J. Curran, S.J. Downing and I.D. Turner (1988), 'Consultation with small business', Department of Employment, London, research paper 66.

Manimala, M.J. (1999), *Entrepreneurial Policies and Strategies: the Innovator's Choice*, London: Sage.

Marino, K.E., R.M. Castaldi and M.J. Dollinger (1989), 'Content analysis in entrepreneurship research: the case of initial public offering', *Entrepreneurship Theory and Practice*, Fall, 51–66.

Merton, R.K. and P.L. Kendall (1946), 'The focused interview', *American Journal of Sociology*, **51**, 541–57.

Morgan, D.L. (1997), *Focus Groups as Qualitative Research*, London: Sage.

Moser, C.A. (1958), *Survey Methods in Social Investigation*, London: Heinemann.

Oppenheim, A.N. (1966), *Questionnaire Design and Attitude Measurement*, London: Heinemann.

Platt, J. (1992), 'Case study in American methodological thought', *Current Sociology*, **40**, 17–48.

Ricoeur, P. (1981), *Hermeneutics and the Human Sciences*, Cambridge: Cambridge University Press.

Shaw, E. (1999), 'A guide to the qualitative research process: evidence from a small firm study', *Qualitative Market Research: an International Journal*, **2**(2), 59–70.

Siu, W.S. and D.A. Kirby (1999), 'Research into small firm marketing: a contextual stepwise approach', *Qualitative Market Research: an International Journal*, **2**(2), 135–46.

Stewart, D.W. and P.N. Shamdasani (1990), *Focus Groups Theory and Practice*, London: Sage.

Wallace, B., A. Ross and J.B. Davies (2003), 'Applied hermeneutics and qualitative safety data: the CIRAS project', *Human Relations*, **56**(5), 587–607.

Vyakarnam, S., A. Bailey, A. Myers and D. Burnett (1997), 'Towards an understanding of ethical behaviour in small firms', *Journal of Business Ethics*, **16**, 15 November, 1625–36.

Yin, R.K. (1994), *Case Study Research: Design and Methods*, London: Sage.

16. A re-visit to the contextual stepwise approach for small firm research*

Wai-sum Siu

INTRODUCTION

In Chapter 15, Kirby proposes the use of a stepwise approach to small firm research. In this chapter, the intention is to describe in more detail how this may be done and to provide a more concrete consideration of the issues involved. While the idea of a stepwise approach came from the attempts of Siu and Kirby (1999a) to build and advance marketing theory, by blending the process model and the contingency approach, they did not, at that time, describe in detail the research methodology issues. In their follow up research (Siu and Kirby, 1999b) they did, however, review the relevant literature on various research designs for small firm marketing and suggest the adoption of a three-stage contextual stepwise approach – adopting a co-ordinated programme of research adjusted in accordance with the situational factors – to examine small firm marketing in more depth.

The contextual stepwise approach argues that adopting a battery of both qualitative and quantitative approaches and techniques is useful to expand the frontiers of marketing knowledge on small firms. However, the research methods listed in the contextual stepwise approach are content analysis, mail survey and personal interview only, other qualitative and quantitative research methods are not examined. Also, the contextual stepwise approach illustrates the usefulness by investigation the marketing practices of Hong Kong small and medium-sized enterprises (SMEs). Hong Kong, before 1997, was a British Colony with Chinese characteristics and is now a Special Administrative Region of China. Hong Kong SMEs have been operating in an interface where the British administrative and legal systems meet with the Chinese socio-cultural values.

The institutional factors of Hong Kong are different from those in other economies, for example China and Taiwan. Notably, the contextual stepwise approach, does not consider adequately the impacts of institutional factors upon small firm operations, nor how should research approaches be changed in order to collect information effectively. The contextual stepwise approach provides researchers with a more 'emic' or culture-specific, insight into Chinese small firm marketing, but fails to acknowledge the importance of 'contextual embeddedness' of small firms in developing other countries (for example Hadjimanolis, 2000; Kim et al., 1993, Tidd et al., 1997). While it is legitimate to query the predominant adoption of an ethnic or culture-free approach to study small firms, it would also need to determine to what extent this 'culture-bound' indigenous approach is useful to explain small firms in other regions or economies. Against this background, this chapter re-visits the contextual stepwise approach. Following the three-stage structure, this chapter reviews the limitations of the contextual stepwise approach and recommends changes for each stage.

STAGE ONE: ETHNOGRAPHIC RESEARCH

Siu and Kirby (1999b) designed a study based on content analyses of newspaper stories about entrepreneurs in Hong Kong. Davis, Hills and LaForge (1985) find that it is very difficult to undertake small firm research because SMEs, compared with large firms, are less willing to co-operate and have no formal marketing policies or decisions. In Chinese society there is a strong preference for secrecy regarding profits and marketing operations and, for reasons which are not altogether clear, Chinese owner-managers prefer to maintain a low profile. Ang and Schmitt (1999) argue that the usual survey research methods may not be very appropriate in a Chinese socio-cultural context, and that in most cases the only means to obtain information is via newspaper reports. Park (1940) regards news as a form of knowledge. He argues that the purpose of news is to locate what everyone needs to know in order to act in the environment, and through their actions to build a common identity. Thus, news stories, which are normally neglected by academic researchers, provide an alternative perspective on the development of entrepreneurship theory.

The contextual stepwise approach distilled small firm marketing models related to marketing activities (Dunn, Birley and Norburn, 1986) and marketing performance (Carson, 1990) and constructed a content analysis schedule to identify the respective marketing practices of Hong Kong SMEs. The study followed the vigorous content analysis procedures (Neuendorf, 2002) and content analysis results and excerpts from the undisguised stories are used to corroborate the empirical evidence.

Published, undisguised news stories, as a source of data for entrepreneurship research, have several advantages over other data sources because they are available from a wide variety of times and places, providing a wider reflection on enterprise culture than is usually the case in management contexts (Czarniawska-Joerges and Guillet de Monthoux, 1994). However, the news stories were not written specifically for the research, and due to the secondary nature of the data of some major issues, for example branding, customer types, and company performance, were not found. This prohibits further analysis. The stories of the Hong Kong SMEs were financial news reports written specifically for small investors who wish to know more about the management capabilities and practices of the owner-manager. If the literacy rate of the specific economy is not high, using published, undisguised news stories does not seem to be a better way to access information. Also, one limitation of the contextual stepwise approach is that it collects undisguised news stories as the only mode of reminiscing, which may have sacrificed some of the natural richness. There are many modes of reminiscing, for example storytelling is one of the diversified narratives. Gummesson (2001) proposes the use of narratives, which are accounts or stories about experiences, to advance theory and knowledge. Thus, future research may examine narratives by storytelling which offer a good ground of a rich and colourful understanding of the marketing practices of SMEs.

Traditionally, the logo-scientific mode of thought has been considered to be scientific and pragmatic, but narratives are regarded as non-scientific and belong to literary genre only. Czarniawska (1997) suggests that narrative requires a plot to bring the stories into a meaningful whole. Boje (2001) further proposes the use of plot analysis, one of the narrative analysis methods, to link a diverse set of events or a succession of incidents together into a narrative structure or meaningful story, so that the embedded situations of how plots get worked out in social systems are identified. Coincidentally, Manimala (1992) proposes the use of analysing stories about owner-managers and their firms to identify the owner-managers' marketing activities and strategic marketing decisions, based on the non-routine decisions of the owner-managers. The narrative approach can make a significant contribution to small firm research. First, it provides a powerful basis for both the generation and testing of theory (Phillips, 1995). Secondly, its can serve as a source of inspiration and model building for business studies (Czarniawska, 1997) and entrepreneurship research (Johansson, 2004). Thirdly, it produces a rich body of knowledge unavailable through other methods of analysis (Boyce, 1995).

A recent study (Siu, 2005) attempts to extend the use of undisguised new stories to other Chinese economies – China and Taiwan – and demonstrates that narratives enhance conceptual, epistemological and methodological reflection in Chinese small firm marketing research. However, the Chinese news stories were prepared by news reporters for propaganda purposes, to support the Chinese central and local governments. The Taiwanese university professors commissioned by the Small and Medium Enterprise Association provide exemplary management practices in the form of cases for native Taiwanese owner-managers. There are thus differences among the Chinese, Hong Kong and Taiwanese stories in terms of the storyteller, the form, the content and the audience. Siu's (2005) study illustrates the attempts to control the cultural factor (Chinese cultural values) and determines small firm marketing practices in different social settings. Different institutional factors should be considered in extending the contextual stepwise approach to other socio-cultural environments.

STAGE TWO: DESCRIPTIVE RESEARCH

The second stage verified insights gained from Stage One and provided a clearer, more systematic picture of the marketing practices of small firms in Hong Kong. At Stage Two the contextual stepwise approach blended the process model (Brooksbank, 1990) and the contingency model (Brooksbank, Kirby and Wright, 1992) in studying Chinese small firm marketing. The marketing process model examines the marketing activities of small firms and the contingency model identifies different types of performing companies.

Among three common survey administered methods – telephone interviews, personal interviews and mail interviews, a mail survey was used for this stage of the study. Though the mail survey is widely criticized (low response rates, a relatively low data reliability and validity being affected by the non-response error), it has proven to be a valuable method of collecting data from the industrial population because it can enable information to be gathered from wide geographic areas at relatively low cost, eliminate interviewer bias, allow respondents to check records, and can be completed at the respondent's convenience (Erdos, 1970; Yu and Cooper, 1982). More specifically it allows the researcher to collect a great deal of data relating to the marketing process and decisions. The anonymous nature of the research method and the confidential assurance offered by the researcher provide a favourable atmosphere for the respondents to give sensitive data, like relative performance in profits, sales and return on investment compared with their major competitors. This helps eliminate interviewer-interviewee bias.

The sampling frame was derived from the *Directory of Hong Kong Industries 1995* and this high quality and readily available sampling frame removed the queries raised by researchers (for example Rosen, 1987; Steele and Yam, 1989; and Yau, Li and Lo, 1986) regarding sampling frame construction and appropriateness of the contact person undertaking survey research in the Chinese socio-cultural environment. A simple probability sampling method, using the random-number generators of the SPSS software for Windows, generated 2,000 sample units.

The instrument involved a four-page, double-sided questionnaire exploring the marketing approaches and practices of small firms in Hong Kong and the page length was regarded by Jobber (1989) as appropriate for an industrial mail survey. The total design method (Dillman, 1978) and professional survey approach (Erdos, 1970) for mail surveys were adopted in designing the questionnaire. In addition, guidelines recommended by small business researchers (Alpar and Spitzer, 1989; Forsgren, 1989) on small firm mail surveys were used to motivate responses. One hundred and eighty-seven useful questionnaires were received from 1,905 effective mailouts, representing a 9.82 per cent response rate. This is only marginally below the normal response rate (10 per cent) in industrial mail surveys, as recognized by Hart (1987), and higher than the response rate to previous mail surveys by Chinese small businesses (Siu and Martin, 1996). Follow-up telephone interviews with 100 randomly selected non-respondents were undertaken to gauge the non-response bias and no overall significant difference was discovered between the respondents and non-respondents.

The 187 returned questionnaires were further screened by the criteria proposed by Brooksbank (1990), Osteryoung and Newman (1993) and Siu and Martin (1992) for Chinese SMEs and 158 firms were eventually analysed. Companies were classified according to a self-assessed measure, using information supplied on the questionnaire and following the approach proposed by Brooksbank, Kirby and Wright (1992). On this basis, 13 (8.2 per cent) of the respondent firms were classified as 'Higher Performer', 97 (61.4 per cent) as 'Average Performer' and 48 (30.4 per cent) as 'Lower Performer'.

Siu et al. (2004) followed and extended the contextual stepwise approach to Taiwan. The sampling frame was derived from the *Taiwan Business Directory* (1999/2000). About 24,000 companies satisfied Brooksbank's (1991) classifications of SMEs. A simple random sampling method was applied by using a sampling probability of 0.1, which generated 2,392 sample units. Deducting 203 returned by the post office as undeliverable, the effective mail-out was 2,189. One hundred and fifty-four useful questionnaires were received. In view of the low response rate given by the Hong Kong survey (Siu and Kirby, 1999), Siu et al. (2004) used follow-up telephone interviews with all non-respondents to motivate and encourage respondents to participate in the study and also to gauge the non-response bias. A predictably high proportion of the respondents claimed not to have received the questionnaire and/or could not spare the time to complete it.

Only 69 useful questionnaires were obtained from the telephone follow-up. In total, 223 useful questionnaires, representing a 10.19 per cent response rate, were used for the data analysis. The response rate was much higher than the response rate of 2.95 per cent found in similar small firm research in Taiwan (Lin et al., 1999).

There are two problems related to the studies of Siu and his colleagues in Hong Kong (1999) and Taiwan (2004). First, the data analysis does not consider the size effect. Larger companies, specifically medium-sized firms (with employment size between 200–500), normally possess many more resources, compared with smaller firms (with employment size less than 200). Hence, they are more likely to attain higher performance. A statistical test should be undertaken to determine the possible effects of firm size upon company performance. To determine the possible effects of firm size, respondents may be grouped into three categories (below 100, 100–199, and 200–499), according to the number of persons employed. If the findings indicate that no statistically significant relationship exists between size and company performance, the researcher can then argue that firm size is not an essential factor contributing to success for the sampled small firms in Hong Kong and Taiwan, rather the higher company performance may be related to marketing practices. Secondly, the reliability of self-assessed measures was queried by researchers and these two studies did not tackle the above problems explicitly.

Though self-assessed measures tend to be biased, Dess and Robinson (1984) believe that in the absence of other objective criteria, self-assessed measures could serve as appropriate and reliable alternative indicators. Also, Bamberger et al. (1989) argue that in cases in which comparisons of cross-industry organizational performance are influenced by external economic factors, self-assessed measures may be even more appropriate than objective measures. Further, research (Dollinger and Golden, 1992; Powell, 1992) reveals that measures of self-reported organizational performance are positively related to objective measures of firm performance. Researchers may need to consider the limitations and conditions of using subjective measures for determining firm performance, should they wish to adopt the contextual stepwise approach.

Nevertheless, the attempt of Siu and his colleagues to extend the contextual stepwise approach from Hong Kong to Taiwan should be commended. First, Hong Kong is a Chinese city with British characteristics because it was a British Colony until 1997 and is now a special administrative region of China. Taiwan was, variously, a Portuguese, a Dutch, a Spanish and a Japanese colony. The island was retroceded to the Republic of China following Japan's defeat and surrender in 1945. A review of relevant literature suggests that Hong Kong is an entrepreneurial society

(Siu and Martin, 1992) whereas Taiwan is a 'boss' island (Shieh, 1992). Recently, institutional analysis (Aoki, 2001) has been widely adopted to describe contextual factors and understand economic development.

Researchers (Lau, 1997; So et al., 2001) specifically point to the importance of understanding the socio-cultural environment and the role of government when applying comparative institutional analysis to Hong Kong and Taiwan. The research findings of Siu et al. (2005) suggest that though China, Hong Kong and Taiwan are 'embedded' in the Chinese culture, differences do exist in the entrepreneurial behaviour and marketing activities of Chinese small firms. They also suggest that the interplay among government intervention, production system and business approach contributes to the differences. Small and medium-sized enterprises in China, under strong government influence, tend to carry out minimal planning in marketing and their marketing activities are implicit. Also under the influence of indigenous Chinese cultural values, SMEs in China are likely to adopt a relation-oriented marketing approach and they place emphasis on building relations with media, rather than advertising.

Though they have minimal marketing expertise, they spend a considerable amount of time and money on marketing. As they have to build their own brands, market research and quality control come to the fore in business operations. Most Hong Kong SMEs operate under the Original equipment manufacturing (OEM) systems. They tend to devote minimal amounts of time and money to marketing and their marketing activities are implicit. The British legal system supports the use of contracts in business transactions and facilitates the development of transaction-oriented marketing activities, for example pricing and product services. Hong Kong is a free economy and SMEs in Hong Kong appear to focus on sales forecasting and adapting to the market environment.

In contrast, Taiwanese SMEs are operated in a politically constrained environment, but economic freedom is tolerated and encouraged by the government. Upgrading from the OEM system to the Original brand marketing (OBM) system, Taiwanese SMEs are trying to develop their own brands. They put a great deal of effort into quality control and invest heavily in marketing. Also, under the influences of indigenous Chinese cultural values, SMEs in Taiwan focus on fostering customer and dealer relations. The economic freedom and also the drive toward building own brands seem to facilitate Taiwanese SMEs' in carrying out explicit marketing activities, and in substantially adapting their marketing plans in response to the specific marketing environment. To redress the balance and place emphasis on the contextual dimension, there is a need to integrate the institutional analysis into the contextual stepwise approach in future studies.

STAGE THREE: FOLLOW-UP IN-DEPTH PERSONAL INTERVIEWS

Although a survey is a valuable method of identifying marketing practices, it provides limited opportunity to investigate the issue in-depth. Siu and Kirby (1999b) undertook 26 in-depth personal interviews with respondents of the mail survey. The process model of Brooksbank (1990) depicting the distinct marketing implementation process of small firms and Yau's (1988) Chinese Cultural Value Orientations were adopted to develop the instrument. McCracken's long interview techniques (1988) were used to guide the interviews, focusing on a series of open questions pertaining to marketing decisions in small businesses. The interviews ranged from an hour to three hours. Interviews were recorded with the consent of the respondents and transcribed accordingly. The scripts were transcribed on a standard word processing package and transformed into ASCII format for further analysis.

The computer-aided qualitative research software, NUD.IST, was used to process the data in ASCII format. The grounded theory approach (Glaser and Strauss, 1967; Strauss, 1987 and Strauss and Corbin, 1990) was adopted to analyse the interview records. Following the grounded theory approach, concepts were drawn from meaningful units of the transcripts.

These concepts were related to each other to produce vignettes to describe marketing actions and strategies of Chinese small firms in Hong Kong. The interview scripts, together with vignettes, were sent to the interviewees for comments. This allowed the researchers to collect reactions and comments about the vignettes from the interviewees as further data which could be incorporated into the proposed proposition or hypothesis. This method of co-inquiry, suggested by Rowbottom (1977), assures the involvement of the interviewees and also allows the researchers to cross-check the interpretations of the interview transcripts. Based on the categorization and concepts generated from the long interview method for data collection, the NUD.IST software package for data processing, and the grounded theory approach for data analysis, a tentative small firm marketing model depicting the influences of Chinese cultural values was constructed.

The contextual stepwise approach allows the researchers to 'see through the eyes of people being studied' (Bryman, 1989, p. 62), and also offers a holistic perspective to examine the phenomenon (Lazega, 1997). It follows a concepts-categories-propositions thread to help ensure conceptual development and density in theory building (Pandit, 1996). Though Siu and Kirby (1999b) provide a detailed explanation on research design, sample design, sampling strategy, instrumentation, and data analysis method and process, two limitations are identified. First, methods used to address the trustworthiness, specifically, credibility, transferability, dependability, and confirmability (Guba and Lincoln, 1981; Miles and Huberman, 1994), for qualitative research are not reported. Secondly, the contextual approach integrates the quantitative and qualitative research methods only. However, a quantitative analysis method could be used to assist grouping the cases, which would in turn confirm the qualitative data analysis results and enhance the confirmability of the entire research.

Researchers (Guba and Lincoln, 1981; Lincoln and Guba, 1985) suggest that compared to the measurement-oriented terms, such as internal validity, external validity, reliability, and objectivity, these analogous terms are more appropriate to the naturalistic paradigm: credibility for truth value, fittingness for applicability, dependability for consistency, and confirmability for neutrality. The credibility criterion involves establishing that the results of qualitative research are credible or believable from the perspective of the participant in the research. To increase credibility, researchers may consider using a series of studies. If informants agree to be interviewed more than one time, interviewers will have chances to verify the data and collect the interviewees' further comments and clarification, which could be incorporated into the original data. Another way to establish the adequacy of a 'fact' is through the triangulation of data sources (Patton, 1990) and 'member checks' (Guba and Lincoln, 1981). Probably, a second informant should be solicited for further interview. In-depth interview data are used as the primary source supplemented with firm public information, like leaflets, firm website, newspapers, as well as direct observation. Transcripts and vignettes were also sent back to the informant for comments. The method of co-inquiry assures the involvement of the interviewees and allows the researcher to cross-check the interpretations of the interview transcripts (Rowbottom, 1977; Miles and Huberman, 1994).

Transferability refers to the degree to which the results of qualitative research can be generalized or transferred to other contexts or settings. Two methods can be used to address the issue of transferability. First, theoretical sampling can be applied to assure the maximum variation. Secondly, Siu and Kirby (1999a) use company performance only as the selection criteria. However, firm size and age may affect the marketing practices and they should be included in the selection criteria. In the naturalistic paradigm, the transferability of propositions to other situations depends on the degree of similarity between the original context and the context to which it is transferred. Thus, thick description of the cases should be provided to allow readers to determine whether the findings are applicable to the new settings (Lincoln and Guba, 1985).

Dependability refers to whether the process of the study is consistent, reasonably stable over time and across researchers and methods. As Lincoln and Guba (1985, p. 316) stated, 'since there can be no validity without reliability (and thus no credibility without dependability), a demonstration of the former is sufficient to establish the latter', researchers should try all measures to attain a high degree of credibility. Lincoln and Guba (1985) also propose 'inquiry audit' in which reviewers examine both the process and the product of the research for consistency to enhance the dependability of qualitative research. Thus, a better approach is using a team and some members are responsible for conducting the interviews independently and the results were reviewed by other research collaborators to test the data variation.

Confirmability refers to the extent to which interpretations are the result of the participants and the phenomenon as opposed to researcher biases. This can be achieved if the researcher can demonstrate the neutrality of the research interpretations, through a 'confirmability audit'. This means providing an audit trail consisting of (1) raw data; (2) analysis notes; (3) reconstruction and synthesis products; (4) process notes; (5) personal notes; and 6) preliminary developmental information (Guba and Lincoln, 1985, pp. 320–21). This audit trail should be developed throughout the data collection and analysis process.

Furthermore, confirmability could be attained if the quantitative analysis results confirm the findings generated from qualitative methods. For example, optimal scaling, a principal component analysis approach with non-linear optimal scaling transformations for ordinal and nominal data (Meulman et al., 2004), may be used to assist the grouping of cases and reveal the major dimensions of variables. According to Young (1981), optimal scaling is a data analysis technique, which assigns numerical values to observation categories in a way, which maximizes the relation between the observations and the data analysis model while respecting the measurement character of the data. By assigning numerical values to the concepts or observation categories, the data could be quantified. Among the commonly used statistical software packages for optimal scaling, the Categorical Principal Component Analysis (CATPCA) routine in the SPSS for Windows, is very user friendly. In fact, CATPCA can be used to analyse complicated multivariate data, consisting of nominal, ordinal, and numerical variables.

In CATPCA, optimal scaling guides the process of quantifying qualitative data and offers a solution on the quantified variables. Biplots, which are joint plots on objects and variables together, offer a graphical display of the results in CATPCA (Gower and Hand, 1996). A straightforward spatial representation is fitted to the data, and different groups of objects can be distinguished in the solution without having to aggregate the categorical data beforehand (Meulman et al., 2004). This method helps to reveal major dimensions of variations and relationships between and among variables and cases. Integrating the quantitative results with findings from the interview scripts will provide critical links or insights into the different groups of data (Miles and Huberman, 1994; Yin, 1994) and gradually build an explanation to 'entertain other plausible or rival expectation' (Yin, 1994, p. 111).

CONCLUSION

The contextual stepwise approach used the stage approach to understand the entrepreneurial and marketing processes of small firms. Each study was designed to build upon what had been learned previously in order to make an incremental contribution to the established knowledge base and allow theory and model building. This allows the research to provide an in-depth and focused analysis of the subject matter. Notably, the contextual stepwise approach can answer research questions which are not able to be answered by relying solely on one research method. Siu and Kirby's (1999b) study confirms that marketing has a positive effect on company performance and at the same time explains and describes how various marketing strategies influence the results. In fact, the contextual stepwise approach answers confirmatory and exploratory questions simultaneously. Secondly, the contextual stepwise approach provides stronger inferences. The survey results identify that marketing practices of Hong Kong SMEs are different from that of their British counterparts. The in-depth personal interview results confirm with the survey findings that Chinese cultural value orientations affect the marketing practices of Hong Kong SMEs. The consistency between the marketing practices quantitatively revealed through the standardized questionnaires and the marketing strategies qualitatively shared by the respondents via in-depth interviews make the inferences from the approach stronger. Thirdly, the contextual stepwise approach offers the opportunity for presenting divergent views. If only the qualitative data were analysed, the influences of the Chinese culture value orientation will be over-estimated.

Similarly, if only the quantitative method was used, the Western marketing principles will be over-emphasised. Using the contextual stepwise approach allows the opportunity for hearing divergent views and provides the platform for theory and model building. The major limitation of the contextual stepwise approach is that the research error in one stage may be transmitted or even multiplied in the following stages. It is essential to ensure that the techniques are applied rigorously, correctly and appropriately. The research error in one stage may be transmitted or even multiplied in the following stages. Should any of the stages make any error, the total research error at the end of the research could be considerable. Thus, users should examine the limitations of each research stage carefully and measures should be taken to minimize the research error. While internal validity, external validity, reliability, and objectivity should be determined for the quantitative methods, credibility, transferability, dependability, and confirmability of each qualitative method should be addressed explicitly and respectively. Also, the contextual factors, which will affect small business operations and also data collection, should be acknowledged. There is a need to integrate the institutional analysis into the contextual stepwise approach.

To conclude, this chapter revisits the contextual stepwise approach and argues that the research methods should be mixed in a way that has complementary strengths and non-overlapping weaknesses. The research methods to be used in the contextual stepwise approach should not be restricted to commonly used methods. Rather, innovative data collection and analysis methods can be put together creatively to answer the specific research questions. This chapter advocates the view that the contextual stepwise approach, adopting a battery of both qualitative and quantitative approaches and techniques in view of the characteristic and limitation of small firms specifically related to the socio-cultural context, is useful to expand the frontiers of knowledge on small firms.

NOTE

*   This chapter is based on Siu, W. and D.A. Kirby (1999b), 'Research into small firm marketing: a contextual stepwise approach', *Qualitative Market Research: An International Journal*, **2**(2), pp. 135–46.

REFERENCES

Alpar, P. and D.M. Spitzer Jr (1989), 'Response behaviour of entrepreneurs in a mail survey', *Entrepreneurship: Theory and Practice*, **14**(2), 31–44.

Ang, H.A. and B.H. Schmitt (1999), 'Introduction to special issue: marketing in the Asia Pacific', *Asia Pacific Journal of Management*, **16**(2), iii–viii.

Aoki, M. (2001), *Toward a Comparative Institutional Analysis*, Cambridge, MA: The MIT Press.

Bamberger, P., S. Bacharach and L. Dyer (1989), 'Human resources management and organizational effectiveness: high technology entrepreneurial startup firms in Israel', *Human Resource Management*, **28**(3), 349–66.

Boje, D.M. (2001), *Narrating Methods for Organizational and Communication Research*, Thousand Oaks, CA: Sage.

Boyce, M.E. (1995), 'Organizational story and storytelling: a critical review', *Journal of Organizational Change Management*, **9**(5), 5–26.

Brooksbank, R. (1990), *This is Successful Marketing*, Bradford: Horton Publishing.

Brooksbank, R. (1991), 'Defining the small business: a new classification of company size', *Entrepreneurship and Regional Development*, **3**(1), 17–32.

Brooksbank, R., D.A. Kirby and G. Wright (1992), 'Marketing and company performance: an examination of medium sized manufacturing firms in Britain', *Small Business Economics*, **4**, 221–36.

Bryman, A. (1989), *Research Methods and Organization Studies*, London; Boston: Unwin Hyman.

Carson, D. (1990), 'Some exploratory models for assessing small firms' marketing performance (a qualitative approach)', *European Journal of Marketing*, **24**(11), 1–51.

Czarniawska, B. (1997), 'Narrating the organization: dramas of institutional identity', Chicago: University of Chicago Press.

Czarniawska-Joerges, B. and P. Guillet de Monthoux (1994), *Good Novels, Better Management: Reading Organizational Realities in Fiction*, Chur, Switzerland: Harwood.

Davis, C.D., G.E. Hills and R.W. LaForge (1985), 'The marketing/small enterprise paradox', *International Small Business Journal*, **3** (Spring), 31–42.

Dess, G.G. and R.B. Robinson Jr (1984), 'Measuring organizational performance in the absence of objective measures: the case of privately held firms and conglomerate business units', *Strategic Management Journal*, **5**, 265–73.

Dillman, D. (1978), *Mail and Telephone Surveys: The Total Design Method*, New York: John Wiley and Sons.

Dollinger, M.J. and P.A. Golden (1992), 'International and collective strategies in small firms: environmental effects and performance', *Journal of Management*, **18**, 695–715.

Dunn, M., S. Birley and D. Norburn (1986), 'The marketing concept and the smaller firm', *Marketing Intelligence and Planning*, **4**(3), 3–11.

Erdos, P.L. (1970), *Professional Mail Survey*, New York: McGraw-Hill.

Forsgren, R.A. (1989), 'Increase mail survey response rates: methods for small business researchers', *Journal of Small Business Research*, **27**(4), 61–66.

Glaser, B.G. and S.L. Strauss (1967), *The Discovery of Grounded Theory: Strategies for Qualitative Research*, New York: Aldine de Gruyter.

Gower, J.C. and D.J. Hand (1996), *Biplots*, London: Chapman and Hall.

Guba, E.G. and Y.S. Lincoln (1981), *Effective Evaluation*, San Francisco: Jossey-Bass.

Gummesson, E. (2001), 'Are current research approaches in marketing leading us astray?', *Marketing Theory*, **1**(1), 27–48.

Hadjimanolis, A. (2000), 'An investigation of innovation antecedents in small firms in the context of a small developing country', *R&D Management*, **30**(3), 23–245.

Hart, S. (1987), 'The use of the survey in industrial market research', *Journal of Marketing Management*, **3**(1), 25–38.

Hills, G.E. and R.W. LaForge (1992), 'Research at the marketing interface to advance entrepreneurship theory', *Entrepreneurship Theory and Practice*, **17** (Spring), 33–59.

Jobber, D. (1989), 'An examination of the effects of questionnaire factors on response to an industrial mail survey', *International Journal of Research in Marketing*, **6**, 129–40.

Johansson, A.W. (2004), 'Narrating the entrepreneur', *International Small Business Journal*, **22**(3): 273–93.

Kim, Y., K. Song, K. and J. Lee (1993), 'Determinants of technological innovation in small firms of Korea', *R&D Management*, **23**(3), 215–26.

Lazega, E. (1997), 'Network analysis and qualitative research: a method of contextualization', in G. Miller and R. Dingwall (eds), *Context and Method in Qualitative Research*, London: Sage, pp. 119–38.

Lau, L.J. (1997), 'The role of government in economic development: some observations from the experience of China, Hong Kong and Taiwan', in M. Aoki, H. Kin and M. Okuno-Fujiwara (eds), *The Role of Government in East Asian Economic Development*, Oxford: Oxford University Press, pp. 41–73.

Lincoln, Y.S. and E.G. Guba (1985), *Naturalistic Inquiry*, Newbury Park, CA: Sage.

Manimala, M.J. (1992), 'Entrepreneurial heuristics: a comparison between high PI (Pioneering-Innovative) and low PI ventures', *Journal of Business Venturing*, **7**, 477–504.

McCracken, G. (1988), *The Long Interview*, London: Sage.

Meulman, J.J., A.J. Van Der Kooij and W.J. Heiser (2004), in D. Kaplan (ed.), *The Sage Handbook of Quantitative Methodology for the Social Sciences*, Thousand Oaks, CA: Sage, pp. 49–70.

Miles, M.B. and A.M. Huberman (1994), *Qualitative Data Analysis*, London: Sage.

Neuendorf, K.A. (2002), *The Content Analysis Guidebook*, Thousand Oaks, CA: Sage.

Osteryoung, J.S. and D. Newman (1993), 'What is a small business', *The Journal of Small Business Finance*, **2**, 219–31.

Pandit, N. (1996), 'The creation of theory: a recent application of the grounded theory method', *The Qualitative Report*, **2**(4), (December), accessed at www.nova.edu/ssss/QR/QR2-4/pandit.html.

Patton, M.Q. (1990), *Qualitative Evaluation and Research Methods*, 2nd edn, Newbury Park, CA: Sage.

Park, R.E. (1940), 'News as a form of knowledge', *American Journal of Sociology*, **45**, 669–86.

Phillips, N. (1995), 'Telling organizational tales: on the role of narrative fiction in the study of organization', *Organization Studies*, **14**(4), 625–49.

Powell, T.C. (1992), 'Organizational alignment as competitive advantage', *Strategic Management Journal*, **13**, 119–34.

Rosen, S. (1987), 'Survey research in The People's Republic of China: some methodological problems', *Canadian and International Education*, **16**(1), 190–97.

Rowbottom, R. (1977), *Social Analysis: a Collaborative Method of Gaining Usable Scientific Knowledge of Social Institutions*, London: Heinemann.

Shieh, G.S. (1992), *'Boss' Island: The Subcontracting Network and Micro-Entrepreneurship in Taiwan's Development*, New York: Peter Lang.

Siu, W. (2005), 'An institutional analysis of marketing practices of small and medium-sized enterprises (SMEs) in China, Hong Kong and Taiwan', *Entrepreneurship and Regional Development*, **17**, 65–88.

Siu, W., W. Fang and T. Lin (2004), 'Strategic marketing practices and the performance of Chinese small and medium-sized enterprises (SMEs) in Taiwan', *Entrepreneurship and Regional Development*, **16**, 161–78.

Siu, W. and D.A. Kirby (1999a), 'Small firm marketing: a comparison of eastern and western marketing practices', *Asia Pacific Journal of Management*, **16**(2), 259–74.

Siu, W. and D.A. Kirby (1999b), 'Research into small firm marketing: a contextual stepwise approach', *Qualitative Market Research: an International Journal*, **2**(2), 135–46.

Siu, W. and R.G. Martin (1992), 'Successful entrepreneurship in Hong Kong', *Long Range Planning*, **25**(6), 87–93.

Siu, W. and R.G. Martin (1996), 'A comparison between Chinese and American small business owner-manager's attitude towards management concepts', *Proceedings of Cross-cultural Management in China*, **2**, 94–103.

So, A.Y., N. Lin and D. Poston (eds) (2001), *The Chinese Triangle of Mainland China, Taiwan, and Hong Kong: Comparative Institutional Analyses*, Westport, CT: Greenwood Press.

Steele, H.C. and E.P. Yam (1989), 'Research in Hong Kong', *The Hong Kong Manager*, **25**(2), 21–27.

Strauss, A.L. (1987), *Qualitative Analysis for Social Scientist*, New York: Cambridge University Press.

Strauss, A.L. and J. Corbin (1990), *Basics of Qualitative Research: Grounded Theory Procedures and Techniques*, Newbury Park, CA: Sage.

Tidd, J., J. Bessant and K. Pavitt (1997), *Integrating Technological, Market and Organizational Change*, Chichester: J. Wiley and Sons.

Yau, O.H.M. (1988), 'Chinese cultural values: their dimensions and marketing implications', *European Journal of Marketing*, **22**(5), 44–57.

Yau, O.H.M., Y.J. Li and T. Lo (1986), 'Marketing and marketing research in China', *Journal of International Marketing and Marketing Research*, **18**(1), 3–18.

Yin, R.K. (1994), *Case Study Research*, 2nd edn, Thousand Oaks, CA: Sage.

Young, F.W. (1981), 'Quantitative analysis of qualitative data', *Psychometrika*, **46**(4), 357–88.

Yu, J. and H. Cooper (1983), 'A quantitative review of research design effects on response rates to questionnaire', *Journal of Marketing Research*, **20** (February), 36–44.

17. Exploring fast-track entrepreneurial thinking by a novel text-analytic method: Pertex

Helge Helmersson and Jan Mattsson

INTRODUCTION

Sarasvathy's (2001) new perspective on entrepreneurship as problem solving is about how one orients oneself when faced with a problem. She suggests two contrasting behavioural orientations termed causation and effectuation. A causation type of behaviour implies that future uncertainty is managed by plans and forecasts. By effectuation, however, future uncertainty is controlled by a continuous and renewed change of goals and assumptions. A future market is not taken for granted, rather the market has to be created in order to reap the benefits from it. In essence, causation is characterized by the logic of prediction and effectuation by the logic of control. Hitherto, effectuation has not been empirically measured. This chapter contributes by using a novel text analytic method (Pertex) to form cognitive models of entrepreneurial orientation from the written accounts of two Swedish entrepreneurs who explain how they took a business idea to market. Clear evidence of causation and effectuation orientations were found. Two orientation models are analysed in depth with important managerial implications suggested.

A COGNITIVE TURN IN ENTERPRISE RESEARCH

An overriding issue in the multidisciplinary field of entrepreneurial research has been the role of the entrepreneur in new venture formation. Trait-based research streams during the last four decades have focused on the personality of the entrepreneur such as: need for achievement (McClelland, 1961; 1965), locus of control (Rotter, 1966), propensity towards risk (De Vries, 1977) and tolerance for ambiguity (Shene, 1982). Nevertheless, it has been difficult to substantiate a special set of personality traits that should characterize the entrepreneur. Similarly, another research stream has emphasized the entrepreneurial role in new venture performance (Sandberg, 1986; Shane and Venkataraman, 2000; Holmquist and Sundin, 2002), which has defined entrepreneurship research in relation to strategic management. However, a persistent effort to link the traits of the entrepreneurial individual to new venture performance has apparently met with little success.

Instead, during the last decade, a recent interest in entrepreneurial cognitions has emerged (Mitchell et al., 2000). In their seminal article they define entrepreneurial cognitions as: 'the knowledge structures that people use to make assessments, judgements or decisions involving opportunity evalu-ation, venture creation, and growth' (p. 97). The aim is to understand how entrepreneurs use simplifying mental models to construct their business perceptions. Recent findings from this stream of research has suggested new and exciting cognitive mechanisms such as: counterfactual thinking and self-justification (Baron, 1998), overconfidence, illusion of control and other cognitive errors (McGrath, 1999; Simon, Houghton and Aquino, 2000) that may shape the entrepreneur's view of business options. For instance, cognitive models are now used to explain the strong heuristic side of entrepreneurial thinking and strategic decision-making (Alvarez and Busenitz, 2001; Alsete, 2002; Sarasvathy, 2001). New qualitative approaches, such as narrative methods, have been suggested to unravel deep-level entrepreneurial cognition (Rae, 2000; Jenkins and Johnson, 1997).

The premise of this chapter is that more advanced methods are needed to analyse deeper-level entrepreneurial cognition and decision-making. We posit that this deeper level cognition is evident in narratives authored by the entrepreneurial person himself/herself. It is the aim of this chapter to present a new text-analytic approach to study entrepreneurial cognitions by probing a recently developed theoretical perspective on two contrasting entrepreneurial orientations.

Causation and Effectuation

Sarasvathy (2001) presents a new perspective on entrepreneurship as problem solving. This new perspective is not about technical problem solving, but rather a personal way of how one orients oneself when faced with a problem. She discusses two main behavioural orientations termed causation and effectuation. The divide between these two concepts is how the entrepreneur manages the planning and organization of a new business venture. A causation type of behaviour implies that future uncertainty is managed by plans and forecasts. For example, the potential market share for a venture is forecasted by existing knowledge and reasonable assumptions about developments. Hence by elaborating formal plans the entrepreneur can control uncertainty.

By effectuation, however, future uncertainty is controlled by a continuous and renewed change of goals and assumptions. For example, a future market is not taken for granted, rather the market has to be created in order to reap the benefits from it. In essence, causation is characterized by the logic of prediction and effectuation by the logic of control (Sarasvathy, 2001, p. 243).

Even if Sarasvathy (2001, p. 249) suggests that effectuation is a novel concept, she also moderates her stance as follows: 'it is necessary to emphasize that effectuation processes are not posited here as "better" or "more efficient" than causation processes in creation artefacts such as firms, markets, and economies. Under what circumstances which types of processes provide particular advantages and disadvantages is an issue to be resolved through future empirical studies'. To test the efficacy of the effectuation approach, relative to that of causation, could then be an interesting way to analyse entrepreneurial decision-making. Prior research on comparing successful and failed entrepreneurs 'have been disappointingly mixed' (ibid, p. 258).

Sarasvathy suggests a rather revolutionary idea as to how effectuation could be studied: 'we need to give up ideas such as the successful personality or clearly superior characteristics of the successful firm or organization. Rather, we need to learn to deal with a rain forest of individuals and firms and markets and societies, intermeshed and woven together with completely coherent yet vastly diverse local patterns that add up to a complex, interdependent ecology of human artefacts' (2001, p. 258). Sarasvathy makes a clear distinction between the successful entrepreneur and the success of the firm. This is explained by the inherent meaning of effectuation – in that the success of the firm created is but one of a range of possible firms. This implies that effectuation posits a plurality of 'failed' firms for any more 'successful' firm that actually gets created by any given entrepreneur.

The normative aspects of effectuation, if any, for the creation of successful firms would have to do with the 'management' of failures rather than with their avoidance (2001, p. 259). Taking effectuation instead of causation as a paradigm we would focus on the question: 'Given who you are, what you know, and whom you know, what type of economic and/or social artefacts can you, would you want to, and should you, create?' (2001, pp. 258–59). Sarasvathy suggests that appropriate methods to use when investigating the propensity of causation and effectuation in entrepreneurial behaviours would be: 'methods such as grounded theory building using case studies and qualitative analyses of detailed decision-making experiments' (p. 261).

To this effect, in this chapter we will apply a new text analytic approach called Pertex (Helmersson, 1992; Helmersson and Mattsson, 2001, 2002; Mattsson and Helmersson, 2005) to analyse the intention of an author of a text produced in a relevant setting. Our aim is to show how effectuation and causation can be identified in normal text generated by entrepreneurs in response to the research question: 'The way I commercialized an innovation by establishing a company'. We structure the chapter in the following way. First, we illustrate how coding and analysis of text fragments are carried out. Secondly, we explain, by using two contrasting examples, how causation and effectuation can be identified from Pertex results and, finally we draw some managerial implications.

THE UNIQUENESS OF OUR APPROACH

Our approach requires that the respondent verbalizes or writes about a narrow topic without the direction of detailed follow-up questions from the researcher. In carrying out traditional in-depth or focus interviews, and in compiling a survey, the researcher has a controlling role in advancing the pre-determined topics or questions or issues. In some respects the results are locked-in before data has been collected (a positivist approach which does not enhance exploratory research). This can be acceptable when a known and well-defined topic is investigated, such as in hypothetico-deductive techniques. However, when exploratory aims are to be fulfilled it is nearly impossible to formulate relevant questions. This permits an exploratory, interpretist approach which aligns well with the purpose of this book.

Sarasvathy (2001) has suggested a number of indications of effectuation and causation behaviours. What seems to be lacking is more empirical testing of how these two different behaviours can be identified in actual behaviours. One option to collect data would be to follow an individual and converse with him and observe the actions and decisions taken – this incorporates attitudes enacted into behaviours. However, such an approach would inevitably be contaminated by the thinking and analysis of the researcher himself and not necessarily capturing the thinking and actions of the individual entrepreneur – this brings in complicated epistemology where the researcher becomes also participant. Our approach is to go directly to the source and collect phenomenological data while seeking to remove, or at least minimize, researcher bias.

We have taken two representatives from a sample of eight entrepreneurs,

Table 17.1   Formatting of the sentence into clauses

Clause No.	Agent	Verb	Orientation borderline	Clause
1	I	(was)	good friend with one of the directors of (company A)	and
2	we	(were allowed)	[–] to a presentation on	
3	[–]	(make)		how
4	we	(could)	[–] their exhaust-air	[–]
5	[–]	(absorb)		

Note: [–] marks Agent, Orientation or Clause borderline not explicitly given in the text.

selected for another study, from a science park location in southern Sweden. Each had established his own company from a technological innovation. We asked the respondents to tell about the process of commercialization of those innovations. In this way, we got an account of how a new market was created. We instructed the respondents to write freely about their experiences of the process of commercialization. Each one of the respondents wrote at least one full page of text, see Table 17.1 above for an example.

In most text analytical approaches an intuitive interpretation has normally been carried out by the researcher as an ad hoc mental operation, by which certain elements have been focused on because these elements have a particular contextual relevance. Hence, it is the interpreter (researcher) who filters content and assigns meaning to the text writer (respondent). This is also the case when one uses computer-based tools such as NUDIST or Atlas/ti.

In Pertex it is the other way around; the author of a text has priority. Pertex generates, in a formal and controllable way, the inherent intention embedded in a given text. We presume that a meaningful text derives its meaning from what the author intended. The standpoint, that the intention of a text can be generated without the researcher taking an absolute interpretative part, however, is quite new. We now focus on the principles behind how the text is coded and organized into a coherent structure, the purpose of which is to depict the intention of the author. The following sentence is reproduced from Appendix 1 (the fourth sentence) and is used to demonstrate how the text is formatted in Pertex:

> I was good friends with one of the directors of (company A) and we were allowed to make a presentation on how we could absorb their exhaust-air.

The verbs in the sentence are crucial because they indicate the activities in the text, however verbs cannot, by themselves, shape meaning to the sentence. Words adjacent to the verbs, however, are able to signal meaning. A clause can be defined around each verb in the sentence. The borderline of each clause is set by 'and', 'to' and 'how'. The words placed in front of the verb are defined as the Agent (generally personal pronouns, considered in parts of speech as the subject). In English the verb is usually followed by an object, which gives the verb meaning. In the Pertex analysis we refer to this as the Orientation. So the words after the verb are construed as that which expresses the Orientation of the clause.

In Table 17.1 the basic conditions for the formatting rules of the Pertex system are demonstrated. We will now explain some of these rules.

Agent is the linguistic unit controlling the activity expressed by the verb. Orientation indicates that which is in focus in the clause. Both Agent and Orientation are always made up of the words, which are in front of, and immediately after, the verb irrespective of what kind of word they are. The verbs were allowed (clause number 2) signal a passive construction, which means that the two verbs form a unit. This is not the case for the two verbs 'could' and 'absorb' (clause numbers 4 and 5), which are both operating in separate clauses.

When formatting, Pertex will automatically replace the implicit denotations of Agent and Orientation, [–], with explicit references to adjacent parts of the text. We will first explain, by using the second clause, how this is done (see Table 17.1). The passive verb unit 'were allowed' has as a consequence that it is not the word 'we' in front of 'the verb', which has the controlling function with regard to allowing something. To the contrary, it is another party, not explicitly mentioned, who allows this to happen. This unknown party is termed Xp and becomes a new and different Agent in the second clause. As the permission is directed towards us, ie 'we', the Orientation of the clause also becomes this word 'we'. In Table 17.2 below we show how the second clause is formatted along these lines.

In the third clause the Agent is implicit. The formatting rule is then to copy the Agent in the preceding clause as the explicit Agent. Consequently, Xp is inserted as Agent in the third clause (see Table 17.2). It may look a bit strange that Xp and not 'we' is inserted as the Agent, which via 'make' is linked to a presentation 'on'. The intention of the author of the text is obvious – to tell that someone, ie Xp, gave permission so that the presentation could be done. However, note that Xp is not the Agent in the fourth and the fifth clause. The mentioned formatting rule, with regard to explicit replacement of an absent Agent in a clause, makes the word 'we' the Agent in the fifth clause.

In the fourth clause we lack an explicit text for Orientation. In this clause it is obvious that 'we could' is referring to that which follows in the next clause. Consequently the formatting rule implies that both the Agent

Table 17.2   Formatting of clauses

Clause No.	Agent	Verb	Orientation borderline	Clause
1	I	(was)	good friend with one of the directors of (company A)	and
2	Xp	(were allowed)	we	
3	Xp	(make)	to a presentation on	how
4	we	(could)	we their exhaust air	*
5	we	(absorb)	their exhaust air	

Note: *marks a technical borderline.

and the Orientation in the fifth clause are inserted as explicit Orientation in the fourth clause. When the text does not contain an explicit border-line for a clause, as in the fourth clause, a technical borderline (*) is inserted.

According to the formatting of clauses in Table 17.2, the sentence as a whole now has three different Agents (I, Xp and 'we') and five different expressions for Orientation. Note that the formatting rules have placed 'we' (firstly used only as Agent) as a part of Orientation in clauses two and four.

When formatting a text it is necessary to perform a lot of different kinds of substitutions when there are implicit references in the text. The example (see Tables 17.1 and 17.2) only shows a few rather simple and common rules of substitution. Natural text often contains implicit references, which can require lengthy textual flows of substitutions, even cyclical ones. It would be too complicated (and not within the scope of this chapter) to expand on all rules of formatting inherent in the Pertex system.

Pertex rests on the axiom that the intention of the author of the text is mirrored by the way the clauses link the Agent and Orientation functions. In the examples above (Tables 17.1 and 17.2) there are the following links between the three different Agents and the five different expressions for Orientation as shown in a binary matrix (see Table 17.3).

Note that the binary matrix in Table 17.3 only shows which unique (and different) portfolio of Agents (I, Xp and 'we') there are. The same is true for the five expressions for Orientation (O1–O5). The matrix contains five rows but only three columns.

The binary Orientation/Agent is now used as an input (data set) to carry out a cluster analysis in which the rows are clustered with the Agents as variables. Using Wards method (Ward, 1963) will yield a hierarchical cluster tree (see Figure 17.1).

Table 17.3   Binary matrix orientation/agent

Orientation	Agent		Xp	we
	I			
01:	good friend with one of the directors of (company A)			1
02:	we		1	
03:	a presentation on		1	
04:	we their excess air			1
05:	their exhaust air			1

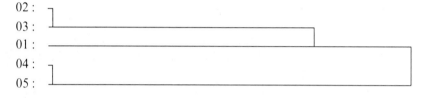

Figure 17.1   Hierarchical cluster tree

To this point the handling of text from formatting to cluster formation has been entirely mechanical. From now on, human interpretation is required to make the intentional message (from the author) clear. The interpretation will strictly follow the hierarchical cluster tree.

In the tree (see Figure 17.1) we have tree clusters; the top-cluster which includes the expressions of Orientation O2+O3, the next cluster comprised of expression from O1, and the final cluster of O4+O5. The textual elements included in these expressions (O1–O5) are shown in Table 17.2 above. We now have the task to put a label on each of the clusters according to their content of textual elements. The top cluster, for example, can be labelled 'Our presentation', cluster two 'Good friend' and the final cluster 'Their exhaust air'. According to the cluster tree, (see Figure 17.1), the first two clusters are joined first, and then the final cluster joins to form 'the root' of the tree. In this root all textual elements (O1–O5) are included.

The final part of the interpretation is about labelling subsequent fusions among the clusters as determined by the tree. In this way, we add and interpret in a consecutive way more and more of the intention of the text. For example, (see Figure 17.2), 'Our presentation' joined with 'Good friend'

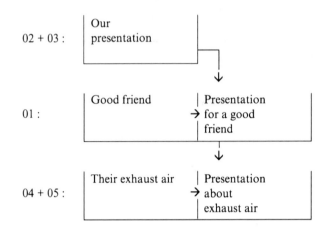

Figure 17.2   Final result from the example

results in 'Presentation for a good friend'. Finally, 'Presentation for a good friend' and 'Their exhausted air' are joined to the root concept of the tree namely 'Presentation about exhausted air'.

This simple example only comprised one sentence, and is therefore unable to illustrate all the intricacies of a longer text. The intention in the sentence is rather straightforward and transparent. The resulting concept 'Presentation about exhaust air' was certainly not surprising. However, the aim was to simplify the explanation of how the Pertex system operates.

We claim the strength of Pertex is in combining formal analysis and human synthesis into one method, which will put more rigor into interpretation. The smallest unit of analysis is the word. By first clustering words we are then able to synthesize and reconstruct the entire text. The complete text is handled without any additions or deletions. If a text is produced in a relevant and coherent way, Pertex is able to detect the intentional message by focusing on how the author has co-ordinated Agents and Orientation in the text. We will now depict how two Swedish entrepreneurs differ in their behavioural orientation (causation and effectuation-driven).

RESULTS: CONTRASTING TWO ENTREPRENEURIAL ORIENTATIONS

We will illustrate how traces of causation and effectuation can be found in the Pertex output from two entrepreneurs. One is termed 'causation-driven' and the other 'effectuation-driven'. As a base for our analysis and argument

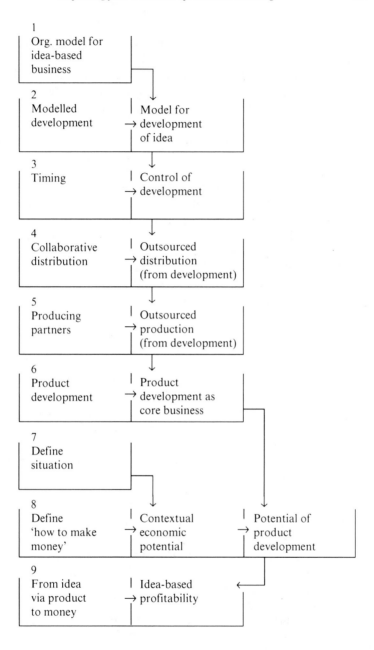

Figure 17.3   Model-driven entrepreneur

we use the cluster trees with Orientation clustered by Agents as variables. The analysis will follow 'the top-down flow' in each tree. We start with the model-driven entrepreneur (see Figure 17.3).

The flow in Figure 17.3 begins with a model that is an ideal model for development (second cluster fusion). Then control is elaborated. With timing and collaboration one can outsource distribution and also production (from the development), which leads to a 'cleansed' product development as the core business activity (sixth cluster fusion). At this point an elaboration of how to make money adapts the rational sequence of thought. The economic potential is context dependent and hence the product development is also linked to this. The bottom-line is idea-based profitability. All in all, this very rational thought pattern is classified as causation-oriented. It deals with how best to make money from an idea. It produces a meta-model of profit making. Context only comes in to moderate the potential of success. The model is given from the start and is then put to use. One can say that this signals an impersonal way (compared to effectuation, which is a highly personal way of planning an emerging venture) of managing a business. The success can be forecasted by plans. The model is in itself an indicator of causation.

In contrast let us look at another entrepreneur who has written the text in Appendix 1. After a Pertex analysis of Appendix 1, we classify this entrepreneur as effectuation-driven. In this cluster tree (see Figure 17.4), the first three clusters deal with exploiting a technical possibility (third fusion) at a very personal level.

The response of financiers and the start-up focus of the entrepreneur decide the establishment of the business and the firm (as a tool for this venture). A consolidation phase is construed from external communication and motivation (by the entrepreneur). We can see, already at this point, that this thought pattern is different. It starts with the person and his possibilities and his attempt to exploit technology commercially by relating it to requirements from financiers and personal focus of interest. By effective external communication the business is consolidated. Nothing is taken for granted. A stepwise approach is demonstrated to secure the entrepreneurial process as such. This is also clear at the end of the tree. Using personal contacts (seventh and eighth cluster), which blends into the creation of personal trust (of the entrepreneur), a highly personal business idea can be established which completes the entrepreneurial task.

In essence, uncertainty is controlled by a continuous change and adaptation of plans. A personal endeavour (means) forms the venture according to necessity. A range of possibilities arises. The final venture is not decided on beforehand as in a model example above. It becomes the outcome of an entrepreneurial process. Effectuation is embedded in the

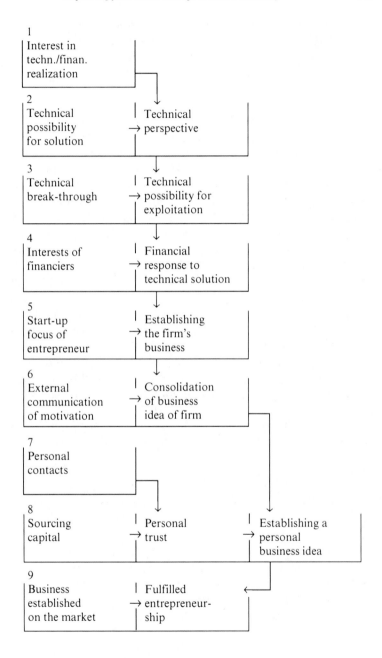

Figure 17.4   Effectuation-driven entrepreneur

Innovative methodologies in enterprise research

way the individual traits and means are interwoven with the attempt to control the venture formation process. Means to do this are a person-centred collaboration with others. Not a model-centric rational planning process to assess the potential of the product.

CONCLUSIONS AND MANAGERIAL IMPLICATIONS

In this way, we claim to be able to assess the degree to which entrepreneurial decision-making (or strategy-making) can be classified as either effectuation-driven or causation-driven. We can hypothesize that these different paradigms of entrepreneurial behaviour can have vast consequences for the outcome of individual ventures and also enrich our understanding of how emergent firms operate. However, effectuation and causation traces are not well-defined phenomena. To the contrary, they often intertwine in the cluster tree and take different positions. It is, therefore, often difficult to interpret the effect of the cluster three on real business outcomes (Sarasvathy, 2001).

Nevertheless, in validating the results we may briefly summarize the careers of the two contrasting entrepreneurs. The model-driven entrepreneur has had a technical focus and has not been sensitive to changing environment and market conditions. To him the model rests supreme. This can be supported by his failure to make a profit during his many years of operations. The effectuation-driven entrepreneur, however, has taken a very different course of action. Not being a technical, but rather commercial, expert, he has constantly taken steps to minimize exposure and cost when creating a new market for himself. He has been profitable from the start.

We suggest that our text approach can help delineate differences between entrepreneurial behavioural orientations. For instance, a systematic study comparing across gender may be relevant in supporting the growth of new small businesses (Holmquist and Sundin, 2002). Another way of taking advantage of our approach could be to compare failures and success stories in retrospect to investigate the propensity for orientations among entrepreneurs. Also potential entrepreneurs, looking for funding, could be the source to trace the kind of orientation arguments carrying weight in these decisions. All in all, we see great scope for the application of Pertex in entrepreneurial cognition research.

REFERENCES

Alsete, J.W. (2002), 'On becoming an entrepreneur: an evolving typology', *International Journal of Entrepreneurial Behaviour & Research*, **8**(4), 222–34.

Alvarez, S. and L. Busenitz (2001), 'The entrepreneurship of resource-based theory', *Journal of Management*, **27**, 755–75.

Baron, R.A. (1998), 'Cognitive mechanisms in entrepreneurship: why and when entrepreneurs think differently than other people', *Journal of Business Venturing*, **13**(4), 275–94.

De Vries, M.F.R. (1977), 'The entrepreneurial personality: a person at the crossroads', *Journal of Management Studies*, **34**, 34–57.

Helmersson, H. (1992), 'Main principles for perspective text analysis via the PC-system PERTEX', *Kognitionsvetenskaplig forskning*, **41**, Lund: Lund University.

Helmersson, H. and J. Mattsson (2001), 'Demonstrating Pertex: a new method for improving text interpretation', *Field Methods*, **2**(13), 115–36.

Helmersson, H. and J. Mattsson (2002), 'Hur förklara en textanalytisk nyorientering?', in Hans Landström, Jan Mattsson and Helge Helmersson (eds), *Ur en forskarhandledares örtagård, en vänbok till Bertil Gandemo, Lund Studies in Economics and Management*, pp. 19–36.

Holmquist, C. and E. Sundin (2002), *Företagerskan: om kvinnor och entreprenörskap*, Stockholm: SNS Förlag.

Jenkins, M. and G. Johnson (1997), 'Entrepreneurial intentions and outcomes: a comparative causal mapping study', *Journal of Management Studies*, **34**(6), 895–920.

Keits De Vries, M.F.R. (1977), 'The entrepreneurial personality: a person at the crossroads', *Journal of Management Studies*, **34**, 34–57.

Mattsson J. and H. Helmersson (2005), 'Eating fast-food: attitudes of high school students', *International Journal of Consumer Studies*, (in press).

McClelland, D.C. (1961), *The Achieving Society*, Princeton, NJ: Van Nostrand.

McClelland, D.C. (1965), 'Need achievement and entrepreneurship: a longitudinal study', *Journal of Personality and Social Psychology*, **1**, 389–92.

McGrath, R.G. (1999), 'Falling forward: real options reasoning and entrepreneurial failure', *Academy of Management Review*, **24**(1), 13–30.

Mitchell, R.K., L. Busenitz, T. Lant, P.P. McDougal, E.A. Morse and B. Smith (2002), 'Toward a theory of entrepreneurial cognition: rethinking the people side of entrepreneurship research', *Entrepreneurship Theory and Practise*, **26**(4), 93–104.

Rae, D. (2000), 'Understanding entrepreneurial learning: a question of how?', *International Journal of Entrepreneurial Behaviour & Research*, **6**(3), 145–59.

Rotter, J.B. (1966), 'Generalized expectancies for internal versus external control of reinforcement', *Psychological Monographs: General and Applied*, **80**(1).

Sandberg, W.R. (1986), *New Venture Performance: the Role of Strategy and Industry Structure*, Lexington, MA: D-C Health and Company.

Sarasvathy, S. (2001), 'Causation and effectuation: toward a theoretical shift from economic inevitability to entrepreneurial contingency', *Academy of Management Review*, **26**(2), 243–63.

Shane, S. and S. Venkataraman (2000), 'The promise of entrepreneurship as a field of research', *Academy of Management Review*, **25**(1), 217–26.

Shene, J. (1982), 'Tolerance of ambiguity as a discriminating variable between entrepreneurs and managers', presentation to the Academy of Management Conference, New York.

Simon, M., S.M. Houghton and K. Aquino (2000), 'Cognitive biases, risk perception and new venture formation: how individual decide to start companies', *Journal of Business Venturing*, **14**(5), 113–34.

Ward, J.E. (1963), 'Hierarchical grouping to optimize an objective function', *Journal of American Statistical Association*, **58**, 236–44.

APPENDIX 17.1 TEXT WRITTEN BY AN EFFECTUATION ENTREPRENEUR (TRANSLATED FROM SWEDISH)

I used to play tennis with (name), professor of chemistry in (town A), during many years. He had obtained several findings but none had been commercialized. The environmental debate was fierce these years and the Environmental Protection Agency was demanding action from industry. (company A) discharged 1400 tons of solvents in (town B). (Name) had developed a compound to with special capacities to absorb (solvents). We discussed different ways in which we could absorb solvents from air. I was good friends with one of the directors of (company A) and we were allowed to make a presentation on how we could absorb their exhaust-air. They went for it and we could show, using a vacuum cleaner and some bits of (compound) how we could retrieve the solvents and recycle them in a liquid form by means of regenerating the (compound) with a stream of gas.

I had been working with innovation as an employee but now I realized that I could be my own man. It was a gamble having a wife at home with four small children but I felt it the right thing to do. I quit my job and we started a joint company (name) in (town A).

(Company A) put in (sum) as a project support. The Development Fund (name) gave the same amount as a loan and we invested (sum). We built the company step by step. We did not proceed until we knew that the steps we had taken really worked. I was given a lot of speeches about the revolutionary method and public interest increased. Not least because of the location in (town A). Soon we got an order from (company B) which were emitting an odour in their production process. We showed that we were able to purify the air completely. (Company B) gave an advance (sum) in (year) and we built the plant together with (company B) and it was operational in (year). It is still in operation today and is purifying the air of (town A)!

(Year) we reached a turnover of (sum) and we had built our own office building at (place). Now it was time to go international. It came out that we had approached friends who had paid in advance and who had not demanded any guarantees. Outside of this group, one demanded bank guarantees. At that time it was impossible to get money for new and innovative companies. The stock market was unthinkable at the time. We sold the company (year) to (name) and moved operations to the US where we are very successful.

I learnt a lot from this. To start without your own money. The agreements must be written in such a way as to not sell our soul. Innovations were more or less impossible to finance in the early stages. The risk capital market did not exist. I took part in the public debate and became a columnist to (daily newspaper) for these issues, consulted for government and together with (name) at (science park) we were able to interest the highest levels of government. The subsequent development has swung around in excesses in what is now termed the new economy.

I found that my competence was about taking charge (of business) in the earlier stages. From idea to sustainable sales. I have never put my own interest for money first. This has made me respected by researchers and I have since then started three other new knowledge intensive firms, which have all become successful. I take a minority share but run the company, often with my own money, as if I owned it all. When things start to roll I hand over command to those who have more competence than I have.

18. The application of Leximancer, a relational content analytical tool in enterprise research – description and evaluation on the basis of an Australian-German research project

Susanne Royer, Martins Bumbieris, Ellen Kittel-Wegner and Damian Hine

INTRODUCTION

This chapter describes the application of a new electronic content analytic tool called Leximancer. Leximancer is an application developed to perform content analysis of text data. It can be used for both explanatory automatic analysis and confirmatory customized content analysis. The tool is employed to analyse data in an ongoing study of changing corporate strategies among large class leading firms, as part of an investigation of how these changing corporate strategies, which increasingly emphasize economies of scope, have an impact on the competitiveness of small firms. The content itself is de-emphasized in this chapter with the focus on the analytical technique.

As it is a relational content analytical tool for text data Leximancer 'is a tool that can be used to automatically analyse the content of document collections and display the extracted information. This information is presented on a conceptual map that provides a birds eye view of the material, representing the main ideas from the text and how they are related. This map is also linked to a browser, allowing users to explore themes throughout the text' (Leximancer Manual, 2005).

The system is intended to include and merge the techniques involved in content analysis (Smith and Grech, 2002), namely: a conceptual overview of data; trend discovery; and a top-down analysis approach, offering the opportunity to access the source text.

The evaluation of the application of the Leximancer in enterprise research involves its suitability for such types of research and discusses its advantages and drawbacks in each step of the research. It is very important to make a comparison between content analysis tool and other types of research strategies (ie case-studies, questionnaires etc). According to Leximancer's own website:

> Leximancer is a tool that can be used to automatically analyse the content of document collections and display the extracted information. This information is presented on a conceptual map that provides a birds eye view of the material, representing the main ideas from the text and how they are related. This map is also linked to a browser, allowing users to explore themes throughout the text. As part of this process, Leximancer performs simple and efficient taxonomy discovery (www.leximancer.com).

APPLICATION OF LEXIMANCER TO THE STUDY

The aim of the study was to explore the impact of changing industry and corporate trends on large and small firms. Innovative efforts and flexibility achievements by larger competitors and their impact on smaller ones are especially investigated. The exploration focuses on the following two aspects with the potential to impact the future economic role of small business in industrialized countries:

- Determination of the extent to which changes in industry structure (eg through outsourcing) contribute to the role for small business in employment growth.
- Identification of limitations to the competitive advantage of small firms given changing corporate strategies in large firms leading to declining rates of outsourcing and the advent of the recreating trend, ie looking at the reintegration that follows disintegration trends in many industry sectors.

The central issue, the impact of changing corporate strategies, is examined through a review of trends in corporate strategies in Germany (as well as in Australia). Thus, the relation to downsizing and outsourcing as well as value chain disintegration and reintegration is addressed. It is these changing corporate strategies which is proposed to have the potential to marginalize smaller firms as employment generators in future in Germany (as well as in Australia).

The recent past is characterized by rapid and unpredictable change combined with increasing competition in many industries leading to new corporate strategies. For example, questions of 'make or buy' in a world of changing patterns of value chain organization became relevant (Bresser et al., 2000). Flatter forms of business organization increasingly dominate in many industries today as a reaction to technological and global developments. Traditionally large organizations have been locked into economies of scale, achieving survival through high volume production, reducing variable costs and proportional fixed costs (Chandler, 1990; Teece, 1993). Increasingly a dynamic situation has emerged where economic efficiencies are still highly relevant but not necessarily achieved in competitive isolation anymore. Alliances, networks and other forms of cooperation supported by sophisticated information and communication technologies (ICT) creating competitiveness through efficiencies and removing reliance on size alone (Ref). Information and communication technologies has made it possible to dramatically reduce transaction costs of cooperative forms.

Aligned with this development, an ever-changing dynamic environment requires flexible actors in global markets. Lead organizations are now able to unlock their corporate strategies to adapt to these developments. In many industries a transfer from individual value chains to collective value chains using a variety of cooperative forms can be observed (Ref). This has implications for the competitiveness of smaller players, which are often locked into certain market niches while taking advantages of flexibility and innovativeness. However, competitiveness based upon these domains are being eroded because of the changing strategies of large organizations. Such unlocking tendencies manifest themselves in restructuring activities within organizations; the establishment of more project-oriented tasks as well as disaggregating of value chains. This enables larger competitors to minimize transaction costs, extend their networks and re-establish a competitive advantage over smaller actors (Williamson, 2000).

In many countries small businesses have played a prominent economic role over the past decade (Acs, 1994). Some countries are highly reliant on these small players for their economic and social well being (OECD, 2002). It is therefore relevant to discover the issues concerning strategy and the shift towards economies of scope, to determine whether they are sporadic or deliberate. The analysis of this situation is the aim of this chapter.

This chapter investigates and analyses: (1) unlocking tendencies regarding corporate strategies in large companies and (2) the adherent implications on the competitiveness of smaller businesses. Since Australia and Germany are two countries where small and medium-sized enterprises (SMEs) play a dominant economic role, the situation in these countries is analysed and compared.

Building on the description of strategic trends in the strategy practice of large players, explanations for the identified patterns and elements are provided. The efficiency of different forms of value chain organization is in the centre of the transaction cost theory. The efficiency criterion here is the sum of production (scale and/or scope) economies on the one hand and co-ordination (transaction) economies on the other hand (Williamson, 1989). A vertically integrated value chain organization is seen as preferable to a disintegrated one with respect to efficiency in situations of high specificity and uncertainty (Monteverde and Teece, 1982; Walker and Weber, 1984; Masten, 1984; Hennart, 1988; Stuckey, 1983). Transaction cost theory sees the reason for the recent tendency to more vertical disintegration in incentive advantages as well as in advantages regarding organization costs (d'Aveni and Ravenscraft, 1994; Mahoney, 1992).

One point of departure for this research regards the explanation of new forms of value chain organization as a facet of corporate strategy in large firms. The results also provide deeper insights into the creation of competitive advantages in the analysed context. They also require a broader analysis than that offered by TCE alone. The dynamic capabilities provide another perspective, and can be seen as an extension of the resource-based view (Amit and Zott, 2001; Collis, 1994). In contrast to the resource-based perspective that often is concerned with value appropriation and the sustainability of competitive advantage (Penrose, 1959; Barney, 1991), the dynamic capabilities view (Teece et al., 1997) explores the ways by which valuable resources are built and acquired over time. In contrast to the resource-based view, not Ricardian but Schumpeterian or entrepreneurial rents are the centre of attention of the dynamic capabilities view. The focal concern of the dynamic capabilities perspective is directed on asset accumulation, replicability and inimitability (ibid, p. 527). However, does the unlocking processes affect the abilities of realizing and sustaining competitive advantages for the investigated firms? To find answers to this question we employ both the resource-based view (Barney, 1991; Grant, 1991; Peteraf, 1993) and the dynamic capabilities view (Eisenhardt and Martin, 2000; Rindova and Kotha, 2001; Teece et al., 1997) to outline the mechanisms of generating competitive advantages in environments characterized by different degrees of dynamism.

SCALE AND SCOPE

This section of this chapter seeks to explain those dynamics with reference to the strategies of both small and large firms. The emphasis of small firms on scope rather than scale has given them a competitive edge in the manufacturing sector over the period under consideration. At the same time, large firms have been downsizing. However, large firms might in future be expected to pick up on the advantages of scope.

Chandler's (1990, p. 17) own definitions of economies of scale and of scope are used in this chapter:

- 'Economies of scale may be defined initially as those that result when the increased size of a single operating unit producing or distributing a single product reduces the unit cost of production or distribution.
- Economies of joint production or distribution are those resulting from the use of processes within a single operating unit to produce or distribute more than one product (we use the increasingly popular term economies of scope).'

Chandler tends almost always to combine the two concepts, whereas other economists tend to separate the two. In actuality, while both can occur simultaneously, firms will focus on either standardization in pursuit of scale, or diversity and flexibility in pursuit of scope. It is difficult for one firm to achieve both scale and scope given resource, management, cultural, structural and skills limitations.

Within the manufacturing sector, large firms have traditionally had a strategic advantage. In explaining the role of large manufacturing firms in the industrial era, Chandler, in his major economic historical work *Scale and Scope* (1990, p. 4) documents the necessity for firm growth in the manufacturing sector in the United Kingdom (UK), United States (US) and Germany between 1880–1948: 'As a result of the regularity, increased volume, and greater speed of the flows of goods and materials made possible by the new transportation and communication systems (at the end of the nineteenth century), new and improved processes of production developed that for the first time in history enjoyed substantial economies of scale and scope. Large manufacturing works applying the new technologies could produce at lower unit costs than could the smaller works'.

The scale imperative is further explained by Chandler in recalling that 'in order to benefit from the cost advantages of these new high-volume technologies of production, entrepreneurs had to make three interrelated sets of investments. The first was an investment in production facilities large enough to exploit a technology's potential economies of scale or scope . . . It was this three pronged investment in production, distribution and management that brought the modern industrial enterprise into being' (1990, p. 4). Scale was not only directed at production but at distribution and in a similar way management, in which the replication of standardized practices created the volume advantage.

Manufacturing is the most capital-intensive sector of the economy. In order for investment returns to be realized, traditionally large-scale production of standardized products has been the path to success. The onset and availability of new technologies through computerization, commercial off-the-shelf technologies and generic software permitted the smaller manufacturing firm to gain a foothold in markets through the product diversity and technological developments permitted. However, given the proportionally large capital base, the process for large manufacturing firms of shifting from scale to scope meant substantial new investments. It was not as simple as for service firms, which relied far more on their human than their physical resources. The time period for conversion from scale to scope will have been substantially greater for manufacturing. This benefited the small innovative manufacturing firm, which could utilize the new technologies to avoid substantial retooling, costs, in terms of both time and resources, and could dramatically increase their product range. Where the impact of economies of scale in traditional industries was greatest, job generation amongst small firms was also greatest. The sector most impacted by the phenomenon was manufacturing.

Methodology in Brief

To gain a general overview about trends and development of strategy it is useful to use a macro level, cross-sectoral approach. Following the market announced strategies of large public companies in two countries, Germany and Australia, will permit analysis of the strategic aims of these large organizations. The identification of drivers and facets of the process of unlocking corporate strategy is undertaken with the newly developed and launched content analysis program LEXIMANCER. This was used to generate conceptual maps highlighting the relationships between, and the relative frequency of, terms in stock exchange announcements and annual reports from sector performance leaders. The data gained from the analysis of the years 2000 and 2003 build the basis for a better description of elements of corporate strategies of the larger players in six industries in Australia and Germany. In three of these sectors small firms dominate (ie, Construction and Engineering, Biotechnology, Software) while in the others large competitors are dominant (ie, Credit Banks, Retail Multiline, Multi-utilities). For each sector two leading competitors have been selected. The database established provides an extensive resource on which to base analyses of lock-ins and unlocking of corporate strategy patterns amongst top performers, utilizing qualitative data of sufficient volume to permit descriptive statistical analyses.

The final aim is to outline certain limitations of unlocking the corporate strategies of large companies and putting the research in relation to strategic options for smaller business. The central issue with regard to this third step is the analysis of the impact of changing corporate strategies. This trend is examined through the review of trends in corporate strategies in Germany and Australia combined with the insights from the theoretical investigation undertaken.

The review was based initially upon desk-top research. Six industry sectors have been selected for further analysis. In three of these sectors small firms dominate while in the other half they do not – large competitors are dominant. The industries chosen where small firms dominate are: (1) Construction and Engineering, (2) Biotechnology and (3) Software. The other three industries taken into account with regard to the analysis are (1) Credit Banks, (2) Retail Multiline and (3) Multi-utilities. From these industry sectors the two leading German competitors have been selected according to share performance (52 week performance in per cent), business volume (turnover of total assets), PEG ratio (Price-Earning-Growth ratio) and market capitalization. The analysis covers the years 2000 and 2003.

The information needed was sourced through press releases and annual reports of years 2000 and 2003. The database established provides an extensive resource on which to base analyses of changing corporate strategy amongst top performers, utilizing qualitative data of sufficient volume to permit descriptive statistical analyses. The collected data for the analysis of the German firms include:

- approximately 270 Press Releases and 10 Annual Reports from the year 2000;
- approximately 623 Press Releases and 12 Annual Reports from the year 2003.

The data were mainly collected from the official websites of the analysed enterprises. Some data (particularly from 2000) had to be scanned and converted to text. Some data were adapted to text (ie, annual reports) because there was too much numerical information as well as repeated symbols (ie, statement, page etc).

PROCESS OF ANALYSIS

The content analysis program Leximancer is used to generate conceptual maps highlighting the relationships between, and the relative frequency of, commonly used terms in a document containing stock exchange announcements or other documents. This section describes how the researchers used this computer program to generate maps regarding sector performance leaders, their interpretation and some problems encountered during this

Table 18.1   Process of analysis with Leximancer

Preprocess text	Text preprocessing is the first phase of processing that is run from Leximancer's main menu. This phase converts the raw documents into a useful format for processing, such as identifying sentence and paragraph boundaries
Automatic concept identification	In this phase, important concepts are automatically identified from the text. As this stage, concepts are simply keywords, such as 'dog' or 'alice'
Concept editing	In this phase of processing, users have the option of deleting automatically identified concepts that are not of interest, adding extra concepts, or merging concepts that refer to the same thing
Concept thesaurus learning	Concepts in Leximancer are collections of words that travel together throughout the text. For example, a term such as 'rifle' may have other terms such as 'ammunition' or 'bullet' that frequently appear with it, and rarely appear elsewhere. The learning phase identifies such clusters of words that surround the main terms given by the preceding two phases
Locate concept occurrences (classification)	Once the concept definitions have been learned, each block of text is tagged with the names of the concepts that it contains. This process is similar to manual coding used in 'content analysis'. However, the benefit of using Leximancer for this task is that it is fast (compared to the time taken for human coders), and is more objective (as opposed to humans, where there is much variability in coding performance)
Mapping	The last phase of processing is 'mapping' in which the conceptual map that displays the relationship between variables is constructed

Source: Leximancer Manual, version 2.1 (2005), p. 15.

process. The whole process can be split up in the six following phases (see Table 18.1).

1.   Splitting Information and Setting up the Text Document

In order for Leximancer to generate concepts and reliable conceptual maps, the text document first had to be altered from its original form, whereby each stock exchange announcement had a title and brief description (sector, company and date) of the announcement before the main content of that announcement. As these headings contained words that were included in the main body of the announcement and had no direct semantic relationship, they had to be erased. Therefore, the document's final format was a series of paragraphs, separated by a single line with no words. Each paragraph was a separate announcement from the relevant company and started with the word 'STATEMENT'.

2. Establishing Effective Configuration of Text Processing Stages

To ensure Leximancer was generating the relevant concepts and most stable conceptual map by processing the document according to certain parameters, the various stages involved in Leximancer's main menu were altered and the conceptual maps were generated a number of times. This also enabled the researcher to gain greater insight into how Leximancer was generating concepts and how altering the text pre-processing, learning and classification phases lead to changes in the conceptual map. On this note, it is necessary to point out that this process may lead to a method that is slightly biased, as the researcher is looking for the conceptual map that is most what the 'desired outcome' or hypothesis of the analysis states. However, it also ensures that each stage is preparing and reading the document, and generating specific concepts for the frequencies and relationships most sought after for conceptual analysis. It further eliminates extraneous factors or parameter settings that may hinder the significant frequencies and relationships of the concepts from being extracted.

As all four stages of text processing configuration need to be run prior to the concept map generation stage, the following will describe briefly the alterations for each stage of processing over a number of conceptual map generation runs (ie, configuration trials). The configuration trials were conducted over approximately nine Leximancer sessions. Throughout eight of these trials various settings were changed – this provided familiarity with first-time use of Leximancer. The relevant alterations were made until it was found that using most of the default settings and changing a few relevant settings was the more optimal methodology for using the program. This iterative process was in line with the non-static process that Leximancer uses itself. The eight trial runs explored changing parameter settings in each of the four stages.

Stage 1: text pre-processing
In this stage, the formatting of information in the text document was defined. Various changes were made to the configurations of the regular expression signifying the start of the document/paragraph (using no words or one line; and/or the word 'STATEMENT').

Stage 2: concept learning
In this stage the main purpose of altering the configuration was the generating and choosing of relevant concepts. Both auto concept generation and manual input of specified concepts from both the Leximancer automatically generated concepts and the researcher's chosen concepts were explored and combined to create the optimum coverage and merging of relevant concepts within the text document. This was an imperative stage for what was to be generated and displayed on the concept map.

In the initial configuration runs, the concepts were automatically generated by Leximancer and then systematically deleted in the next processing stage if they were of no relevance. This included names. Later the 'no name' function was activated – however names, for example of companies, were still included in the auto generation and thus had to be manually deleted. The number of concepts to be generated by Leximancer increased over trial runs from 40 up to 140 for the final run (as described later). It was found that each time the concepts were generated automatically some concepts were added or deleted across runs. One hundred and forty concepts resulted in generating the most effective coverage of automatic seed words. Other parameters that were explored were boilerplate cut-off and bi-gram sensitivity to examine how these affected the quality and quantity of automatic concept generation.

Stage 3: classification and indexing
In this configuration stage the automatic concepts generated from the previous stage were edited. Eventually manual concepts were created from the automatic seed words and importation of autoseeds from previous sessions was found to be most useful. The concepts were also merged if they were very closely related to or were the same concepts (eg innovation/ innovative). The learning threshold was also varied across runs and eventually the number of iterations that took place during automatic concept generation dictated at what parameter this function should be set at.

Stage 4: mapping
The two options of Gaussian or linear map generation were explored. Initially the Gaussian map was used as the Leximancer manual states that this emphasizes the similarity between the conceptual context in which the words appear (p. 44). However, for the purpose of generating a map that has the greatest stability and representation (ie, after running the clustering several times and noting a similar positioning of the concepts between runs) the linear map is purported to be the best option. As reported later, the Gaussian map was chosen for the final run as it did display stability and also displays the concepts being spatially close if they appear in semantically similar environments (Leximancer manual, p. 44). This is of greater

importance in the current study than of the frequency with which the concepts co-occur in the text (as the linear map displays).

From this stochastic process of using Leximancer for the concept map generation, it was found that by varying and revising the parameters specified, the concept map generated was sometimes too cluttered or not representative of what was in the text document. The frequency (or direct relationship) lines on the map after some runs also appeared to be non-specific in revealing the strength of co-occurrence between a concept and other concepts. It was through this experimental use of Leximancer that it was discovered that the most effective text processing configuration was by maintaining most of the Leximancer default settings and that by changing a few parameters in each of the stages, this could lead to the most significant alteration and outcome for the generated conceptual map.

3. Final Configuration of Text Processing Stages and Map Generation

In the final session whereby the current maps were generated, the configuration was as follows.

Stage 1
The first configuration within this stage involved pre-processing of the raw documents by converting them into a useful format for processing. Leximancers default settings were maintained for this first section of text preprocessing configuration.

The second configuration section defined how the information in the text document was formatted. For the start of the document 'STATEMENT' was listed as the regular expression that signified the starting line of each document (ie each stock exchange announcement within the text document). This allowed easier browsing for Leximancer by breaking up the long text document. STATEMENT was also defined as the start of each paragraph within the text document, thus signifying a change of topic at the paragraph boundary. All other functions within this second configuration stage were left at Leximancer's default settings.

Automatic concept selection, the third configuration stage within the preprocessing section involved two components. First, in a completely separate run to the final map generation run shown here, automatic seed words were automatically extracted from the data by choosing the 'find automatic concepts' option. The total number of concepts chosen was 140. This was to gather as many concepts relevant in the text document as possible, and also to generate as many seed words as possible for the concepts to be defined by. These were later manually imported as seed words and concepts, as described in the next section.

For the next option, no names were to be identified, this leading to a natural mixture of words and names, the names of which were then all deleted manually. An alternative option that was not realized at time of Leximancer use was that this name option could be set at 1, which would then generate one name from the document and could then be deleted from the automatic seeds list. This would save time deleting unwanted names from the seed list.

Other options that were changed from default settings were a strong boiler plate cut-off was chosen and bi-gram sensitivity was set at 2. All other options were left at Leximancer's default settings.

Stage 2

In this stage, the automatic concept seeds from the previous processing phase were edited. First, any two concept seeds that seemed to be related to the same concept were merged. All the automatically generated seeds from this previous session (external seeds file) were imported into the concept list and the automatic concept seeds were totally deleted. These imported concepts were then systematically chosen or deleted according to relevance within the document and kept for the main Leximancer run, where they were manually inserted. Relevance within the document relates to the splitting up of the selected concepts into categories. These were as follows:

Table 18.2   Categories and concepts in the study data generated by Leximancer

Category	Concept
Relational term	Venture, relationship, alliance, network, partnership, joint
Collaboration process term	Support, people
Scope term	Portfolio, global, technology, range, international
Newness term	Improve, opportunity

Other concepts not generated by Leximancer but generated by the researchers were also inserted into the concepts list manually in the main run. See Table 18.3 opposite.

It is important to reiterate that the automatic seed words were generated from a previous Leximancer session, and were then imported into the main Leximancer session where the concepts were then manually entered by 'creating concepts'. The other option chosen in the learning phase was the learning threshold which was set at 16, slightly above the default setting. Increasing the learning threshold will increase the number of words to be

Table 18.3   Categories and concepts in the study data generated by the researchers

Category	Concept
Relational term	–
Collaboration process term	Mutual, agreement
Scope term	Product range
Newness term	Innovation, new

included in each concept. This was done as the number of iterations viewed from the previous Leximancer concept and map generations involving the same settings as this main run (1 in 4 iterations) was slightly low. All other options in the learning phase were kept at Leximancer's default settings.

Stage 3
All the options for the settings in the classification and indexing stage were kept at Leximancer's default settings.

Stage 4
A Gaussian map was chosen for the map generation phase. Map Generation and Interpretation – The conceptual map was viewed in Netscape and changes were made to the interface. The map was reset and then learned a number of times in order to test cluster stability. As stated earlier, if re-rotating the concepts after resetting the map does not change the clustering or position of concepts in relation to each other on repeated map generations using the same processing configurations, then the cluster map is likely to be representative. The Gaussian conceptual map generated from the above parameters for the final run of Leximancer proved to be stable upon relearning, with variations only within rotations and reflections.

One problem that arose with the reclustering function (ie resetting the map, then 'learn') in the map interface was that once the map had been reclustered and re-rotated, the previous or original map from the Lexmiancer session was not accessible. It would be beneficial for the user to go back to previous rotations/clusterings in order for a more direct and efficient referencing to other clusterings to test stability of the map. Once the concept map had been established in this way, it was viewed at 100 per cent and then at 50 per cent. The 50 per cent map was chosen in order to show the more relevant concepts and view clearer, less cluttered frequency lines between a concept and other concepts. Therefore, maps were generated and hard copied (including one 100 per cent map, one 50 per cent map without any frequency lines and eleven 50 per cent maps with frequency lines for each concept).

In the last phase of the process, the list of related entities was built. In Table 18.4 the most important concepts found in 2000 are summarized. Table 18.4 gives an overview over the 2003 data. Table 18.6 then compares the 2000 and 2003 results. In these tables the frequencies and the relational counts are provided, however it is in the maps that the relationships are most clearly visually interpreted.

The results in Table 18.6 provide a solid indication of the move by sector leading large corporates toward strategies and processes that can be categorized as economies of scope. Processual developments, with a focus on how strategies are enacted, rather than a more simplistic product or service focus, support the central tenet of the study.

These relationships are then represented as a map. A raw version of such a map, which matches the data above, is presented below. More detailed maps ensue, based upon the Australian data, which provide a more comprehensive view of the relationships. Unfortunately this is one of the drawbacks of Leximancer that will be referred to later in this chapter, the difficulty converting the maps to a usable format.

CREATING A HARD COPY OF THE MAPS

In order to get a copy of the map generated by Leximancer, it was necessary to get a copy of the map from the screen (Alt-Print screen keyboard function) and then paste into a Microsoft Word document. This proved difficult in that the size of the map in Leximancer could not be changed and so in Microsoft Word the viewing percentage had to be increased to 150 per cent in order for the map to be printed out at an acceptable size. The map was then imported into Adobe Photoshop and the outer edges with the map generation information were cropped, so just the map itself remained. The contrast was boosted in order to get a clear print out of the map, however this created a problem whereby the connecting lines needed to be distinguished in terms of brightness relating their strength of direct co-occurrence in the text document and by increasing the contrast, this made the brightness of the lines uniform. Thus a balance had to be found between increasing the brightness and contrast in order for the map to be clear, and the connecting lines to be distinguishable in their relative brightness. A function to increase the map size for printing purposes would be desirable in the Leximancer program.

Table 18.4　Relevant concepts in the 2000 data

Concept	2000	
	Absolute count	Relative count (%)
risks	163	23.1
financial	142	20.1
systems	124	17.6
process	100	14.2
services	95	13.5
customers	87	12.3
basis	75	10.6
corporate	75	10.6
products	68	9.6
capital	68	9.6
information	65	9.2
operations	65	9.2
project	61	8.6
work	59	8.3
operating	55	7.8
consolidated	55	7.8
sales	52	7.3
employees	50	7.1
assets	50	7.1
growth	45	6.4
time	43	6.1
German	39	5.5
world	39	5.5
integration	38	5.4
technology	36	5.1
Internet	35	4.9
income	34	4.8
equity	33	4.6
industry	33	4.6
interest	31	4.4
e-business	31	4.4
global	31	4.4
Germany	29	4.1
shares	28	3.9
stock	27	3.8
partners	27	3.8
leading	26	3.6
period	25	3.5
software	23	3.2
power	20	2.8
joint	17	2.4
subsidiary	12	1.7
NYSE	8	1.1

Table 18.5   Relevant concepts in the 2003 data

	2003	
Concept	Absolute count	Relative count (%)
management	789	27
processes	762	26.1
solution	664	22.7
information	483	16.5
integration	460	15.7
industry	396	13.5
financial	370	12.6
software	330	11.3
global	314	10.7
technology	309	10.6
operating	294	10
leading	265	9
applications	248	8.5
Germany	245	8.4
Mysap_Customer_ Relationship_Management	214	7.3
world	209	7.1
provide	186	6.3
nucleic	181	6.2
capital	181	6.2
project	170	5.8
assets	161	5.5
income	159	5.4
bank	136	4.6
shares	129	4.4
work	125	4.2
German	106	3.6
interest	96	3.2
consolidated	95	3.2
shareholders	78	2.6
research	76	2.6
Sap_Netweaver	71	2.4
agreement	70	2.4
contract	55	1.8
stock	31	1
Entirex_Communicator	23	0.7

Table 18.6   Comparison of the 2000 and 2003 results

2000		
Concept	Absolute count	Relative count (%)
risks	163	23.1
financial	142	20.1
systems	124	17.6
process	100	14.2
services	95	13.5
customers	87	12.3
2003		
Concept	Absolute count	Relative count (%)
management	789	27
processes	762	26.1
solution	664	22.7
information	483	16.5
integration	460	15.7
industry	396	13.5

MAP RESULTS

The conceptual map was reset and then learned a number of times in order to test cluster stability. As stated earlier, if re-rotating the concepts after resetting the map does not change the clustering or position of concepts in relation to each other on repeated map generations using the same processing configurations, then the cluster map is likely to be representative. Once the concept map had been established in this way, it was viewed at 100 per cent and then at 50 per cent. The 50 per cent map was chosen in order to show the more relevant concepts and view clearer, less cluttered frequency lines between a concept and other concepts.

The conceptual maps for two of the strongest findings in the maps are presented in this chapter. Technology is at the centre of these maps, meaning that it is the most relational term to all other terms in the analysis. Conceptually, technology is at the heart of innovation and of economies of scope through process innovations such as information technology as an enabler, or in terms of the generic and specialized technologies which create the competitive advantage for the high performers in this analysis.

A visual assessment of the map indicates three groupings of related concepts (or constructs) each of which can be considered an aspect of economies of scope:

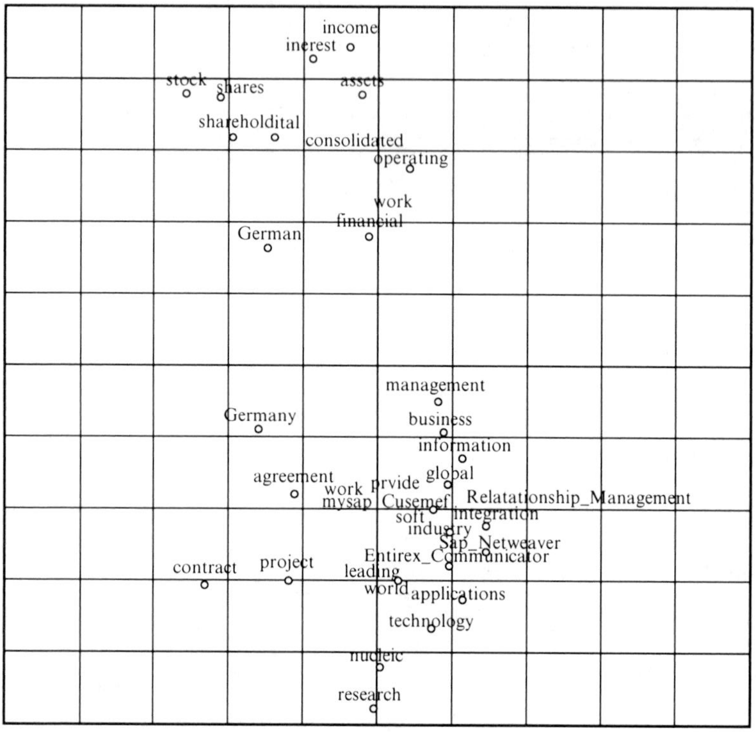

Note: Iterations = 1000.

Figure 18.1   A raw map based upon the German data

- Those concepts above the centre line can be grouped under a Collaboration banner;
- Those on the right hand side can be grouped under a Strategy banner and
- Those in the bottom half can be grouped under a Scope focus banner.

Collaboration – under this banner come familiar related words such as 'joint', 'venture', 'relationship', 'agreement', 'alliance', 'partnership', and 'mutual'. It is clear that these are grouped in a positive light, as they are associated with the word 'global'.

Strategy – the most obvious strategy related terms being 'strategy', 'long-term', as well as positive ideas of growth, opportunity, international, as well as being an indication of the complexity of strategy in the term portfolio.

Scope focus – while economies of scope are generally recognized as concentrating resources on enhancing product range and expanding into new

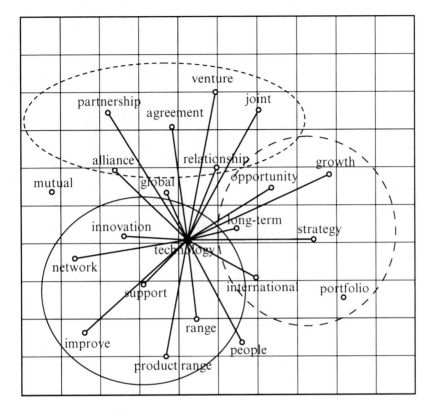

Note: Iterations = 1000.

Figure 18.2 Technology as the central concept (100%)

markets, it is also recognized that the 'economies' aspect of the term refers to efficiency, improvement and cost reduction. Therefore, in this grouping of words and terms those such as 'range', 'product range', 'people', 'innovation', 'network', 'support', tell the scooping side of the story, while the words such as 'improve' indicate process innovation. It is also clear that each of the three groups are intrinsically linked and therefore the groupings are interdependent.

The map below is set at 50 per cent, so that only the strongest associations are indicated. Even under this resolution the groupings are clear. These may also be indicative of the central concepts in each of the groups. It does provide a basis for interpretation, though the visual assessment is somewhat subjective. In the 50 per cent view, to augment this, it is valuable to include the frequency counts for these maps.

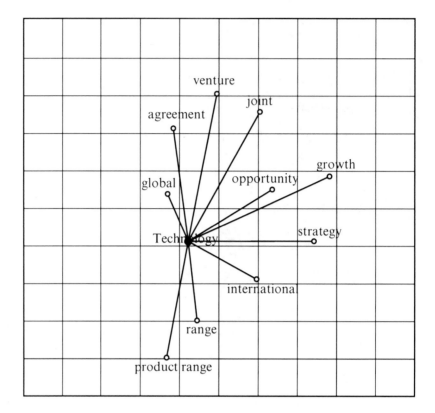

Note: Iteration = 1000.

Figure 18.3   Technology as the central concept (50%)

CONTENT IMPLICATIONS

What is presented here and summarized in these two graphs and the supporting frequencies, is a portrayal, directly from high performing large
firms in the Australian economy, using their own announcements, of a
focus on those strategies and techniques that can be brought under the
auspices of economies of scope. These are the very same techniques and
strategies that have made smaller nimble firms so competitive in the last
30 years. It is clear that the competitive attributes of economies of scope
are accessible to the larger firms. Furthermore, these firms have benefited
from these techniques and strategies in terms of growth, revenues and
profitability. They are sector leaders and they come from a wide variety of
sectors from banking and finance, to manufacturing, retail, resources and

mining, and construction. It is, therefore, not just firms in one sector which have gained the economies of scope advantage. It may be though, that the diffusion of these scope approaches will vary between sector, according to the ability of larger players in the sector to change. This would be expected to be closely linked to the level of capital intensity in the sector and to what extent the changes are competence enhancing or competence destroying (Tushman and Anderson, 1986). However, it is a chicken and egg situation. Those employing the scope approaches will be able to change more readily and adapt more easily than those who continue a scale focus in their strategy.

Given the scenario that larger firms have started to solve the scope puzzle, the choices facing the smaller firm become more difficult. For many small firms at this juncture the choice is between maintaining the innovative path and selecting the commercialization path. Over the last two decades this has been a difficult decision for small firms to make. It is the choice between scope and scale. To this point the scope path has been a relatively easy choice to make as it maintains the creativity focus and the R&D imperative. Yet if the potential scenario, outlined in the proceeding paragraphs does eventuate, the choice for the growing small firm will be confounded even further. Where scope no longer provides the same advantage as previously, this does not become an optimal choice. Scale on the other hand has been proven to be disadvantageous.

If the shift in focus is followed through with consistent strategies (albeit diverse ones), then the advantages gained by small firms will be eroded and their share of employment and employment growth will decline in the future. Once the larger firms work through their 'scale crisis' to the 'scope solution', then their competitiveness can be regained. Once again small firms (or at least the majority of them) will be at the whim of large firm strategy.

The consequence of this shift will be the limiting of success of small firms. Friedman's (1972) prediction of 'small business as an entity with a limited life, which will decline as industries and economies grow due to their inability to compete on the basis of their lack of economies of scale', will be shown to be partly correct. However, rather than being the inability to compete through economies of scale for small firms which will see their advantage eroded, it will be large firms' achieving scope which will swing the competitive pendulum.

However, we have countered the assumption that advantage achieved through economies of scope are exclusively the domain of small business. Economies of scope is about achieving competitiveness through a diverse product range (while still achieving low cost and efficiency), it has little to do with firm size. It is the innovative firms, those able to achieve a sustainable product stream, which will be advantaged, regardless of size. This then does not preclude the innovative, entrepreneurial small firms from being competitive. However, they will not be alone in future as the pioneers of new markets and the effective exploiters of niche markets.

ADVANTAGES OF LEXIMANCER

One general challenge of qualitative research is how to process large amounts of data to gain objective information and results. It is suitable to analyse a large amount of data to get a first impression of the most important concepts (overview of books, discussions, laws, debates etc). With reference to this specific study, the major means for listed companies to inform the economy of their actions and strategies is through press releases, company announcements and annual reports. The analysis of such data is generally labour and time intensive. Leximancer, more than other comparable techniques, offers a relatively expeditious approach to the analysis. The analytical steps provided in this chapter are the most comprehensive. It is possible to simply undertake an analysis of an entire body of literature (such as a book, a series of annual reports, press clippings, or other voluminous textual data) without any seeding.

Through this technique it is possible to obtain crucial information about the strategy of enterprises while maintaining a high degree of impartiality on the researcher's part, generally considered to be an issue in content analysis. Leximancer can display major relational concepts, providing results in a relatively short time and with limited effort. However, this package also offers greater depth of analysis and a more structured approach to this analysis if required. To some extent this is akin to both exploratory and confirmatory analytical approaches being catered for according to need.

Another advantage of Leximancer is the relational intensity between concepts, which raises the value of this tool beyond that of a simple frequency count. The maps permit conceptual groupings somewhat reminiscent of factor analysis in quantitative analysis.

SOME DRAWBACKS OF LEXIMANCER

Leximancer cannot be used as a purely explanatory tool for research. To maintain the intention one should work with concepts to remove noise words. There are many unnecessary terms being included in many of the analytical rounds. Unless these are eliminated the clarity of the concepts which emerge are diminished, while some crucial concepts may emerge only several times in the text and hence are ignored or overlooked.

Leximancer can be applied to novel type texts very well. However, there are some problems arising when one is dealing with short press releases and fragmented annual reports. Due to the structure of the text being analysed, there are many concepts arising that are not crucial for the research. Furthermore, some consideration needs to be given to the authoring style and typical format of the text being analysed. This is the same for any text analysis, yet can create bias where terminology, jargon, expected words and phrases are not taken account of. Again this is part of the process to reduce bias in the analysis.

Displaying the maps is also difficult for paper presentation, however this is being addressed. Finally, Leximancer displays most the important concepts and the intensity of the relationship only between them. Most other concepts are not included in this analysis because of the frequency counts. It is important to ensure that words are not double counted, or on the other hand that frequencies are underreported due to the unnecessary separation of words and terms.

CONCLUSION

This chapter has presented content material on a study which is continuing to be conducted on the shifting corporate strategies of sector leading corporates and the implications these strategies potentially have on small firms. The study required an analytical tool which could provide content analysis beyond simple frequency counts and could assist in analysing concept and construct relationships with a view to developing a strong conceptual framework. Leximancer, a relatively new analytical tool offered the solution to the analytical dilemma. While the application of the analytical tool takes some time and effort to manage, the results of the Leximancer analysis are solid, and will enhance the progress of the study referred to in this chapter. Other researchers are encouraged to experiment with this tool, as with other techniques and tools outlined in this book.

REFERENCES

Acs, Z.J. (1994), '*Where New Things Come From*', **16**(5), 29–31.
Amit, R. and C. Zott (2001), 'Value creation in e-business', *Strategic Management Journal*, **22**(6/7), 493–520.
Barney, J.B. (1991), 'Firm resources and sustained competitive advantage', *Journal of Management*, **17**(1), 99–120.
Bresser, R.K.F., M.A. Hitt, R.D. Nixon and D. Heuskel (eds) (2000), *Winning Strategies in a Deconstructing World*, Chichester: John Wiley & Sons.

Chandler, A. (1990), *Scale and Scope: The Dynamics of Industrial Capitalism*, Cambridge, MA: Harvard University Press.

Collis, D.J. (1994), 'Research note: how valuable are organizational capabilities', *Strategic Management Journal*, **15**, Winter Special Issue, 143–52.

D'Aveni, R.A. and D.J. Ravenscraft (1994), *Economies of Integration versus Bureaucracy*.

Eisenhardt, K.M. and J.A. Martin (2000), 'Dynamic capabilities: what are they?', *Strategic Management Journal*, **21**(10/11), 1105–21.

Friedman, M. (1972), *Capitalism and Freedom*, Chicago: University of Chicago.

Hennart, J.-F. (1988), 'Upstream vertical integration in the aluminium and tin industries', *Journal of Economic Behaviour and Organization*, **9**, 281–99.

www.leximancer.com/overview.html (1984), accessed 3 March 2005, *Administrative Science Quarterly*, **29**, 373–91.

Mahoney, J.T. (1992), 'The choice of organizational form: vertical ownership versus other methods of vertical integration', *Strategic Management Journal*, **13**, 559–84.

Masten, S. (1984), 'The organization of production: evidence of the aerospace industry', *Journal of Law and Economics*, **27**, 403–17.

Monteverde, K. and D. Teece (1982), 'Supplier switching costs and vertical integration in the automobile industry', *Bell Journal of Economics*, **13**, 206–13.

Organization for Economic Co-operation and Development (OECD) (2002), *Science, Technology and Industry Outlook*, Paris: OECD.

Orr, S., R. Millen and D. McCarthy (1999), 'Beyond downsizing: recreating in Australia', *Management Decision*, **37**(8), 657–70.

Reynolds, P. (1996), 'A new look at the small business role in economic growth', presentation to the 41st World Small Business Conference, Stockholm.

Revesz, J. and R. Lattimore (1997), *Small Business Employment*, Canberra: Australian Industry Commission.

Rindova, V.P. and S. Kotha (2001), 'Continuous "morphing": competing through dynamic capabilities, form, and function', *Academy of Management Journal*, **44**(6), 1263–80.

Smith, A.E. and M. Grech (2002), *Application of the LM Text Analysis System to Human Factors Research*.

Stuckey, J. (1983), *Vertical Integration and Joint Ventures in the Aluminium Industry*, Cambridge, MA.

Teece, D. (1993), 'The dynamics of industrial capitalism: perspectives on Alfred Chandler's scale and scope', *Journal of Economic Literature*, **31**, March, 199–225.

Teece, D.J., G. Pisano and A. Shuen (1997), 'Dynamic capabilities and strategic management', *Strategic Management Journal*, **18**(7), 509–33.

Tushman, M. and P. Anderson (1986), 'Technological discontinuities and organizational environments', *Administrative Science Quarterly*, **31**, 439–65.

Walker, G. and D. Weber (1984), *A Transaction Cost Approach to Make-or-buy Decisions*,

Williamson, O.E. (1989), 'Transaction Cost Economics', in R. Schmalensee and R.D. Willig, *Handbook of Industrial Organization*, **1**, Amsterdam: Elsevier Science Publishers, pp. 135–82.

Williamson, O.E. (1999), 'Strategy research: governance and competence perspectives', *Strategic Management Journal*, **20**, 1087–108.

19. Innovative methodologies in enterprise research: tackling the question of the role of the state from a macro and micro perspective

Rachel Parker

INTRODUCTION

Recent research indicates that small firms are a key source of growth, employment and innovation in modern economies (Baldwin and Picot, 1995; Clay et al., 1994; Hoffman, 1998; Konings, 1995). The competitiveness of small enterprises is explained in terms of the orientation of contemporary economies towards rapidly changing consumer markets and niche markets in combination with an increased role for information and knowledge in both new and existing industries. In this environment, small flexible enterprises are regarded as having an advantage over large bureaucratic organizations (Bryson et al., 1997; Delapierre et al., 1998; Hoffman, 1998; La-Rovere, 1998).

The increased emphasis on small and medium-sized enterprises (SMEs) can be explained in part by the emergence of the knowledge economy associated with the growth in high technology industries and knowledge-based services. Of particular significance has been the digitalization of information and the increasing importance of information and communications technologies (ICTs) both in terms of the ICT sector's share of value added, growth and employment and also in terms of its impact on employment and productivity in other industry sectors (Daveri, 2002; Pohjola, 2002). For some, innovation, entrepreneurship and geographical clustering of knowledge firms in sectors such as ICT is a defining characteristic of the new economy (Audretsch and Thurik, 2001).

In response, small business and the ICT sector have become a focus of industrial policy initiatives in the OECD countries (OECD, 2005; Delapierre et al., 1998; La-Rovere, 1998). Many industry policy programs dealing with innovation and export in ICT contain specific provisions for small firms. The presence of dynamic small firms in the ICT sector is regarded as critical to industrial competitiveness in the new economy (Baldwin and Picot, 1995; Clay et al., 1994; Hoffman, 1998; Konings, 1995).

It is therefore desirable to better understand how public policy impacts on the competitiveness of small firms in knowledge sectors such as ICT. This chapter takes a unique approach to the analysis of the influence of public policy on small firms by combining a macro-comparative institutional analysis with a micro-analysis of firm level interviews. While these methods are not unusual in entrepreneurship and small business research, the combination of the two different levels of analysis is unique and provides original insights into the understanding of policy impacts on small firms.

In addition to combining macro and micro-level analysis this chapter adopts a comparative method. Cross-national comparison allows for the testing of general theories through 'comparative checking' (Sartori, 1991, p. 245). Two countries were chosen as the basis of comparison – Australia and Sweden. The countries were chosen because both are small market economies yet they have very different political, social and economic environments, given that Australia is a typical Anglo-Saxon competitive market economy and Sweden is a co-ordinated market economy (Soskice, 1999). State–economy relations vary significantly across the two countries facilitating a comparison of the impact of the state on entrepreneurial activity, the critical operative variable in this chapter.

The empirical analysis involves two different data sources. The first empirical component of this chapter is a micro-level analysis of the findings of 11 interviews with ICT SMEs in Australia and Sweden. The interview results explain the influence of different variables on innovation amongst ICT SMEs in the two countries. The second dimension of the empirical research involves a comparison of the environment of ICT SMEs in Australia and Sweden, relying primarily on quantitative data collected by national statistics bureaus and the Organization for Economic Co-operation and Development (OECD). The dimensions of the institutional environment of the two countries that are relevant to SMEs and for which data is collected are those identified in the initial micro-level interview data. The final section of this chapter draws out the implications of the empirical research for conceptions of the role of the state in the knowledge economy. In particular, it is suggested that a key role for the state in the knowledge economy is to build competence amongst a variety of actors (Eliasson, 2000).

METHODS

In combining macro and micro methods, this chapter is able to provide insights into the role of the state in promoting small business and entrepreneurship that are unable to be gained from either macro or micro techniques used in isolation. The micro-level interview analysis allows for depth and complexity to be taken into account in the exploration of the perceptions of small firms, while the macro level analysis allows for the inclusion of institutional and political variables which constitute the context of small business and entrepreneurial activity. The micro-level analysis is essential to the identification of relevant political and institutional variables which are scrutinized in the macro-level analysis. As such, the two levels of analysis are both complementary and inter-dependent.

The empirical research involves a comparative method and is based on two types of data – qualitative data derived from firm interviews and quantitative data collected by national statistics bureaus and the OECD. The interview data is used for the purpose of theory building. The quantitative data and cross-national comparative method are used for the purpose of theory testing. As with most exercises in theory building, some initial insights were extracted from the literature dealing with the role of the state in the knowledge economy (Audretsch and Thurik, 2001; O'Riain, 2000; Eliasson, 2000). This literature formed the basis for the construction of interview questions, but which were sufficiently broad to allow for important explanations to emerge that were not previously accounted for in the literature.

Interviews were conducted with 11 ICT SMEs – seven in Australia and four in Sweden. Interviewees were asked to explain the way in which different variables in the external environment of the firm impacted on innovation within the firm. Firms passed through an initial screening process in that all firms participating in the study had reported that they had introduced at least one major new product innovation into the market in the last three years. Interviewees were the senior managers of the SME. The interviewees were asked questions concerning the nature of the innovation, the capabilities of the firm which led to the innovation and the importance of employee skills, collaborations with external organizations and access to finance. The interview finished with a general question which enabled the interviewees to identify any additional factors that had contributed to, or impeded, the innovative output or competitiveness of the firm.

From the interviews it was possible to identify a set of variables that appeared to be important in influencing entrepreneurial activity. These variables formed the basis for a comparison of the institutional environment of entrepreneurship in Australia and Sweden in the macro-level analysis.

As such, the second stage of analysis involves comparative techniques. Cross-national comparison only rarely involves the comparison of many countries because of the difficulties of data-collection. Cross-country comparison involving few countries, with many variables, can be based on either the most similar or most different research design. The most similar approach involves the selection of countries that are similar in many respects, but different in relation to the variables under consideration. This allows the researcher to control those variables that are similar across the two countries, for it is assumed that the similarities do not provide an explanation for the differences that are observed. This is a common technique in comparative research and is particularly popular in relation to area studies, for example comparative analysis of Latin American countries or Asian, African, Anglo-Saxon or European countries. In contrast, the most different design involves the selection of countries which can be regarded as different in many properties, but for which there is similarity in the variables under consideration (Pennings et al., 1999, p. 45; Landman, 2003, pp. 29–34; Sartori, 1991, p. 250).

The most similar research design was utilized for the purpose of the study. Australia and Sweden were chosen for the basis of comparison because they can be regarded as similar in many respects, but they are different in relation to the variables under consideration in this chapter. There is a long tradition of research involving comparison of Australia and Sweden. This is because both are small countries, have similar levels of economic development (both are advanced economies), both have democratic political systems and both have fairly high levels of dependence on resources. However, the countries differ in relation to variables of relevance to this study including their political-economic models (see Table 19.1 below) and levels of entrepreneurial activity (see Table 19.2 below). Utilizing the model developed from the interview results, the second dimension of the empirical analysis involves a comparative analysis of the environment for entrepreneurship in Australia and Sweden, relying on quantitative data obtained from national statistics bureaus and the OECD. A comparison of the two countries is used to test the model developed from the qualitative interview data. The implications for the role of the state in promoting entrepreneurship are discussed in the final section of this chapter.

MICRO-LEVEL ANALYSIS OF SMALL FIRM INTERVIEWS

Initial analysis of the interview results revealed four important factors contributing to SME innovation and competitiveness – the first concerned issues relating to the market for SMEs, which included the importance of niche rather than consumer markets. The second concerned the role of the public sector. Two further themes emerged with respect to employee skills and access to finance. The following discussion seeks to explain how these different factors were of importance to the SMEs.

THE SME MARKET

The ICT SMEs interviewed in this study did not have the capacity to participate in consumer markets and as such depended on the presence of local customers in niche markets whether large private or public sector organizations. The products of the SMEs were specialized and differentiated between users, and their customers were either public sector or large private sector companies.

The clearest illustration of the importance of differentiation to the competitiveness of the SMEs that were interviewed can be drawn from the SME involved in internet security, whose products were used for the verification of internet transactions. In this market, the competitiveness of the SME was linked to the fact that standardization in the security market is insecure. It was the differentiated and tailored nature of the product provided by the SME that was its competitive advantage.

The importance of niche markets for SMEs was also apparent with respect to relatively early start-ups that were commercializing new technologies. While these technologies may have had a broader application of relevance to consumer markets, the SMEs depended on well-established corporations in existing industries rather than consumers as their initial market. For example, a Swedish SME developed a computer super-processor capable of very high speeds and with potential wide-spread application including consumer markets for desk-top computers. However, in order to avoid problems with marketing and distribution channels, the SME was initially approaching major industrial customers who could reap large financial savings from application of the technology in manufacturing processes and in relation to bio-infomatics.

Further explanation of the importance of niche markets to SMEs was revealed in the interview with an SME whose products were used for imaging, in that an important aspect of the competitiveness of that SME was that it was not tied to film based systems for imaging in speed detection devices as were some of the larger MNCs in the market. This enabled the SME to move rapidly into digital systems, which was an important basis of its competitive advantage.

The firms interviewed in this project therefore suggested that local niche markets were important for SMEs. The SMEs interviewed needed to either distinguish themselves from larger competitors, for example, by offering a new technology that was superior to technologies to which larger competitors were tied, or by participating in a market in which differentiation was the basis of competitiveness, such as the internet security market. The SMEs interviewed did not have the marketing and distribution channels of larger organizations and were therefore unable to penetrate larger consumer markets. It would therefore seem that public policies which impact on local niche markets for technology intensive products would be important to SMEs.

THE ROLE OF THE PUBLIC SECTOR

The public sector played a critical role as an important customer to several of the SMEs interviewed in the study. Interviews indicated that some SMEs used the reputation of a domestic public sector customer as leverage for entering international markets. This seemed to be a factor relevant to all Australian SMEs, although its importance varied for different SMEs. In Sweden, some SMEs relied exclusively on private sector customers. This is possibly because Swedish SMEs were able to rely on the presence of large private sector multinational corporations (MNCs) as major customers. As Australia has few domestic MNCs in key medium-technology industry sectors it would seem to have a weak source of private domestic users of SME products and heightened dependence on public sector users.

One of the clearest examples of dependence on public sector users was an Australian SME involved in the development and supply of imaging software used in conjunction with speed detection devices. The major users of the SME's products were police and transport authorities. The SME operated in a jurisdiction that was early in introducing legislation to facilitate the use of speed detection devices. It was able to leverage into international markets after acquiring a major domestic public sector user of its products in the early stages. The local transport authorities and policing organizations had global connections and communication channels through which the SME was able to develop a global reputation.

Other SMEs also provided examples of the dependence of SMEs on public sector users. Both an Australian and Swedish SME were involved in the design and supply of kiosks utilizing public touch-screen technology. Major users of the technology were public sector organizations such as those providing public information, job-search facilities or gaming facilities. In the case of the Australian SME, the public sector gaming authority was a source of a major innovation in using touch-screen technology in the gaming industry, which had previously relied on machines with push-buttons or handles. With respect to the Australian SME, the establishment of a presence in the local Australian market was a launch pad for markets in the United Kingdom (UK), United States of America (USA) and Europe.

Across the SMEs there are many examples of important public sector customers. An Australian SME involved in the development of security for the verification of internet transactions had a federal government defence organization as its major customer in the early stages. From that customer base it was possible to move into the area of international financial transactions, such that the SME acquired the business of an international stock exchange, which required security for internet transactions. An Australian SME involved in sound technology and conferencing had major users in the government telecommunications carrier and emergency services departments as well as public education institutions responsible for distance education. Another Australian SME relied on government road maintenance customers for use of its road measurement technology used to detect roughness on road surfaces.

Several of the interviews therefore revealed the importance of the public sector as a user of SME products. Other interviews showed the way in which public sector programs can assist SMEs. For example, the Australian government trade commission, Austrade, was important for one Australian SME in obtaining information about potential international customers and identifying specific contacts for the SME to pursue.

It would seem that given the problems SMEs face due to their limited resources and weak distribution and marketing channels, niche markets driven by public sectors users are of importance as are public sector programs, such as those which assist firms to penetrate export markets and therefore compensate for weak marketing and distribution channels.

EMPLOYEE SKILLS AND COMPETENCE

The interviews indicate that innovation depends on the availability of a highly skilled workforce with technical knowledge and industrial or commercial competence. As senior management in one of the SMEs explained, the knowledge required in internet security is less scientific and more commercial than people think. Knowledge of the industries such as banking and government, which were important users of the technology, was critical to the development and application of the technology.

The important combination of technical and commercial competence is clear in relation to one of the Swedish SMEs in which two of the founders had previously worked in a well-known Swedish company responsible for the development and commercialization of image processing electronics. In one of the Australian SMEs, the managing director had previously worked in the public sector Road Research Board, which had provided him with important industry knowledge and networks necessary for the development and commercialization of road surface quality measurement and intelligent transport systems, including tolling technologies. In two of the Swedish SMEs, employees had industrial experience in major Swedish companies such as Ericsson, ABB and Tetra Pak, which meant that their competence went beyond a narrow technical focus.

The cases therefore suggest that public policy initiatives with the potential to impact on the availability of both technical skills and industrial competence are of importance to SMEs in new technology sectors.

ACCESS TO VENTURE CAPITAL AND COMPETENT FINANCIERS

In some cases, sources of finance for innovation were internal to the firm and therefore did not appear to be a factor that public policy initiatives might influence in a positive way. Interviews revealed that in situations in which it was necessary to raise money external to the firm, the presence of competent venture capital funds was an issue.

In the case of one of the Swedish start-up SMEs, a 12-month discussion had resulted in the SME receiving funding from TeknoSeed, a venture capital company supporting early stage projects which had been set up by the Foundation for Technology Transfer in Sweden in 1997 as part of its role in encouraging university-industry collaboration in the south of Sweden. This indicates the importance of an organizing role for the public sector in creating a venture capital (VC) source. The advantage of having competent financiers was also demonstrated by the Swedish SME in that TeknoSeed used an ICT investment company to help evaluate the potential for the SMEs' technology, which subsequently led to the investment company itself providing funding for the commercialization of the technology.

An Australian SME also indicated the importance of finance to SMEs by highlighting the impediments created by command and control management philosophies that resulted in a low risk and conservative attitude to the development and commercialization of new technologies. In this case, the board of directors had held back financial support for technologies that the managing director had believed had huge potential because, as the managing director perceived it, the board did not have knowledge of the technology or the industry.

The lack of industry knowledge and competence amongst financiers was identified as a problem in several interviews. As one interviewee put it, 'VC companies are financial and not industrial – they do not have "intelligent money", they have only "financial money" '. This is suggestive of the need for public policy initiatives that affect not only the availability of the finance, but also the supply of competent financiers.

A MACRO LEVEL ANALYSIS OF THE POLITICAL AND INSTITUTIONAL ENVIRONMENT OF SMEs IN ICT IN AUSTRALIA AND SWEDEN

The above discussion has summarized the major findings of the interviews with SMEs in Australia and Sweden. Several propositions emerge from the micro-level interview analysis which can feed into a macro-level analysis. First, SMEs in new technology sectors are competitive in niche and differentiated markets and public sector customers are often critical to the creation of markets for SMEs. As such, the micro-level analysis suggests that aspects of the macro-level environment such as the non-consumer market for ICT are important for SMEs. Turning to the macro-level environment, the dominance of large industrial MNCs in Sweden may be regarded as a positive factor for stimulating SMEs in ICT – as would the relatively well-funded public sector. In contrast, Australia has a very weak base in medium and medium-high technology industries, which might limit the potential for niche markets for ICT innovations. The public sector would therefore appear to be of greater importance in Australia as potential users of ICT SMEs innovations, although it remains relatively underfunded in comparison with the Swedish public sector (see Table 19.1 below).

Secondly, the micro-level interview analysis suggests that SMEs in new technology sectors depend on employees with good technical skills as well as commercial or industrial competence, once again indicating the importance of the macro-level institutional environment. The Swedish education system has a stronger orientation towards training in engineering, manufacturing and computers than does the Australian education system, which might be expected to constitute an important source of graduates with technical expertise in Sweden (see Table 19.1). In addition, Sweden has a well-developed mechanical engineering sector, several key firms in ICT such as Ericsson and Electrolux (electronics) and an overall larger number of MNCs per capita. As such, there is potential for graduates to acquire industrial experience with leading Swedish companies, whereas in Australia the engineering sector remains small in comparison to Sweden (see Table 19.1).

Table 19.1   A macro-level institutional analysis of the environment of small firms in ICT

Measure	Australia	Sweden
Industrial competence		
Export specialization in high technology industries, 1999[1]	0.5	1.10
High and medium-high technology industries as % of business value added, 1999[2]	5.7	10.0
Skills and competence of the workforce		
Proportion of population whose highest educational attainment is at least upper secondary, 2001[3]	65.0	83.0
Proportion of Tertiary Type A graduates in engineering, manufacturing and construction, 2000[4]	7.9	20.5
Proportion of tertiary graduates in computing, 2000[4]	4.6 (Tertiary Type A)	3.1 (Tertiary Type A) 20.1 (Tertiary Type B)
Public sector		
Size of government – government expenditure % GDP, 2000[6]	31.9	55.1
Venture Capital		
Size and orientation of venture capital market[7]	Size below OECD and EU, orientation to high technology sectors and new firm start-ups below EU and OECD	Size around OECD level (above EU level). Orientation towards high technology sectors and new firm start-ups slightly above EU but below OECD

Source and Note: See appendix to Table 19.1, p. 317.

Thirdly, interview results suggest that SMEs seeking to commercialize radical new technologies depend on access to venture capital and this depends in part on the competence of financiers to evaluate the technology. At a macro-institutional level, both industrialists and the high level of engineering and technology skills amongst the workforce might be expected to contribute to competence with the venture capital market in Sweden. In addition, the overall size of venture capital funds in Sweden is higher than in Australia and there is a stronger orientation towards high

Table 19.2   Distribution of enterprises by size class of firms in ICT

Size class of firm	No. of employees				
	0–4	5–19	20–99	100+	Total
Australia	18 936 (84.3)	3048 (13.6)	854 (3.8)	187 (0.8)	22 475 (100.0)
Sweden	27 085 (85.4)	3039 (9.6)	1321 (4.2)	280 (0.9)	31 725 (100.0)

Note: Percentage of total in brackets.

Source: Statistics, Sweden, Centrala företags och arbetsställeregistret (CFAR) Företag och anställda efter näringsgren SN192 och storleksklass. (År) 1993–2002 and ABS Information Technology Australia 2000–01, 8126.0, pp. 23–24.

technology investments within Swedish venture capitalist funds than there is in Australia.

Sweden would therefore seem to have a stronger macro-institutional environment in areas identified in the interviews as impacting on SME innovation. This might help to explain Sweden's relatively high number of SMEs in ICT when compared with Australia. Table 19.2 shows that Sweden has either a similar or larger number of small enterprises in ICT sectors than does Australia, despite the fact that Sweden has a population and economy that is around half the size of Australia's. This macro-level data adds support to the proposition derived from the micro-level analysis that certain characteristics of the institutional environment of small firms are important to their competitiveness.

The combination of macro and micro level analysis is suggestive of the importance of the state in building competence.

The firm level interviews have identified a series of factors in the institutional environment that appear to impact on innovation and competitiveness amongst SMEs. A macro-level comparison of the institutional environment of Australia and Sweden indicates that Sweden has a stronger institutional environment for knowledge intensive SMEs, which helps to explain Sweden's higher level of SME activity in the ICT sector.

At a more specific level, interview analysis has shown that public policy initiatives might aim to foster competent public or private sector users that might form the basis of niche markets for ICT SMEs. This is not necessarily a field for public policy intervention in countries such as Sweden in which the institutional context of the domestic industry base is already strong. However, in countries such as Australia, which has a limited medium and high technology industry base, the role of the public sector as a competent user may be of critical importance. Furthermore, drawing on the concept of the flexible development state, it might be possible for the state to improve domestic niche markets in ICT by attracting foreign direct investment (FDI) such that local industry might act as suppliers to imported foreign capital (O'Riain, 2000).

The second dimension of the environment of ICT to be identified as important in the interviews – the skills and competence of employees – is also a potential field of public policy intervention at a macro-level. In particular, education and training policies might be altered to provide an increased emphasis on training in engineering and computing where there are existing deficiencies in the institutional environment, as revealed by the macro-level data for Australia.

The lack of supporting industries which might act as a training ground for new graduates in countries such as Australia might also be addressed through policies to attract FDI such that transnational corporations (TNCs) operating in the local environment might then provide a source of industrial experience for new graduates, and might therefore help build industrial competence to enhance the technical skills of the workforce.

Finally, the environmental constraints on commercialization characteristic of the institutional environment in Australia and in particular problems with access to competent venture capital sources might be addressed through initiatives which improve the supply of venture capital funds, for example, through public venture capital initiatives such as TeknoSeed and Industrifonden in Sweden. With time, as the industrial competence of the economy improves through initiatives to attract FDI and develop the skills of the local workforce, the competence of VC funds might also be expected to improve. Furthermore, the state might assist local SMEs to tap into global venture capital sources.

CONCLUSION

These policy initiatives are captured within the idea of the flexible development state (O'Riain, 2000) and recent contributions to our understanding of the role of the state in the entrepreneurial economy (Audretsch and Thurik, 2001). However, whereas the literature reviewed in the first part of this chapter has emphasized the role of the state in influencing inputs into the science, technology and commercialization environment (as well as interactions between different actors and institutions within that environment), the empirical research reported in this chapter is suggestive of a clearer role for the state in building industrial competence as a mechanism for supporting SMEs in ICT. Competence bloc theory provides a basis for understanding the critical role of competence in stimulating new economy industries.

The concept of the competence bloc provides a framework for interpreting the empirical findings and for elaborating on elements of the national political, social and economic framework that explain the performance of SMEs in knowledge intensive sectors such as ICT. As explained above, the idea that building competence is a critical component of support programs for SMEs in knowledge sectors such as ICT moves beyond existing understandings which emphasise the role of the state in influencing inputs and interactions within the economic system. Importantly, competence bloc theory seeks to explain new industry formation or the conditions which are necessary for the 'innovative and entrepreneurial selection process to take place' (Eliasson, 2000, p. 220) and the 'selection of winning technical and economic solutions' (Eliasson, 2000, p. 221).

According to this view, science and technological resources or inputs do not in themselves enhance industrial competitiveness unless they are applied commercially. It is the commercial application that is the focus of the concept of the competence bloc, which highlights the importance of competent actors including customers, innovators, entrepreneurs, venture capitalists and industrialists (Eliasson, 2000, pp. 220–23). This would suggest that the role of the state is more complex than simply providing a sound infrastructure in terms of education and research and must take into account factors affecting the commercialization of knowledge, particularly in terms of the competence of actors within the innovation system. According to Eliasson, the role of industrial policy is to ensure that there is an adequate supply of competent actors to stimulate new economy industries.

The unique combination of macro and micro-level analysis has shown that competence building is a critical element of the role of the state in the knowledge economy. Interview level data has shown that the supply of competent users in niche markets, the skills of the workforce and the capability of the financial sector to evaluate the viability of potentially successful technologies are important to SMEs. A macro-level analysis has shown how the institutional environment, which is partly constructed by the state, impacts on SMEs by influencing those variables identified as important in the micro-level analysis. As such, the combination of these techniques has provided a depth of understanding of the role of the state that is not possible through the use of either micro or macro level analysis in isolation.

REFERENCES

Audretsch, D. and R. Thurik (2000), 'Capitalism and democracy in the 21st century: from the managed to the entrepreneurial economy', *Journal of Evolutionary Economics*, **10**(1), 17–34.

Audretsch, D. and R. Thurik (2001), 'What is new about the new economy: sources of growth in the managed and entrepreneurial economies', *Industrial and Corporate Change*, **10**(1), 25–48.

Baldwin, J. and G. Picot (1995), 'Employment generation by small producers in the Canadian manufacturing sector', *Small Business Economics*, **7**, 300–23.

Bryson, J., D. Keeble and P. Wood (1997), 'The creation and growth of small business service firms in post-industrial Britain', *Small Business Economics*, **9**(4), 345–60.

Clay, N., T. Creigh and W. Stephen (1994), 'SMEs and employment in the European community: an industrial perspective', *Revue-d'Economie-Industrielle*, **67**, 71–88.

Daveri, F. (2002), 'The new economy in Europe 1992–2001', *Oxford Review of Economic Policy*, **18**(3), 345–62.

Delapierre, M., B. Madeuf and A. Savoy (1998), 'NTBFs – the French case', *Research Policy*, **26**(9), 989–1003.

Eliasson, G. (2000), 'Industrial policy, competence blocs and the role of science in economic development', *Journal of Evolutionary Economics*, **10**, 217–41.

Hoffman, K. (1998), 'Small firms, R&D, technology and innovation in the UK: a literature review', *Technovation*, **18**(1), 39–55.

Konings, J. (1995), 'Job creation and job destruction in the UK manufacturing sector', *Oxford Bulletin of Economics and Statistics*, **57**, 5–24.

Landman, T. (2003), *Issues and Methods in Comparative Politics: An Introduction*, London: Routledge.

La-Rovere, R. (1998), 'Small and medium sized enterprises and IT diffusion policies in Europe', *Small Business Economics*, **11**(1), 1–9.

OECD (2005), *SME and Entrepreneurship Outlook*, Paris: OECD.

Pennings, P. H. Keman and J. Kleinnijenhuis (1999), *Doing Research in Political Science: An Introduction to Comparative Methods and Statistics*, London: Sage.

Pohjola, M. (2002), 'The New Economy in growth and development', *Oxford Review of Economic Policy*, **18**(3), 380–96.

O'Riain, S. (2000), 'The flexible development state: globalization, information technology, and the "Celtic Tiger"', *Politics and Society*, **28**(2), 157–93.

Sartori, G. (1991), 'Comparing and mixcomparing', *Journal of Theoretical Politics*, **3**(3), 243–57.

Soskice, D. (1999), 'Divergent production regimes: coordinated and uncoordinated market economies in the 1980s and 1990s', in H. Kitschelt, P. Lange, G. Marks and J.D. Stephens (eds), *Continuity and Change in Contemporary Capitalism*, Cambridge: Cambridge University Press.

APPENDIX TO TABLE 19.1

1. OECD (2001a), *Science, Technology and Industry Scoreboard*, Paris, OECD, p. 208. The export specialization data measures the share of the exports of the particular industrial grouping in the country's total manufacturing exports, divided by the share of total OECD exports of that industrial grouping in total OECD manufacturing exports.
2. *Ibid*, p. 203.
3. OECD (2002a), *Education at a Glance*, Paris, OECD, p. 54, (excluding ISCED 3C).
4. *Ibid*, p. 61. This includes Tertiary Type A and B. Tertiary Type A Education (ISCED 5A) 'are largely theory based and are designed to provide sufficient qualifications for entry to advanced research programmes and professions with high skill requirements, such as medicine, dentistry of architecture'. Tertiary Type B Education (ISCED 5B) 'are typically shorter than those of Tertiary Type A and focus on practical, technical or occupational skills for direct entry into the labour market' (OECD 2002, pp. 375–76).
5. OECD (2002b), *Science, Technology and Industry Outlook*, Paris, OECD, p. 300.
6. OECD (2001b) *OECD in Figures*, Paris, OECD, pp. 36–39.
7. Baygan and Freudenberg (2000), Figure 14, p. 31. For measurement problems and limitations on comparability see Baygan and Freudenberg (2000), pp. 11–13. High technology is defined as information and communication technology, biotechnology and medical/ health related sectors. Investment in early stages and expansion refers to the share of total venture capital investment financing firms in their early stages of expansion (thus excluding buyouts and other investments).

20. Conclusion: maintaining the innovative momentum

Damian Hine and David Carson

The entrepreneurial small business sector is rightfully regarded as a major generator of innovation in national economies. Research into this sector also needs to be innovative to meet the needs of this sector and to enhance its competitiveness. In this book we have compiled a diverse range of methodologies and analytical techniques which are designed to build an innovation agenda in enterprise research, to maintain parity with the innovation that occurs within the industry sector itself. Each of the approaches outlined in the chapters has been tested in the field. Each offers a real alternative or a supplement to traditional techniques and standard approaches, which themselves standardize the nature of the research being conducted and have the potential to stifle innovation. In essence, an innovative phenomenon requires an innovative methodology.

It is acceptable to employ standardized methodologies and research designs in well-established research fields such as clinical and organizational psychology. Entrepreneurship, and enterprise research generally, have not reached the same level of maturity as a research field. There is much yet to know in the area, the frontiers of knowledge are quite expansive. To open new doors on this knowledge base we must always be open to those new, innovative techniques which can offer different perspectives, views and interpretations of the phenomena we are exploring. Not only are qualitative techniques still appropriate in many areas of enterprise research, there is scope for the application of techniques which can increase our knowledge base more extensively than many traditional techniques.

Furthermore, the small business sector is a very challenging area in which to undertake research. Response rates are very difficult to achieve and in many cases there is little inclination on the part of entrepreneurs and small business owners to respond, particularly as their focus is usually on their own firm and their orientation is toward day-to-day survival. The value of research, which aggregates across an industry sector, or attempts to explain the intentions, practices, problems or orientation of an entire population, may well be lost on an individual small business owner or manager.

As a result, researchers must seek out techniques in their research that can take account of these issues, while maintaining rigour in their research. It is important for researchers to have at their disposal a range of techniques in their research arsenal (or toolkit) to employ, dependent upon the context and situation they find themselves in during their study.

We encourage researchers to add to this innovative effort, employ and even develop new methodologies specific to enterprise research designed to meet its specific needs. It is feasible also that two or more of the techniques described in this book could be combined. For instance, it is possible that convergent interviewing could be employed and the data analysed, while in the field, using Pertex or Leximancer. Innovation is as much about successful repackaging as it is about radical new-to-the-world concepts and processes.

While we have introduced and explored quite a number of novel approaches to enterprise research within the chapters of this book, in no way is the list of methodologies and techniques explored within these pages an exhaustive one. They should be regarded more as a sample of innovative techniques and methodologies, a platform upon which other innovative techniques can be launched and promulgated.

This book has been developed with the strong support of Edward Elgar Publishers. It is one in an emerging series on research methodologies. We certainly encourage other researchers to offer their insights in ensuing books published through Edward Elgar Publishers, given that these publishers have displayed the same innovative outlook we are trying to promote through this book.

It behoves the researchers in this field to maintain this innovative agenda. While it is important for all disciplines to gain credibility and forge their place in the array and hierarchy of research fields, given that enterprise research borrows its theoretical perspectives largely from other disciplines including but not restricted to psychology, marketing, micro-economics, sociology, anthropology, accounting and financial management the challenge of creating a distinct identity for the discipline is a significant one. It is as much through the development of distinctive and rigorous methodologies that most disciplines build their status as their theoretical contribution. In the enterprise research field, we have the benefit of a strong theoretical foundation from the supporting disciplines we rely upon and work with, however an over reliance on the extant methodologies practiced in these disciplines brings into question the legitimacy of enterprise research as an independent discipline. Innovative methodologies can achieve the dual goals of theory building and methodological distinction. We should aim to achieve the aim of a clear, definable discipline so that the enterprises we research are given the recognition they deserve according to their contributions to their economies.

CONCLUSION

Both David and Damian would like to very sincerely thank all the contributors to this book and the staff of Edward Elgar Publishers for their enormous contribution to this book. We hope that the book achieves the success it deserves and that the field of enterprise research gains accordingly. We most particularly thanks Edward Elgar himself for his foresight in supporting this book from the first pitch, to its proposal and subsequent publication. We hope he is rewarded for this foresight and for his support.

Index